DISCARD

THINKING GLOBALLY, COMPOSING LOCALLY

Rethinking Online Writing in the Age of the Global Internet

Edited by
RICH RICE
KIRK ST.AMANT

UTAH STATE UNIVERSITY PRESS
Logan

© 2018 by University Press of Colorado

Published by Utah State University Press
An imprint of University Press of Colorado
245 Century Circle, Suite 202
Louisville, Colorado 80027

 The University Press of Colorado is a proud member of
the Association of University Presses.

The University Press of Colorado is a cooperative publishing enterprise supported, in part, by Adams State University, Colorado State University, Fort Lewis College, Metropolitan State University of Denver, Regis University, University of Colorado, University of Northern Colorado, Utah State University, and Western State Colorado University.

∞ This paper meets the requirements of the ANSI/NISO Z39.48-1992 (Permanence of Paper)

ISBN: 978-1-60732-663-2 (paperback)
ISBN: 978-1-60732-664-9 (ebook)
https://doi.org/10.7330/9781607326649

Library of Congress Cataloging-in-Publication Data

Names: Rice, Rich (Richard Aaron), editor. | St.Amant, Kirk, 1970– editor.
Title: Thinking globally, composing locally : rethinking online writing in the age of the global Internet / edited by Rich Rice, Kirk St. Amant.
Description: Logan : Utah State University Press, [2017] | Includes bibliographical references and index.
Identifiers: LCCN 2017025369| ISBN 9781607326632 (pbk.) | ISBN 9781607326649 (ebook)
Subjects: LCSH: Language and the Internet. | Intercultural communication. | Composition (Language arts)—Study and teaching. | Media literacy—Cross-cultural studies. | Digital communications—Cross-cultural studies. | Education—Data processing—Cross-cultural studies.
Classification: LCC P120.I6 T47 2017 | DDC 808.00285—dc23
LC record available at https://lccn.loc.gov/2017025369

Nicholas Alexander Brown composed the graphic panels that appear at the beginning of each section in this book.

CONTENTS

FIGURES

TABLES

ACKNOWLEDGMENTS

It is impossible to acknowledge all of the people who have helped support and bring this collection together. It has been a successful example of the process of contacting, conveying, and connecting. Of course, our contributors deserve credit first and foremost. Each chapter has gone through many revisions and updates over the last several years, as diverse scholarship and perspectives regarding intercultural and global technical communication emerge constantly. Our contributors' students, and well as our own students at Texas Tech University and Louisiana Tech University, inspired the need for this research. Students reviewed ideas and writing in this collection indirectly and directly as part of our engagement as integrated scholars in our teaching, research, and service. Our colleagues from our institutions, from professional conferences we attend and present at, and from the international schools we've worked with, have helped enormously.

Rich Rice was awarded a U.S. Fulbright-Nehru Scholars Award in 2014, which enabled him to focus his research on global technical communication and this collection. Thank you, sincerely, Fulbright. His serving as a visiting research scholar in India at the Central University of Kerala in 2011, Delhi University in 2014, and Ashoka University (also in 2014), was instrumental to this work. Serving as a visiting research scholar in China at Southeast University in 2017, too, was very helpful. The research was sponsored by Texas Tech University in a variety of ways, too, such as through the TTU Transdisciplinary Research Academy; the Teaching, Learning, and Professional Development Center and the Multicultural Course Transformation Project; the Humanities Center; the Provost's Office; the Service-Learning Faculty Fellow Program; and the College of Arts & Sciences. The Council for Programs of Technical and Scientific Communication provided a research grant in support of this work. And we thank Dr. Kanika Batra, whose scholarship and insights in postcolonial literature, gave an important interdisciplinary eye to the project.

Kirk St.Amant wishes to thank Mark D. Hawthorne and Victoria Mikelonis—whose combined mentoring introduced him to computing, culture, and communication—and Beth L. Hewett and Christa Ehmann

Powers for providing the initial opportunity to examine the teaching of writing in international online spaces and he wishes to thank the Eunice C. Williamson Endowment made possible through the State of Louisiana Board of Regents Support Funds. Kirk wishes to especially thank his daughters, Lily St.Amant and Isabelle St.Amant, for being a continued source of inspiration for all he does.

We also wish to thank Nicholas Alexander Brown, who is a doctoral student in Rhetoric and Composition at Texas Christian University. His research examines multimodal rhetoric and comic books, and he composed the graphic panels at the beginning of each section in this book. And a sincere thanks goes to Michael Spooner (associate director), Laura Furney (assistant director and managing editor), Dan Miller (production and marketing designer), Kylie Haggen (editorial assistant), and Charlotte Steinhardt (sales and marketing assistant) at the University Press of Colorado. We also thank Utah State University Press, manuscript reviewers, and the entire editorial staff who helped prepare this collection for publication. Without your work and service this publication wouldn't exist. Please, continue to share it with your colleagues and students.

THINKING GLOBALLY,
COMPOSING LOCALLY

Earth (the not too distant future)
The P.U.C.K. Center for Communication

Introduction

THINKING GLOBALLY, COMPOSING LOCALLY
Re-thinking Online Writing in the Age of the Global Internet

Rich Rice and Kirk St.Amant

Audience—it is one of the central components of the writing process. We consider audience carefully, first, to meet a group's reading expectations. In some cases, the audience is created in our minds. It's imagined, and we address presumed reading preferences the best we can (consider Ong, 1975). In other cases, we conduct specific sorts of research (e.g., rhetorical or audience analyses) to learn more about a group's background and communication needs. Using this information as a guide we attempt to craft targeted messages (such as St.Amant, 2015). Regardless of the process, one key tenant remains the same: when we write, it is to convey information to a group in a way that recognizes the communication needs of group members (Caroll, 2010).

Online environments add new levels of complexity to understanding audience because the notion of group changes. In such environments, audience is always more diverse, varied, and in many cases global in scale. We must adapt, and we must do so quickly. To successfully invoke online audiences that are global in nature, the writing process requires a *kairotic* approach of working to contact participants in just the right way, to convey just the right information, and to connect with readers at just the right time in a sustained or even transactional process. Thus, communicating online involves moving beyond traditional borders or notions of groups, exploring functional more so than political geographies, and valuing economic, social, and cultural ties rather than only territorial group tensions (Getto & St.Amant, 2014).

THE GLOBAL NATURE OF ONLINE AUDIENCES

Online media often give us a means to bypass such boundaries of space and time. That is, information communication technologies allow us

DOI: 10.7330/9781607326649.c000

to almost instantly share information and ideas with individuals half a world away. Thus, when we write online, our audience theoretically becomes anyone who has is interested in our topic and who has online access. Moreover, the global spread and distribution of online access also allows an audience to quickly and directly respond to our ideas. As a result, the rhetoric triangle—which traditionally includes reader, writer, and text—must expand to include location and modality. Where and who our audience is, in addition to what tool they're using to access our content, must be considered carefully. Audiences today are often large and diverse; they also have the potential to be relatively interactive. All of these factors come to bear when we consider the question "Who is our audience in the age of global online access?"

Let's examine this question further. As of this writing, the potential international audience for our online work is huge: some 3.7 billion persons worldwide, and growing rapidly. It is also a culturally diverse one, comprised of some 353 million with online access in Africa, roughly 385 million persons online in Latin American and the Caribbean, 637 million in Europe, 142 million in the Middle East, 28 million in Oceana/ Australia, and almost 1.9 billion individuals who have online access in Asia. (For the most current statistics on international online access, see "The Internet Big Picture" [2017] through *Internet World Stats: Usage and Population Statistics* [2017] at http://www.internetworldstats.com.) Such a degree of diversity in global cyberspace, moreover, is a relatively recent development.

At the turn of the millennium, only 361 million persons worldwide were connected to online environments (The Internet big picture, 2017). In addition, most of these individuals were located in North America—particularly the United States and Canada (almost 1/3 of all individuals with online access) or in Western Europe (almost another 1/3 of all individuals with access) (Internet users in the Americas, 2017; Internet penetration in North America, 2017; Internet in Europe stats, 2017). The majority of today's Internet users, by contrast, represent not only a greater percentage of individuals from Asia, Africa, and Latin America, but also an increase in the number of online participants from emerging economies. For example, as of this writing, the number of individuals with online access in China alone (some 722 million persons) is almost twice that of the number of Internet users in the United States and Canada combined (roughly 363 million persons). Similarly, India's 465 million persons with online access constitutes over half the entire population of Europe (roughly 739 million persons). Moreover, it is in these emerging economies of the world where the prospects for markedly increasingly online access are the greatest. China, for example, saw the number of individuals with online access within its borders grow from 22.5 million persons in 2000 to over 700 million by 2017—and this number accounts for only half its total population (Internet penetration in Asia, 2017). Thus, as global access to online environments continues to expand, it will likely be non-Western cultures and the citizens of emerging economies that account for a large percentage of this growth. While not everyone is reading what we write, of course, this gives significant cause for rethinking contexts surrounding audience.

RETHINKING WRITING CONTEXTS FOR ONLINE AUDIENCES

Scholars around the world are calling for changes in education to focus on preparing students for becoming global citizens (Darling-Hammond, 2010). Such change must equip students with twenty-first century technology skills needed to become employable, prepare individuals who live and work with diverse cultures, and focus on solving complex world issues (Zhao, 2009, 2010).[1] Given all of these complexities, those of us who teach or research writing or communication studies must consider what these factors mean in terms of writing online and intercultural communication competence. For example, who is our intended, actual, and inadvertent audience? Who can we communicate with via writing through these environments, and how do we do so effectively? How can we use online writing to engage in greater international discussions as well as to create greater international communities? What sorts of intercultural communication competencies must we develop and foster? These are but a few of the questions for which we must consistently rethink our answers.

In truth, this situation can seem overwhelming. The challenge becomes determining the best initial step or framework to consider in trying to address these questions. The purpose of this collection is not to answer every nuanced question related to writing online in global contexts. (Online writing is forever evolving.) Indeed, we want to suggest that new answers must be developed for each unique context, ingroup/outgroup relationship, and audience. Rather, the overarching objective of this volume is to identify areas that can serve as starting points for fields within technical communication and writing studies and can help individuals focus on and approach frameworks they can use to begin to understand varied and diverse contexts for online writing. Central to this objective is creating a model or approach that can guide how we think about, examine, and address online writing situations in terms of composition and rhetoric when borders or boundaries are more fluid and ever-changing, even hyperconnected.

RETHINKING PERCEPTIONS OF GLOBAL COMMUNICATION

Most of us have encountered the concept of the "borderless world." The central notion is that online media have leveled many of the conventional limitations of space and time by providing near instantaneous access to people around the world. So prevalent has this notion of open international online access become that a relatively new metaphor of the "flat earth" has entered the public consciousness. Popularized by *New York Times* journalist and writer Thomas L. Friedman, the flat earth perspective represents the idea of a world free of boundaries and barriers. It is a world in which a convergence of online access, geopolitical developments, and economic approaches allows for information, ideas, and digital goods and web-based services to move across the globe as easily as a hockey puck seems to slide across the flat surface of an ice rink. We know this to be a less than perfectly true framework.

The paradigm, in fact, can be misleading. Consider extending the metaphor. As anyone who has traversed an ice rink can attest, just because the surface of the rink appears to be flat and open does not necessarily mean that surface is smooth or even. Rather, such surfaces tend to be covered by a wide array of dips and divots and cracks and bumps that create a certain degree of pull or drag or friction on any object that tries to move across. In much the same way, an array of technological, political, economic, cultural, and linguistic factors can exist and create a similar kind of pull or drag or friction that affects how smoothly or quickly or directly information can move from point to point in global cyberspace. Thus, while the earth might appear to be increasingly flat from the perspective of international online communication, it is far from frictionless.

These aspects slow, shift, or impede movement, affecting the supposedly smooth travels of ideas, information, goods, and services across the seemingly flattened realm of international online spaces. As with an ice rink, these friction points in global cyberspace can vary from the easily observed to the seemingly imperceptible. In every case, such friction points affect the free flow of information across the globe. Thus, a key to navigating international online writing contexts is to first identify friction points, attempt to understand them, and then devise writing approaches for specific audiences that allow us to account for or address friction points through effective communication practices.

This collection approaches the study of online writing in global cyberspace by keeping friction points in mind. The idea is to identify areas that appear to add to friction points or obstruct the effective flow of information when trying to share our online writing with greater global audiences. Doing so provides those of us engaged in technical communication and writing studies with a mechanism for identifying friction points associated with such writing contexts. We can then examine ideas of context and audience in further detail in the hopes of developing online writing strategies or approaches that effectively account for and address them. How do we proceed?

RECONSIDERING APPROACHES TO WRITING ONLINE

Friction points and the flat earth concept clearly relate to the notion of audience. With the hockey metaphor of flattened spaces, the "puck" we wish to slide across the ice is content or what we have written, texts we compose when we use writing to share our ideas with others. When we use online media to connect to or write for greater, global audiences, our goal is to use texts to convey information to that audience in ways that are easy to access or to be coherent or understandable and well considered or usable. To do so, we must account for friction points that could affect aspects of access, comprehension, and usability across a range of globally distributed readers. In this way, there are three main kinds of friction points: those that affect *access* (can your audience get to what you have composed), those that affect *comprehension* (can your audience understand what you have composed as you intended it), and those that affect *action* (can your audience make use of or act upon the information provided as intended).

While these factors are very broad in scope, they can be examined, understood, and addressed in terms of three sorts of variables: (1) *technology*, or what technologies (e.g., hardware, software, and networking) are used to compose and to access online texts; (2) *culture*, or what aspects of language, rhetoric, and culture need to be considered when creating texts to share ideas with international online audiences, and (3) *laws*, or what legal aspects (e.g., censorship, data disclosure, and copyright law) affect sorts of texts individuals can create, share, and access via international cyberspace (see St.Amant, 2013; St.Amant & Rife, 2014; Sun, 2012). These categories are broad, but they represent starting points for identifying where friction points can occur. For those of us in technical communication and writing studies, the question becomes what kinds of friction points must we identify, examine, and attempt to address to work effectively within and when preparing our students for writing online in larger global contexts (see Internet world users by language, 2017; and Most common languages used on the Internet as of June 2015, 2015, to help consider the complexity).

To address this question, we propose the "3Cs of writing in global online contexts." The objective of this approach is to isolate the study of writing-related friction points into three central, overarching realms connected to using online media in order to compose for globally distributed readers. When writing online for broader, international audiences, individuals attempt to accomplish three, interconnected general and overarching processes—contacting, conveying, and connecting:

- *Contacting*: To share ideas and information effectively with a global audience, the writer must be able to access or make contact with that audience. To this end, the first and perhaps most important step of writing online for greater global audiences involves selecting the online medium or media that allow one to contact the targeted audience effectively. Section I: Contacting contains chapters spanning the use of digital notebooks (Josephine Walwema); experience mapping (Minh-Tam Nguyen, Heather Turner, and Benjamin Lauren); literacy development in international public forums (J. C. Lee); ePortfolios and blogfolios (Cynthia Davidson); and 4C4Equality and usability as networked engagement (Liz Lane and Don Unger).

- *Conveying*: Just because one can contact a given audience to share a composition does not inherently mean that audience will understand the ideas conveyed or the writer's purpose for sharing that information. Conveying becomes readily apparent if a given international audience responds to or acts upon a given composition in the manner intended *or* unintended by the author. Thus, this friction point involves factors that can affect an international audience's ability to comprehend conveyed ideas and desired responses or actions intended by the author. Section II: Conveying contains chapters spanning connections in Internet-mediated learning environments (Suzanne Blum Malley); massive open online courses (MOOCs) and world Englishes (Kaitlin Clinnin, Kay Halasek, Ben McCorkle, Susan Delagrange, Scott Lloyd Dewitt, Jen Michaels, and Cynthia L. Selfe); writing resources across the global information divide (Amber Engelson); activity and actor-network theory (Beau S. Pihlaja); and digital composing practices in Turkey (Mª Pilar Milagros).

- *Connecting*: It is one thing to share information globally via an online medium. It is a far different exercise to use online media to create a system of interaction whereby author and reader continually shift roles and exchange information to engage in a greater discussion. Thus, maximizing the potential of writing online in global contexts involves connecting in ways that build a continually interacting community around a shared area of interest. Section III: Connecting contains chapters spanning writing centers and online feedback (Vassiliki Kourbani); distributed agency in digital environments (Lavinia Hirsu); transnational activism (Katherine Bridgman); multimodal literacies among Bhutanese refugees in the United States (Tika Lamsal); and glocalization through Google Apps for Education (Daniel Hocutt and Maury Brown).

The central notion of the 3Cs approach (contacting, conveying, connecting) is that composing through text and other media is a powerful mechanism for creating and maintaining communities in international contexts. Consider what global strategist Parag Khanna (2016) calls "connectography," which is how connectivity has enabled us to build a global network civilization and work toward overcoming some geopolitical problems. When done effectively, online composing is ideally suited for creating greater global communities around shared interests and objectives.

In technical communication and writing studies, we can use this 3Cs approach to identify, understand, and address various friction points that can affect the success or effectiveness of writing in online global contexts. Doing so allows us to achieve central objectives related to connecting with global audiences, in order to do the following:

- Identify potential friction points that could impede the exchange of ideas when writing in international, online contexts;
- Understand how an item creates friction or affects aspects of contact, conveying, and/or connecting when writing in global online contexts; and
- Develop approaches for addressing or mitigating friction points when writing online to ensure participants meet the objective of effectively engaging with global audiences.

In technical communication and writing studies, we must focus more on the expanded rhetorical triangle to better understand complexities of audience and purpose.

By using this 3Cs approach to guide our research and teaching practices to address these factors, those of us in technical communication and writing studies can better understand and better prepare our students to compose online in the age of global cyberspace. Of course, these areas are broad and in scope, and vary significantly with each context, as the contributors in this collection demonstrate. We offer a polyvocal perspective in this collection, with views from a variety of scholars, positions, and approaches. As such, this collection builds on the work and approach of Blake Scott, Bernadette Longo, and Kathy Wills's (2007) *Critical Power Tools: Cultural Studies Approaches to Technical Communication.* Our text explores ways in which we can understand embodiment

(Fleckenstein, 2003, 2009; Fleckenstein, Hum, & Calendrillo, 2007), as well as technological ecologies and sustainability (DeVoss, McKee, & Selfe, 2009). That is, with diverse genres and voices within this collection we work to (inter)connect a representative picture of writing research related to global contexts.

Specifically, entries in this collection represent examples that explore these 3Cs areas to overview how a particular friction point can affect composing online for globally distributed audiences. There are five chapters in each of three sections. Each chapter provides insights for better identifying and understanding friction points, and models how we in technical communication and writing studies might approach this idea of friction points in our research and teaching practices. Thus, chapters contained here are informational (they provide an overview of a given idea), exemplary (they provide a model for how to approach the idea of friction points in teaching and research), and foundational (they offer starting points from which others can launch further inquiry into a given friction point area). It is the hope of the editors that readers will view these collected entries as an invitation to engage in a greater discussion of and debate of these friction point issues and overall practices related to writing online for global contexts.

Note

1.   See, for instance, the Global Learning, Information Literacy, and Intercultural Knowledge and Competence rubrics from the Association of American Colleges and Universities (AACU) VALUE Rubric Development Project (AACU, 2017).

References

AACU. (2017). VALUE rubric development project. *Association of American Colleges and Universities*. Retrieved from https://www.aacu.org/value/rubrics

Caroll, L. B. (2010). Backpacks vs. briefcases: Steps toward rhetorical analysis. In C. Lowe & P. Zemliansky (Eds.), *Writing Spaces Readings on Writing Vol. I* (pp. 45–58). Anderson, SC: Parlor Press.

Darling-Hammond, L. (2010). *The flat world and education: How America's commitment to equity will determine our future.* New York, NY: Teachers College Press.

DeVoss, D., McKee, H., & Selfe, R. (2009). *Digital writing research: Technologies, methodologies and ethical issues.* Cresskill, NJ: Hampton.

Fleckenstein, K. (2003). *Embodied literacies: Imageword and a poetics of teaching.* Carbondale, IL: Southern Illinois University Press.

Fleckenstein, K. (2009). *Vision, rhetoric, and social action in the composition classroom.* Carbondale, IL: Southern Illinois University Press.

Fleckenstein, K., Hum, S., & Calendrillo, L. (2007). *Ways of seeing, ways of speaking: The integration of rhetoric and vision in constructing the real.* Carbondale, IL: Southern Illinois University Press.

Getto, G., & St.Amant, K. (2014). Designing globally, working locally: Using personas to develop online communication products for international users. *Communication Design Quarterly, 3*(1), 24–46. https://doi.org/10.1145/2721882.2721886

The Internet Big Picture. (2017). *Internet World Stats: Usage and Population Statistics.* Retrieved from http://www.internetworldstats.com/stats.htm

Internet in Europe stats. (2017). *Internet World Stats: Usage and Population Statistics.* Retrieved from http://www.internetworldstats.com/stats4.htm

Internet penetration in Asia. (2017). *Internet World Stats: Usage and Population Statistics.* Retrieved from http://www.internetworldstats.com/stats3.htm#asia

Internet penetration in North America. (2017). *Internet World Stats: Usage and Population Statistics.* Retrieved from http://www.internetworldstats.com/stats14.htm#north

Internet users in the Americas. (2017). *Internet World Stats: Usage and Population Statistics.* Retrieved from http://www.internetworldstats.com/stats2.htm

Internet world stats: Usage and population statistics. (2017). *Internet World Stats: Usage and Population Statistics.* Retrieved from http://internetworldstats.com/links.htm

Internet world users by language. (2017). *Internet World Stats: Usage and Population Statistics.* Retrieved from http://www.internetworldstats.com/stats7.htm

Khanna, P. (2016). *Connectography: Mapping the future of global civilizations.* New York, NY: Random House; https://www.ted.com/talks/parag_khanna_how_megacities_are _changing_the_map_of_the_world

Most common languages used on the Internet as of June 2015. (2015). *Statista.* Retrieved from https://www.statista.com/statistics/262946/share-of-the-most-common-languag es-on-the-internet

Ong, W. J. (1975). The writer's audience is always fiction. *Publications of the Modern Language Association, 90*(1), 9–21. https://doi.org/10.2307/461344

Scott, B., Longo, B., & Wills, K. (Eds.). (2007). *Critical power tools: Technical communication and cultural studies.* Albany, NY: SUNY.

St.Amant, K. (2013). Finding friction points: Rethinking the flat earth model of globalization. *conneXions: International Professional Communication Journal, 1,* 125–132.

St.Amant, K. (2015). Reconsidering social media for global contexts. *Intercom: The Magazine of the Society for Technical Communication.* Fairfax, VA: Society for Technical Communication. 16–18.

St.Amant, K., & Rife, C. M. (Eds.). (2014). *Legal issues in global contexts: Perspectives on technical communication in the international age.* Amityville, NY: Baywood.

Sun, H. (2012). *Cross-cultural technology design: Crafting culture-sensitive technology for local users.* New York, NY: Oxford University Press. https://doi.org/10.1093/acprof:o so/9780199744763.001.0001

Zhao, Y. (2009). *Catching up or leading the way: American education in the age of globalization.* Alexandria, VA: Association for Supervision and Curriculum Development.

Zhao, Y. (2010). Preparing globally competent teachers: A new imperative for teacher education. *Journal of Teacher Education, 61*(5), 422–431. https://doi.org/10.1177 /0022487110375802

SECTION I

Contacting

To access and communicate effectively with an audience through the use of online media. Friction points include topics related to the technological, the linguistic, and the cultural.

1

DIGITAL NOTEBOOKS
Composing with Open Access

Josephine Walwema

ABSTRACT

Online media have brought previously disparate communities together and have altered how people around the globe interact. Complicated problems now profit from degrees of collaboration never before possible, and the writing classroom can create opportunities for learning with online media in this context. Using online media such as digital notebooks can facilitate dialogic inquiry where participants can interact with peers from other cultures as they compose locally for global readerships. This chapter relates promises and challenges of such multicultural composing processes in digital spaces.

Keywords: collaboration, invention, cross-cultural rhetoric, digital notebook, online media, participatory writing technologies, transnational

INTRODUCTION

The global proliferation of online media and Internet access enables individuals from different cultures and nations to interact in different ways. Activities such as crowdsourcing, crowd funding, user reviews, and social media groups are a few that characterize online interaction. Moreover, such interaction is not limited to nation states. It is often global, fueled by open access to content and passion for causes. Because digital media allow people around the world to access more content more quickly, the capacity to bridge the gap between local concerns and international dialogue is now possible. Live tweets from crisis spots around the world have, for example, informed the reporting of media organizations such as *The New York Times*, but with a more globalized focus (see The Choices Program: Teaching with the News). If this paradigm can revolutionize the news and impact global dialogue, what new, global context for teaching writing as a "transnational

DOI: 10.7330/9781607326649.c001

literacy practice[s]" does it offer (Hawisher, Selfe, Kisa, & Ahmed, 2010, p. 58)? Digital notebooks, in turn, represent a ready platform for students to interact and collaboratively compose with peers locally and globally.

Digital notebooks describe a range of participatory writing technologies in which a topic initiated by the writer is opened up for collaborative engagement with others. Because the collaboration begins at the conceptual level, the process allows for a cumulative flow of information where, through a back and forth, participants add, comment on, correct, and edit content. Here is how writer Ta-Nehisi Coates, who originated the phrase *digital notebooks,* openly invited the site's dedicated group of commenters (who he calls *the horde*), "On things I am not sure on, I'll state my opinion rather gingerly and then hope my commenters can fill in the gaps" (Coates, 2008, para. 1).

Coates's used the phrase "Talk To Me Like I'm Stupid" to invite commentary on various topics ranging from Hermeneutics, Revolutionary Island, Locke's State of Slavery and War, Victorian Fashion, to Financial Derivatives (Coates, 2011). He was rewarded with comments (content) explicating topics beyond their dictionary definition. Coates turned his comments section into a remarkable array of analyses, discussions, debate, and virtual reading group where people learned from each other. Such a form of crowdsourcing helps engage citizens in public issues by blending data, video, and social networking tools. It connects writers with the communities they serve by leveraging their knowledge and lived experiences to generate knowledge from the ground up.

Unlike the easy displays emanating from simple Google searches, the kind of knowledge that comes from this active back and forth is significant for its ability to shape the reality of its immediate audience. And that is an important element in interactive and collaborative global composing because it demonstrates that a genuine intellectual community can be formed, even on Internet.

I contend therefore that digital notebooks hold enormous promise for knowledgeable and skillful collaborative composing and open up more global communicative possibilities for students. Further, digital notebooks come with a built-in pedagogical system that (a) broadens the perspectives of the writer, (b) prompts real time revision, (c) heightens the writers' audience awareness, and (d) promotes metacognition through self-reflection. In this chapter, I examine how digital notebooks can support collaborative composing and promote transnational literacy practices.

THE INTEGRATION OF ONLINE MEDIA
INTO COMPOSING PRACTICES

Making online media a regular composing space—akin to word processing—is still a work in progress. The extant literature on online media in composition tends to emphasize ancillary components such as peer review (Bradley, 2014), revision, or online reflective practices of student writers (Ross, 2014). Other literature (e.g., Kirby & Crovitz, 2012) suggests ways to "incorporate technology" into writing, but in so doing, implies it is an add-on. Moreover, such literature draws from functional approaches to composition as means for teaching skills (Guth & Helm, 2010) rather than as forums that can promote collaborative educational experiences among disparate global learners. Further, articulated differences between so-called traditional composition—where the technology of word processing is an "instrumental tool of writing" (Porter, 2009)—and new media in which the actual work of composing occurs, suggest the need for more work.

Those shortcomings aside, the consensus on online media indicates it has heralded a "writing and reading renaissance" (Garcia, 1997) or, as Lunsford puts it, "a literacy revolution" (cited in Thompson, 2009) that permeates the composition class. Studies of online media have also led to it being referred to by various names, including the following:

- Digital (e.g., Porter, 2009; Eyman, 2012; Losh, 2014)
- New media (e.g.,Wysocki, 2004; Ball & Kalmbach, 2010)
- Multimedia (e.g., Faigley, 2003)
- Multimodal (e.g., Kress, 2005; Selfe, 2007; Palmeri, 2012)
- Online (e.g., Warnock, 2009)
- Web writing (Santos & Leahy, 2014).

Such dissimilar terms, as Lauer (2014) notes, "depend more on the audience to whom we are speaking than any external definition of the term itself" (p. 73). Currently, the term *digital* is evoked to refer to cutting-edge technologies of meaning—making and managing content.

As indicated, digital notebook technologies and related approaches to writing are increasingly gaining widespread use. They cultivate an inquisitive culture that appreciates uncertainty and encourages interpretation. In the process of creating meaning, absolute truths are set aside and complexities examined, making for a more informed writer. The implication is digital notebooks are spaces that allow for unbridled access to a global connected community that can collaboratively contribute to, compose, and critique ideas to prompt real-time revision, reflection, and review. Digital notebooks are collaborative software applications that allow several people to work together in real time.

Aside from individual writers, MIT runs Climate CoLab for an online community of people concerned about climate change. Here, individuals brainstorm and share ideas on how to combat climate change in their own localities before sharing those solutions globally. Thus, while Web 2.0 has seemingly integrated the tools of collaborative composing, "education 2.0 remains an aspiration" (Carr, Crook, Noss, Carmichael, & Selwyn, 2008, p. 1). Given their obvious scope of communication in the twenty-first century, digital notebooks, are products of our time that can influence how we make meaning. They deserve their place in the composition classroom.

Because the potential of digital notebooks highlights the ability to improve students' language skills along with their intercultural communicative competence (Guth & Helm, 2010), educators can leverage students' social-media skills into academic composing strategies. Students can be taught to use these spaces for educational purposes because, as Thorne and Black (2007) find, online exchanges support more meaningful interactions rather than fixate on learning the content. Students can thus interact in situ to initiate and further global conversations on issues of interest within the writing classroom.

Composing Globally

The nature of communication has fundamentally changed. We are now grounded in the networked textual and image world in which we can instantly and globally communicate. Thus we don't simply draw information from the web; we actively participate in and contribute via blogs, social media platforms, and "comments" sections of online articles. It is thus essential composition teachers train students to be participatory in a world that has radically redefined what expertise means. To compose successfully in the twenty-first century, one must excel at verbal and written expression and at the use and manipulation of images.

One of the more promising approaches to building expertise is through *collaborative composing*. To promote collaborative composing in this global context, educators have to work closely with students through direct instruction to engage the theory of composition and guided application of practice using digital tools. Educators also need to be guided by identifying barriers that can affect how students interact and collaboratively compose with peers from other nations and cultures. Such barriers are numerous, but I focus on two:

- cultural differences
- linguistic differences including communication expectations, patterns, practices, and the language of interaction

Granted, addressing cultural and linguistic barriers veers into intercultural communication. However, one of the ways rhetoric examines the available means of persuasion is through assessing the role of social practices in meaning making. Because this essay focuses on composing collaboratively for textual production, examining the sociocultural aspects that shape meaning is important. As such, educators and students will need a "repertoire of complex and interrelated skills" (Cook, 2002, p. 7) and multiliteracies pertinent to the twenty-first century—in short, a hybrid of literacies (Cook, 2002, p. 7; Selber, 2004). For this author, the literacies most applicable to collaborative global composing are

- digital literacies—to collaboratively compose; instantaneous and wide access; direct reach
- rhetorical literacies—to address specific audiences, purposes, and medium of delivery
- cultural/social literacies—to negotiate meaning by learning local communication patterns

To develop these literacies learners need to develop a cosmopolitan and global perspective necessary to look beyond their own communities. The concept of cosmopolitanism, understood here as an embodiment of cultural identity formation and promoting global citizenship through transnational communication (Appiah, 2006; Hull, Stornaiuolo, & Sahni, 2010, p. 331), can help bridge cultural communication differences among students.

Competencies for Collaborative Writing in Global Contexts

Here, I discuss the competencies necessary for participating in/co-authoring digital notebooks.

Digital Literacy

When we speak of digital literacy, we speak of a functional literacy beyond the ability to comprehend the "core competencies of the Internet" (Giles, 2005, p. 900) in which students can search, navigate, assemble, and evaluate texts for their information quotient. We aspire, instead, to a digital literacy of multimodal texts. To be digitally literate, as Lanham (1995) asserts, is to be "skilled at deciphering complex images and sounds as well as the syntactical subtleties of words" (p. 200). Lanham's definition speaks to digital skills that are broad in scope and cutting edge. Hull & Nelson (2009), in turn, suggest digital texts require "transliteracies" to engage not just across platforms, but also beyond barriers and territories. Without these literacies, students' ability to collaborate would be greatly compromised.

Becoming "transliterate" (Hull & Nelson, 2009) to engage diverse ideas and construct "text across geographical spaces" in multimedia (p. 87) supports this goal of collaborative global composing. It builds on categories of "new literacy studies" (Gee, 2005) that include knowing the sociocultural contexts where discourse is rooted. Because the digital interface brings together users and technologies in an "attempt to broker solutions" (Johnson-Eilola, 2004, p. 201) so that meaning is produced in the content rather than transmitted from sender to receiver, such writing has been deemed a twenty-first century technology (Wysocki, 2004; Johnson-Eilola, 2004). However, Hull and Nelson (2009) suggest the ability to negotiate differences and meaning across territories is a literacy consistent with the twenty-first century because it involves more than technological competence. It is also about engaging the cultural and linguistic sense of people beyond students' own territorial and geographical boundaries. Engagement is what in the end makes global interconnectedness possible. In addition, it makes the composing process transparent and the resulting knowledge collaborative and transactional. It thus democratizes meaning making, which is important for cultivating global ideas (Berlin, 1987).

Meaning making is central to composing in online media and its communal nature as Yancey (2009) discusses, and can act as a means to cultivating global citizenship. As Yancey contends, an improved form of composition is capable of rendering, even cultivating, state and global citizen writers in a communal literacy and "writers of the future" (p. 1). That way, as students collaborate in a community of inquiry (Garrison, Anderson, & Archer, 2010) at a lateral level, they can stake out and contest claims with peers from different cultures and nationalities based on a sociocultural understanding and a consideration of each others' values. Such is what digital notebooks do.

Cultural Literacy

Cultural and structural differences, linguistic challenges, and belief systems are a few of the barriers students would need to overcome to successfully write collaboratively in global contexts (Hartley, 2011; Volet & Jones, 2012; McCalman, 2014). Existing research on multilingualism and the cultural challenges pertaining to writing (e.g., Bawarshi & Reif, 2010; Sofianou-Mullen & Mullen, 2011; St.Amant & Rife, 2014; Leonard, 2014) suggests approaching culture as a people's view of what they deem un/acceptable behavior. Ongoing and extensive research on the communities with which students are paired can reveal sources of ambiguity and contextualize stylistics and wording (Walwema, 2016)—what Leonard (2014) calls "rhetorical attunement." Such attunement can be attained through a translingual approach that "assumes multiplicity" (p. 228), yet makes it possible to negotiate meaning across culture. It is a literacy developed over time.

In addition to culture, McCalman (2014) suggests developing a global awareness entails overcoming language differences among communicants. Such differences can be indicative of socio-economic status constituting "the dialects of [the speakers'] nurture" (NCTE, 1974) or may belong to the category of Global Englishes (Schneider, 2014). Acknowledging language differences even among native speakers from the same country is an important first step in intercultural communication (Galloway & Rose, 2014). Exposing learners to Global Englishes sensitizes them and makes them more receptive to ideas originating from those speakers (Cheung & Sung, 2014).

Related to linguistic understanding is acquiring the intercultural competence that limits instances of miscommunication (Dooly, 2011; Bradley, 2014). Writing collaboratively, for example, often involves peer critique. Couched in established norms here in the United States, students offering peer critique engage in a delicate balance of praise tempered with gentle critique (Bradley, 2014). Not so with Asian or even Latin American cultures. Guardado and Shi (2007), for example, have found some members of certain Asian cultures associate critique with negativity and see it as putdown. Such (U.S.) norms might prevent collaborative composing with cultures where people are more interested in "maintaining harmony" than upsetting the balance established within the group.

Cultural understanding can be learned as long as educators and students recognize the multilayered nature of communities. Knowing communities are comprised of individuals who interact outside of their dominant groups is important (Wilson & Peterson, 2002; Walwema, 2016). Intercultural interaction is therefore not only situated and dynamic; it also "requires high levels of sensitivity and a genuine mutual search for reciprocal understanding" (Ujitani & Volet, 2008, p. 297). And that mutual search for reciprocal understanding is rhetorical.

Understanding belief systems, cultures, and language also lies at the heart of the participatory nature of writing a "digital commons" (Yancey,

2009, p. 5) within the commonly understood rhetorical notion of audience and of publishing in an era where readers are co-creators of texts (White & Le Cornu, 2011; Stark & Fins, 2012). Thus, understanding belief systems can never be approached with a broad brush that assumes homogeneity on account of ethnicity or nationality, given the "participatory," "collaborative," and "distributed" nature of digital technologies.

In laying the groundwork for collaborative composing, media scholars (McLuhan, Fiore, & Agel, 2001; Benjamin, 2008; Hansen, 2014) who examine communities and their relationship to media have not only uncovered the constraints and affordances of different media forms throughout history, but have found that the significance of media is "derived from its status both as a material thing embedded within social practices, and through its capacity to facilitate communication, and thus social relationships" (Gershon & Bell, 2013, p. 261). Media are therefore tools whose possibilities and even risks can be leveraged for social and communicative purposes. They can, for example, enable new forms of interaction and collaboration, as I expand in the next section.

Overcoming Barriers to Global Collaboration

Global (In)Differences

An important dimension of literacy in the connected world is one that necessitates respect for differences, values, and belief systems represented by others—the realm of cosmopolitanism. As Hull and Stornaiuolo (2010) write, cosmopolitanism as conceptualized by philosopher Kwame Appiah, once a theoretical pursuit has made a resurgence in the wake of globalization and related proliferation of online media and Internet access. Part of the attraction of cosmopolitanism is that it presents a vision of global democracy and world citizenship (Appiah, 2006). With that vision comes the capacity to engage multiculturally across the globe and, in doing so, to synthesize new knowledge through a dynamic exchange of ideas and information.

To be cosmopolitan is to acknowledge others' humanity by, first and foremost, being grounded in one's own interpretive community. From that place of stability, one can then become aware of others' differences, cultivate a tolerance and understanding of those differences, enhance one's standing while transcending it to engage other cultures (Appiah, 2006). For example, Gershon and Bell (2013) find texting as a technology has significantly rebranded Papua New Guinea by "simultaneously" grounding it more locally while infusing it with a "cosmopolitan identification" (p. 259). In Papua New Guinea, cosmopolitanism has helped mediate local and global communication scenarios to bridge cultural literacy and to promote intercultural communication. With a cosmopolitan *ethos*, students using digital notebooks as communication spaces can engage epistemological differences beyond their localities more substantively.

Language and Difference

Other epistemological differences are centered on language. While students in general have appropriated the digital networking tools of actively talking through issues of shared interest with a wide range of speakers, that skill has not been adopted in the writing classroom. Yet understanding language and difference is a necessary step in promoting rhetorical literacy through digital notebooks.

No doubt students collaborating with other speakers of English might encounter language variances, which may interfere with intentionality. To address such disparities, Horner, Lu, Royster, and Trimbur (2011) call for a "translingual approach" in which language varieties are not perceived as barriers, but as avenues for meaning making (p. 303). Similarly, Galloway and Rose (2015) study of Global Englishes found that exposure to other Englishes helps normalize language differences. Educators have to work with students to examine phrases, expressions, and other ranges of English language use for their rhetorical and communicative possibilities and not their perceived errors or inferior status. After all, students are constantly reading texts and listening to speakers whose Englishes do not necessarily conform to what is considered standard in their own communities. Popular culture has, for example, been credited with Britishism finding its way into American vocabulary (Yagoda, 2016) just as rap and hip-hop music aesthetics set the standard for artistic expression in the arts, normalizing Black English in the process.

Recognizing and acknowledging such differences moves learners to focus on deliberation. Moreover, in respecting those differences, an element of critical inquiry that examines who/what deems a language standard can be broached and a healthy respect for other Englishes upheld. That way, participants are communicating at a lateral, rather than a top-down level of understanding.

To aid in comprehension, digital notebooks can be outfitted with resources devoted to deconstructing differences in terminology without compromising the integrity of shared projects. Such a page mimicking the *sidebar* in newspapers can accommodate adjacent information that is separate but contextually connected to the project (see, for example, "Explore the Past," 2017).

Culture and Difference

At its most basic level, language is intertwined with culture, which itself comes with a set of values and belief systems. Using students' knowledge of web tools within digital notebooks can be instrumental in abridging those cultural gaps. As noted earlier in this essay, cultural differences can be an obstacle in transnational collaboration.

Studies in intercultural rhetoric in the context of communication (Connor, 2004; Connor, 2011; Atkinson, 2012) have broached ways to examine the pedagogical consequences of difference or similarity among cultures. After focusing on contrastive rhetoric whose emphasis was on the influence of first language patterns on ESL, Connor (2011) offered cross-culture as a way to generate useful yet "idealized descriptions of cultural practices" and intercultural research that focuses on cultural interconnection (Atkinson, 2015, p. 426). Since then, St.Amant (2016) has found that through cross-cultural and intercultural communication, designers of communication ought to identify the "different world view of the cultures interaction" to determine how those differences factor into the communication process (p. 12). In short, knowing fellow communicants beyond their national identities is a significant step in communicating globally.

Useful online resources to aid in this comprehension in digital notebooks include the Hofstede Center and the United Nations Human Development Index (HDI). While the Hofstede model has been critiqued for drawing broad conclusions, the toolkit located at https://geert-hofstede.com/countries.html, which allows users to scan global cultures in order to develop insight and acquire strategies to develop content fit for a particular culture, can serve as a starting place for debunking assumptions on given cultures. For its part, the HDI's focus on human development can help orient discussion on people and their needs and less on perceived cultural indicators (Sarat-St. Peter, 2016). Both these resources can provide rhetorical cues that aid in collaboration. For as St.Amant (2006) notes, "the point at which one is expected to mention a particular special topic can be crucial to establishing credibility" (p. 60). These tools can be synchronously present during the composition process as source material embedded within the project for a multimodal effect.

Digital Notebooks: Epistemological Differences in Dialogue

One of the cosmopolitan tenets for collaboration is *dialogue*. Let us note from the outset that dialogue should not always lead to consensus, but rather that it facilitates learning about others through those cross-cultural interactions. Dialogue and self-reflexivity help promote deliberate ways of speaking about others' differences in ways that make living in a global world a more conscious and conscientious act. And digital notebooks come with a twenty-first century capacity for dialogue in facilitating transnational communication.

To promote transnational collaboration, there has to be a conscious effort to interact with others outside our default social networks, that is, those similar to us in race, class, and even ideological outlook (boyd & Ellison, 2007). Such cooperation requires initiation. If as educators we reframe digital notebooks as educational avenues for collaborative writing projects, we can overcome that initial hurdle of being contained in balkanized communities. We can help our students go outside of their social networks to engage others. For within cosmopolitanism is a tradition of philosophy and social action capable of shaping knowledge through diverse perspectives.

Moreover, collaborative composing on a global scale is supported by the communal nature of literacy in which knowledge in digital spaces is not the purview of one expert, but rather of "experienced peers or co-conspirators" (Mills, 2010, p. 235) in a participatory framework.

Application: Teaching with Digital Notebooks Collaborative Writing Project

We are in a rich moment of open experimentation. As we attempt to broaden the reach and scope of academic research in networked environments, we, as scholars can stop theorizing about networked collaboration and launch collaborative projects. For example, Stanford's Cross-Cultural Rhetoric pioneered collaborative writing for globally distributed students from universities around the world beginning with Sweden and expanding to Singapore, Russia, Egypt, and New Zealand (Stanford, n.d.). Those collaborative ventures were facilitated by technologies such as video-conferencing, wikis, and collaborative blogging. Given the increased accessibility of the Internet and wider adaptation of digital tools for teaching and learning, expanding this venture is seamlessly possible.

In the next section, I describe one approach in digital notebooks that can be adapted for globally distributed students as a collaborative composing project. It begins with an overview, stated goals, and offers resources to complete the project.

Sample Collaborative Task

Overview

Students will research and write about contemporary issues affecting their communities and explore ways to make the issue relevant to (inter)national audiences. They will develop content promoting a contemporary issue of national importance to that country. Collaborators must deem the issue important.

Topics may range from emerging health issues, communicable diseases, education, national security, and nation-states (e.g., Britain's exit from the EU [Brexit], refugee stories, sanitation, food insecurity, to name a few). To get started, students might scan the editorial pages of at least FIVE major newspapers in that country (see Abasi, 2014 on the role of editorials). They might also familiarize themselves with non-mainstream media types like bloggers, and others who are keyed into the topical issues in that country at a particular time.

At the onset of the collaborative venture, scholars should identify a topic and then ask:

- What theoretical and philosophical foundations can broaden my exposure and understanding of this topic?
- How is this topic informed by both contemporary and historical contexts?
- What primary and secondary verifiable sources exist on this topic?

These goals can be realized through Porter's (2009) heuristic for developing courses in writing with online media. For this particular purpose, the key elements of that heuristic are, *Access/Accessibility*-concerning questions about user connectedness to Internet-based information, openness for collaborative composing and access; *Interaction*-concerning the range of engagement, avenues for inquiry and dialogue among people and information made possible by digital designs; and *Distribution/ Circulation*-concerning the technological publishing options for reproducing, distributing, and circulating digital information (p. 208).

Collaborators can rely on more publicly collaborative spaces like Wikis, Dropbox, and Google Docs and have them configured for the composing project so only individuals in the group are granted access. Digital notebook technologies require accountability. From the moment participants agree to collaborate, their presence will be visible as will a record of their work.

Digital Notebooks
The following technologies facilitate the collaborative process:

- https://docs.google.com
- https://www.dropbox.com
- https://www.wikispaces.com
- https://www.google.com/fusiontables

Digital notebooks already reflect the current social structure that moves away from hierarchical to lateral communication. Collaborators engage in researching, writing, and contributing their knowledge to the notebooks during the composing phase. Such hands-on engagement heightens their sense of audience awareness and, hopefully, prompts them to be rigorous and measured in their contribution. In turn, the participatory acts broaden the writers' perspectives even as they prompt real-time revision.

Resources
- Geert Hofstede's cultural map: https://geert-hofstede.com/countries.html
- United nations Human Development Index (HDI): http://hdr.undp.org/en/content/human-development-index-hdi
- Institutional resources in nation states (agencies, newspapers sites, blogs)

The resources are entry points for social-cultural literacy. Through them, collaborators become aware of and are acquainted with others and with that understanding progressively begin to relate better with them. The instructor outlines the process phases as a form of guided instruction so collaborators are assured of being in the right moment at every phase.

Phase I: Framing the Issue
Let's suppose that students in the United States wish to investigate the Zika virus. Their initial research might start from the United States, specifically in states that have reported cases (Center for Disease Control and Prevention, 2016). Given every confirmed case of Zika in the United States to date is travel-related, students might be led to follow the trail, which might lead them to Brazil, a country that is at the epicenter of the virus (Dadario, 2016). While students might rely on outlets like the Centers for Disease Control, and the National Institutes of Health, and the *New York Times* among other sources, they might want to expand their research to Brazil itself to interrogate the resources and to collaborate with peers there. Grouped into collaborative communities of inquiry, students would research the topic locally and globally. This

phase sets the direction and tone of the investigation so that they can later critically analyze the content emerging from that research.

Objectives
Students will

- Review a timeline of Zika from its initial detection to today.
- Identify what resources are being deployed to convey risk associated with Zika.
- Convey the short term and long-term effects of the virus.
- Generate visual displays in the form of medical cartography and infographics to help inform the public.

Phase II: Gathering (Re)Sources
Students explore how this subject might resonate globally. What resources would work best to broaden the issue and to reflect a shared sense of understanding? Are other nationalities affected by the same concerns raised locally? What are their particular circumstances? How are those issues resolved or left unresolved in those communities? This stage allows for new situated knowledge and a broadening of competencies of research, analyses, and framing. In this phase, contributors are encouraged to contribute primary material, offer personal insights, and share instantiations of the outbreak and its effects. Contributions include digital assets in the form of images, videos, web texts, slides, and screen captures—keeping copyright and accessibility principles in mind. These assets can all bring multimodality to the text.

Phase III: Analyzing
In this phase, students begin to compose their arguments in their forum of choice—Google Docs, FusionTables, or Wikis. They frame the context; outline the conceptual framework and research reflecting scholarship on the topic. Additionally, they explore the historical background, descriptions and definitions of key topics to be covered. They also analyze the sources for their meaning, challenging assertions and assumptions, calling for clarity and examples, identifying patterns, formulating theories and drawing conclusions.

Phase IV: Write-up, Finalizing, Publishing
All assets gathered, ideas interrogated, the writing phase takes the project to completion—including references, formatting, and

generally ready the text for sharing. The final write-up is the collective responsibility for making meaning out of the content and giving it the proper structure. Throughout these phases, members can cycle back to revisit initial views, amend, expand, or self-correct as their knowledge of the issue grows.

To allow for immediate visualization of the extent and magnitude of Zika distribution, students can look into mapping software to create maps that show epidemiological data such as Google Fusion Tables, which uses Google Maps to map data. Researchers such Welhausen (2015) have found that communicating health risks in intercultural contexts calls for "explanatory text and or visuals to more fully contextualize" the information so as to minimize the perception of risk among the general public (p. 244). In visual communication and data visualization, "the meaning of visuals often seems intuitive" (Welhausen, 2015, p. 250; Kress & van Leeuwen, 1996). Thus, the public can be counted upon to interpret visuals without a great deal of explanatory information making data visualizing a useful genre in collaborating globally to impact global dialogue and to promote transnational literacy. For their part, students would be motivated to inform, educate, and invite participation from the community by pointing them to resources and information they can use.

Maps based on empirical evidence, can support evidence-based decision making including intervention strategies and travel advice. Such an immediate impact of scholarship can be motivating for students. The fact that open source application software can be freely accessed by all for purposes of composing and easy distribution of text that carries local and global importance is an added benefit. Moreover, such visualized texts can serve as the basis upon which narratives can be constructed.

Assessment

Students collaboratively develop a set of criteria to rate the material.

Reflection

Students reflect on the collaborative process and how the text was informed by collaboration right from conception to completion; rate how knowledge of culture, rapprochement of linguistic, belief systems and cultural differences informs their writing. What changed in terms of content and design as the project shifted from local to global focus? The reflection achieves the dual purpose of digital notebooks with a greater focus on the kind of cultural literacy grounded in cosmopolitanism to encourage cooperation and awareness.

CONCLUSION

Composing collaboratively in digital notebooks provides pedagogical value in learning from one another and in promoting global connectedness. Some of the built-in pedagogical benefits that come with digital notebooks include a heightened sense of audience awareness where real readers are responding to the writing without the assessment sword hanging over the work. Further, a participatory audience focuses on important points and manages information overload. Such a collaborative venture enhances knowledge retention by promoting just in time learning that seems to have been gotten firsthand. Such benefits have been registered by many collaborative ventures including the MIT Climate CoLab, Stanford University's cross-cultural rhetoric collaborative project (with Örebro University in Sweden in 2006) and, indeed, Coates's "talk to me like I'm stupid" outreach. Among other things, collaborators realized gains such as lateral intercultural and rhetorical literacy within the aegis of cosmopolitanism, not to mention the interconnections made across territorial and geographical divides.

Collaborative and participatory modes of writing promote instantaneous revision and self-editing. As students write and read each other's writing, they encounter competing perspectives and different approaches to framing ideas. Given these dialogic exchanges, students are compelled to consider alternative perspectives and to substantively revise their work to meet the rhetorical goals of the project. Further, because such an ongoing peer review and revision process is transparent without diminishing the writer's expertise, revision takes on a more prominent place as part of the composing process. What's even better is that visualizing the revision process allows students to seamlessly review drafts in real time as peer critique becomes more supportive than controverting.

Participants can examine how a more multimedia focused approach that integrates writing, speech, images, color, sound, and animation, transcends language and cultural differences, while offering opportunities for authentic self-representation. Such research can test how indeed the transnational nature of collaboration helps students maintain their sense of self, voice, language, culture, and *ethos* while conveying it to others. Together, they can harness the tacit, dynamic, and even explicit aspects of meaning making.

Digital notebooks as collaborative composing spaces with global peers taps into a diverse intellectual audience and leads to a transliterate society that is also cosmopolitan. They can be the starting place for accommodating differences and smoothing over dissimilarities. The necessary dialogue with people of other cultures helps build social responsibility and the goodwill to promote the wellbeing of all people.

References

Abasi, A. R. (2014). Evaluative choices and rhetorical impact: American learners of Persian as a foreign language writing to appraise. *International Journal of Applied Linguistics, 24,* 224–249. Retrieved from https://doi.org/10.1111/ijal.12024

Appiah, K. A. (2006). *Cosmopolitanism: Ethics in a world of strangers.* New York, NY: Norton.

Atkinson, D. (2012). Intercultural rhetoric and intercultural communication. In J. Jackson (Ed.), *Routledge handbook of language and intercultural communication* (pp. 116–129). New York, NY: Routledge.

Atkinson, D. (2015). Writing across cultures. In F. Sharifian (Ed.), *The Routledge handbook of language and culture* (pp. 417-430). New York, NY: Routledge.

Ball, C. E., & Kalmbach, J. R. (Eds.). (2010). *RAW: (Reading and writing) new media.* Cresskill, NJ: Hampton Press.

Bawarshi, A. S., & Reif, M. J. (2010). *Genre: An introduction to history, theory, research and pedagogy.* Anderson, SC: Parlor Press.

Benjamin, W. (2008). *The work of art in the age of mechanical reproduction.* London, England: Penguin UK.

Berlin, J. A. (1987). *Rhetoric and reality: Writing instruction in American colleges, 1900–1985.* Carbondale, IL: Southern Illinois University Press.

boyd, d. m., & Ellison, N. (2007). Social network sites: Definition, history, and scholarship. *Journal of Computer-Mediated Communication, 13*(1), 210–230. Retrieved from https://doi.org/10.1111/j.1083-6101.2007.00393.x

Bradley, L. (2014). Peer-reviewing in an intercultural wiki environment—Student interaction and reflections. *Computers and Composition, 34,* 80–95. Retrieved from https://doi.org/10.1016/j.compcom.2014.09.008

Carr, D., Crook, C., Noss, R., Carmichael, P., & Selwyn, N. (2008). Education 2.0? Designing the web for teaching and learning: A commentary by the technology enhanced learning phase of the Teaching and Learning Research Programme. Retrieved from http://eprints.ioe.ac.uk/6217/1/Selwyn2008education.pdf

Center for Disease Control and Prevention. (2016). Zika virus disease in the United States, 2015–2016. Retrieved from https://www.cdc.gov/zika/geo/united-states.html

Cheung, C., & Sung, M. (2014). Global, local or glocal? Identities of L2 learners in English as a Lingua Franca communication. *Language, Culture and Curriculum, 27*(1): 43–57.

Coates, T.-N. (2008, August 4). "It's yours": A short history of the horde. *The Atlantic.* Retrieved from https://longreads.com/2015/02/04/its-yours-a-short-history-of-the-horde/

Coates, T.-N. (2011, April 27). Talk to me like I'm stupid: Locke's state of slavery and war. *The Atlantic.* Retrieved from https://www.theatlantic.com/personal/archive/2011/04/talk-to-me-like-im-stupid-lockes-state-of-slavery-and-war/237935/

Connor, U. (2004). Intercultural rhetoric research: Beyond texts. *Journal of English for Academic Purposes, 3*(4), 291–304. Retrieved from https://doi.org/10.1016/j.jeap.2004.07.003

Connor, U. (2011). *Intercultural rhetoric in the writing classroom.* Ann Arbor, MI: University of Michigan Press. Retrieved from https://doi.org/10.3998/mpub.3488851

Cook, K. C. (2002). Layered literacies: A theoretical frame for technical communication pedagogy. *Technical Communication Quarterly, 11*(1), 5–29. Retrieved from https://doi.org/10.1207/s15427625tcq1101_1

Dadario, A. (2016). Living in the epicenter of Zika. Retrieved from https://blogs.unicef
.org/blog/living-in-the-epicenter-of-zika

Dooly, M. A. (2011). Crossing the intercultural borders into 3rd space culture(s):
Implications for teacher education in the twenty-first century. *Language and
Intercultural Communication, 11*(4), 319–337. Retrieved from https://doi.org/10.1080
/14708477.2011.599390

Explore the past . . . shape the future: History and current issues for the classroom.
(2017). Retrieved from http://www.choices.edu

Eyman, D. (2012). On digital rhetoric. Web log comment. Retrieved from http://www
.digitalrhetoriccollaborative.org/2012/05/16/on-digital-rhetoric

Faigley, L. (2003). The challenge of the multimedia essay. In L. Bloom, D. Daiker, & E.
White (Eds.), *Composition studies in the new millennium* (pp. 174–187). Carbondale, IL:
Southern Illinois University Press.

Galloway, N., & Rose, H. (2014). Using listening journals to raise awareness of Global
Englishes in ELT. *English Language Teaching Journal, 68*(4), 386–396. Retrieved from
https://doi.org/10.1093/elt/ccu021

Galloway, N., & Rose, H. (2015). *Introducing global Englishes.* Abingdon, Oxon:
Routledge.

Garcia, M. (1997). *Redesigning print for the web.* Indianapolis, IN: Hayden-McNeil.

Garrison, D. R., Anderson, T., & Archer, W. (2010). The first decade of the community
of inquiry framework: A retrospective. *Internet and Higher Education, 13*(1–2), 5–9.
Retrieved from https://doi.org/10.1016/j.iheduc.2009.10.003

Gee, J. P. (2005). The new literacy studies: From 'socially situated' to the work. *Situated
Literacies: Reading and Writing in Context, 2,* 177–194.

Gershon, I., & Bell, J. A. (2013). Introduction: The newness of new media. *Culture, Theory
& Critique, 54*(3), 259–264. Retrieved from https://doi.org/10.1080/14735784.2013
.852732

Giles, J. (2005). Internet encyclopedias go head to head. *Nature, 438*(7070), 900–901.
Retrieved from https://doi.org/10.1038/438900a

Guardado, M., & Shi, L. (2007). ESL students' experiences of online peer feedback.
Computers and Composition, 24(4), 443–461. doi:10.1016/j.compcom.2007.03.002

Guth, S., & Helm, F. (Eds.). (2010). *Telecollaboration 2.0: Language, literacies and intercultural learning in the 21st century.* New York, NY: Peter Lang. Retrieved from
https://doi.org/10.3726/978-3-0351-0013-6

Hansen, M. B. (2014). *Feed forward: On the future of 21st century media.* Chicago, IL:
University of Chicago Press. Retrieved from https://doi.org/10.7208/chicago/9780
226199863.001.0001

Hartley, J. (2011). *The uses of digital literacy.* New Brunswick, NJ: Transaction.

Hawisher, G. E., Selfe, C. L., Kisa, G., & Ahmed, S. (2010). Globalism and multimodality in a digitized world. *Pedagogy: Critical Approaches to Teaching Literature, Language,
Composition, and Culture, 10*(1), 55–68. doi:10.1215/15314200-2009-020

Horner, B., Lu, M. Z., Royster, J. J., & Trimbur, J. (2011). Opinion: Language difference
in writing: Toward a translingual approach. *College English, 73*(3), 303–321.

Hull, G., & Nelson, M. E. (2009). Literacy, media, and morality: Making the case for an
aesthetic turn. *Future of Literacy Studies,* 199–227. Retrieved from https://doi.org
/10.1057/9780230245693_11

Hull, G. A., & Stornaiuolo, A. (2010). Literate arts in a global world: Reframing social
networking as cosmopolitan practice. *Journal of Adolescent & Adult Literacy, 54*(2),
85–97. Retrieved from https://doi.org/10.1598/JAAL.54.2.1

Hull, G. A., Stornaiuolo, A., & Sahni, U. (2010). Cultural citizenship and cosmopolitan
practice: Global youth communicate online. *English Education, 42*(2), 331–367.

Johnson-Eilola, J. (2004). The database and the essay: Understanding composition as
articulation. In A. Wysocki, J. Johnson-Eilola, C. Selfe, & G. Sirc (Eds.), *Writing New*

Media: Theory and Applications for Expanding the Teaching of Composition (pp. 199–235). Logan, UT: Utah State University Press.

Kirby, D. L., & Crovitz, D. (2012). *Inside out: Strategies for teaching writing.* Portsmouth, NH: Heinemann.

Kress, G. R. (Ed.). (2005). *English in urban classrooms: A multimodal perspective on teaching and learning.* Psychology Press. Retrieved from https://doi.org/10.4324/9780203397305

Kress, G., & van Leeuwen, T. (1996). *Reading images: The grammar of visual design.* New York, NY: Routledge.

Lanham, R. A. (1995). Digital literacy. *Scientific American, 273*(3), 198–199.

Lauer, C. (2014). Expertise with new/multi/modal/visual/digital/media technologies desired: Tracing composition's evolving relationship with technology through the MLA *JIL. Computers and Composition, 34*(December), 60–75. Retrieved from https://doi.org/10.1016/j.compcom.2014.09.006

Leonard, R. L. (2014). Multilingual writing as rhetorical attunement. *College English, 76*(3), 227–247.

Losh, E. M. (2014). *The war on learning: Gaining ground in the digital university.* Cambridge, MA: The MIT Press.

McCalman, C. L. (2014). International instructor preparing teachers for multicultural classrooms in the United States: Teaching intercultural communication competence online. *New Directions for Teaching and Learning, 2014*: 73–81. Retrieved from doi:10.1002/tl.20098

McLuhan, M., Fiore, Q., & Agel, J. (2001). *The medium is the massage: An inventory of effects.* Corte Madera, CA: Gingko Press.

Mills, K. A. (2010). A review of the "digital turn" in the new literacy studies. *Review of Educational Research, 80*(2), 246–271. Retrieved from https://doi.org/10.3102/0034654310364401

National Council of Teachers of English. (1974). *Students' right to their own language. NCTE Resolution no. 74.2.* Urbana, IL: National Council of Teachers of English.

Palmeri, J. (2012). *Remixing composition: A history of multimodal writing pedagogy.* Carbondale, IL: Southern Illinois University Press.

Porter, J. (2009). Recovering delivery for digital rhetoric. *Computers and Composition, 26*(4), 207–224. Retrieved from https://doi.org/10.1016/j.compcom.2009.09.004

Ross, J. (2014). Performing the reflective self: Audience awareness in high-stakes reflection. *Studies in Higher Education, 39*(2), 219–232. http://dx.doi.org/10.1080/03075079.2011.651450

Santos, M. C., & Leahy, M. H. (2014). Postpedagogy and web writing. *Computers and Composition, 32*(June), 84–95. Retrieved from https://doi.org/10.1016/j.compcom.2014.04.006

Sarat-St Peter, H. (2016). Designing with HDR data: What the human development report can tell us about international users. *Communication Design Quarterly Review, 4*(1), 60–72. Retrieved from https://doi.org/10.1145/2875501.2875506

Schneider, E. W. (2014). New reflections on the evolutionary dynamics of world Englishes. *World Englishes, 33*(1), 9–32. Retrieved from doi:10.1111/weng.12069

Selber, S. A. (2004). *Multiliteracies for a digital age.* Carbondale, IL: Southern Illinois University Press.

Selfe, C. L. (2007). *Gaming lives in the twenty-first century.* New York, NY: Palgrave Macmillan. Retrieved from https://doi.org/10.1057/9780230601765

Sofianou-Mullen, F., & Mullen, J. W. (2011). Critical thinking, critical writing in composition courses at the American University in Bulgaria. *The American-Style University at Large: Transplants, Outposts, and the Globalization of Higher Education, 257.*

St.Amant, K. (2006). Globalizing rhetoric: Using rhetorical concepts to identify and analyze cultural expectations (specialized knowledge) related to genres. *Hermes—Journal of Language and Communication Studies, 37,* 47–66.

St.Amant, K. (2016). Introduction to the special issue: Cultural considerations for communication design: Integrating ideas of culture, communication, and context into user experience design. *Communication Design Quarterly Review, 4*(1), 6–22. Retrieved from https://doi.org/10.1145/2875501.2875502

St.Amant, K., & Rife, M. C. (2014). Legal issues in global contexts: Examining friction points on the flat earth. In K. St.Amant & M. C. Rife (Eds.), *Legal issues in global contexts: Perspectives on technical communication in an international age* (pp. 1–5). Amityville, NY: Baywood.

Stanford. (n.d.). Cross-cultural rhetoric: Developing intercultural competences through collaborative rhetoric. Retrieved from http://ccr.stanford.edu/globalexchange.htm

Stark, M., & Fins, J. J. (2012). The self, social media, and social construction. *American Journal of Bioethics, 12*(10), 38–39. Retrieved from https://doi.org/10.1080/15265161.2012.708094

Thompson, C. (2009). Clive Thompson on the new literacy. *Wired Magazine, 17*(9). Retrieved from https://www.wired.com/2009/08/st-thompson-7

Thorne, S. L., & Black, R. W. (2007). Language and literacy development in computer-mediated contexts and communities. Cambridge, England: Cambridge University Press. *Annual Review of Applied Linguistics, 27*, 133–160. Retrieved from https://doi.org/10.1017/S0267190508070074

Ujitani, E., & Volet, S. (2008). Socio-emotional challenges in international education insight into reciprocal understanding and intercultural relational development. *Journal of Research in International Education, 7*(3): 279–303. Retrieved from https://doi.org/10.1177/1475240908099975

Volet, S., & Jones, C. (2012). Cultural transitions in higher education: Individual adaptation, transformation and engagement. *Advances in Motivation and Achievement, 17*, 241–284.

Walwema, J. (2016). Tailoring information and communication design to diverse international and intercultural audiences: How culturally sensitive ICD improves online market penetration. *Technical Communication (Washington), 63*(1), 38–52.

Warnock, S. (2009). *Teaching writing online: How and why*. Urbana, IL: National Council of Teachers of English.

Welhausen, C. A. (2015). Visualizing a non-pandemic: considerations for communicating public health risks in intercultural contexts. *Technical Communication (Washington), 62*(4), 244–257.

White, D. S., & Le Cornu, A. (2011). Visitors and residents: A new typology for online engagement. *First Monday, 16*(9). Retrieved from https://doi.org/10.5210/fm.v16i9.3171

Wilson, S. M., & Peterson, L. C. (2002). The anthropology of online communities. *Annual Review of Anthropology, 31*(1), 449–467. Retrieved from https://doi.org/10.1146/annurev.anthro.31.040402.085436

Wysocki, A. F. (2004). Opening new media to writing: Openings and Justifications. In A. F. Wysocki, J. Johnson-Eilola, C. L. Selfe, & G. Sirc (Eds.). *Writing new media: Theory and applications for expanding the teaching of composition* (pp. 1–41). Logan, UT: Utah State University Press.

Yagoda, B. (2016). Not one-off Britishism. Retrieved from https://britishisms.wordpress.com

Yancey, K. B. (2009). Writing in the 21st century: A report from the National Council of Teachers of English. Retrieved from http://www.ncte.org/library/NCTEFiles/Press/Yancey_final.pdf

2

DISJUNCTURE, DIFFERENCE, AND REPRESENTATION IN EXPERIENCE MAPPING

Minh-Tam Nguyen, Heather Noel Turner, and Benjamin Lauren

ABSTRACT

Experience maps are a research practice used to visualize the interactions people have with a service, product, organization, or institution. An experience map might work to accurately identify how people access information or use product documentation. While documenting "experience" appears to emphasize user exigency, designing maps that meets these needs is iterative and involves representing a complex process of identifying doing, thinking, and feeling activities while working to understand culturally situated interactions. Our chapter argues experience maps can unintentionally disempower or marginalize certain participants or ways of being in the world. We argue cross-cultural experience is not a transparent concept, but one that is always changing.

Keywords: autoethnography, ethics, experience mapping, intercultural communication, globalization, participatory design, researcher stance

INTRODUCTION

Experience maps are a research practice for visualizing the interactions individuals have with an organization or institution. An experience map can identify how people access information about a product or policy by searching a website, calling customer service, or using product documentation. Writers use and design experience maps to understand "the holistic customer experience, demonstrating the highs and lows people feel while interacting with [a] product or service" (Adaptive Path, 2013). While documenting "experience" appears to naturally emphasize exigency, designing maps that represent experiences accurately involves a complex process of identifying doing, thinking, and feeling while working to understand culturally situated interactions. When working to

DOI: 10.7330/9781607326649.c002

understand culturally situated interactions, experience maps can unintentionally disempower or marginalize certain participants, emotions, or behaviors. The chapter argues cross-cultural experience is not a transparent concept, but is always changing. Experience maps are often designed and used in workplaces and classrooms that are globally connected.

WHAT IS AN EXPERIENCE MAP?

Because organizations value understanding how customers interact with products and services, professional and technical writers often collect and visualize information about a customer's experience in order to improve it. One method for visualizing such information is alignment diagrams, explained by Kalbach (2015) as "any map, diagram, or visualization that reveals both sides of value created in a single overview. They are a *category* of diagram that illustrates the interaction between people and organizations" (p. 4). Alignment diagrams have two purposes: to illustrate an organization's products, services, and processes and to visualize an individual's experience as they interact with these products, services, and processes (Kalbach, 2015). Alignment diagrams contribute to understanding a customer's experience, which is key to empathizing with someone's needs as they navigate services. As a form of alignment diagram, experience maps help us visualize the customer experience in ways that create empathy across an organization.

Organizations often use experience maps to show the how components of their services and products interact with customers to construct an experience. Kalbach (2015) explains, "they influence decision making at all levels and lead to consistency in actions" (p. 13). At the heart of an experience map lies the customer journey model, an archetypal journey created from an aggregate of all customers going from point A to point B as they attempt to achieve a goal or satisfy a need (Adaptive Path, 2013). Alignment diagrams are a strategic tool for capturing and presenting insights into customer interactions across an organization's ecosystem of products and services.

In today's workplace, writers might work with teams that develop and design alignment diagrams like experience maps. In addition, students might assemble alignment diagrams during internships or in coursework when studying user research, technical and professional writing, content strategy, or digital and technical contexts. When developing skills in alignment diagramming, students learn to understand customer experience from a broader perspective instead of narrowly focusing on the usability of content or a system. Alignment diagrams

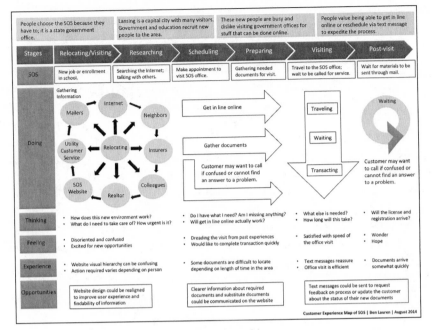

Figure 2.1. SOS Automobile Registration Experience Map

can also demonstrate how work fits into a broader customer experience, further illustrating how the activities of people interconnects across departments, organizations, companies, and even fields. Alignment diagrams, thus, help to visualize the larger workplace ecosystem. Figure 2.1 provides a sample experience map (the type described in this chapter) assembled to visualize the process of registering a car with Michigan Secretary of State.

Advantages and Disadvantages of Experience Maps

Experience maps offer individuals valuable information about interactions they have with and in different contexts. By articulating and plotting the touch points a person encounters when working with a product or service, experience maps identify behavioral trends and act as a catalyst for change. Figure 2.1, for example, demonstrates how the Secretary of State could offer text message surveys to assess visitor experiences after registering a car using the service. The biggest advantage of experience maps is the ability to reveal the pain points—or problems—of a particular experience, which are used to design interventions that improve a customer's experience. Experience maps thus offer insights into customer behaviors often left unsaid or unseen during everyday transactions. In addition, experience maps help visualize wayfinding, or spatial problem solving (e.g., how persons use websites to find information).

Despite such benefits, experience maps can also fall short as a method of studying users. First, experience maps can do a poor job representing cultural differences. When synthesizing multiple, cross-channel maps of the same experience, feelings emanating from certain touch-points have the potential to become homogenized and essentialized. This makes it easier to erase experiences that exist beyond the scope of paths most commonly taken. For example, someone might not consult a website prior to a visit at the Secretary of State (SOS), and as a result, would not know the documents needed to register their car. Also experience maps can privilege certain experiences while simultaneously granting too much power to the map-maker to decide what experiences matter. Kalbach (2015) explains, "As the mapmaker, it's up to you to decide on what aspects to include and which to leave out" (p. 20). The training of the mapmaker thus plays a significant role in how maps are perceived.

Problems with Designing Experience Maps

Experience maps depend greatly on visual representation of people's activities, thoughts, and emotions, and decisions about these representations are often made by the mapmaker. As Barton and Barton (2004) explained, maps are inherently ideological and can reinforce hegemonic processes and practices. As such, maps can be inclusive or exclusive documents. Therefore, Barton and Barton (2004) call for "a new politics of design, one authorizing heterodoxy—a politics where difference is not excluded or repressed, as before, but valorized" (p. 245). A mapmaker's response to difference and representing difference on an experience map can shape how organizations position customers. So, a major problem in assembling an experience map is how cultural difference is responded to and represented. And, as Dragga and Voss (2001) note, an important ethic is at stake as well, for we must represent people and activities using visuals that emphasize their humanity in meaningful and equitable ways. Such factors represent challenges to those creating experience maps.

As a starting point, Adaptive Path (2013) published a well-known guide to constructing experience maps that outlines steps a company uses to map a customer's journey, and it introduces language like "touch points," which is "a point of interaction between a person and any agent or artifact of an organization" (p. 6). It also defines concepts like "channel" as "a medium of interaction with customers or users" (p. 6). The focus on interaction is important because that is how an experience map identifies exigencies and captures experiences. At heart, experience mapping focuses on the stories people tell about interacting with a company or organization and pays attention to the "highs" and "lows" of those activities as a way to improve the customer's journey. As a method, experience mapping has the potential to provide opportunities for changing how people interact with a company over time while completing tasks, buying products, or engaging with materials. Conversely, the training of the mapmaker represents a point of contention, especially relating to how different ways of thinking, feeling, acting, and living in the world are represented visually. One approach for responding to cultural differences surfaces in stronger training in critical research practice.

Global Contexts and Researcher Stance

Sullivan and Porter (1997) argue researchers need to understand how they are framing themselves in research. Extended to experience mapping, this argument suggests researchers should understand how epistemological leanings influence what is discovered and how those discoveries are represented and understood by others. Researchers must therefore be cognizant of how the map defines good and bad, highs and lows, disruptions, contradictions, opportunities, and so on.

Experience mapping certainly emphasizes rigor through iteration and collaboration, but so far, the method does not directly address frameworks for ensuring a variety of realities are represented as unfamiliar or perhaps unfamiliar. John Law (2004) explains, "while standard methods are often extremely good at what they do, they are badly adapted to the study of the ephemeral, the indefinite and the irregular" (p. 4). Methodologies, moreover, are inherently political. They have histories and make arguments about ways of seeing and understanding. John Cresswell (2008) calls this a "world view" or a philosophy that each methodology presupposes. A researcher's choice of methodology constructs, sustains, and produces realities, which ultimately influences the user's broader experience. A team interpreting a person's story largely controls the reality created by the experience map. As global contexts and audiences continue to grow more complex, capturing experience accurately presents many challenges with no simple solution. Arjun Appadurai (1990) explains how we might conceive of experience as in a constant state of flux.

In "Disjuncture and Difference in the Global Cultural Economy," Appadurai (1990) describes models of understanding how international interactions among cultures are somewhat limited. Instead, he argues we should imagine a cultural economy "as a complex, overlapping, disjunctive order" (p. 296). At root, "the complexity of the current global economy has to do with certain fundamental disjunctures between economy, culture and politics" (p. 296) and as such, Appadurai presents a basic framework for "exploring such disjunctures" (p. 296). The framework consists of "five dimensions of global cultural flow." The concept of flow is important because Appadurai is arguing that we see culture as comprised of several scapes, or formations, and sets out to define each one. He further explains, "The suffix scape also allows us to point to the fluid, irregular shapes of these landscapes, shapes which characterize international capital as deeply as they do international clothing styles" (p. 297). The five -scapes presented are ethnoscapes, mediascapes, technoscapes, finanscapes, and ideoscapes.

Appadurai (1990) argues each scape is constantly evolving, shifting, and overlapping in unpredictable ways. He defines each: ethnoscapes are the "landscape of persons who constitute the shifting world in which we live" (p. 297); technoscapes are "the global configuration, also ever fluid, of technology, and of the fact that technology, both high and low, both mechanical and informational, now moves at high speeds across various kinds of previously impervious boundaries" (p. 297); finanscapes are "global capital" such as "currency markets, national stock exchanges, and commodity speculations" (p. 298); mediascapes are "the distribution of the electronic capabilities to produce and disseminate information [. . .] and to the images of the world created by media" (pp. 298–299); and ideoscapes are "concatenations of images, but they are often directly political and frequently have to do with ideologies of states and the counter-ideologies of movements explicitly oriented to capturing state power or a piece of it" (p. 299). Positioning these categories as overlapping and constantly evolving demonstrates a need for flexible methods of capturing people's experience as they seek to participate in civic and work life.

Building on Appadurai's work, Godwin Agboka (2012) argues there is a need for more localized accounts of culture that help uncover the individual factors encompassing cultural experiences. Agboka thus tasks technical communicators with straying away from "large culture" ideologies that often see culture from a decontextualized and macro rather than a micro perspective. Focusing on the individual mechanisms of a culture can lead to more accurate understandings of how culture is discursively created and negotiated by the agents within a given cultural context. Sun (2012) too discusses the importance of a dialogic cross-cultural approach to technology design, which sees culture "as an open set of practices and as an energetic process with meanings, objects and identities flowing across sites in diffuse space-time" (p. 25). Situating definitions of culture as dialogic or discursive is necessary to understand how individuals in a society create, share, and produce meaning. Importantly, experience mapmakers must have a methodological response for appropriately assembling the rich and dynamic experiences that represent global contexts and audiences.

Methodological response to these overlapping realities and experiences becomes important in cross-cultural information design, where the impression of a person's journey is often based on our own understanding and communication conventions. As communication conventions are rhetorically and culturally situated, the experience map can be seen as a form of invention that is likely based on a mapmaker's (perhaps limited) knowledge of a set of practices for approaching a relatively complex event that is treated as static—as a snapshot in time. For example, Laura Gonzales and Rebecca Zantjer give one methodological response that illustrates how user-localized translation practices can lead to improved technical communication outcomes, especially when working to convey meaning across cultures (Gonzales and Zantjer 2015). As Law (2004) explains, "The argument is no longer that methods discover and depict realities. Instead, it is that they participate in the enactment of those realities" (p. 45). A mapmaker's training to work with cultural difference can be unknowingly filtered through a set of practices that may or may not be able to effectively represent diverse ways of thinking, acting, and feeling.

Experience Maps as Participatory

One response is to treat the experience map as a participatory document. While the experience map is generally based on user behaviors, it must also capture the other thinking and feeling people do. Adaptive Path emphasizes the process of discovery through collecting data from users while building the map. Meanwhile, Sullivan (2014) makes the case for encountering users as methodologically necessary to this form of inquiry. The encountering Sullivan (2014) argues for can occur in a sort of third-space, or a safe space open to other ways of being in the world.

Thirdspace offers an openness to approaching the role of culture in a person's journey and interaction with information. Soja (1996) describes thirdspace by extending an "invitation to enter a space of extraordinary openness, a place of critical exchange where geographical imagination can be expanded to encompass a multiplicity of perspectives that have heretofore been considered by the epistemological referees to be incompatible, uncombinable" (p. 5). Soja (1996) also explains a thirdspace epistemology works with other approaches and ideas "without privileging one over the other; where one can be a Marxist and post-Marxist, materialist and idealist, structuralist and humanist, disciplined and transciplinary at the same time" (p. 5). When we extend such theory to methods like experience mapping, they quickly become less practical. Yet, as a mindset for understanding how to approach mapping experience, thirdspace offers a participatory mindset open to the experiences of other ways of being, unfamiliar contexts, and ways of understanding. Participation is key to designing valuable experiences for people and experiences must be co-constructed.

The invocation of thirdspace as an epistemological grounding for experience mapping is grounded in research addressing globalization and its impact on communication. As Homi Bhabha (1994) explains,

> The borderline work of culture demands an encounter with 'newness' that is not part of the continuum of past and present. It creates a sense of the new as an insurgent act of cultural translation. Such art does not merely recall the past as social cause or aesthetic precedent; it renews the past, refiguring it as a contingent 'in-between' space, that innovates and interrupts the performance of the present. (p. 10)

The in-between space references in this quotation can also be thought of as a thirdspace used to disrupt dominant ways of understanding people's experiences, exigencies, and motivations. Casting "the in-between" as thirdspace also creates a space devoted to change and co-learning. As noted, participatory methods are well suited for explaining and understanding behavior not easily categorized. Simonsen and Robertson (2013) argue, "Inviting users to such collective discussions and reflections requires a trustful and confiding relationship between all participants" (p. 5). Such dialogue can provide the intervening moment Bhabha discusses, particularly to make experience maps about how cultures learn and discover.

Research Questions

Given experience maps award a great deal of decision-making power to mapmakers, we focused our research on testing a central hypothesis: Experience maps can treat cultural difference as outlier behavior rather than important user experience. Our case study focused on the following research questions:

- What sort of decisions must be made when mapping collective experiences?
- How can experience maps better represent disjuncture and difference?
- How can experience maps as a method be made more participatory?

Methods

Because this project is a case study, the results are limited in that they are not generalizable and may not apply to other cases. However, our work acts as a starting point for thinking through the role of culture in experience mapping. To create our study, we followed Mary Sue MacNealy's (1999) suggestions and used four basic steps to create a strong ethnographic case study. The first was "preparing for the project" (p. 224) by conducting a literature review, developing a plan, and choosing a specific mapping template to follow. We selected the *doing, thinking,* and *feeling* approach as offered by Adaptive Path (2013) because it most aligned with our research questions.

We also agreed on a common experience to map: working at a coffee shop, though we defined working loosely as reading/writing activities. We agreed working at a coffee shop would provide a common experience and help map a common reaction. To conduct our study, each of us visited at different times during the same week (we each reserved a day/time to avoid overlapping). We gave each other another week to assemble our individual experience map prior to meeting to discuss our experiences.

Second, we discussed "collecting the data" (p. 224) where we used our experience mapping template more directly. The template suggested we write down what we were doing, thinking, and feeling. We wrote field notes before, during, and after our experience that focused on these prompts. Then, we each assembled our own experience maps before meeting and talking about what we learned. The experience maps were especially useful because they represented our experiences visually, which provided clear indications of where disjuncture occurred.

Third, we spent time collectively "interpreting the data" (MacNealy, 1999, p. 224) and asking an outside party to help us verify our findings. To analyze our experiences, we discussed our individual doing, thinking, and feeling categories, specifically where we discovered overlap and divergence across our experiences. Then, we attempted to represent each of our experiences as a collective map by hand-drawing on a

24×36-inch piece of poster paper. During this process, we used a sort of think-aloud protocol to hyper-communicate our thought-process. We also wrote down findings during this period of time, noting where we could not reconcile our maps and the issues we came across through our collective dialogue. We next took all of the information we wrote down and assembled it on sticky notes and worked to create affinity diagrams of our findings so that we could uncover themes.

To assemble our affinity diagrams, we used Goodwin's (2009) approach to keep the process simple. Thusly, we wrote each finding down on a sticky note and created organic categories through iteration: the process was recursive as we continued to refine our diagram. Then, we took a picture of our final affinity diagram and took the stickies down. We also asked a third party to use our stickies to create categories based on our findings. Once this person (Kristi Wiley, a WIDE Graduate Researcher) finished her diagram, we compared results and talked through any differences to reconcile them. For example, the results we named "Issues of Space" Kristi called "Coffee Shop." We believed many of the differences were in how we defined the categories and represented our own general understanding of the research project.

Finally, we spent time "reporting the results" (MacNealy, 1999, p. 224) before and after our analysis using thick description, affinity diagramming, and experience mapping. Our goal was to report results before and after our analysis to test our hypothesis that experience maps, while useful, can also make it difficult to represent all experiences in equitable and ethical ways, creating a potential issue for behavior that may appear to be "outlier." Our experiences are explained in further detail below, and our results follow our experiences.

Anatomy of Experiences at Rad Coffee Co.

For this project, the first thing we decided was in what coffee shop we were going to work. After a discussion of available choices, we decided on "Rad Coffee," (pseudonym) a fairly new and locally owned shop in Lansing, MI.

Ben's Experience

Prior to visiting Rad Coffee, I did an Internet search to learn its location and general background on the company. I had never heard of Rad before, so I wanted to know how far I was going to drive. Once I learned about the company from the website, I started to make plans to drive over. Generally, I don't like working in public, and since the coffee shop was on the other side of town, I was somewhat frustrated that I had to drive to go somewhere and work when instead, I could have worked from home. Still, I felt curious and a bit excited because I love coffee and coffee shops, and I had wanted to visit Rad since I first heard about it.

Once I arrived at Rad, I was not sure where to park. I circled for a moment, and decided to park in the street. I looked around for a sign to indicate that the parking was by permit only, but did not find anything. I did not feel totally comfortable parking in the street because I had received tickets before for parking in an area that was for residents only, but I decided if there was no sign then all was well.

Once inside, I was startled both by the busy and small environment of Rad. The place seemed filled to capacity. Even so, there was no line for ordering, so I walked up to the counter. The music seemed a bit too loud for me to focus, though I liked the song, so it seemed somewhat less intrusive. I noticed as people sat alone they had headphones on. Within just a few moments I decided there was no way I would work at Rad. It was too loud and busy. I did not want to order coffee. I was ready to leave. Instead, I sat down at the only open seat at the coffee bar. The seat was a tall stool. The person next to me shift uncomfortably, clearly unhappy with my choice. The environment quickly began to feel claustrophobic.

After a few moments, a space opened up at a table and I darted over, coffee in hand. The table provided a very different experience. I decided to stay and work instead of leaving once I finished with my coffee. From the table, I felt a bit more peace because I was more comfortable. The environment still felt busy, but I was in my own space with my computer and a plug so I could tune it out. Also, I started to notice the design of Rad. It was sort of rustic, but hip. The design was clearly building off of its city location with exposed brick and industrial design finishings. I decided to then begin to work.

At ten minutes in, I wanted to leave. The chair felt uncomfortable. Typing was difficult because the table was small and kept seesawing. Too often I was distracted and lost my train of thought. I tried to do some writing but kept finding myself people watching when I'd look up to think about a phrase or sentence. Also, the music just felt too loud. With small tables and loud music, it seemed like I would never get work done here. Then, I started to notice the heat. The place felt hot, and it was getting hotter. I pulled out a book and decided to try to get some reading done. However, since the place was so busy, people kept going in and out. I wanted to go hide in the back so I could concentrate, but the coffee shop was too small. There was nowhere else to hide—I had

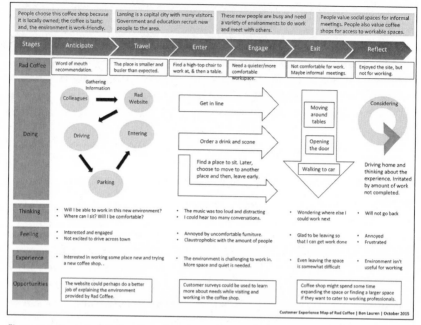

Figure 2.2. Ben's Rad Coffee Shop Experience Map

the best seat in the house. At this point, I realized I was checking the clock at five-minute intervals. Finally, I decided to get up and leave. I opened the door and felt the cold of the fall weather as I left the heat and noise behind me. As I walked to my car, I felt relieved and knew it was unlikely that I would ever go back to Rad to work. I might go back to chat with someone, but not to work. (See Figure 2.2 for the map of these experiences.)

Minh-Tam's Experience

The act of going to a coffee shop to get work done is not a novel experience for me. Because I have gone through the motions of locating, driving, entering, and working in a coffee shop before, my expectation of mapping my experience at new establishment was routine and mundane. However, when I embarked on this trip, my observation of all the touchpoints and feelings surrounding them were laced with meticulous details that often get overlooked during a common practice like visiting a coffee shop.

Since I had never heard of Rad before, I tried to do some research about it by visiting their website. Although the website was easy to navigate and offered basic information, I found myself needing to know more. It was at this point where I turned to third-party review sites to glean more information about this coffee shop. Upon scanning reviews, I was filled with anxiety as I read through the mixed reviews and could only anticipate the long lines, the crowded and uncomfortable seating, the long wait times, etc. But there were glimmers of hope as many of the reviews talked about the good coffee, free street parking, and the many outlets for working. These factors weighed heavily for me when deciding where to work and made me feel more at ease. With this information in mind, I was ready to map out my trip to Rad Coffee.

Later that week, I headed to Rad to get some work done. Before leaving, I made sure I had all the materials I needed to make the trip as painless and productive as possible—charger, books, journal, writing utensils, etc. By this time, I was feeling prepared. I had researched where it was and realized it was very close to where I lived, making the act of traveling quite easy and quick. However, parking gave me pause because street parking was not available (at a distance that I felt comfortable walking), so I decided to park behind the shop, not knowing if I had to use the metered spots or not. At this point, I decided to park in a non-metered lot adjacent to Rad Coffee but wondered if my car was okay being in a lot for another establishment.

After parking, I made my way toward the entrance of the coffee shop, which was much smaller than I anticipated. I felt immediately discouraged, as smaller spaces are more difficult to work. Along with that, it was packed the day I visited, making it even more difficult to navigate the space and figure out the infrastructure. I started asking myself questions—what should I do first? Should I find a place to sit? Should I get in line to order a drink? Ultimately, I decided to find seating first because, at this point, empty seats were scarce. The only place unoccupied was a bench at the back wall, which didn't have a crucial element: a nearby outlet. Because my computer was on low battery, I needed access to an outlet, so sitting there for a prolonged time was not realistic. Instead, I decided to get in line to order a cup of coffee with the hopes that an open seat near an outlet was made available.

With this in mind, I made my way toward the front of the shop and stood in, what I thought, was the line to order. What I thought was going to be a standard process turned out to be quite confusing. As I was approaching the barista to order, another man came and stood right in front of me and placed his order. Feeling disoriented, I questioned the structure of ordering—was there a line? Was I standing in the right place? Despite this, I was able to get an order in and found a vacant spot near the front to sit. As I sat down and unpacked my things, I was

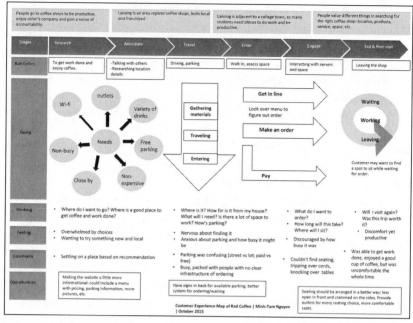

Figure 2.3. Minh-Tam's Rad Coffee Shop Experience Map

struck by how small the tables were. The cramped space disrupted my preferred workflow of going between my computer and writing notes, referencing my books, etc. After situating my belongings at the table, my order was ready. While getting up to retrieve my coffee, I tripped over a power strip housing the chargers of my neighbors' computers—another reminder of how crowded and hectic this place was.

From there, my time at Rad Coffee was spent drinking and working. Although the chairs were highly uncomfortable, I was able to be productive during the remainder of my time there. As I finished up the tasks I set out for myself that day, I packed up my things and got up to leave. Upon standing, I, embarrassingly, knocked the table, which produced a loud bang, bringing attention from everyone around me. On the way out, the baristas said a friendly "goodbye" and I left Rad Coffee wondering, "Will I ever go here again?" (see Figure 2.3).

Heather's Experience

Because I live close to this coffee shop and visit it regularly to do work or to have meetings, my experience was not novel, but I encountered similar touchpoints to my collaborators. After we agreed to visit this coffee shop and map our experiences, I began anticipating my work experience at this location. Would there be a crowd? Would I be able to locate a seat next to an outlet? Feeling anxious, I traveled the short distance from my home to the coffee shop with my laptop and charger.

As the coffee shop came into view I saw that the parking spaces on the front street were full, which made me think that inside would be crowded. I found a parking space around the back of the shop and walked from my car to the front, noticing that the line for ordering reached the door. I entered the coffee shop, maneuvering around the crowd, feeling anxious and worried that I would not find a seat, let alone find a seat by an outlet. As I walked to the back of the coffee shop, I noticed that a seat up front became available, and I went to grab it. Feeling a bit more relaxed as I set down my bag, I grabbed my wallet and got in line to order a drink. The line comprised seven to eight people crowding uncomfortably between the small space (maybe room from two to three people) between the counter and the entrance, making it difficult for customers to enter and exit the coffee shop, as well as form a line.

As I waited in line, I was wondering how long it would take to make my espresso drink, because there is only one espresso machine. I also wondered if my drink (pumpkin flavored) would be out because of the crowd and the time of year (fall).

As the line progressed and it became my turn to order, I reached the counter and chatted with the barista, who I know from my previous trips. I asked about the availability of my drink, I placed my order, and then waited at my seat for my name to be called. It took approximately thirteen minutes to receive my drink from the time I placed my order. I started working, noticing how extremely hot the temperature of the room was, as well as how much the sun was coming through the front window I was at that did not have a blind.

Eventually my drink was called, but by the time I got my hot coffee I had already felt overheated and did not want to drink it. I tried to work for an hour, but felt so hot that I could not concentrate and ended up leaving. As I left feeling annoyed, I wondered if I would come to this shop if it was not a convenient distance from my house. (See Figure 2.4 for a map of these experiences.)

Results

Through our experiment, we saw four distinctive categories emerge as we attempted to reconcile our experiences into one map. We believe these categories create issues mapmakers might consider and a close

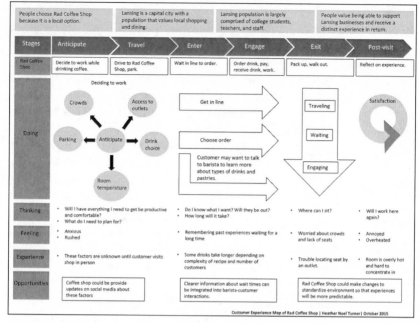

Figure 2.4. Heather's Rad Coffee Shop Experience Map

consideration of them can help make the practice of experience mapping more productive in cultural contexts. Our results emphasize disjuncture and difference between the three of us, particularly when we work to represent our experiences in equitable ways. What follows in Table 2.1 are terms and definitions for each of these categories.

Template

Because experience maps are a sort of narrative or retelling of a person's experience, they require a beginning, middle, and end. Thus, we discovered our template allowed little room for mapping out experiences that were interrupted; rather, the template required an experience to be mapped according to its design. For this reason, experience maps do not account for experiences cut short by elements beyond a customer's control (such as a malfunctioning product or an emergency), and they also require answers to prompts that might not be relevant to a user's mindset. For instance, while Ben was parking, he did not feel any specific way, but realized he needed to fill out an emotional state, so he chose one to represent his emotions at the time. In this way, as mapmakers work to capture holistic experience in global contexts, they may find similar issues with predetermined templates.

Table 2.1. Analytical Categories.

Category	Definition
Template	Refers to the form and genre of experience maps specifically related to layout, order, templates, sections, etc.
Purpose	Refers to the intended outcomes and takeaways of assembling experience maps.
Emotional Response	Refers to the feelings and thoughts surrounding each touch point accounted for in the experience map.
Space and Place	Refers to the physical layout of the coffee shop, as well as the spaces and places we engaged to reach the coffee shop.

Although the template provided a basic guideline for how to organize, present, and format our experiences, we found the existing structure also created other meaningful constraints. For example, as demonstrated by Figure 2.2 and Figure 2.3, Ben and Heather both stuck closely to the template, despite having different orientations to the experience (Heather was a repeat customer and Ben was new). In contrast, Minh-Tam decided to change the template and move elements around, which created challenges when we later worked to assemble our collective experiences into a single map. As a result, Ben began to rework his template to better represent his experience. As we worked to combine our experiences, we quickly discovered that, as a result of formatting issues, our individual purposes shifted, and it became easier to see the overlap and differences between our experiences.

Experience maps make it difficult to account for every relevant detail about an experience. For example, the embarrassment Minh-Tam felt after knocking the table over seemed relevant, but how that influenced her overall experience at the coffee shop was not easily captured by her experience map. Of course, it is neither plausible nor useful to present the entirety of an experience, but the accidental omission of a touch point or the influence of a single experience and how it affects recollection can be crucial for assembling a map, particularly in intercultural situations where communication and behavior can contain a great deal of nuance. So, it appears definitions of effective experiences are highly contingent on business goals and outcomes instead of participant exigencies.

Purpose

To be effective, the mapmaker must have a predefined purpose in mind. For instance, in Figure 2.4, Heather mapped out the elements she anticipated interacting with as she decided to work at Rad. Similarly, in Figure 2.3, Minh-Tam outlined her needs for deciding where to work. However, in Figure 2.2, Ben mapped out the progression of his actions in his first stage of the map, which focused less on the anticipated space where the experience map would take place, and focused more on his journey to get there. Earlier we found that the value of experience maps relies quite heavily on the template of those maps. It became more clear when we took into consideration our past experiences and existing orientations to the coffee shop we chose to visit. As mentioned earlier, Heather's map was largely informed by her past knowledge of the coffee shop—understanding wait times, seating, space, and so on, influenced the way she presented her data. Because of this, we found it too difficult to create a map from two vastly different vantage points: the new and repeat customer.

We also discovered that the mapmakers purpose must be clear: the goals for the map must be collectively understood before collecting data. We discussed our goal long before beginning the experience map, but since experience is so broad it quickly became difficult to understand what sort of timeline to use. The timeline could have begun as soon as we decided on a coffee shop to visit or it could have begun the day of our visit to the coffee shop. Similar things could be said about the end of our experiences. Choosing this timeline proved difficult because it eliminated particular experiences that could have been relevant. While this result is intuitive, it also demonstrates that representing holistic experience is subject to a set of goals and outcomes predefined by mapmakers.

Emotional Response

Our emotional responses to stimuli differed among the three of us. For example, new customers Ben and Minh-Tam anticipated their visit in dissimilar ways. (Ben felt "interested" and "engaged" while Minh-Tam felt "overwhelmed.") These variations in emotional manifestations continued throughout our comparisons of our maps and culminated in our different exit strategies. Although all three of our feelings regarding the post-visit had a negative valence, Minh-Tam felt discomfort, Heather felt annoyance, and Ben felt defeat and frustration. Representing emotional response across groups of people can be difficult because there is no way to predict how that response might change with time and our own expectations of the environment. These small distinctions in emotional response resonate in the ways we interacted with the spaces we occupied, while also being informed by our own cultural experiences and differences.

Space and Place

All three maps paid close attention to the space(s) we inhabited before, during, and after our visit. One such element was travel. For Heather and Minh-Tam, living in close proximity to the coffee shop made travel quick and convenient. However, despite the shared convenience of proximity, Minh-Tam was concerned about finding the location since it was her first time visiting while Heather did not map out this concern. Of more importance was how we responded to the physical space—the coffee shop itself. While all three of us seemed to think the environment was small, Ben focused more on the music and the size of the overall environment. Minh-Tam discussed the tables and cramped space, and Heather did not comment on the size of the environment, instead noting the temperature of it. Our focus on spatiality also emphasized the importance of our individual culturally situated expectations by illuminating unique exigencies and contexts.

Discussion

Our work demonstrates the importance of researcher stance when assembling alignment diagrams in global contexts. Our case study also suggests areas of inquiry that require further development. While we believe our research is a preliminary look at experience maps as a method, we also assert experience maps require careful methodological and epistemological training, particularly as maps are developed in global contexts. While a participatory framework appears to help address these issues, we also believe our results demonstrate some practical advice as writers begin to work with experience maps in different cultural contexts.

Here, we address each of our results by providing suggestions for writers implementing experience mapping:

- *Experience map templates must be flexible, not static.* Our results show the role of the template is an item experience mapmakers must consider. Templates have the potential to preclude diverse ways of doing, thinking, and feeling. Templates should therefore be flexible and not static. For instance, the template may use visuals or color that do not represent experience in culturally appropriate ways. Or, the template may require including information that is not relevant (at a specific moment) as well.
- *The purpose of experience maps may not align across cultures, so spend time understanding your cultural context.* As Appadurai (1990) notes, culture is constantly shifting in unpredictable ways. Focusing on space and place is a productive way for thinking through experience maps while working to accurately represent unfamiliar cultural contexts.
- *When agreeing on a purpose for a map focus on understanding people's needs (and cultural contexts) first.* In global contexts, you should spend some

time understanding how people's needs vary from your own cultural context. As a team, you should spend some time addressing cultural context in your work.

- *Timelines for the map should be addressed ahead of time.* Work with your participants to identify when an experience began and when it ended. Your goal is to determine a timeline that represents holistic experience, which may vary across different cultures and audiences.
- *Use a participatory approach.* Your experience map can engage participants in the development of the map. Show them your finished product to learn if it is representative of their experience. Seek feedback and enter into a dialogue that seeks to better understand the holistic experience of people.

We believe these items provide researchers new to experience mapping with advice for working with the method or issues to consider when designing an experience map. For students or instructors, our work helps to illuminate some of the issues that may surface when working to address disjuncture, difference, and cultural representation.

CONCLUSION

The chapter emphasizes the importance of maintaining critical research practices through methodological approach in experience mapping. Researchers must understand how their own cultural context influences the experiences they represent for people. As researchers work through these ideas, they can bring methods like participatory design and experience mapping together, particularly as they are informed by critical research practice.

We do not mean for our research to be a complete guide for doing experience mapping. Rather, as teachers of professional writing, we believe students must understand how designing artifacts such experience maps can be opportunities to advocate for ways of being in the world. In doing so, professional writers need methods to help them understand how to represent people's behaviors, exigencies, and experiences across a variety of culturally situated environments. But people who are mapping these experiences must also practice critical reflection about their own understanding of users and how it influences the experiences they create. Through teaching effective methods of mapping experiences in global contexts, we can address disjuncture and difference and continue to think through ways of actively engaging audiences in more equitable and ethical ways.

References

Adaptive Path. (2013). Adaptive path's guide to experience mapping. Retrieved from http://mappingexperiences.com

Agboka, G. (2012). Liberating intercultural technical communication from "large culture" ideologies: Constructing culture discursively. *Journal of Technical Writing and Communication, 42*(2), 159–181. Retrieved from https://doi.org/10.2190/TW.42.2.e

Appadurai, A. (1990). Disjuncture and difference in the global cultural economy. *Theory, Culture & Society, 7*(2), 295–310. Retrieved from https://doi.org/10.1177/02632769 0007002017

Barton, B. F., & Barton, M. S. (2004). Ideology and the map: Toward a postmodern visual design practice. In J. Johnson-Eilola & S. A. Selber (Eds.), *Central works in technical communication* (pp. 232–252). New York, NY: Oxford University Press.

Bhabha, H. K. (1994). *The location of culture*. London, England: Routledge.

Cresswell, J. (2008). *Research design: Qualitative, quantitative, and mixed methods approaches.* (3rd ed.). Thousand Oaks, CA: Sage.

Dragga, S., & Voss, D. (2001). Cruel pies: The inhumanity of technical illustrations. *Technical Communication (Washington), 48*(3), 265–274.

Gonzales, L., & Zantjer, R. (2015). Translation as a user-localization practice. *Technical Communication, 62*(4), 271–284.

Goodwin, K. (2009). *Designing for the digital age: How to create human-centered products and services.* Indianapolis, IN: Wiley.

Kalbach, J. (2015). Mapping experiences: A complete guide to creating value through journeys, blueprints, and diagrams. Sebastopol, CA: O'Reilly Media.

Law, J. (2004). *After method: Mess in social science research.* New York, NY: Routledge.

MacNealy, M. (1999). *Strategies for empirical research in writing.* Boston, MA: Allyn and Bacon.

Simonsen, J., & Robertson, T. (2013). *Routledge international handbook of participatory design.* New York, NY: Routledge.

Soja, E. W. (1996). *Thirdspace: Journeys to Los Angeles and other real-and-imagined places.* Cambridge, MA: Blackwell.

Sullivan, P. (2014). User experience and the spectacles of the small: On mundane change and encounters. *Proceedings of Annual SIGDOC Conference.* Colorado Springs, CO. DOI:https://doi.org/10.1145/2666216.2692335

Sullivan, P., & Porter, J. E. (1997). *Opening spaces: Writing technologies and critical research practices.* Greenwich, CT: Ablex.

Sun, H. (2012). *Cross-cultural technology design: Creating culture-sensitive technology for local users.* Oxford, England: Oxford University Press. Retrieved from https://doi.org /10.1093/acprof:oso/9780199744763.001.0001

forums' as potential educational spaces. Trena M. Paulus (2007), for example, established online forums had several advantages to offer in this area. These advantages stemmed from the online forum's asynchronicity, which James Purdy (2009) explains adds value to the writing experience. However, even earlier research on technology instruction extrapolated effective suggestions for online forum use. For example, Davis and Brewer's (1997) early work on e-conferences suggested frequent and required forum posts enabled learning by fostering a regular and ongoing conversation within the classroom—a finding echoed by others. Similarly, DeSanctis et al. (2003) explain digital compositions most benefit the classroom when they enable information sharing in high volumes, for it facilitates knowledge production according to Etienne Wenger's "community of practice" (DeSanctis et al., 2003, pp. 573–574). Similarly, Brian W. King's (2015) research finds that public, online writing communities not only socialize users, but often help them refine and reflect upon their work. In such contexts, the regular pacing of comments amid a strong community dynamic facilitated professional training through new media technologies (pp. 573–574). Such findings match those of Ruti Gafni and Nitza Geri, who discovered requiring and grading online forum writing as a part of course design strengthened overall classroom learning (Gafni & Geri, 2010, pp. 339–341). Timothy J. Ellis and William Hafner also discuss comparable classroom implementation that strengthens pedagogical practice, and they assert instructors can design and implement forums autocratically in order to meet specific learning goals while requiring regular posting (Ellis & Hafner, 2008). The chapter builds on such findings, adding to them by examining one successful online forum dedicated to international discussions of a central topic.

Often, the scholarship discussing online forums as learning tools assumes collaborative interactions established throughout forum participation facilitate learning outcomes. For example, Anderson and Kanuka's (1997) study directly and explicitly connects focal ideas (i.e., the benefits of forums used for professional education) to collaborative learning—an area of composition research that has influenced many pedagogies over the past three decades. Many of these works that examine the value user-generated content contributes to learning environments stem from the assumption people will help each other learn through the collaboration that forms in cooperative new media environments. In "Collaborative Learning and the 'Conversation of Mankind,'" for example, Kenneth Bruffee (1984) explains collaborative learning has a "social context for conversation" in which conventions facilitate learning within a communal conversation (p. 642). Online communities dominated by user-generated content often exhibit such collaboration, and this chapter draws connections to the community's role in the enforcement of rules—both implicit and explicit. Such communal interaction, support, and guidance facilitate self-instruction in the absence of teachers, assignments, and graded criteria.

Kathleen Blake Yancey (2004) has indicated many people develop their literacy skills online without the direct intervention of classroom structures (pp. 298–302). Autonomous learning occurs in public spaces, aligning most with Henri Holec's (1981) original vision of learners with "the ability to take charge of [their] own learning," independent of instructors (emphasis removed from the original, p. 3). Such forms a key difference between open online forums and classroom forums, for users in the former must exhibit a greater degree of autonomy to succeed in the learning environment than users in the latter group. Most notably, those who become confused, frustrated, or disinterested in an open online forum can leave the community: an option not available to students who participate in online forums as a graded part of a class.

Individuals with low degrees of technological literacy—a population that conversations on online learning sometimes miss—have higher potential for confusion or frustration. Many implicitly assume Mark Prensky's (2001) concept of the digital native when discussing today's online learning environments, despite frequent challenges to the concept since its inception. In 2008, findings from the Organization for Economic Co-operation and Development (OECD) and the Centre for Educational Research Innovation (CERI) synthesized the variables contributing to digital literacy as "Access," "Previous Experience," "Frequency of Use," and "Confidence Level" (OECD & CERI, 2008). In addition, Sue Bennett, Karl Maton, and Lisa Kevin discuss the digital native's popularity, explaining that pervasive "moral panic" among academics often inspired it, rather than rigorous, proven research that queried the accuracy of digital nativity (Bennett, Maton, & Kervin, 2008, p. 783). Erika Polson (2011), in turn, characterizes the global population of skilled Internet users as a new and growing, global middle class; this, she feels, best describes populations that dominate many online arenas (pp. 145–149). However, the global populations of potential students for online classes far exceed this digital middle class; thus, the ability to engage diverse, global students effectively in online classroom environments requires further research and scholarship. The trajectory of research into online forums and people's usage thereof provides a context through which to understand the online forum as it exists today.

The research reported here builds on such past works to analyze the writing and community interaction on an international, public forum in order to develop strategies that can benefit classroom-based forum use.

RESEARCH METHODS

The chapter's findings on Standard English usage occurred amid a larger, IRB-exempted ethnography of knowledge making in online forums for amphibian hobbyists (the online forum *Caudata*). The original project used interviews, usage diaries, participant observation, and rhetorical and textual analysis to develop a rhetorical ethnography of knowledge making online. The focus of the study was an international online forum for newt and salamander hobbyists who exhibited a range of ages as well as degrees of literacy, fluency, and expertise on the topic. As Christine Hine (2009) explains, when studying digital media, it becomes incredibly difficult to delineate field sites' boundaries, particularly when the digital landscape so often overlaps and blurs into other online environments and off-line practices or communities (pp. 1–4). To facilitate a clear delineation amid a potential overlap, the field site remained exclusively online, and it included forum articles, thread posts (conversations), and stickies (permanent threads).

The larger project featured a narrow, purposive pool of participants comprised of two women and four men (referred to by pseudonym) ranging in age from eighteen to sixty. They displayed diverse educational backgrounds ranging from high school to vocational, college, or advanced degrees, and the two native English speakers and four nonnative English speakers with varied degrees of fluency represented many nations: England, Germany, Italy, The Netherlands, Poland, and the United States. While their interviews provided core material for much of the larger work that informs this chapter, they take a secondary role here, providing support for findings obtained through textual analysis.

Amid the studies of how volunteer participants and forum members learned, wrote, engaged with the forum, and created new knowledge for their special interest hobby, the original project analyzed the particular forum environment, its rules, and its moderators' and administrators' approaches, as well as the individual and community reactions thereto. While the project originally used ethnographic methods for human subject research, the narrower findings reported here employed practices of rhetorical analysis of closed conversations on the public forum, none of which include the interview participants' contributions. In this way, the public text of the forum combined with the private interviews of participants to garner understandings of writing in online forums. While analyses of cultural, environmental, and social variables help develop an understanding of how and why forum members use language, these form a background—muted from the original driving force that they brought to the larger project from which this work grew. Participant data from interviews and usage diaries provide support for conclusions drawn from rhetorical and textual analysis of the forum.

FOCUS OF THE CHAPTER

As a forum that specializes in the care, maintenance, and breeding of newts and salamanders, *Caudata* holds a great deal of English language information people cannot easily locate elsewhere. One subject, Piotr Szott, specifically mentioned before finding *Caudata,* he could not locate specific information in his native Polish (P. Szott, personal communication, December 18, 2012). In addition, each of the six, international participants mentioned the wealth of reliable information found on *Caudata* as a central reason they turned to the forum. The international community affects language use across the forum, which requires interactions take place in Standard English. As the forum's rules state:

> We require that English speakers not write in nonsense words (such as those used in text messages). Please refrain from the use of words like "gonna," and please use good grammar and punctuation. Remember that new subjects and sentences warrant the use of a capital letter. Proper punctuation will make your message much easier to understand, and thus improve the discussion. Banning won't occur for such offences, but we actively encourage moderators and users to lower the reputation of users who insist on speaking drivel. Nonnative English speakers will not be penalized for grammatical errors. (Clare, 2013, post 1)

A general bias against non-standardized usages underlies this policy, as indicated by the term "nonsense word" and the word "drivel." The final statement "Non-native English speakers will not be penalized for grammatical errors" indicates forum administrators prioritize clear and effective communication across a diverse community with varied levels of English-language fluency.

Participant data reinforced this finding. One participant, Adam, discussed this quite directly stating some informalities, such as common or colloquial names for newt and salamander species, lead to "confusion because popular names are not standardized. I try to use scientific names along with popular names. Also, some bodily functions and behaviors are difficult to describe because people do not know the

proper terms. So, I will be lenient when someone uses the word 'poop'!"
(Adam, personal communication, February 12, 2013). Moderators
enforce rules with care and critical awareness to address the rhetorical
context of each forum thread.

That administrators, moderators, and members collaborate to enforce
Standard English usage rules across the forum indicates a communal
goal for effective communication. When individuals challenge this goal,
a cooperative effort begins to shift writing toward the accepted norm. For
example, when diztorcion, a forum user from the United States, wrote
an unpunctuated post asking for help with his pets, another user replied
by asking diztorcion to adjust to the Standard English the community
preferred as slang and abbreviations might confuse nonnative English
speakers. Diztorcion then offered to remove his post from the forum
until a moderator replied, "[t]here is no need to earse [*sic*] your thread,
the question is legitimate. Just try to be careful when typing your texts—
it's also good practice to help improve your English!" (diztorcion, 2008,
post 4). Following Jin Sook Lee's (2006) research, which showed that
low-stakes, nonstandard online writing forms socialize Korean language
learners well but decrease their ability to distinguish standard from non-
standard language forms, these amphibian forums' supportive insistence
on Standard English may help users develop standard fluency. Through
a cooperative team effort, the community quickly teaches newcomers
through a combination of example, instruction, and explicit rules.

Like diztorcion, other forum members who deviate from explicit
and implicit community rules face communal reprimand. Members
and moderators intervene regularly to provide polite and productive
criticism and direction. For example, amid a thread by one user named
ammar, a moderator (Jennifer) enters the conversation to provide constructive suggestion for ammar's informal writing style:

> Ammar, there are many wonderful people on this forum who are willing
> to share their experience and advice with those in need. It will help if you
> post your question in a) the correct area [a topic-appropriate subforum]
> and b) in a format of English that others can understand. I personally
> have difficulty interpreting your slang. There are many users on the forum
> for whom English is not their first language but still make the effort. As
> Ester pointed out people are more likely to help you if your posts are more
> intelligible. (ammar, 2005, post 10)

Jennifer's guidance demonstrates how moderators can explain their suggestions to ensure productive rather than punitive responses.

As this conversation continues, Jennifer positively reinforces ammar's
appropriate use of Standard English, reinforcing and rewarding his

efforts to adhere to the forum's norms. As ammar's writing improves, Jennifer notes, "Ammar, I notice in your last post here that you are expressing yourself a bit more clearly. Thank you! Keep it up, and we will try to help" (Jennifer posting in ammar, 2005, post 26).

Like the moderator, the forum participants prefer Standard English above abbreviations and informalities. Anne, Kees, Adam, and Gabriella all expressed this preference during their interviews, thought their opinions varied. Kees explained, "I think it should be avoided. A forum isn't a chat room" (Kees, personal communication, January 31, 2013). Adam's slightly more stern interview responses revealed "[t]ext-speak or slang is not welcomed as far as I am concerned" (Adam, personal communication, February 12, 2013). Anne's response featured the most dislike of informal, incorrect, or abbreviated English language usage: "I loathe hate and despise it" (Anne, personal communication, March 17, 2013). Anne explained her severe dislike for slang, in particular, writing that "[i]t frustrates me that it [slang] has become more acceptable to use across forums. [. . .] I appreciate that text speak and slang is part of the evolution of our language, but I do not think it is appropriate on international forums. [. . .] I fear I may have to accept it one day" (Anne, personal communication, March 17, 2013).

While linguistic informalities could overtake the forum, Anne is able to encourage correct use amid a forum with clearly stated policies to that effect. Other forums where rules and communal mores do not necessitate Standard English usage, certainly display less standard usages. For example, when apologizing for his informalities after a reprimand from the community, FredLikesNewts (2004) posted, "[s]orry for not using proper grammer [*sic*], punctuation and all of that stuff, the only other forums ive [*sic*] been to are for video games and its [*sic*] not really enforced to use proper grammar considering [*sic*] all of the little kids and gamer slang" (post 4). FredLikesNewts's posting indicates many forums have fewer rules guiding language usage. However, as an international community of amphibian hobbyists, *Caudata* attracts nonnative English speakers, and this factor influences the forum's rules and their enforcement.

Each forum member undergoes a process of socialization into the rules, guidelines, and mores of the community, and the forum members, administrators, and moderators provide continual and constructive correction and guidance as needed to facilitate this process. Through repeated contact with the forum, members can appropriate a language usage that suits the community to which they belong. In the case of *Caudata*, the international dynamic makes Standard English essential to clear communication and engagement, a point that one participant reinforced when she confessed her frequent reliance on translation software to help read others' English-language posts (Gabriela, personal communication, February 1, 2013). In these ways, the community shapes the forum's rules, their enforcement, and the resulting language use across the community. These components converge to create an effective international learning community.

The community achieves adherence to convention, not only through clearly stated rules, but also through a social community dynamic that enforces the implicit and explicit communal values. For example, *Caudata* repeatedly engages in debates on whether to mix species within one enclosure. Citing such staple arguments of predation, toxicity, and aggression among other claims, the community maintains the dominant and strongly held conviction owners should house animals in species-specific enclosures rather than in mixed-species environments. Often, a newcomer raises this issue, hoping to defend or justify mixing to the community while seeking information on a given amphibian, but such defense does not succeed.

Two particular threads demonstrate this pattern while illustrating variation in rhetorical approach: cheese's (2008) thread, "I need a definitive answer!" and Bunnygirl's (2009) thread, "Tiger salamander with frog." These represent two common approaches newcomers take to the community. In each case, the original posters (OP) hopes to combine varied species of amphibian species within a single enclosure. However, their opening tones differ. The community that commonly opposes mixing species of amphibians opposes both opening posts. Throughout both conversations, forum members move through each of the community's common claims, providing opposition to species mixing, and creating an argument in favor of a single-species tank. Because people react passionately to this issue, moderators enter each of the threads, ensuring the conversation remains respectful and polite.

Seasoned site veterans rarely raise such conversations. Instead, new members initiate a debate on species mixing, most likely because, as Peter Berger and Thomas Luckmann explain, "it is more likely that one will deviate from programs set up for one by others than from programs that one has helped establish oneself" (Berger & Luckmann, 1966, p. 62). As those community members who have engaged over a long period of time help direct and correct the conversations of the newer members, they have more reinforced mores, and fewer explicitly raised debates that challenge the communally accepted norms.

After these conversations, cheese and Bunnygirl left rather quickly, having minimal forum participation in the interim. cheese posted nine times over that week before his postings stopped; he continued reading active threads for three months before all activity on his account stopped. Bunnygirl stayed within the community a little longer, posting nineteen times over the next year; once these posts had stopped, she continued to read for two years and seven months after initiating her species mixing conversation. In other words, without belonging to the forum community, both members left. Their reputation points, a use-generated scoring system where members rate each other based on the helpfulness and accuracy of their posts, indicate their lack of belonging.

Cheese has negative reputation points, which means that the community disapproved of his information and contributions. Bunnygirl has one reputation point, suggesting she learned enough from the community to advise someone well at some point in time. Ultimately, individuals who cannot share the values of the community leave quickly, as cheese did. While Jie Chi Yang, Benazir Quadir, and Nian-Shing Chen have shown that ratings systems can motivate those who wish to belong to a community, members like cheese and Bunnygirl do not, as their reputation points indicate (Yang, Quadir, & Nian-Shing, 2015).

cheese's and Bunnygirl's threads illustrate two approaches to OP's tones. The former opens with an exclamation point, indicating the somewhat hostile nature of many of cheese's posts in this thread. The latter has a question mark showing that Bunnygirl has more openness to feedback than cheese, even when other users' suggestions defy her hopes. The opening posts also reveal tonal and attitudinal differences between the two. The opening post for cheese's (2008) I need a definitive answer! reads as follows:

> I am planning on starting a Japanese FBN [fire bellied newt, Cynops pyrrhogaster] tank. I know about the fish that can be mixed with them. I would just like to know how to go anuran, and (probably not) reptilian wise. Before I get a bunch of "stick to the rules" types, I know that it's "Amphibian 101" to not mix. However, I have seen so many more community FBN success stories than failures. And, about 90–95% of the failures are to mixing them with FBT's [fire bellied toad, Bombina orientalis] which I would never run the risk of doing. I want kind answers, please. (cheese, post 1)

By comparison, the opening post for Bunnygirl's (2009) forum thread, "Tiger salamander with frog?" seems shorter, more polite, and more inquisitive: "Hello, / I was just wonderign [*sic*] if anyone had ever kept their tiger with any species of arboreal frogs. Assuming that they have the same habitat, and requirements, and foos [*sic*] items this seems like it would work out great. one [*sic*] is terrestrial and one arboreal. /

Thanks!" (Bunnygirl, post 1). In addition, both members' deviations from communal norms show through their lack of Standard English, as both cheese and Bunnygirl use initialisms to refer to species types throughout their threads, and Bunnygirl's post features errors: all discursive practices discouraged by forum rules and the community. This reveals their new initiate status into the community and that they have not yet learned the Standard English and rhetorical conventions of the forum.

These discussions indicate that, amid open, online forums that exhibit regular engagement from their members, the community plays a crucial role in language use involving everything from Standard English to tone. While open online forums differ from classroom forums, instructors can replicate the advantages of regular forum engagement to facilitate learning.

APPLICATION OF IDEAS

Members of an international online forum learn rules and mores through interaction with the community. The collaborative environment favors certain linguistic norms that can provide individuals with the opportunities and guidance to practice and strengthen their communication skills over time. The voluntary nature of members' engagement represents a crucial difference between open, online forums and those that mandate participation. In the *Caudata* forum, cheese and Bunnygirl illustrate the potential to lose members who cannot or will not conform to the explicit and implicit rules and guidelines of the environment. Consequently, the community that remains exhibits high levels of engagement and adherence to the forum. While instructors might face difficulties replicating the success of an open online forum, they can use certain strategies to simulate the learning that happens in public arenas.

The community dynamic is central to the success of a forum like *Caudata*. A wide array of members contributes on a regular basis, and this ensures a fluid and ongoing conversation in which members can become friendly and comfortable with one another. This facilitates corrective comments and adherence to guidelines as members, administrators, and moderators can approach correction politely, nonconfrontationally, and respectfully, as the examples have shown. Davis and Brewer's (1997) early research into online forums matches this finding. They noted requiring frequent posts toward the course grade allowed the online conversation to gain a fluid pattern that facilitated classroom learning. DeSanctis et al. (2003) found a similar success in online learning environments. Their project determined high amounts of information exchange and online conversation facilitated community building and the learning that results from it. These findings align with Gafni and Geri's (2010) discovery that, without a grade requirement, students post far less frequently, and therefore, the forums facilitate classroom learning less (pp. 339–341). Instructors can develop guidelines that necessitate regular posting as a graded course component to ensure the classroom community develops a regular routine of engagement from the start.

The examples of the international, open, online forum also show communities benefit from explicit rules the community itself (vs. only designated moderators or administrators) can enforce. Instructors can do many things to create and develop such rules and encourage their enforcement. For example, Ellis and Hafner (2008) encourage an autocratic approach wherein instructors encourage self-reflection amid specific learning goals. A more democratic approach might entail developing forum rules with students, allowing their feedback and suggestions to shape policy, thereby encouraging engagement throughout the term, through students' personal investment in the forum and its creation. As the previous section has mentioned, Berger and Luckmann (1966) assert "it is more likely that one will deviate from programs set up for one by others than from programs that one has helped establish oneself" (p. 62). The more teachers directly involve students with the creation and shaping of forum rules, the more likely students will support and endorse them. Furthermore, forum members in open online communities often bear the responsibility of directing new members to the rules vs. leaving such tasks to moderators or administrators. To this end, an instructor can take a role that has less direct involvement with the forum community, allowing it to become a peer-to-peer community shaped by the course, its goals, and its outcomes. The more invested students become in that space, the more they see it as their own, and the more likely they will participate regularly and form a learning community.

Within the preceding section's examples of forum writing and rule enforcement, all posts remained respectful and polite. While not all public Internet writing demonstrates fair and even-handed approaches, these examples illustrate the accomplishments of successful and supportive constructive feedback. As with the Standard English policy, politeness of tone begins in the forum rules, and members, site administrators, and moderators regularly demonstrate its appropriate employment. To replicate such a discussion environment, instructors can include a clear forum policy regarding appropriate tones of, which works particularly well if the community mutually agrees upon and evenly enforces such a policy.

Perhaps of most direct importance to the forum's functioning, rules should be clear, logical, and explained. In *Caudata*, the rules explain "Proper punctuation will make your message much easier to understand, and thus improve the discussion" (Clare, 2013). Here, a concrete example opens the sentence amid a discussion of conventions and correctness. Rather than sit alone as a rigid rubric item, correctness pairs with its purpose—clarity in communication which the online forum environment requires—and so the rule itself becomes clearer and easier to both endorse and enforce.

Online forums are wonderful learning spaces, and one must acknowledge the extent to which guidelines, community, and engagement make this the case. To harness their potential in a classroom requires self-reflexive pedagogy and careful design and classroom implementation. While mandatory forums can take many shapes, teachers must grade them, require regular posting as part of the course assignments, and ensure clear and carefully thought out rules that benefit not only the learning goals of a course. Ultimately, instructors can shape online forum environments in a myriad of ways. As with other learning tools, care, precision, and pedagogical consideration can help develop a self-reflexive practice that fosters clear and situated guidelines to help the classroom forum become a learning environment that can help students achieve a course's learning outcomes.

CONCLUSION

In "Key Differences between Web 1.0 and Web 2.0," Graham Cormode and Balachander Krishnamurthy remark that new media environments exhibit "co-mingling of commentators and creators, and every visitor has the opportunity to click, comment, create, etc." (Cormode & Krishnamurthy, 2008, sec. 5.2, n.p.). The collaborative space of new media environments ensures rapid change, as the space and its participants continually respond to the subtle need of internal and external variables. The chapter reviews how one international, public, online forum environment successfully uses such "co-mingling." The chapter suggests practices instructors can adopt, such as the use of clear and self-reflexive guidelines and rules, the requirement of regular, graded engagement with forum writing, and using the classroom forum as a peer-to-peer learning community. These practices can foster active and dynamic online participation in which the members, as well as site creators (teachers), actively enforce communally determined rules and policies.

The chapter examines approaches that can help global students learn in new media environments. The online forum of study, *Caudata*, has explicit rules and guidelines that encourage Standard English usage to develop English-language use among native and nonnative English speakers. Often, the general public assumes slang, text-speak, abbreviations, incorrectness, and other informalities dominate new media environments. Instead, Susan Herring (2001) depicts e-grammar as a set of choices that suit rhetorical situations of computer-mediated communication. She deliberately prefers the term "e-grammar" over "netspeak," because it aligns Internet writing with grammar and rules, distancing it from the assumptions of random unregulated usage that lacks a set of conventions. One might expect to find e-grammar to dominate all modes of user-generated content with equal ubiquity, but as the examples of forum posts and participants' attitudes indicate, online writing can take a variety of approaches that have more or less tendency toward informalities over Standard English.

The chapter analyzes forum rules regarding Standard English usage on *Caudata*, a public forum for amphibian enthusiasts, finding that the language use that pervades the majority of *Caudata's* threads defies the expectation that Computer Mediated Communication inclines toward e-grammar and away from Standard English. While *Caudata* shares many features with other forums, it distinguishes itself from other online arenas that allow less traditional language usage. Ultimately, the international community affects the language used because Standard English has become a requirement in order to meet the needs of nonnative English speakers, which manifests in the forum rules that favor Standard English except in the case of nonnative English speakers' errors. This reveals clear and cooperative communication between diverse participants with multiple degrees of fluency as one of the forum's underlying goals.

As the examples provided here reveal, the greater community chides many forum members if they do not follow the implicit and explicit community rules. Perhaps most importantly, moderators also contact members to positively reinforce their endeavors with Standard English, as demonstrated through ammar's postings. Direction and correction from fellow forum members, moderators, and administrators socialize each user into the culture and customs of the given forum community. Members thus learn to enact the writing and the role of an appropriate forum poster who belongs within the community. The international community necessitates Standard English usage, and this factor affects the forum rules, the moderators' enforcement of language use, and the members' use of language.

Future research can continue to examine classroom forum policies and the efficacy of their implementation. The findings reported here suggest scholars can learn much from public environments in which people self-instruct without the guidance of instructors, assignments, or syllabi. Thus, future research can continue to explore these connections, expanding into other new media environments for beneficial policies and practices to implement amid global, online learning environments of learners with diverse and varied skill sets.

References

ammar. (2005). Help me and brenden feeding problem!! Online forum comment. Retrieved from http://www.caudata.org/forum/f46-beginner-newt-salamander -axolotl-help-topics/f47-newt-salamander-help/35942-help-me-brenden-feeding -problem.html

Anderson, T., & Kanuka, H. (1997). On-line forums: New platforms for professional development and group collaboration. *Journal of Computer-Mediated Communication, 3*(3). Retrieved from http://onlinelibrary.wiley.com/doi/10.1111/j.1083-6101.1997 .tb00078.x/full

Bennett, S., Maton, K., & Kervin, L. (2008). The digital native debate: A critical review of the evidence. *British Journal of Educational Technology, 39*(5), 775–786. Retrieved from https://doi.org/10.1111/j.1467-8535.2007.00793.x

Berger, P. L., & Luckmann, T. (1966). *The social construction of reality: A treatise in the sociology of knowledge.* Garden City, NY: Anchor Books.

Bruffee, K. A. (1984). Collaborative learning and the "conversation of mankind." *College English, 46*(7), 635–652. Retrieved from http://www.jstor.org/stable/376924; https://doi.org/10.2307/376924

Bunnygirl. (2009). Tiger salamander with frog. Online forum comment. Retrieved from http://www.caudata.org/forum/f46-beginner-newt-salamander-axolotl-help-topics /f47-newt-salamander-help/61870-tiger-salamander-frog.html

cheese. (2008). Phase one of JFBN tank, what next? Online forum comment. Retrieved from http://www.caudata.org/forum/f46-beginner-newt-salamander-axolotl-help-top ics/f47-newt-salamander-help/56987-phase-one-jfbn-tank-what-next.html#post162625

Clare, J. (2013). Terms of service (forum rules). Online forum comment. Retrieved from http://www.caudata.org/forum/forum_rules.htm

Cormode, G., & Krishnamurthy, B. (2008). Key differences between Web 1.0 and Web 2.0. *First Monday, 13*(6). Retrieved from https://doi.org/10.5210/fm.v13i6.2125

Davis, B. H., & Brewer, J. P. (1997). *Electronic discourse: Linguistic individuals in virtual space.* Albany, NY: State University of New York Press.

DeSanctis, G., Fayard, A. L., Roach, M., & Jiang, L. (2003). Learning in online forums. *European Management Journal, 21*(5), 565–577. Retrieved from https://doi.org/10 .1016/S0263-2373(03)00106-3

diztorcion. (2008). Skinny newt. Online forum comment. http://www.caudata.org /forum/f46-beginner-newt-salamander-axolotl-help-topics/f47-newt-salamander -help/36777-skinny-newt.html

Ellis, T. J., & Hafner, W. (2008). Building a framework to support project-based collaborative learning experiences in an asynchronous learning network. *Interdisciplinary Journal of E-Learning and Learning Objects, 4,* 167–190.

FredLikesNewts. (2004). Ordering eastern newts from biological supply? Online forum comment. Retrieved from http://www.caudata.org/forum/f46-beginner-newt-salamander-axolotl-help-topics/f47-newt-salamander-help/56199-ordering-eastern-newts -biological-supply.html

Gafni, R., & Geri, N. (2010). The value of collaborative e-learning: Compulsory versus optional online forum assignments. *Interdisciplinary Journal of E-Learning and Learning Objectives, 8,* 335–343.

Griffin, J., & Minter, D. (2013). The rise of the online writing classroom: Reflecting on the material conditions of college composition teaching. *College Composition and Communication, 65*(1), 140–162.

Herring, S. C. (2001). Computer-mediated discourse. In D. Tannen, D. Schiffin, & H. Hamilton (Eds.), *Handbook of discourse analysis* (pp. 612–634). Oxford, England: Blackwell.

Hine, C. (2009). How can qualitative Internet researchers define the boundaries of their projects? In A. N. Markham & N. K. Baym (Eds.), *Internet inquiry: Conversations about method* (pp. 1–20). Thousand Oaks, CA: Sage.

Holec, H. (1981). *Autonomy and foreign language learning.* Oxford, England: Pergamon Press.

King, B. W. (2015). Wikipedia writing as praxis: Computer-mediated socialization of second-language writers. *Language Learning & Technology, 19*(3), 106–123.

Lee, J. S. (2006). Exploring the relationship between electronic literacy and heritage language maintenance. *Language Learning & Technology, 10*(2), 93–113.

Organisation for Economic Co-Operation and Development (OECD) & the Centre for Educational Research and Innovation (CERI). (2008). Retrieved from http://www .oecd.org/redirect/dataoecd/39/51/40554230.pdf

Park, N., Lee, K. M., & Cheong, P. H. (2007). University instructors' acceptance of electronic courseware: An Application of the technology acceptance model. *Journal of Computer-Mediated Communication, 13*(1), 163–186. Retrieved from https://doi.org /10.1111/j.1083-6101.2007.00391.x

Paulus, T. M. (2007). CMC modes for learning tasks at a distance. *Journal of Computer-Mediated Communication, 12*(4), 1322–1345. Retrieved from https://doi.org/10.1111 /j.1083-6101.2007.00375.x

Polson, E. (2011). Belonging to the network society: Social media and the production of a new global middle class. *Communication, Culture & Critique, 4*(2), 144–163. Retrieved from https://doi.org/10.1111/j.1753-9137.2011.01099.x

Prensky, M. (2001). Digital natives, digital immigrants. *On the Horizon, 9*(5), 1–6. Retrieved from https://doi.org/10.1108/10748120110424816

Purdy, J. P. (2009). When the tenets of composition go public: A study of writing in Wikipedia. *College Composition and Communication, 61*(2), 351–373.

Yancey, K. B. (2004). Made not only in words: Composition in a new key. *College Composition and Communication, 56*(2), 297–328. Retrieved from https://doi.org /10.2307/4140651

Yang, J. C., Quadir, B., & Nian-Shing, C. (2015). Effects of the badge mechanism on self-efficacy and learning performance in a game-based English learning environment. *Journal of Educational Computing Research, 54*(3), 371–394. Retrieved from https://doi .org/10.1177/0735633115620433

4

RECONSTRUCTING *ETHOS* AS DWELLING PLACE
On the Bridge of Twenty-First Century Writing Practices (ePortfolios and Blogfolios)

Cynthia Davidson

ABSTRACT

As writers find ways to respond to complex interactions in networked and global spaces, revisiting the rhetorical idea of *ethos* as dwelling place becomes critical. Following ideas from Heraclitus (1971), Heidegger (1977), and Cordova (2013), maintaining virtual residencies can *bridge* two visions of writing—one as fragmentary, convergent, modular, and rhizomatic, the other as shaper of the rational—through *interactivity* and *reflection*. ePortfolios and blogfolios represent networked residencies—or teachable models of multimodal textuality that can reveal the relationship of writing to technology.

Keywords: architectonic, Aristotle, blogfolios, Cordova, cyborg, digital, digital space, ePortfolio, *ethos,* Heidegger, hybridization, interactivity, lifeworld, multimodality, network, New London Group, Plato, *poiésis,* reflection, virtual space

INTRODUCTION

Because of recent shifts in the literacy landscape, people must communicate clearly on the Internet in multiple and rapidly changing environments. As such spaces undergo frequent updates and are actively monitored, revisiting the rhetorical idea that *ethos* is a dwelling place is imperative (Cordova, 2013). *Ethos* has established its position in contemporary media literacy in the form of a rhetorical appeal, agency, ongoing transactional rhetoric, and responsive online space. Connected across physical and online spaces simultaneously, writers must achieve status as literate cyborgs—people of imagination and materiality working to find their *ethos* as a dwelling situated across networks.

DOI: 10.7330/9781607326649.c004

WHERE DO CYBORGS DWELL?

In *Writing Space,* J. D. Bolter (2001) states that scholars like Walter Ong theorize writing shapes the analytical mind, making it "easier to see logical relationships and to subordinate one idea to another" and to unify one's views (p. 191). It is a Cartesian perspective reflecting "I write, therefore I think," and this view influences many composition researchers who have studied writing as a cognitive process (see Emig, 1971; Perl, 1979; Flower & Hayes, 1981; Berthoff & Stephens, 1988; Berthoff, 1990; Olson, 1996). However, critics of this pseudo-Cartesian model and its "autonomous, rational ego" are now considered influential voices in global cultural theory, including Bourdieu (1984); Lyotard, Bennington, and Massumi (1984); Baudrillard (1994); Butler (2005); Gergen (1991); Haraway (1991); and Landow (1997)—who argue for variations of the multiple and fragmented material self (Bolter, 2001, p. 197).

In *The Cyborg Manifesto,* Donna Haraway (1991) creates a representation of the postmodern digital reader/writer (the cyborg) as "a cybernetic organism, a hybrid of machine and organism, a creature of social reality as well as a creature of fiction" (p. 149). The cyborg has a modular existence that finds contingent alliances and provisional completions on an ad hoc basis. By design, nothing is sacred, eternal, or unbroken as the cyborg constructs and is constructed by a web of lived experiences described socially by networks and rhetorically by hypertext. Connections tend toward the rhizomatic (see Deleuze & Guattari, 1987) and associative rather than the linear and hierarchically or institutionally prescribed. Although Haraway's purpose was to address the changing role of feminism in the post-Reagan era, the connection of her cyborg to readers and writers is a rich one, as hypertext promotes and requires this associative turn (see Landow, 1997).

The cyborg as a metaphor for postmodern readerly/writerly identity emphasizes its agency; the cyborg may be the icon of a personalized network of relational parts, but it presents itself as an integrated unit. Cooper (2011) defines a composing agent as one who "through conscious intention or free will causes changes in the world" and agency as "an emergent property of embodied individuals" (p. 421). What remains suspect is the environment in which the cyborg operates and forms relationships—textually and socially. Although Haraway's cyborg is a creation of contingency and connection, Craig Malkin (2013) views cyborgs as incapable of strong human connections. Malkin was inspired by the "wormhole theory" of virtual communication proposed by Case (2011) in her talk for TEDWomen 2010, "We Are All Cyborgs Now" (http://tinyurl.com/casetedtalk). After viewing Case's talk, Malkin (2013) observed how cyber-communication affects our ability to relate: "The very constrictions of time and space that permit magically instantaneous communication also mean that the more we reach out with this second, cyberself, the less human we become; we only know ourselves—and are known—in bits and pieces." Malkin concludes invoking the need to retain our "all" and reject the "crudely pixelated self of cyberspace." If the cyborg dwells in fragments through dispersion, it cannot build a self, which must be formed through reflection, and it will not be able to form satisfactory relationships.

Unlike Haraway, Malkin addresses the Cartesian ideal of an integrated self and rejects postmodern fragmentation as a viable way of life. Rather than finding sustenance in rhizomatic networks, his cyborg is potentially a homeless stray, a reactive, button-pushing, link-clicking aberration without love. Malkin's concerns reflect an important node both in current public opinion and in scholarship on global networking communications and power relations—one that emphasizes the importance of selling trust through visual cues in media (see Castells, 2007, p. 243). Now that global and social networks inscribe the postmodernism into everyday life, how can educators afford to observe, accept, and celebrate freedoms afforded by its fragmentation and dispersion without considering the potential sustainability for students who live with these practices? To answer this question, I first consider Heidegger's (1971) work on dwelling, materialized in his example of the *bridge*, as the foundation of sustainable networked living. I next examine how hypertext and its derivatives can remediate print text (see Bolter & Grusin, 2000) and become a bridge on which the modern cyborg may dwell. In identifying a bridge as a dwelling place, Heidegger opened a transitional node where a space for networking can be a place for developing *ethos* as dwelling and become a space for composing identities.

THE *ETHOS* OF DWELLING ON THE BRIDGE

Heidegger (1971) offers a bridge as the model of a "built thing" in which one might dwell, demonstrating how his thoughts of dwelling are never far from considerations of technology (p. 146). Reflecting on the roots of building (German *bauen*, Gothic *wunian*) led him to conclude dwelling relates to staying, remaining in peace, and being preserved from danger (*sparing*) (Heidegger, 1971, pp. 146–147). The bridge not only spares and preserves, but also frees: "Saving does not only snatch something from a danger. To save really means to set something free into its own presencing" (p. 148). Heidegger is quick to exemplify dwelling as a shelter from harm and exposure—one that facilitates travel, crossing-over from place to place. By this emphasis, Heidegger (1971) portrays the web-like nature of dwelling and its role as the facilitator of networks (pp. 150–151). Optimistically, this staying-within-gathering quality of the bridge releases the dweller from the tension invoked by the fragmentary postmodern condition and the isolation and fixedness of the separatist Cartesian ego. It also produces value through *techné*, which Heidegger sees as the definition of art and the foundation of all technology (p. 157). The bridge represents a built thing that lets dwelling exist, for "[b]uilding accomplishes its nature in the raising of locations by the joining of their spaces" (Heidegger, 1971, p. 157).

For the bridge depicted by Heidegger, one can see a gesture to Plato's desire for a *techné* of virtue in the act of dwelling. Heidegger also alludes to the role of character and intent inherent in Aristotle's virtue-evaluation: dwelling becomes the home of the virtuous character. Yet *poiésis* and *praxis* must retain their distinctive characters because there is freedom to act in networks, and free will allows for actions both virtuous and not. The Internet gets much of its overarching character from this distinctive freedom, and the impact of this freedom is the source of much concern to critics of the Internet's effects on society. The bridge (with the virtual spaces of the Internet being perhaps its most striking and important manifestation) is a place of *praxis*, a *poiésis* where actions occur.

Heidegger's bridge evokes the origin point of the human communicating across networks and becoming cyborgian. For instance, Heidegger (1971) articulates the effect of the bridge on human experience of time and distance as that state "in which everything is neither far nor near [. . .] without distance" (p. 164). Perhaps it is this "unearthly" (Heidegger, 1971, p. 164) quality that disturbs Malkin about the cyborg who has access to others through technological wormholes. But what are those wormholes if not bridges—"built things" that allow the potentiality for dwelling through gathering-while-staying? Rather than identifying the collapse of time and distance as dehumanizing, Heidegger implies it is perhaps the essence of humans to find dwelling in these new scenes. We can see this applied in Appadurai's (1996) description of the potential volatility caused by "global processes involving mobile texts and migrant audiences" that "create implosive events that fold global pressures into small, already politicized areas producing locality in new, globalized ways" (p. 8)—a wormhole-like effect that causes a rewriting, or perhaps rewiring, or both, of the world our students must learn to compose in. Appadurai (1996) evokes this wormhole image in his descriptions of once fixed local diasporas "of hope, of despair, of terror" imagining new cultures for themselves through mass mediation and mobility (p. 5).

In this scenario, dwelling on this made-thing by *techné*, the bridge, also becomes the source of unforced discovery and perhaps of creativity. In "The Question Concerning Technology," Heidegger (1977) asserts technology is not by nature instrumental, but it opens a space for what is real to emerge (p. 5). He defines this essential revelatory quality of technology by contrasting it with the gridlike, managerial and organizational concept of *enframing* (p. 13), described as a "setting-up which sets upon man, i.e., challenges him forth, to reveal the real, in the mode of ordering, as standing-reserve" (p. 10). The challenge to order and to create standing-reserves defines enframing, not technology itself, as the shaper of manufacturing (p. 14). While enframing (a concept that can be related to global capitalistic practices in a very practical sense—see Joronen, 2010—as well as to educational assessment—see Henry, 2013) does not deny the revelatory, creative nature of technology, it can conceal it: "in the sense of *poiésis*, let[ting] what presences come forth into appearance" (p. 9). It is only within the awareness of the "coming to presence of technology" that we might discover the "innermost destructible belongingness," or "the arising of the saving power" (p. 17). The "indestructible belongingness" infers *reflection* on the technological "question" might lead to results both human and deeply social in nature. If the cyborg can access this saving power, Malkin's fears for its loveless, socially-bankrupt future might be waylaid. Saving power could arise through *reflection* on, and perhaps within, technology itself. Reflection is also linked to dwelling, which allows for freedom of movement from location to location. The bridge is thus "akin to the essence of technology and, on the other, fundamentally different from it" (pp. 18–19).

Rhetorically, the bridge might represent a commonplace as developed by Aarseth (1994). Aarseth investigates nonlinearity as a rhetorical device that allows readers to negotiate hypertexts by actions such as forking and jumping. Ball and Moeller (2007) define this perspective as cultural anthropology, "whereby the critic observes the making of meaning through the process of interacting with a text." The presentation of a new media text's material elements (primarily visual, aural, and spatial) is available to the reader for interpretation and meaning-making. The bridge as a location inhabited by bodies and minds better describes new media writing where the reader/participant does not approach the text from without, but from the center, from within. The bridge as a dwelling, however, further describes the reader/participant's ability to pause and reflect and to claim that location as a place of social connection and pleasure.

Writing has long proved to be such a location. ePortfolios are consciously structured to serve as locations for composing, archiving, linking to related content, and paying attention to the work of thinking, as well as responding to audiences. The idea of "portfolio thinking" (McLagan, 2000), provides a robust system for facilitating this kind of reflection. Cordova (2013) asserts a "reengagement with an understanding of *ethos* as dwelling place [. . .] can enhance a pedagogy of multiliteracies disposed toward the praxis of designing liberatory futures" (p. 146) (see also Selber, 2004). In the local lived reality, or lifeworlds (Habermas, 1985; Cordova, 2013), of people's lives, global society requires each person to facilitate connections with other lifeworlds through architectonic spaces of digital composition-delivered across bridges that connect these local lived realities. These networks provide the potential for members of these global communities to tell their stories. The bridge of Heidegger's metaphor is the hoped-for reality of global networking.

Heidegger's response to Heraclitus reveals the foundation of the relationship between *ethos* and reflection. In "Towards a Phenomenology of Dwelling," Guenther (2002) examines Heidegger's translation of Heraclitus's *ethos anthropoi daimon*, which she identifies as the inspiration for his reclamation of *ethos* as dwelling place. The Greek word for "to lacerate" or "divide" is *daiomai*; Guenther (2002) concludes the *daimon* is "what splits me against myself, making me not quite coincide with myself; it both is me and goes beyond me, exceeding my grasp, resisting every attempt to comprehend it once and for all" (p. 40). For Guenther, the split within the self is bound up with encounters with other beings: "Indeed, my encounters with other beings not only show me who I am; in a fundamental sense, they make me who I am" (p. 40). The *daimon* or divinity is *ethos* in the sense of a calling to different practices of living through interactions with others and also a dialogue within oneself (reflection). This is different than a common sense of *ethos* we encounter in rhetorical practice, which "has customarily been understood as 'credibility' and thus moral character or ethics, which along with *logos* and *pathos* form Aristotle's three artistic proofs (*pistis*) as central components in argumentation" (Cordova, 2013, p. 147).

The definition of *ethos* as credibility evokes a "stored-up" device reminiscent of Heidegger's (1977) standing reserve. Aristotelian situated *ethos* frequently becomes part of an arsenal of argumentation that organizes credibility (often viewed as reputation) as one of several rhetorical *tools*. Modern argument often embraces situated *ethos* as a defense against rhetorical vulnerability. Invented *ethos* is shaped to meet the needs and expectations of a specific audience for a specific situation (Crowley &

Hawhee, 2011, pp. 3–4). Invented *ethos* thus has much in common with *ethos* as dwelling place. Invented *ethos* is performed, and audiences can be physically present, and rhetor and audience would share verbal interactions or exchanged nonverbal cues of approval or disapproval. No matter their previous reputation, orators needed to adjust quickly to audience response, to be sensitive to *kairos*. *Ethos* was not given by nature, but was developed by habit (Crowley & Hawhee, 2011, pp. 1–3).

Globalization has a pervasive effect on the habits that shape *ethos*. Cowen (2003) remarks isolation and trade are two powerful influences on the *ethos* of artists; while isolation can "inject self-confidence and a sense of magic into an art," trade widens an artist's circle of influences (p. 17). Cowen's definition of *ethos* as "the special feel or flavor of a culture" is in sync with the definition of *ethos* as dwelling place (p. 17), but is disturbing in the sense that it essentializes *ethos* as the ground of a market force in a capitalistic "global shopping mall" (p. 17). Cowen's description of "niche *ethos*" as "cultural communities [that] are typically independent of geography, as their ethoses are transmitted through means other than spatial proximity," however, relate directly to new media texts as digital dwelling spaces (p. 17).

The sense *ethos* has to be actively practiced is in line with it as a dwelling place, and the importance of sensitivity to *kairos* becomes exponentially intrinsic to its development in the global networks of the digital age. The Internet and affiliated digital cultures have provided citizens with a series of personal and cultural "wormholes" through which they time/distance travel and respond to audiences daily. The idea we live online (rather than simply communicate) is not strictly academic; it has suffused popular culture as well. Appadurai (1996) evokes this wormhole image in his descriptions of once fixed local diasporas "of hope, of despair, of terror" imagining new cultures for themselves through mass mediation and mobility (p. 5). And as Lim (2014) writes, "Across the humanities and social sciences, the past three decades have witnessed 'a spatial turn', a shift toward geographically sensitive work with attentiveness to context, difference and the pre-eminence of locale" (p. 2).

But is living online the same as dwelling? The answer perhaps lies in the New London Group's (1996) call for a multiliteracies pedagogy that embraces the designing of social futures and invokes the cultivation of lifeworlds as the path to true education (Habermas, 1985). Dwelling online is a reflective vs. reactive, practice. As Zubek (2015) notes, this reflective "paying attention" fosters critical thinking in the global community where often citizens simply do not see the point of resistance, slowing down, or letting anything disrupt functionality on the grid. In a sense, reflection syncs with Selber's (2004) second and third multiliteracies, as reflection disrupts the filters of authorized vision (critical literacy) and allows for its reconstruction in the production of new media texts (rhetorical literacy). As mentioned previously, "portfolio thinking" provides a robust system for facilitating this kind of reflection.

Many, including Shirky (2010) and Rheingold (2000), have argued the world has undergone a revolution in how we obtain and process information. In this context, one form of risk mentioned by Appadurai (1996) is the potential volatility caused by "global processes involving mobile texts and migrant audiences" that "create implosive events that fold global pressures into small, already politicized areas producing locality in new, globalized ways" (p. 8). Appadurai provides Salman Rushdie's *The Satanic Verses'* impact on Muslim communities as an example of this kind of implosion. More recently, the attack on the offices of the French magazine *Charlie Hebdo* ended in tragedy as gunmen in France shot and killed twelve people, including the editor and several cartoonists, for unflattering depictions of the Prophet Mohammed (see http://www.bbc.com/news/live/world-europe-30710777).

Appadurai's example shows in the globally-networked sphere, there is much more at stake than individuals losing or gaining control over their cyborg destinies. In his examination of the relationship of Heidegger's work on technology to present-day globalism, Joronen (2010) notes how the cyber-networking of the planet has turned the world into an enframing "governed by technical command revealing the whole of the earth as nothing but a reserve on call for the networks of its commanding orderings. By implicitly indicating fundamental leveling and ever-heightening possession of the space of the earth, such ordering of things has turned the earth into a planetary resource to be used up by the manipulative powers of technological societies" (p. 3).

When Heidegger wrote "The Question about Technology," Joronen reminds us,

> it was still 'intellectually respectable' to ignore his views about gigantic, total, and global characters of the logic intrinsic to technological revealing. However, during the last few decades we contemporaries have become increasingly satiated with awareness about the matter that we now live in a technological age, witnessing its global trajectories. (p. 5)

It would be naïve to claim learning to "dwell online" via environments such as ePortfolios or crafting a cherished place in a virtual world can even begin to solve the social and economic problems facing society. However, encouraging students to form social connections online through academic work meaningful to them recalls Audre Lorde's (1984) statement, "Without community, there is no liberation [. . .] but community must not mean a shedding of our differences, nor the pathetic pretense that these differences do not exist" (p. 112). The statement echoes Cordova's (2013) hope for "a pedagogy of multiliteracies disposed toward the praxis of designing liberatory futures" (p. 146).

In scope, global *ethos* would seem counterintuitive to the idea of the local lifeworld. Global *ethos*, however, should be determined by local lifeworlds—connected by the same bridging network that produces enframing. The bridge, that also evokes the "bridge between culture and personality," which Hall (1976) called "[p]ossibly the most important aspect of culture" (p. 240), is a useful metaphor for global *ethos* as dwelling place. As discussed, Guenther (2002) examines Heraclitus's *ethos anthropoi daiomai* as resisting "every attempt to comprehend it" and "splits me against myself." The split with oneself is one we see explode online as people react to, respond to, and occasionally, reflect on others whose actions, opinions, and beliefs differ from their own. As Zubek (2015) explains, the danger of globalization often involves a despair related to making an impact, to fostering agency, to doing anything but react and perhaps, if lucky, survive. The ability to dwell in the *kairotic* moment of response to difference is often a life-changing skill that determines if a relationship with others is sustainable, online or off. These responses are usually public online, and have effects far beyond the individuals who initiate them. Between rapid-fire reaction and disillusioned shutting-down lies the dwelling place of the reflective, globally-networked citizen, the cyborg.

Can consideration of our cyborg nature get us to better intercultural understanding? Manfred Clynes's original definition was "the exogenously extended organizational complex functioning as an integrated homeostatic system unconsciously" (Madrigal, 2010). It was meant to define a way of extending the human experience. The later development of the term by Haraway (1991) weave together humanness with the machine and the animal in a reconfiguration of proscribed patriarchal boundaries. There is a movement toward appropriation of the term to designate less than human, not more, as represented by Malkin (2013) and hinted at by Case (2011). However, the focus of Appadurai (1996) on mobile texts, migrant audiences, and the role of the imagination in the development of new lifeworlds made possible by mass mediation supports the idea of a global movement toward cyborg consciousness. The new diasporas he describes are not determined by geography, but by the intersections of "taste, pleasure, and politics" (p. 8). An example may be found in Noodin, Pitawanakwat, and Sheldon's (2015) work with the preservation of Anishinaabemowin language and culture. The multilayered mediation of poetry, story, and song offers a webtext that becomes a preservational arc (see http://ojibwe.net).

Current scholarship in translingual practice also promotes cyborg consciousness through negotiated difference. Canagarajah (2012) challenges the romantic notion of pristine cultural lifeworlds with gated vernaculars and limited access to dominant global discourses. He instead encourages codemeshing, which "enable multilingual users to both recognize the dominant conventions and also insert qualified changes for voice" (introduction). He describes this practice as cosmopolitanism—one in which differences are normative and meaning is negotiated, and writing as well as speaking communities are marked as contact zones ripe for this process (see Pratt, 1991). Through characteristics of envoicing (retaining non-dominant writing practices in discourse), recontextualization (providing multiple avenues/clues to those who are unfamiliar with non-dominant practices), interaction (openly sharing insights about discourse and negotiating for better uptake), and entextualization (reconfiguring discourse in response to negotiations), Canagarajah (2012) encourages writers to negotiate differences of style and grammatical choices with their audience (p. 127). He also suggests classroom practices can encourage the development of performative competence that models this process, and recognizes the role of technology in codemeshing (p. 19).

Through written online textual environments such as the ePortfolios and blogfolios discussed later, writers may find a grounding for codemeshing and the negotiation of differences mentioned by Canagarajah (2012). Here, codemeshing is not only practiced between speakers of English and others; it is also a feature of creating online identity spaces (what I am referring to as *ethos* as dwelling place) that starts with one scale (such as a professional niche or for a particular course or genre) and expands to include other facets of a writer's identity.

EPORTFOLIOS AND BLOGFOLIOS

Appadurai's (1996) discussion of "global processes involving mobile texts and migrant audiences" that "create implosive events that fold global pressures into small, already politicized areas producing locality in new, globalized ways" (p. 8) has pedagogical and political implications if thought of as a metaphor for the intersection of a student, pathways of learning, consumption and understanding of new discourses, texts, and ideas, and production of new media texts, and invites codemeshing and negotiation of differences (Canagarajah, 2012). In the remainder of this essay, I examine the rhetorical, theoretical, and social relations of writing practices that build *ethos* for cyborgian online residents (i.e., those who dwell there): ePortfolios and blogfolios. Students fold the pressures of their learning process into local spaces that provide them in imaginative, potentially global ways.

ePortfolios are robust performance support systems for identity management, saving and preserving valuable content, reflection, and interactivity. An ePortfolio is hypertextual (linking a hub module to auxiliary modules—although there is nothing to prevent all modules from having an equal weight or status), and fragmentary (no one part of it is the whole, and the parts have value in relation to one another). In most cases, ePortfolios invite commenting and linking by visitors to other online texts. However, most ePortfolio programs allow for extensive customization of privacy settings, so that the scope of interactivity is under the control of the owner.

Jenkins (2006) defines convergence as "the flow of content across multiple media platforms, the cooperation between multiple media industries, and the migratory behavior of media audiences who will go almost anywhere in search of the kind of entertainment experiences they want" (p. 2). ePortfolios foster convergence in they increase the smooth integration of cultural components from the perspective of the individual; ePortfolios are hybridizations of culture viewed through the lens of an individual's experiences as represented by his or her artifacts, the reflections on them, and the connections that she or he makes between them. As representations of culture through the perspective of an individual's voice, ePortfolios are also representations of lifeworlds (Habermas, 1985). In producing such a lifeworld we see the real world is much larger and more complex. ePortfolios engage all the rhetorical relations of multimodal texts listed by Cordova (2013, pp. 145–154).

Yancey (2013) claims although print portfolios have been strongholds in writing classrooms and programs for over two decades (Belanoff & Dickson, 1991; Yancey & Weiser, 1997), they "offer fundamentally different intellectual and affective opportunities than electronic portfolios do" (p. 19). Stating "what we ask students to do is who we ask them to be," Yancey defines a "Web sensible" ePortfolio as one which does not simply transfer print to an HTML environment, but "through text boxes, hyperlinking, visuals, audio texts, and design elements not only inhabits the digital space and is distributed electronically but also exploits the medium" (p. 20). ePortfolios offer readers multiple navigational paths and often include instructions from the author to guide them through the reading experience (p. 27). Web-sensible ePortfolios are remediations (Bolter & Grusin, 2000) of print portfolios, including and converging upon other older media (such as television, itself remediated through video) (p. 28).

Bolter and Grusin (2000) define "remediation" as a pattern older and newer media establish throughout the ages, an oscillation "between immediacy and hypermediacy, between transparency and opacity," explaining the process of hypermediation as an effect of remediation that creates greater awareness of older media that may have earlier been transparent (p. 22). The print portfolio was a remediation of a book (Yancey, 2013, p. 28), calling attention to the holistic quality of a semester's writing in view of the fragmentation of the individual pieces of writing. The process of writing is also remediated in the ePortfolio as the process of writing itself becomes remediated through the web and multimedia. ePortfolios remediate the awareness of the space in which information is made accessible and tangible, removing it a degree from the material but increasing its potential for modular chunking and fluidity—making it more *bridgelike* in the Heideggerean sense. Portfolios are "exercises in deeply reflective activity" that remediate the process of reflection, making it potentially an activity to be shared with chosen publics rather than a semi-private ritual between student and teacher, and perhaps a few peers (Yancey, 2013, p. 30).

Another remediation of writing space that occurs in an ePortfolio is a gallery (Yancey, 2013, p. 30). Sometimes ePortfolios recall museum exhibitions of the self, especially in the showcase mode. In an article on a community ePortfolio gallery project for Native Americans in Augustana, Cambridge (2013) writes about the remediation of a museum (p. 156). The project is a modular "ePortfolio city" that bears a resemblance to Heidegger's bridge; taken as a metatext, it offers a location to the fragmentary stories and perspectives that represent the community. Groups like this working together in online spaces benefit from "protopublic spaces" (Eberly, 2000) where "individuals can share their private experiences and ideas with trusted others and develop the skills they need to present them effectively in more fully public forums" (Cambridge, 2013, p. 173). These are also referred to as "middle spaces" by Bass and Bernstein (2008) in a study of faculty communities (Cambridge, 2013, p. 173). They recall the "third spaces" of Soja (1996), shared community spaces away from home and work. Cambridge's project recalls Appadurai's (1996) statement about "subversive micronarratives," the "transformation of everyday subjectivities through electronic mediation and the work of the imagination," creating a "diasporic public space"

(p. 10) that can give rise to political movements and energies, as well as Canagarajah's (2012) negotiation of differences. The ePortfolio has the potential to disrupt totalizing narratives received from the influences of dominant cultures.

ePortfolio scholars call attention to a greater need for the integration of ePortfolios and social media or features that enhance social activity between writers and readers or between collaborators. Middlebrook and Sun (2013) argue that, while the educational benefits of both ePortfolios and blogging are documented, students are "better served if blogging is employed as a venue for developing their writing, critical thinking, and technology skills in conjunction with their disciplinary and professional identity" (p. 134). Calderòn and Buentello (2006) define these as blog-folios, "a union with 'the customization power of the weblog and the evidence showroom of an ePortfolio'" (as cited in Middlebrook & Sun, 2013, pp. 125–126). As one of my students reflected on the relationship between blogs and ePortfolios:

> Instead of just listing your qualifications, skills, and experiences on a single piece of paper, ePortfolio allows you to further elaborate on this while also incorporating imagery and various other types of media to offer a visually appealing experience for the viewer. In contrast, blogs serve as more of a reflective medium that allows the user to express him or herself without limitation. (Milano, personal communication, August 3, 2014)

Also advocating for more social features in ePortfolios, Klein (2013) claims that "ePortfolio systems can emphasize social media alongside professional presentation, encourage students to develop individual voices and produce a range of content. The content, which can be trans-lated across media and contexts, puts students' intellectual leadership, analytical ability, and personal creativity on display" (p. 58). Rice (2013) has called for deepening faculty teaching statements "to embrace, much like ePortfolio performance support systems, individual identity *and* rhetorically situated networked spaces" (p. 51)—or to become more hypercirculatory, social, reflective, and multimodal. Such a space allows teachers to showcase their individual strengths (and those of their stu-dents) in a way that scores cannot, and offers the potential to connect the texts that compete, contrast, and collide, intellectually, aesthetically, and culturally, displaying the full dynamic of their teaching lives. This is also Canagarajah's (2012) negotiation of differences again, modeled by teachers in situations that matter to the construction of their own professional *ethos*. While Canagarajah (2012) spoke primarily of negoti-ated literacy spaces between speakers, there is the possibility of writers of multimodal, multifaceted identity texts such as ePortfolios to negotiate their own competing texts through reflection as they negotiate a professional identity with a larger, external audience.

While the "tool" of the ePortfolio is technological, the process and presentation of reflection is not technological, but akin to it. We should remember this, or we risk essentializing the ePortfolio as "just another tool." Henry (2013) describes ePortfolios as tools situated in a "standing reserve" state (with reference to Heidegger, 1977), "waiting to be used, where they are then placed into a larger structure (enframed), the computerized network or the network of the pedagogical, referring to the teacher/teachers who place the works together into a collection of class work" (Henry, 2013). Henry is correct about the situation of ePortfolios as standing reserve for a variety of purposes and about how ePortfolios are "enframed" in larger orders. Standing reserves are always organized, presumably for the purpose of revealing what technology can do, but the act of ordering can become a dominant end unto itself. Henry asserts ePortfolios are primarily instrumental tools that can be assessed for effectiveness. While applications of ePortfolios in institutional settings for specific assessment uses are certainly organizational and instrumental, Henry's assertion that ePortfolios are by definition tools need to be challenged in light of Heidegger's definition of *ethos* as dwelling place. Heidegger (1977) writes, "Because the essence of technology is nothing technological, essential reflection upon technology and decisive confrontation with it must happen in a realm that is, on the one hand, akin to the essence of technology and, on the other, fundamentally different from it" (pp. 18–19). ePortfolios, as constructed technological spaces for content and reflection, seem tailored to this purpose. Heidegger's definition of technology's essence as nothing technological seems to demand the tool be considered in relation to multiple local uses: not just for assessment, but for their impact on lives, bodies, and communities.

One way in which ePortfolios combine the work of assessment of learning with the lives affected by that learning is detailed by Madden (2015) in a study of how nontraditional students in her program at Notre Dame de Namur University. Madden found value in narrative identities created through ePortfolios "which aim [. . .] to create a text that represents a student's identity in a way that allows others to connect with their passion and struggles" (p. 95). She noted "new understandings about the shared world that they inhabit, both within the classroom and in broader community networks" occurred as a result of the ePortfolio project. Madden remarks on how students from backgrounds that do not conform to the grid of traditional college expectations formed counter-narratives to resist dominant cultural narratives, and noted that this seemed relevant for any marginalized group of students (p. 96).

The role of ePortfolios in storytelling, especially in the fostering of these potentially subversive counter-narratives, stands outside instrumentality. Madden explains "[n]arrative imagination is essential to constructing a story of self in which time, authenticity, and meaning are engaged in discourse about both past and current learning and future possibilities of being" (p. 97). Such is the counterpoint to Appadurai's "global processes involving mobile texts and migrant audiences" that "create implosive events that fold global pressures into small, already politicized areas producing locality in new, globalized ways" (p. 8). The ePortfolio of a nontraditional student contains juxtapositions that produce a locality for that life with its earned wisdom, connections, and human capital.

Expectations for ePortfolios often run much higher than the reality (Yancey, 2013, p. 32). But there are creative turns in ePortfolio construction that surprise and delight, such as its potential for extended storytelling in genres that are generally fixed (e.g., resumés). An example is the ePortfolio of Emily Madsen, a Stony Brook University student whose Digication ePortfolio has received over a million views internationally. Much of the interest is related to Madsen's interactive Work History and Resumé, which does not initially look different than any online resumé (see Figure 4.1).

Madsen's resumé page is organized to guide the reader, offering navigational tips at the top. The first-glance text of the resumé appears fairly linear, organized chronologically. The familiar setup is reassuring to people used to "flat" CVs. The white background is also familiar, crisp, and professional-looking. But notice that the navigation panel to the left is much fuller than the text that is immediately visible. Clicking on any of the links will take the reader to a different page with a narrative about the professional or educational experience listed there. Some pages, like "In the Heart of the Lavender Capital of North America," provide multimedia content. Many pages serve more than one purpose, as they promote Madsen's own narratives and the places and programs she attended.

The hub-like nature of ePortfolios demonstrates they are constructed to be virtual residencies as well as bridges. One can also see the influence of Walter Ong's theoretical constructions of writing as rational mind-shaper (cited in Bolter, 2001) in current ePortfolio theories. That is, they portend the connection-building of the fragmentation of modern educational experience, displayed through a

Work History and Resume

Stony Brook University Orientation and Family Programs

Orientation Leader

Technology and Instructional Design

ePortfolio Consultant and Media Assistant

Promoting ePortfolios at the SBU General Job and Internship Fair

SCALA Screens

▸ 2013 Teaching & Learning Spring Colloquium

SBU Faculty Center ePortfolio Consultant and Media Assistant

Promoting ePortfolios at the SBU General Job and Internship Fair

SCALA Screens

▸ 2013 Teaching &amp; Learning Spring Colloquium

Aquaculture

Coast Seafoods

Port Discovery Seafarms

Port Discovery Oyster Hatchery

Introduction: Logistics and Set-Up of Hatchery

Daily Operations and Problem Solving

High School - Retail & Farm Jobs

Lavender Farms: Jardin du Soleil and Purple Haze

Other Relevant Experience

Science at SEA

W e l c o m e

Listed below is my resume. To the left are links to pages containing more information about my work experience. However, clicking on any of the blue underlined words in my resume below will take you to a page containing more information about the item listed.

I hope you enjoy reading through these pages!

Emily Marie Madsen

emily.madsen@stonybrook.edu

Education

State University of New York (SUNY) Stony Brook University

Major: Biology

Specialization: Developmental Genetics

Minor: Marine Science

Field Work Experiences

University of the West Indies - Discovery Bay Marine Laboratories

Undergraduate Study Abroad Experience - Jamaica

January 2013

- Studied coral reef biology and processes
- Developed and executed individual research project under the supervision of SBU faculty

Sea Education Association (SEA)

Science at Sea Oceanography Program - Woods Hole, MA

August 2010

- Participated in classes, lectures, field trips, laboratory activities
- Conducted research aboard the SSV Corwith Cramer for ten days
- Graduated with High Honors

Work Experience

Figure 4.1. Emily Madsen, ePortfolio Work History Page (see https://stonybrook.digica tion.com/emily_madsen/Welcome/published).

series of artifacts upon which reflections are crafted as a personal narrative that allows a student to become better conscious of what s/he has learned. ePortfolios are thus constructed primarily for the display of and reflection about artifacts while blogs are more conversational, informational, and dialogic; connecting these creates an ideal platform for what ePortfolio scholars Light, Chen, and Ittelson describe as "global bridges" (Rice, 2013, p. 47). They claim "today, most students can expect to explore cultures and have life experiences, and world views that are different from other people they must learn and work with" (Light, Chen, & Ittelson, 2011, p. 59; Rice, 2013, p. 47). In a blogfolio, a blog can be an artifact within an ePortfolio, but one that harbors continuing interactivity (an important pillar of Canagarajah's (2012) negotiated differences) due to commenting and feedback as well as authorial reflection.

CONCLUSION

In a globally-networked world, writers are cyborgs who need to manage multiple selves that bridge the distance between digital/virtual and physical realms. The mission involves skills that are as equally important as those required for crafting and organizing a logical, well-supported argument or editing one's writing for clarity. If writers must feel confident in their ability to navigate sustained conversations over time and distance, they might *dwell* in their digital writing spaces while navigating the "wormholes" Case celebrates and Malkin cautions against. The predicament of cyborgian writers is one that recalls Heidegger's (1971) definition of dwelling on a bridge as related to remaining in peace and being preserved from danger. It exemplifies dwelling as not only shelter from harm and exposure, but as that which facilitates crossing-over from place to place (Heidegger, 1971, pp. 146–147) in a world built of networks.

I identified composing through networks as the *techne* from which the dwelling place (*ethos*) of the cyborg is constructed. Heidegger (1971) offers a bridge as the model of a "built thing" in which one might dwell, demonstrating how his thoughts of dwelling ("the manner in which mortals are on the earth") are never far from consideration of the question of technology (p. 146). New media texts situated in networks are the bridges where *ethos* can be constructed and inhabited. Heidegger's bridge evokes the current origin point of the human communicating across networks, one critical moment of *becoming cyborgian*.

In his discussion of the enframing power and saving power of technology, Heidegger (1977) links reflection to dwelling, the gathering-while-staying of the built thing, the bridge. The bridge is "akin to the essence of technology and, on the other, fundamentally different from it" (pp. 18–19). Reflection is also a *political* (and therefore global) issue. Reflection is paying attention, noticing where one dwells, offering "disruptive paths of attention" as an alternative to being overwhelmed by "global processes and neoliberal dynamics" (Zubek, 2015). Rhetorically, the bridge is in the sense developed by Aarseth (1994) whereby nonlinearity is seen as a rhetorical device that allows readers to negotiate hypertexts (Ball & Moeller, 2007). The presentation of a media text's material elements (primarily visual, aural, and spatial) is available to the reader for interpretation and meaning-making. The relationship between *ethos* and reflection explored by Guenther (2002) examines Heidegger's translation of Heraclitus's *ethos anthropoi daimon*, which she identifies as the inspiration for his reclamation of *ethos* as dwelling place. Guenther emphasizes the role of habit in producing *ethos*.

I then examined, through Appadurai (1996), the effects that global-ization has had on the habits that create *ethos*. He evokes Case's (2011) image of contemporary communication through technology as a series of "wormholes" in his descriptions of once fixed local diasporas "of hope, of despair, of terror" imagining new cultures for themselves through mass mediation and mobility (p. 5). I connected this power to the abil-ity to imagine new futures through making connections. Appadurai's (1996) discussion of "global processes involving mobile texts and migrant audiences" that "create implosive events that fold global pres-sures into small, already politicized areas producing locality in new, globalized ways" (p. 8) has pedagogical and political implications if we think of this as a metaphor for the intersection of a student, pathways of learning, consumption and understanding of new discourses, texts, and ideas, and production of new media texts. I also related new media identity text creation to Canagarajah's (2012) notions of codemeshing and negotiation of differences from both an internal process.

ePortfolios and blogfolios can serve as models of multimodal textual-ity while revealing to students the evolving nature of writing as the "built thing," the bridge of Heidegger's dream, which allows cyborgs to dwell and reflect, rather than simply respond and react, in global networks. In these examples, students can fold the pressures of their learning process into local spaces that provide them.

References

Aarseth, E. J. (1994). Nonlinearity and literary theory. In G. Landow (Ed.), *Hyper/text/ theory* (pp. 52–86). Baltimore, MD: Johns Hopkins University Press.

Appadurai, A. (1996). *Modernity at large: Cultural dimensions of globalization.* Minneapolis, MN: University of Minnesota Press.

Ball, C., & Moeller, R. (2007). Reinventing the possibilities: Academic literacy and new media. *The Fibreculture Journal, 10.* Retrieved from http://ten.fibreculturejournal.org /fcj-062-reinventing-the-possibilities-academic-literacy-and-new-media

Bass, R., & Bernstein, D. (2008). The middle of open spaces: Generating knowledge about learning through multiple layers of open teaching communities. In T. Iiyoshi & V. Kumar (Eds.), *Opening up education: The collective advancement of education through open technology, open content and open knowledge* (pp. 303–317). Cambridge, MA: MIT Press.

Baudrillard, J. (1994). *Simulacra and simulation.* Ann Arbor, MI: University of Michigan Press.

Belanoff, P., & Dickson, M. (Eds.). (1991). *Portfolios: Process and product.* New York, NY: Heinemann.

Berthoff, A. E. (1990). *The sense of learning.* Portsmouth, NH: Heinemann.

Berthoff, A. E., & Stephens, J. (1988). *Forming, thinking, and writing.* Portsmouth, NH: Boynton/Cook.

Bolter, J. D. (2001). *Writing space: Computers, hypertext, and the remediation of print* (2nd ed.). New York, NY: Routledge.

Bolter, J. D., & Grusin, R. (2000). *Remediation: Understanding new media.* Cambridge, MA: MIT Press.

Bourdieu, P. (1984). *Distinction: A social critique of the judgement of taste.* Cambridge, MA: Harvard University Press.

Butler, J. (2005). *Giving an account of oneself.* New York, NY: Fordham University Press. Retrieved from https://doi.org/10.5422/fso/9780823225033.001.0001

Calderón, M. A. M., & Buentello, J. R. (2006). Facilitating reflection through ePortfolios at technológico de Monterrey. In A. Jafari & C. Kaufman (Eds.), *Handbook of research on ePortfolios* (pp. 486–495). Hershey, PA: Idea Group Reference.

Cambridge, D. (2013). From metaphor to analogy: How the National Museum of the American Indian can inform the Augustana Community portfolio. In K. V. Wills & R. Rice (Eds.), *ePortfolio performance support systems: Constructing, presenting, and assessing portfolios* (pp. 155–180). Fort Collins, CO: The WAC Clearinghouse; Anderson; SC: Parlor Press. Retrieved from https://wac.colostate.edu/books/eportfolios/chapter9.pdf

Canagarajah, S. (2012). *Translingual practice: Global Englishes and cosmopolitan relations* (Kindle version). Retrieved from https://amazon.com

Case, A. (2011, January 11). *We are all cyborgs now.* [Video.] Retrieved from https://www.youtube.com/watch?v=z1KJAXM3xYA

Castells, M. (2007). Communication, power and counter-power in the network society. *International Journal of Communication, 1*(1), 1–29. Retrieved from http://ijoc.org/index.php/ijoc/article/view/46/35

Cooper, M. M. (2011). Rhetorical agency as emergent and enacted. *College Composition and Communication, 62*(3), 420–449.

Cordova, N. I. (2013). Invention, *ethos*, and new media in the rhetoric classroom: The storyboard as exemplary genre. In T. Bowen & C. Whithaus (Eds.), *Multimodal literacies and emerging genres,* 143–163. Pittsburgh, PA: University of Pittsburg Press. https://doi.org/10.2307/j.ctt6wrbkn.10

Cowen, T. (2003). Does globalization kill ethos and diversity? *Phi Kappa Phi Forum, 83*(4), 17–20.

Crowley, S., & Hawhee, D. (2011). *Ancient rhetorics for contemporary students.* London, England: Longman.

Deleuze, G., & Guattari, F. (1987). *A thousand plateaus: Capitalism and schizophrenia.* (B. Massumi, Trans.). Duluth, MN: University of Minnesota Press.

Eberly, R. A. (2000). *Citizen critics: Literary public spheres.* Urbana, IL: University of Illinois Press.

Emig, J. A. (1971). *The composing processes of twelfth graders.* Urbana, IL: National Council of Teachers of English Press.

Flower, L., & Hayes, J. R. (1981). A cognitive process theory of writing. *College Composition and Communication, 32*(4), 365–387.

Gergen, K. J. (1991). *The saturated self: Dilemmas of identity in contemporary life.* New York, NY: Basic Books.

Guenther, L. (2002). Towards a phenomenology of dwelling. *Canadian Journal of Environmental Education, 7*(2), 38–46. Retrieved from https://cjee.lakeheadu.ca/index.php/cjee/article/view/254

Habermas, J. (1985). *The theory of communicative action, volume 2: Lifeworld and system: A critique of functionalist reason.* Boston, MA: Beacon Press.

Hall, E. T. (1976). *Beyond culture.* Garden City, NY: Anchor Press.

Haraway, D. J. (1991). A cyborg manifesto: Science, technology, and socialist-feminism in the late twentieth century. In D. J. Haraway (Ed.), *Simians, cyborgs, and women: The reinvention of nature* (pp. 149–181). New York, NY: Routledge.

Heidegger, M. (1971). *Poetry, language, and thought.* New York, NY: Harper Perennial.

Heidegger, M. (1977). The question concerning technology. In W. Lovitt (Ed.), *The question concerning technology and other essays* (pp. 3–35). New York, NY: Garland.

Henry, T. P. (2013). Toward a technological theory of ePortfolios. *Computers and Composition Online* (Winter). Retrieved from http://www2.bgsu.edu/departments /english/cconline/winter2013/eportx

Jenkins, H. (2006). *Convergence culture: Where old and new media collide.* New York, NY: New York University Press.

Joronen, M. (2010). *The age of planetary space: On Heidegger, being, and metaphysics of globalization* (Doctoral dissertation). Turku, Finland: University of Turku. Retrieved from http://www.doria.fi/bitstream/handle/10024/66733/AnnalesAII257Joronen.pdf?se quence=1

Klein, L. F. (2013). The social ePortfolio: Integrating Social media and models of learning in academic ePortfolios. In K. V. Wills & R. Rice (Eds.). *ePortfolio performance support systems: Constructing, presenting, and assessing portfolios* (pp. 57–74). Fort Collins, CO: The WAC Clearinghouse; Anderson, SC: Parlor Press. Retrieved from https://wac.colostate.edu/books/eportfolios/chapter3.pdf

Landow, G. P. (1997). *Hypertext 2.0: The convergence of contemporary critical theory and technology.* Baltimore, MD: Johns Hopkins University Press.

Light, T. P., Chen, H., & Ittelson, J. (2011). *Documenting learning with ePortfolios: A guide for college instructors.* San Francisco, CA: Jossey-Bass.

Lim, M. (2014). Seeing spatially: People, networks and movements in digital and urban spaces. *International Planning Development Review, 36*(1), 51–72. Retrieved from http://proxy.library.stonybrook.edu/login?url=http://search.ebscohost.com/login .aspx?direct=true&db=hus&AN=94281890&site=eds-live&scope=site; https://doi.org /10.3828/idpr.2014.4

Lorde, A. (1984). The master's tools will never dismantle the master's house. In A. Lorde & C. Clarke (Eds.), *Sister outsider: Essays and speeches* (pp. 110–114). Berkeley, CA: Crossing Press.

Lyotard, J.-F., Bennington, G., & Massumi, B. (1984). *The postmodern condition: A report on knowledge.* Minneapolis, MN: University of Minnesota Press.

Madden, T. M. (2015). Reimagining boundaries: How EPortfolios enhance learning for adult students. *International Journal of ePortfolio, 5*(1), 93–101. Retrieved from http://www.theijep.com/pdf/IJEP151.pdf

Madrigal, A. C. (2010, September 30). The man who first said "cyborg," 50 years later. *The Atlantic.* Retrieved from http://www.theatlantic.com/technology/archive/2010 /09/the-man-who-first-said-cyborg-50-years-later/63821

Madsen, E. (2011, February 14). Emily Madsen. Retrieved from https://stonybrook.digi cation.com/emily_madsen/Welcome/published

Malkin, C. (2013). Can cyborgs fall in love? *Psychology Today.* Retrieved from https://www .psychologytoday.com/blog/romance-redux/201301/can-cyborgs-fall-in-love

McLagan, P. A. (2000). Portfolio thinking. *Training and development, 54*(2), 44–51.

Middlebrook, G., & Chih-Yuan Sun, J. (2013). Showcase hybridity: A case for blogfolios. In K. V. Wills & R. Rice (Eds.), *ePortfolio performance support systems: Constructing, presenting, and assessing portfolios* (pp. 123–133). Fort Collins, CO: The WAC Clearinghouse; Anderson, SC: Parlor Press. Retrieved from https://wac.colostate.edu/books/eport folios/chapter7.pdf

New London Group. (1996). A pedagogy of multiliteracies: Designing social futures. *Harvard Educational Review* (Spring, 1996), 60–93. Retrieved from http://hepg.org /her-home/issues/harvard-educational-review-volume-66-issue-1/herarticle/design ing-social-futures_290

Noodin, M., Pitawanakwat, A., & Sheldon, S. (2015). *Ojibwe.net.* Retrieved from http://ojibwe.net

Olson, D. R. (1996). *The world on paper: The conceptual and cognitive implications of writing and reading.* New York, NY: Cambridge University Press.

Perl, S. (1979). The composing processes of unskilled college writers. *Research in the teaching of English, 13,* 317–336.

Pratt, M. L. (1991). Arts of the contact zone. *Profession 1991,* 33–40. New York, NY: MLA Press.

Rheingold, H. (2000). *The virtual community: Homesteading on the electronic frontier.* Cambridge, MA: MIT Press.

Rice, R. (2013). The hypermediated teaching philosophy ePortfolio performance support system. In K. V. Wills & R. Rice (Eds.), *ePortfolio Performance Support Systems: Constructing, Presenting, and Assessing Portfolios* (pp. 41–55). Fort Collins, CO: The WAC Clearinghouse; Anderson, SC: Parlor Press. Retrieved from https://wac.colo state.edu/books/eportfolios/chapter2.pdf

Selber, S. (2004). *Multiliteracies for a digital age.* Carbondale, IL: Southern Illinois University Press.

Shirky, C. (2010, June 4). Does the Internet make you smarter? *The Wall Street Journal.* Retrieved from https://online.wsj.com/news/articles/SB1000142405274870402530 4575284973472694334

Soja, E. W. (1996). *Thirdspace: Journeys to Los Angeles and other real-and-imagined places.* Oxford, England: Blackwell.

Yancey, K. B. (2013). Postmodernism, palimpsests, and portfolios: Theoretical issues in the representation of modern work. In K. V. Wills & R. Rice (Eds.), *ePortfolio Performance Support Systems: Constructing, Presenting, and Assessing Portfolios* (pp. 19–38). Fort Collins, CO: The WAC Clearinghouse; Anderson, SC: Parlor Press. Retrieved from https://wac.colostate.edu/books/eportfolios/chapter1.pdf

Yancey, K. B., & Weiser, I. (1997). *Situating portfolios: Four perspectives.* Logan, UT: Utah State University Press.

Zubek, I. (2015, March 29). Open your eyes: Globalization and the politics of attention. *E-International Relations: Students.* Retrieved from http://www.e-ir.info/2015/03/29 /open-your-eyes-globalization-and-the-politics-of-attention

5

CONSIDERING GLOBAL COMMUNICATION AND USABILITY AS NETWORKED ENGAGEMENT
Lessons from 4C4Equality

Liz Lane and Don Unger

ABSTRACT

The chapter traces the development of 4C4Equality (4C4E), an initiative implemented through the Conference on College Composition and Communication (4Cs). The initiative's purpose is to make conference goers more responsive to issues important to residents of the cities that host each year's conference. From 2014 to 2016, 4C4E provided tactics to allow attendees to support local struggles for marriage equality and LGBTQ rights. Through the initiative, we developed networked engagement as a method for connecting global concerns to local activism. The method draws from research on global communication and usability in writing studies and adjacent areas to develop a view of audience and a sense of purpose that emphasizes usefulness over a uniform critique or set of practices.

Keywords: audience, engagement, context, global communication, LGBTQ, networks, usability

INTRODUCTION

The 4C4 Equality initiative (4C4E) partially formed as a response to a Writing Program Administration (WPA) LISTSERV discussion in Fall 2013.[1] The discussion weighed the merits of boycotting the 2014 Conference on College Composition and Communication (4Cs) due to Indiana legislation that proposed amending the state constitution to ban same-sex marriage (House Joint Resolution-3, or HJR-3). Emails posted to the LISTSERV detailed how conference sites were selected, the logistics of moving the conference, aspects of organizing a boycott, and actions people could take to demonstrate support for marriage

DOI: 10.7330/9781607326649.c005

equality. The discussion, however, gave little attention to the local residents affected by a constitutional ban. In addition, participants largely ignored actions underway in Indiana to oppose HJR-3. As the discussion progressed, graduate students and faculty at Purdue University met to address how opposition to HJR-3 expressed through the LISTSERV could be channeled to influence Indiana politics. The primary points of discussion were

- What could 4Cs do?
- How could we help the organization do it?

Seemingly simple questions, both required well-considered and well-planned answers.

This chapter outlines how we answered those questions. In doing so, we trace 4C4E's development as an initiative aimed at making 4Cs responsive to residents of the conference's host cities. First, we examine the online and local organizing resulting from similar state legislation aimed at curtailing the rights of people who identify as LGBTQ. In analyzing two different approaches, namely a boycott popularized through social media and a coalition built through local organizing, we begin to develop networked engagement as a method for bringing these approaches together. Next, we filter our concept of networked engagement through scholarship on global communication and examine the complexities of working among audiences when navigating global issues and local concerns. Then, we outline how a rhetorical understanding of use helped us develop tactics these audiences might employ in their daily online and face-to-face interactions. Following this discussion, we briefly document 4C4E's work at three different instantiations of 4Cs, namely the

- 2014 conference in Indianapolis, Indiana
- 2015 conference in Tampa, Florida
- 2016 conference in Houston, Texas

Finally, we reflect on the tactics developed for and implemented through each conference. By tracing these changes, we illustrate how networked engagement serves as a flexible method for addressing rhetorical situations that shift based on the location.

ACTIVISM, COALITIONS, AND NETWORKS

To understand what 4Cs could do to help fight Indiana's HJR-3, we considered tactics posed on the WPA LISTSERV. Specifically, we researched boycotts over similar legislation. One stood out in particular: In 2004, Seattle activists organized the "Virginia is for Haters" campaign, a boycott to protest the Virginia General Assembly's passage of HB-751, the "Affirmation of Marriage Act" ("Why the Boycott?," 2004). Though the Virginia law reached further, it was comparable to Indiana's HJR-3 where proponents sought to amend the state constitution to define marriage as being between a man and a woman. However, Virginia's amendment additionally prohibited any legal recognition of same-sex relationships. The organizers of "Virginia is for Haters" waged a social-media campaign encouraging supporters to choose alternate vacation destinations, to stop buying products from Virginia-based companies (particularly J. Crew and Altria), and to call the Virginia tourism board to file complaints ("Why Boycott? Because More than Marriage Is at Stake," 2004). Individuals could also support the boycott by purchasing t-shirts, bumper stickers, and various items from the campaign's Cafe Press store. Finally, organizers encouraged supporters to send receipts from products and services they purchased in lieu of spending money on Virginia-based companies or in the state itself to then Governor Mark R. Warner's office ("Quantifying the Boycott," 2004).

Although it is impossible to trace the campaign's impact on the legislation, it is clear the boycott had a chilling effect on at least some Virginians. In a blog posted to the Seattle newsweekly *The Stranger*, Dyana Mason (2004), a community organizer and the Executive Director of Equality Virginia, discussed how the boycott hampered local efforts to push-back against the legislation because it echoed the legislation's implied call: Virginia is not your home, and you should leave. Still, the boycott's initiators might have seen it as a symbolic effort at shaping debate around the legislation, and it succeeded in that regard. In fact, online media turned the boycott's slogan into a common trope, employing it whenever they reported subsequent legislation aimed at curtailing the rights of LGBTQ Virginians. For example, in 2010 when Governor Bob McDonnell removed non-discrimination protections for LGBTQ state employees, the slogan "Virginia is for Haters" served as a headline in articles and blogs from *Huffington Post, Daily Kos,* and others (Brantley, 2010; Cluchey, 2010; Drew, 2010; Spaulding, 2010). In some sense, the slogan and the social-media campaign worked so effectively they limited responses to subsequent legislation by channeling the debate into questions of love versus hate and avoidance from afar rather than taking local action. Still, we were encouraged that a seemingly small, media-savvy group had such an impact on the discourse surrounding LGBTQ rights in Virginia.

For a similar boycott of 4Cs in Indianapolis, such a strategy might have worked for some involved in the WPA LISTSERV discussion, but it would not have worked for those of us living and working in Indiana. However, the "Virginia is for Haters" campaign was not the only strategy that emerged from opposition to the "Affirmation of Marriage Act." Equality Virginia's grassroots approach pointed us toward another option: We could leverage 4Cs attendees' intellectual, social, and financial resources to oppose HJR-3 in Indiana. We characterize Equality Virginia's approach as grassroots because their tactics connected various audiences. Equality Virginia organizers traveled throughout the state to host informational meetings; they used the organizers' and sympathizers' professional and personal connections to build "The Commonwealth Coalition," which was composed of dozens of community-based organizations, student groups, and small businesses ("HB 751 and the 'Marriage Amendment,'" 2010).

At the time, Equality Virginia's success was unprecedented in terms of organizing statewide support for LGBTQ rights. Organizers raised a million dollars and met their goal of one million votes in opposition to HB-751 ("HB 751 and the 'Marriage Amendment,'" 2010). While these numbers were not enough to stop the amendment, Equality Virginia had succeeded in creating a coalition that could serve as a model for LGBTQ activism around the nation. For us, their success raised questions about how we could establish something similar through 4Cs. Our initial question changed from "What could 4Cs do?" to "How could we work with or through 4Cs to establish a network that channeled some of the members' collective resources into a specific location, working alongside local people?"

As our question became more focused, the complexity of the problem became more apparent. We realized organizing something similar through 4Cs and in Indianapolis meant establishing connections among a number of audiences with myriad concerns and political leanings, including the following:

- Conference organizers and attendees (i.e., academics working at various universities around the world and in a number of different disciplines)
- Representatives of social-benefit and social-justice organizations (ranging from college student groups, to an organization of LGBTQ-identified and -friendly business owners, to regional chapters of national civil rights organizations)
- Local LGBTQ people and allies who were not affiliated with any of these institutions

We wanted to draw in people who would have supported a boycott, and we wanted to connect their outrage, desire for action, and resources with the grassroots organizing already happening in Indiana. We began to approach this issue as one of engaging in a network useful for all these audiences. We employed the term network rather than coalition because the former encompasses the work of both "Virginia is for Haters" and Equality Virginia. Thinking of our work as engaging in or developing a network allowed us to draw from tactics the activists behind "Virginia is for Haters" used to make the fight against HB-751 meaningful to those outside Virginia as well as the tactics that Equality Virginia's organizers used to build a statewide coalition. We dubbed the work emerging around this networked conception 4C4Equality (a portmanteau of 4Cs and equality groups organizing around similar issues). It is not another organization per se, but a method emerging from how online activism and local organizing could coordinate to reach different audiences.

In characterizing 4C4E's method as networked engagement, we address how scholarship on global communication and usability inform this method. Research on global communication helps locate a writer among the global and local concerns of various audiences and among global (or distributed) and local (or place-based) practices at points where they overlap, connect, or break down. Imagining 4C4E as engaging with global and local audiences helps us connect the ethical concerns of conference goers to the lived experiences of LGBTQ people in Indiana, who bear the brunt of laws like HJR-3. Similarly, research on usability moves back and forth among macro-level issues (i.e., one's ethics) and micro-level considerations (i.e., one's day-to-day life). Furthermore, such research emphasizes how a writer brings multiple perspectives into the composing process. In our work, such a sensibility combines practices involved in "Virginia is for Haters" and Equality Virginia's approaches without chastising one approach and championing the other.

HOW GLOBAL COMMUNICATION ADDRESSES AUDIENCE

One of the challenges in bringing these approaches together involved defining our audiences. We intended to target 4Cs, a professional organization of writing studies scholars who convene an annual three-to-four-day conference. Thus, part of our audience was distributed around the world and located in various universities and communities, and contact with this audience would be primarily Internet-based and aimed at building support for 4C4E. On the other hand, we wanted to connect with people located in the conference's host city of Indianapolis. This meant calling on contacts we had developed ourselves and creating new contacts by attending meetings for local groups organizing against HJR-3.

To work through these complexities, we looked for scholarship that provided theoretical guidance and practical strategies and initially turned to scholarship on service learning and community engagement. Commonly, such research focuses on how scholars establish relationships among institutions or workplaces and community-based organizations. For example, Thomas Deans (2000) characterizes service learning as writing with, for, or about communities, and Jeffrey T. Grabill (2001) addresses how institutions and communities rhetorically construct one another (p. 89). In both cases, audience refers to local people, and the researcher aims to establish deep, vertical roots in one geographic place or with one community partner over a number of projects or courses (e.g., Scott, 2008). The research often focuses on developing sustainable products for community organizations (e.g., Getto, Cushman, & Ghosh, 2011). While we identify with this work, particularly its focus on bringing the perspectives of local people into complex issues or helping to enhance the work of community organizations, we found this research inadequate in considering how to connect to both distributed audiences (e.g., an academic field) and local audiences. To bring these audiences together, we turned to global communication scholarship, for it better addresses audiences in terms of our question.

Scholarship on global communication in technical communication approaches the interplay of distributed and local audiences by attending to the complex contexts in which the writer works or locates him/herself and by demonstrating how such contexts are unstable. The scholarship emerges from familiar contexts, such as academic and corporate workplaces. In these contexts, writers navigate the complex of economic, political, cultural, and linguistic influences faced by employers, employees, users, and other audiences (Warren, 2002; Thayer & Kolko, 2004; Mangiron & O'Hagan, 2006; Major & Yoshida, 2007; Agboka, 2013).

To work through these issues, global communication scholarship develops a layered approach to context. The first layer includes the writer's location in a research site with more or less discernible geographic boundaries (a region, city, neighborhood, company, and in some cases community) even when multiple groups or populations interact in that context. The layer informs traditional notions of service learning and community engagement described previously. The second layer includes the writer's location in a company, industry, or institution. By addressing these layers, we began to develop a complex view of audience that helped us understand the contexts and the layers we would be working with through 4C4E. Furthermore, digging deeper into these layers helped us approach our audience as a network.

Global communication scholarship addressing the academy helped us consider this second layer, a writer's location, as geographically distributed. Such research focuses on networking higher education both in the teaching offered in F2F and online courses and in sharing research or creating and carrying out international projects with others located around the world (Suárez-Orozco & Qin-Hilliard, 2004; Cargile Cook & Grant-Davie, 2005; Starke-Meyerring, Duin, & Palvetzian 2007; Starke-Meyerring & Wilson, 2008). These scholars generally agree traditional models of higher education and the skills, experiences, and resources these models offer do not meet the challenges of globalization. These scholars characterize globalization as a phenomenon involving "a far-reaching shift in the means of production" where goods and services are produced "in global networks that allow service producers to take advantage of the most favorable production conditions around the world (e.g., in terms of labor costs, labor rights, environmental regulations, and other policies)" (Starke-Meyerring, Duin, & Palvetzian, 2007, p. 141). The shift in the means of production and distribution involves emerging, often Internet-based, digital tools.

In the epoch of globalization, a writer's work, and therefore the writing instructor's work, takes shape at various points along an internationally distributed, or networked, chain of production and distribution. In fact, the writer locates him/herself at different points or nodes in such networks as circumstances change (Castells, 2004). Rich Rice and Zachary Hausrath employ "glocal" thinking as a tactic that helps the writer consider these nodes and how they are linked. Such thinking helps the writer "maximize productive dialectical and transactional exchange(s) between people" because it provides a dynamic sense of audience (Rice & Hausrath, 2014, p. 20). We see glocalization, defined as "globally dispensed products or ideas designed to accommodate users in local markets," as useful way to conceive of 4C4E's work (Tharpe, 2001; as cited in Rice & Hausrath, 2014, p. 20). To develop 4C4E as an initiative creating a sustained relationship among 4Cs members and annual conference sites (vs. a single intervention at the 2014 conference), we needed to consider our work as developing and implementing a method and not simply a uniform message taken up by different audiences.

The method reflects how we understand context and audience as being networked, and it relates to where we locate ourselves in this network at different times and places. Table 5.1 illustrates the relationship

Table 5.1. Our Contexts and Audiences for the 2014 Conference on College Composition and Communication in Indianapolis, Indiana.

Distributed and Local Contexts	Audiences
Indiana	State Residents
Indianapolis	City Residents
Conference Hotel and Convention Center	Individual Businesses and Offices
	Local Workers
	Passersby
	Western Indianapolis/Downtown Residents
4C4E Organizers	Graduate Students
Local Social Justice and Social Benefit Organizations	Indiana Equality Action
	Indy Rainbow Chamber
	Freedom Indiana
	Indy Pride, Inc.
	Pride Lafayette
	Campus-Based LGBTQ Organizations
Nearby Academic Institutions	Ball State University
	Butler University
	Indiana University
	Indiana University-Purdue University Indianapolis
	Purdue University
	Ivy Tech Community College
Disciplinary Bodies	4Cs Members
	4Cs Chair
	4Cs Executive Committee
	4Cs Caucuses and Special Interest Groups
	WPA LISTSERV

between contexts and audience we developed through our research on global communication. In it, we list some of the contexts where we locate ourselves as writers doing work to oppose HJR-3 in Indiana. While it is impossible to address all the contexts or to include all the audiences with a stake in issues of LGBTQ rights and marriage equality in Indiana, we focused on those contexts where 4C4E organizers had contacts or connections.

Even as Table 5.1 represents only a partial list, figuring out what we could do with or through 4C4E and 4Cs became more concrete. We had a list of individuals who would be affected by any action we took through the conference. We could then use this list to address how or where we related to these audiences, what aspects of the issue these audiences would be interested in, etc. Drawing from global communication scholarship, we began considering how these audiences might *use* what we created to address the issue of marriage equality in Indiana.

DEFINING USE AS PARTICIPATION *IN SITU*

Technical communication has devoted considerable attention to understanding use as the negotiation of complex systems, composed of but not limited to audiences (or users), writers, technical documentation, and things (products, objects, technologies, etc.). Such research investigates use through overlapping frameworks related to and derived in part from usability studies. These frameworks include user-centered design (Johnson, 1998), productive usability (Simmons & Zoetewey, 2012) and participatory localization (Agboka, 2013), among others. While these frameworks differ, scholars employ rhetorically rich definitions of use to orient their research. These definitions guide the questions they ask about who their audiences are in a particular context, what use means to these audiences, and what role a writer plays in helping these audiences work with one another. Still, each framework depicts use differently. By examining the similarities and differences, we began to see how each framework positions use in relation to context and audience. It is this relationship we were particularly interested in exploring when considering how 4C4E could be useful.

Traditionally, a usability researcher might examine how users and/ or testers behave—that is, how users interact with technologies and with documentation meant to explain how such technologies work. They also consider how usability testers assess these interactions, consider design changes, and implement these changes. Such usability testing amounts to what Robert Johnson (1998) calls a systems-centered approach. The approach gives little attention to how users engage with technologies in their everyday lives. Instead, a systems-centered approach depicts how the writer or designer intends for a technology to work under laboratory conditions. To bring user experience into the design process, Johnson (1998) develops a user-centered approach, which argues for a complex of use centered on the user and radiating outward to their rhetorical situation—into the "global activities that users are apt to be involved with either during the design, dissemination, or end use of technological systems or artifacts" (learning, doing, and producing); then, to the constraints that "larger human networks place on technological use" (institutions, disciplines, and communities); and finally, to the "outer edges" of culture and history, which shape a user's understanding of use and how she applies technologies (pp. 36–39).

Johnson's work describes the complex layers involved in considering use and users; his work thus helped us consider how to put users at the center of 4C4E. Still, we needed a clearer idea about what this might mean in online and local contexts. W. Michele Simmons and Meredith Zoetewey's scholarship on productive usability (Simmons & Zoetewey, 2012) and Godwin Agboka's (2013) research on participatory localization offer examples of user-centered approaches that aim to increase civic participation in these different contexts. According to these perspectives, productive usability focuses on civic organizations' online presence, and participatory localization deals with the impact that multinational corporations on local people.

In defining productive usability, Simmons and Zoetewey (2012) distinguish it from traditional usability by parsing the terms "usable" and "useful." Traditional usability raises questions about how a website's design is usable, and designers employing such techniques provide "self-evident navigation, scannable layouts, and links distinguishable at a glance" (Simmons & Zoetewey, 2012, p. 251). Productive usability raises questions about how a website's design is useful, and designers are concerned with how the website affords "in-depth and multifaceted explorations that complex problem solving requires" (Simmons & Zoetewey, 2012, p. 253).

Simmons and Zoetewey offer of examples of where traditional usability principles fail to accommodate users' needs on civic websites. To understand these needs, they conducted a three-and-a-half-year community-based, service-learning project where graduate and undergraduate students developed websites for community organizations. In the course of designing these sites, Simmons, Zoetewey, and their students used interviews and protocol analysis to "collect data on how citizens wanted to use these websites" (p. 259). In coding responses, four themes emerged. Simmons and Zoetewey compared these themes to criteria associated with conventional usability. They used the *IEEE Professional Communication Society's Technical Communicator's Glossary* entry for "usability" to represent such criteria (Simmons & Zoetewey, 2012, p. 266). They found while these themes about use mapped on to traditional usability criteria, the traditional criteria could not address all the concerns users had. In the end, Simmons and Zoetewey argue increasing civic participation online means civic websites "must go beyond functional usability to productive usability," and they offer general principles to "challenge, or at least temper, the familiar usability precepts" (Simmons & Zoetewey, 2012, p. 275).

While Simmons and Zoetewey discuss productive usability in online contexts, Godwin Agboka (2013) offers participatory localization as a framework that addresses local contexts where multinational corporations' technologies, products, and the activities surrounding these products exert power. Agboka argues that in order to change these power relations, a technical communicator brings local people into the processes through which these products and accompanying documentation get designed, and implemented, or distributed. His research examined the packaging and documentation that accompanies sexuopharmaceuticals produced by Chinese companies for Ghanaian consumers. He reviewed when the documentation helped and did not help consumers use the products. In instances where they did not help, he asks why not. Agboka finds the failure to provide instructions useful to Ghanaian people reflects a tension between local knowledge and global knowledge systems. Participatory localization works at this tension. It is not enough for technical communicators to focus on localization as changing the way they say something or even to change the way they make something. Rather, they need to understand how use relates to local practices and values. Agboka, in turn, characterizes participatory localization as a "more intuitive and user-sensitive localization approach that is reflective of sociopolitical issues existing at the user's site" (p. 45). Participatory localization relies on an "ethnographic, participant-observer approach [. . .] that requires careful, humble, and thorough outsider involvement with local users and in which users and designers coconstruct knowledge" (p. 43).

Participatory localization identifies difference and offers a sensibility about how the technical communicator works in politically charged situations to make sure local people's voices have a hearing and their needs addressed in developing products and technologies that affect their everyday lives. This means involving users throughout the design process. It also means long-term involvement where a technical communicator approaches local users in ways that support, respond to, and influence practices rather than trying to change or *correct* them.

Examining use through these frameworks reveals the rhetoricity that weaves through writing designed to increase participation in online and local contexts. Each framework considers how the term "user" applies to audiences with different identities, experiences, practices, and needs. It also considers use as technical knowhow. Each scholar characterizes their work differently: Agboka (2013) refers to participatory localization as social justice work; Simmons and Zoetewey (2012) describe productive usability as an approach for increasing civic involvement; and Johnson (1998) offers user-centered design to foster user participation. Still, their frameworks overlap in how they depict the relationship between use and participation.

"Use" describes how participation happens *in situ*. In this sense, use and participation are always shifting. However, these concepts are often taken for granted and depicted as static terms in product development where use means interacting with the product in the way a designer dictates. Each framework recognizes the need to change our ideas of use. Furthermore, each scholar argues that changing these perceptions will not happen spontaneously. It involves long-term, complex rhetorical work that relies on one's ability to convey this concept to others and apply it in everyday life. Such work includes developing tactics for contacting and connecting with various audiences who may or may not understand why we need to change anything. These tactics might include figuring out how to win someone's active or passive support, how to work around certain audiences who want to block such participation for whatever reason, and how to discuss these relationships from multiple perspectives. While these frameworks do not provide step-by-step manuals, they provide ways of thinking about use as participation with different audiences and in different contexts.

In developing networked engagement as a method to guide 4C4E's work, we needed to consider how putting users at the center meant advancing a concept or theory about participation and developing tactics that made sense for different people in their daily lives. Thus, to the extent 4C4E pushes a uniform message or critique, that message has to do with why people need to participate: we needed to consider where people could advance their own rationales for supporting marriage equality and LGBTQ rights. We also needed to consider different products or objects and the messages they allow people to convey on these issues.

CHANGING IDEAS ABOUT PARTICIPATION

To develop our approach, we considered our audiences' relationships to networks in multiple senses:

- How they engaged with and located themselves within various contexts (their universities, fields of study, home communities, etc.)
- How they engaged with online spaces related to the conference and the host city

- How they engaged with local spaces related to the conference and the host city

While this list demonstrates the complexity of our work, it presents a simple depiction of the rhetorical situation surrounding HJR-3 discourse in Indiana and beyond during Fall 2013.

Looking more closely at the opinions within even one of these layers identifies some of the challenges we faced as we began implementing the initiative. For example, in examining the discussion going on in writing studies, we reprint some excerpts from the WPA LISTSERV discussion regarding 4Cs' response to HJR-3 here. These quotes capture the perspectives individuals in writing studies expressed when news of HJR-3 first spread to 4Cs attendees planning their conference trip to Indianapolis in 2014 (Indiana as CCCC Site 2013):

- "I'm wondering why CCCC is going ahead with holding our national convention in Indianapolis, especially given CCCC's commitments to GLBTQ equity?"
- "We wouldn't plan a conference in a state that prohibited interracial marriage, and for that reason, we should also refuse to hold our conference in a state that prohibits same sex marriage."
- "We are always already deep in politics, and [. . .] it is not only a professional but a political act to hold our flagship conference in particular places at particular times. Encouraging us to protest (but come! spend money!) [. . .] is encouraging us to become more deeply complicit in the homophobic laws in Indiana."
- "Convention siting is incredibly complicated, and people of goodwill act in good faith to make the best decisions possible. Second, a decision made 4 or 5 years in advance of a convention can never anticipate conditions further down the road."
- "Actually, what would help is to come, be visible, and show that the kind of prejudice being displayed here will hurt the economy and jobs. You will also be a support for the community living [in Indianapolis]."
- "In the past we've moved conferences to other states in order to protest various regressive or harmful laws. Doing so has given us a way to protest such laws [. . .] but at considerable financial cost to the organization. Because we enter into contracts very far in advance of the actual meetings, we can't anticipate what might happen legislatively within the states on the docket."

As these excerpts demonstrate, there was considerable discussion of avoiding the conference, taking action at the conference to voice public disagreement to HJR-3, and changing the conference location. As the LISTSERV discussion progressed, we saw a need for someone to coordinate the engagement work being discussed, such as showing support for local businesses who opposed HJR-3 and raising awareness among the 4Cs membership about the struggle for LGBTQ rights in Indiana and beyond. We note none of these responses suggested speaking with local people about what work was already going on to fight HJR-3. The omission raised questions about how 4Cs and academic conferences relate to the places that serve as conference sites.

The organizers of the annual 4Cs conference often organize events or entertainment that showcase local or regional customs, food, and talent. For example, when the 2011 4Cs conference was in Atlanta, Georgia, a group of Cherokee performers sang a traditional song at the conference's opening session to highlight issues of indigenous people in Georgia (Powell, 2012). Beyond specific conference panels and caucus discussions, however, little public discourse about indigenous people in the Georgia area or issues that might affect them occurred. Efforts such as these, thus, do attempt to connect academic conferences to their host cities' landmarks or culture, but these connections are often superficial. We wanted to conference attendees to interact with local residents beyond simply observing cultural performances or consuming local products.

As we observed these attempts toward bridging each year's 4Cs conference site with local contexts, we recognized a need to foster different relationships that bring conference attendees and local audiences together through a model of networked engagement. To better understand this goal, we focus on the purpose of global communication and its effect on local audiences, detailing how we worked in various contexts and with various audiences to carry out our work.

IMPLEMENTING A USEFUL APPROACH

While Table 5.1 overviews audiences and contexts involved in our work in Indianapolis, understanding how we could adapt our purpose for each perspective meant moving from research on global communication to research on usability and user-centered design (see "How Global Communication Addresses Audience" below). To be sure, 4C4E's overarching purpose can be summed up by our revised slogan, "How do you write for change?" Making this slogan meaningful through the discourse we advanced around participation, the practices we used to organize 4C4E's work at 4Cs, and the materials we provided to conference goers meant considering how each audience could have a hand in making the initiative useful *and* usable. It meant advancing a flexible definition of participation and developing ways for attendees to engage with each issue. An attitude toward usefulness and usability belies such considerations.

Usefulness characterizes the writer as one who supports others' participation rather than one's personal critique. Simmons and Zoetewey (2012) address how usefulness has a long history in technical communication, and point toward Barbara Mirel's (2004) work in defining the concept "as the ability to do better work, not just use an application more easily" (Mirel, 2004, as cited in Simmons & Zoetewey, 2012, p. 252). Simmons and Zoetewey consider usefulness as an approach to designing (or redesigning) civic websites to meet citizens' needs. These needs relate to developing a sense that ease of use affords participation, and participation enables users to develop expertise. In terms of 4C4E, we translate "expertise" to mean a sense of ownership over the types of support our audiences develop in relation to the initiative or the issue of same-sex marriage rights.

Such work provides a sense of how participation looks different when considered at different phases of the project (e.g., when materials are being designed, once they get implemented, and in assessing in what ways they proved useful or failed to do so). For 4C14, we developed a three-phase approach that considers how the initiative can be useful to different audiences in each phase (see Table 5.2). In describing these phases in some detail, we tease out how networked engagement considers usefulness throughout the design and implementation process.

4C14 IN INDIANAPOLIS, INDIANA

In the first phase of the 4C4E initiative (November 2013 to January 2014), we reached out to various audiences to discuss our ideas and highlight discussions that were taking place on the WPA LISTSERV. We began contacting people who posted specific suggestions to the LISTSERV discussion regarding what participation might look like through 4Cs or at the conference. In addition, we contacted LGBTQ organizations throughout Indiana, including community- and college campus–based organizations, and we attended events in Lafayette, IN, to discuss the initiative with community and campus leaders (e.g., the Director of the Purdue University's LGBTQ Center, organizers of Purdue University's Krannert School of Management Out at Work Conference, and executive board members of Pride Lafayette, Inc.). We met on Purdue's campus and online to research the history behind the fight for marriage equality in Indiana, to discuss our perspectives,

Table 5.2. 4C4E's Three-Phase Approach to Networked Engagement.

4C4E's Three-Phase Approach	
PHASE 1	Bringing various audiences into the research and design process
PHASE 2	Offering our materials to 4C14 attendees at the conference and engaging with them over how they can demonstrate support
PHASE 3	Soliciting feedback and assessing our work through postcards, surveys, conversations, and web analytics

and to develop ideas for the materials we could provide conference attendees so that they could demonstrate their support for marriage equality in Indiana. Phase 1 culminated with the development of materials organized around the slogan, "How do you support marriage equality in Indiana?" These included the following:

- A website that documented all of our work
- A Twitter account where we shared information about HJR-3 and LGBTQ rights in Indiana as well as updates on 4C4E's work at 4Cs
- Buttons with the 4C4E logo
- Stickers with the 4C4E logo
- An online maps locating LGBTQ-owned and -friendly Indianapolis area businesses
- Customer cards demonstrating support for LGBTQ-owned and -friendly businesses
- Customer cards encouraging business owners to identify as such[2]
- Postcard-checklists connecting these materials together and suggesting additional ways that conference attendees could demonstrate support[3]

The second phase took place at 4Cs in Indianapolis (March 19–22, 2014), and sixteen volunteers staffed a table during the conference. At the table we offered our materials, engaged in discussion with conference attendees regarding same-sex marriage in Indiana and issues related to LGBTQ rights in the states they called home. Also, we asked attendees to fill out and return a postcard-checklists and complete an online survey about the initiative so we could develop a better sense of how our initial organizing needed to be adapted for future conferences. To this end, we recognize most of the audience for our materials was drawn from a specific group of English, writing, communications, and rhetoric educators, including graduate students, adjunct and contingent faculty, and tenure-track faculty. The audience represents a relatively broad swathe of people within the 4Cs community, but it is narrow considering the class backgrounds, race, and formal education of each person.

From the outset, we made the assumption most 4Cs attendees have some sort of technological know-how—they Tweet during the conference, they blog about sessions, and they likely have a Wi-Fi enabled devices with them throughout the conference. After we met and talked with a few conference attendees and read the results of our survey, we realized this assumption was incorrect. In effect, we targeted an even smaller number of participants through our largely digital presence. In moving forward, we recognize the need for an equal representation of printed and digital materials.

In the third phase, we assessed the response to our materials from 4C14 to reshape the initiative to meet our audience's needs at future 4Cs conference sites. We collected and assessed data in two ways: By tracking the conference Twitter activity through its #4C14 hashtag and by dispatching our hashtag (#4C4E), using a digital tracking script to trace how conference attendees shared information on social media about the conference and the HJR-3 issue. We also distributed a digital survey that contained questions about participant experience with the 4C4E initiative at the conference. The digital survey received forty-two responses and approximately ninety total Tweets under the #4C4E hashtag. We used these results to revise our materials for 4C15 in Tampa, adapted our social-media approach, and realized the changing needs of our audiences, their contexts, and how they used tools and information.

Our efforts to attract representatives from local organizations to 4C14 resulted in few connections. This may be due to any number of factors, including not establishing deep enough connections with these organizations—which relates to the brief period we had to organize the initiative (about five months) and our limited resources; a lack of interest or resources on the part of these organizations; or any number of other factors. In addition, we were unable to organize events offsite to bring together conference attendees and local people involved in the fight against HJR-3. Therefore, 4C4E participants were almost exclusively attendees of the 4C14 conference.

It should be noted that this conference requires a hefty financial registration and travel commitment. The number of 4Cs members and professionals in attendance thus varies year to year based on the location of the conference and cost of travel from one's home institution or state. In a sense, any attendee who stopped by our conference table was "participating," as they heard the 4C4E mission statement from our table volunteers, picked up tangible materials, or visited the website on the public iPads. However, we had a group of specific participants who took our digital survey made available on iPads at the table and emailed to various LISTSERVS after the conference.

4C15 IN TAMPA, FLORIDA

Using the information gathered from audiences at 4C14, we brainstormed (early Fall 2014) ideas for engaging with 4Cs attendees at the 2015 conference in Tampa, Florida. Because we would not be locals at this conference site and did not want to define local issues for others, we initiated work for the 2015 conference by distributing a "Call for Pitches" on social media and to LISTSERVS in the writing studies field. Through this call, we identified local/Tampa-area partners interested in working with the 4Cs audience. As we saw it, our role was to support their work. This included discussing our experiences with them and providing advice as requested, contributing to or commenting on draft materials as requested, and helping to promote their work during the 4C15 conference.

Our partners for 4C15 represented a group of tenure-track and nontenure track faculty from the University of Tampa (U Tampa). These individuals designed a semester of curricula for communications and writing classes built around the issues of privilege and marriage equality. Their aim was to use their U Tampa classrooms to investigate these issues in local communities. Their efforts produced a website that promoted their campaign, "Let's Talk Equality,"[4] and the site featured mini documentaries about privilege, video interviews with Tampa couples fighting for marriage equality, poster designs promoting social justice and equality, and a directory of Tampa businesses that support marriage equality. In our initial discussions with these partners, they expressed they were inspired to bring such assignments into their classrooms because of 4C4E's work in Indianapolis.

4C15 took place on March 19–22 at the Tampa Convention Center. We adapted our 4C4E presence to account for the physical conference locale and new spaces Conference Chair Joyce Locke Carter made available to attendees (such as the bustling Action Hub). As in Indianapolis, we maintained a table in the main thoroughfare of the convention center. At the table, we distributed 4C4E materials and an updated postcard-checklist with suggested actions that attendees could take in Tampa during the conference. This table also displayed work from our U Tampa partners. In the Action Hub, we featured work from U Tampa students, and we also organized a two-hour showcase on March 21 where our U Tampa partners presented their students' work. At this showcase, about forty 4C15 attendees visited and learned about issues in the local Tampa community.[5]

Finally, in the Action Hub, we collected video interviews in which attendees described the community engagement work they were conducting at their home institutions. After the conference, we compiled these videos and made them available on our website to promote our network for 4Cs 2016 in Houston.[6]

4C16 IN HOUSTON, TEXAS

For 2016, we sought to expand the scope of our initiative and begin building 4C4E as a broader network. We had spent two years designing engagement tactics for the 4Cs conference in two different cities, and based on the conversations we had with conference goers, we sensed a need to put scholars who identify with a number of different frameworks and describe their work in many different ways in contact with one another. As we saw in our 4C15 work, there are many writing studies faculty who seek to use writing as a mechanism for change. These individuals, however, often struggle to connect with like-minded colleagues or to find resources that can help reach their goals or sustain their work.

Furthermore, we wanted to take the infrastructure we had developed through the 2014 and 2015 conferences and make it accessible to others without having to recreate it each year. Because 4C4E is not an organization or a body directly related to or sponsored by 4Cs, having a presence at each conference meant appealing to the 4Cs conference chair for resources and space. While we found the chairs to be sympathetic and supportive, they changed each year (from Adam Banks in 2014, to Joyce Locke Carter in 2015, and finally, to Linda Adler-Kassner in 2016). To make the initiative sustainable, we had to consider how the work we had carried out at 4Cs could be translated to digital spaces so connections we made would not disappear after the conference ended and attendees returned home.

In our work at 4C 2016 in Houston, Texas, we began to address these issues by remediating 4C4E as a digital network and encouraging conference goers to add their work to a Google Map.[7] On this map, participants identify the framework they use to describe their work (e.g., activism, action research, community engagement, service learning, etc.). They also provide a description of their work in the placemark on the map. Along with the video interviews conducted at the 4Cs 2015, this map serves as an initial step in developing 4C4E's digital presence as a space where scholars, activists, community organizers, and others can connect with one another by discussing stories about their work, sharing strategies and tactics, and contributing open-source documents that others may adapt to their local contexts. The shift in 4C4E's orientation reflects a goal of being useful that we have maintained from the initiative's earliest days and one that connects to the scholarship on global communication described previously (i.e., connecting with and meeting the needs of a distributed audience).

CONCLUSION

As we consider 4C17 and beyond, we continue the process of carrying out and promoting networked engagement by seeking local connections, investigating local issues, adapting the initiative to the needs of the audiences in different host cities, and continuing to develop our digital presence. In the end, we believe discussing the initiative's history and trajectory addresses two interrelated questions central to networked engagement:

- How do we develop a sensibility about service and engagement that does not lock us into one view of such work?
- How do we contribute to work in place where we are not locals without demanding that such work fall in line with our particular perspectives?

In a theoretical sense, we believe these questions get at the heart of global communication and the complexities of usability. They shape our future goals, which include developing a digital "starter kit" with Creative Commons licensed materials, such as logos, images, templates for deliverables, and a report detailing our approach and suggesting how others may adapt it to meet their needs. We see possibilities for generating support around various issues through other academic conferences and local partnerships. The materials document and reflect a method for implementing our approach and articulate a rationale for connecting a conference and its attendees to the conference's host city. Therefore, we hope what we have learned about working with local audiences, designing useful materials, and implementing global communication tactics can be useful for others interested in like-minded community engagement initiatives. We leave it to the organizers of these initiatives to decide what issue they organize around.

Notes

1. The entire WPA LISTSERV conversation from this time can be accessed at http://tiny url.com/WPAfall2013. The specific thread in question regarding Indiana's legislation can be accessed at http://tinyurl.com/WPAIndiana4C14.

2. 4C14 involvement materials: https://4c4equality.wordpress.com/2014-4c4e-initia tive/participation.

3. 4C14 engagement checklist: https://4c4equality.files.wordpress.com/2014/01/4c 4e-checklist_final.pdf.

4. University of Tampa's "Let's Talk Equality" project: http://utletstalk.wixsite.com/let stalkequality.

5. 4C15 Action Hub and initiative recap: https://4c4equality.wordpress.com/4c15 -recap.

6. 4C15 Action Hub interviews with attendees: https://4c4equality.wordpress.com /4c15-recap/news-and-interviews.

7. 4C16 map: https://4c4equality.wordpress.com/4c16-recap/writing-for-change -map/.

References

Agboka, G. (2013). Participatory localization: A social justice approach to navigating unenfranchised/disenfranchised cultural sites. *Technical Communication Quarterly*, *22*(1), 28–49. https://doi.org/10.1080/10572252.2013.730966

Brantley, M. (2010, February 17). Virginia is for haters. Retrieved from https://www.ark times.com/ArkansasBlog/archives/2010/02/17/virginia-is-for-haters

Cargile Cook, K., & Grant-Davie, K. (2005). Introduction. In K. Cargile Cook & K. Grant-Davie (Eds.), *Online education: Global questions, local answers* (pp. 1–12). Amityville, NY: Baywood.

Castells, M. (2004). Informationalism, networks, and the network society: A theoretical blueprint. In M. Castells (Ed.), *The network society: A cross-cultural perspective* (pp. 3–45). Northampton, MA: Edward Elgar. Retrieved from https://doi. org/10.4337/9781845421663.00010

Cluchey, D. (2010). Virginia is for haters. Retrieved from http://www.huffingtonpost .com/daniel-cluchey/virginia-is-for-haters_b_529206.html

Deans, T. (2000). *Writing partnerships: Service-learning in composition*. Urbana, IL: National Council of Teachers of English.

Drew. (2010, February 11). *Republican Bob McDonnell: Virginia is still for haters*. Retrieved from http://www.dailykosbeta.com/stories/836300

Getto, G., Cushman, E., & Ghosh, S. (2011). Community mediation: Writing in communities and enabling connections through new media. *Computers and Composition*, *28*(2), 160–174. https://doi.org/10.1016/j.compcom.2011.04.006

Grabill, J. T. (2001). *Community literacy programs and the politics of change*. Albany, NY: State University of New York Press.

HB 751 and the "Marriage Amendment." (2010, April 30). Rainbow Richmond: LGBTQ history of Richmond, VA. *Outhistory.org*. Retrieved from http://outhistory.org/exhib its/show/rainbow-richmond/in-the-twenty-first-century/hb-751

Indiana as CCCC Site. (2013, October/November). Retrieved from https://lists.asu.edu /cgi-bin/wa?A1=ind1310

Johnson, R. R. (1998). *User-centered technology: A rhetorical theory for computers and other mundane artifacts*. Albany, NY: State University of New York Press.

Major, D. L., & Yoshida, A. (2007). Crossing national and corporate cultures: Stages in localizing a pre-production meeting report. *Journal of Technical Writing and Communication*, *37*(2), 167–181. https://doi.org/10.2190/2780-1R37-4W67-38K7

Mangiron, C., & O'Hagan, M. (2006). Games localization: Unleashing imagination with the "restricted translation." *Journal of Specialised Translation, 6,* 10–21.

Mason, D. (2004, June 1). Virginia is for haters. *The Stranger.* Retrieved from http://www.thestranger.com/seattle/virginia-is-for-haters/Content?oid=18627

Mirel, B. (2004). *Interaction design for complex problem solving: Developing useful and usable software.* San Francisco, CA: Morgan Kaufman.

Powell, M. (2012). *Stories take place: A performance in one act.* Keynote address presented at Conference on College Composition and Communication in Missouri, St. Louis.

Quantifying the Boycott. (2004, June 5). Retrieved from https://web.archive.org/web/20040605234941/; http://www.virginiaisforhaters.org/archives/000542.html#more

Rice, R., & Hausrath, Z. (2014). The necessity of teaching intercultural communication competence in literacy classes. *Journal of College Literacy and Learning, 40,* 19–34.

Scott, J. B. (2008). The practice of usability: Teaching user engagement through service-learning. *Technical Communication Quarterly, 17*(4), 381–412. https://doi.org/10.1080/10572250802324929

Simmons, W. M., & Zoetewey, M. (2012). Productive usability: Fostering civic engagement and creating more useful online spaces for public deliberation. *Technical Communication Quarterly, 21*(3), 251–276. https://doi.org/10.1080/10572252.2012.673953

Spaulding, P. (2010, March 8). David Mixner: "Virginia is for haters"—and what needs to be done about it. *Shadowproof.* Retrieved from https://shadowproof.com/2010/03/08/david-mixner-virginia-is-for-haters-and-what-needs-to-be-done-about-it

Starke-Meyerring, D., Duin, A. H., & Palvetzian, T. (2007). Global partnerships: Positioning technical communication programs in the context of globalization. *Technical Communication Quarterly, 16*(2), 139–174. https://doi.org/10.1080/10572250709336558

Starke-Meyerring, D., & Wilson, M. (2008). *Designing globally networked learning environments: Visionary partnerships, policies, and pedagogies.* Rotterdam, The Netherlands: Sense.

Suárez-Orozco, M. M., & Qin-Hilliard, D. B. (2004). Globalization: Culture and education in the new millennium. In M. M. Suárez-Orozco & D. B. Qin-Hilliard (Eds.), *Globalization: Culture and education in the new millennium* (pp. 1–37). Berkeley, CA: University of California Press.

Tharpe, M. (2001). *Marketing and consumer identity in multicultural America.* Thousand Oaks, CA: Sage.

Thayer, A., & Kolko, E. B. (2004). Localization of digital games: The process of blending for the global games market. *Technical Communication (Washington), 51,* 477–488.

Warren, T. L. (2002). Cultural influence on technical manuals. *Journal of Technical Writing and Communication, 32*(2), 111–123. https://doi.org/10.2190/T79F-V84A-NARA-NFLY

Why the Boycott? Because more than marriage is at stake! (2004, June 23). Retrieved from https://web.archive.org/web/20040623171212/http://www.virginiaisforhaters.org

SECTION II

Conveying

To share information effectively with the intended audience so that readers are able to understand ideas being conveyed and act on or respond to texts in the manner intended by the author. Friction points are rhetorical, such as online channels viable across cultures and use.

MESSAGE READY TO **CONVEY** IN 3... 2... 1... AND GO. SATELLITE ACTIVE, MESSAGE SENT.

6

LUDIC IS THE NEW PHATIC
Making Connections in Global, Internet-Mediated Learning Environments

Suzanne Blum Malley

ABSTRACT

In the study described here, the author presents an analysis of five years' worth of asynchronous discussion board exchanges from 663 college students at four institutions in three countries (the U.S., South Africa, Russia). In these interactions, playful discourse serves as a rhetorical strategy for initiating and developing social connection through small talk, or "phatic" communication, in a global such international contexts.

Keywords: conveying, discussion boards, global, knowledge-building, Internet-mediated learning environment, ludic, phatic, relational, small talk, transactional, writing classrooms

INTRODUCTION

In Internet-mediated, asynchronous learning environments (IMLEs), teachers and students cannot look for raised hands, cocked eyebrows, nodding heads, or other paralinguistic cues to facilitate communication. The act of conveying ideas can thus be quite complicated because simply presenting oneself as dictated by the practices of embodied greetings or of embodied "small talk" does not work. In such contexts, how does one engage in the interactions essential to fostering meaningful relationships and create effective online communities? Essentially, how does one engage in the "small talk" interactions essential to forging the connections needed to build online communities in international classroom settings?

In this chapter, I share ideas on how student writing in an IMLE offer insights into the peer-to-peer writing teachers typically hope for when designing courses. Further, I argue small talk, or "phatic" (Malinowski, 1989) introductory functions are foundational to social connections and

DOI: 10.7330/9781607326649.c006

that those functions often require playful, funny, wry, non-serious, non-earnest, or ludic-as-phatic discursive strategies to successfully negotiate interpersonal connections. I believe to be interculturally competent, we must develop specific ludic-as-phatic negotiations in online spaces to understand our audiences and to move into deeper, more substantive learning and knowledge building.

VALUING THE PHATIC

Anthropologist Bronislaw Malinowski coined the term "phatic communion," defining it as "a type of speech in which ties of union are created in a mere exchange of words" (Malinowski, 1989, p. 315). One of Malinowski's goals was to support the assertion by Ogden and Richards that all language and linguistic processes derive power from context (p. ix). In doing so, Malinowski sparked debate about and research into just what "phatic" utterances do and mean. As Malinowski explained, "'phatic communion' serves to establish bonds of personal union between people brought together by the mere need of companionship and does not serve any purpose of communicating ideas" (Malinowski, 1989, p. 316).

Despite a persistent perception as unimportant, linguists have now widely acknowledged that phatic communion, often referred to as "small talk," is anything but superfluous, frivolous, secondary, or irrelevant (Laver, 1975; Senft, 1995; Coupland & Coupland, 1992; Brown & Levinson, 1987; Jaworski, 2000; McCarthy, 2003; Holmes, 2006; Holmes & Schnurr, 2006; Holmes & Marra, 2004). Instead, small talk has been identified as a primary rhetorical/discursive strategy for creating "the bonding and respecting behaviors, in local conversational routines, that are the social fabric of communities" (Coupland, 2003, p. 5).

In truth, small talk is just as important when it is not "talk" at all. In face-to-face studies of conversation and small talk, interlocutors have a tremendous amount of paralinguistic, nonlexical components of speech and material information to draw on to "read" each other and to "guide conversational management" (Gumperz & Berenz, 1993, pp. 91–92) as they check on their lines of communication. In a digital, networked, text-only scenario, however, gesture, tone of voice, facial expressions, shared physical space, etc. are absent from the conversation or are added in elaborate Unicode emoticons. In other words, the mechanism for writers to create "small talk" and to establish and maintain lines of communication requires a distinct way of writing in order to create Umberto Eco's moment of "primary indexicality," (Eco, 2000, p. 14), the tug-of-the-jacket or tap on the shoulder for attention.

Small talk in digital, networked spaces has also been characterized negatively in many of the same ways that phatic utterances have historically been judged: as meaningless, as inconsequential, and as a waste of time. In educational contexts, the informality of language and the tendency for participants in digital, networked communicative environments (MOOs, discussion boards, LISTSERVs, etc.) to playfully get "off-task" and "waste time" has been noted in a variety of contexts (Cogdill, 1996; Basharina, 2007; Belz, 2002; Rouzie, 2001; Rouzie, 2005). Negative perception is reflected in popular media reports on how digital communication is causing the demise of the English language and the demise of "real" social skills. Yet research on social media and digital communication does not support either supposition (see Androutsopoulos, 2010; Crystal, 2009; Haas et al., 2011; Thurlow, 2003).

Despite the public condemnation, communication in digital networked spaces is "real" communication after all. In fact, researchers repeatedly find in "non-talk" digital, text-based contexts, small talk is more prevalent and perhaps more important (Thurlow, 2003; Thurlow & Poff, 2012; Thurlow & Bell, 2009; Naaman, Boase, & Lai, 2010; Androutsopoulos, 2010; Crystal, 2009; Schandorf, 2012). In their examination of instant messages of college students, for example, Haas et al. (2011) found students "creatively inscribe into their written conversations important paralinguistic information" (p. 380). In other words, the relational cues and signals, or the phatic messages, conveyed by paralinguistic information in face-to-face communication must be *written* in some form or another, making discursive small talk and relational text important areas of inquiry in digital and global writing studies.

Across the research in this area is a consistent pattern of recognition that fun, funny, playful, quirky, or ludic aspects of the discourse of digital writing play a central role in establishing and maintaining open lines of communication. As critics suggest, there is quite a bit of nonsense and goofing off that goes on in online exchanges. Yet what the critics miss is there is something rhetorically purposeful and intentional about how writers, texters, and instant messagers in digital, networked spaces use the playful, funny, and joking paralinguistic cues to establish and maintain social connections. In short, if this type of phatic conversation does not happen, then other, more substantive conversations do not happen either.

PLAYFULNESS AND PHATIC COMMUNION

The playfulness of the "nonsense" in texts in online exchanges has been recognized as a means of performing identity and of creating and maintaining social relationships online. Baym (1993), for example, acknowledged the important role of wit and humor in the creation of *ethos*. Later, Fernback (2003) observed how wit and humor attract and sustained attention in online communities, particularly in the absence of identifiable, typically embodied characteristics of "brawn, money, or political clout" (Fernback, 2003, p. 213). Much of this early discussion expressed an underlying concern about real work not getting done or "real" meaning not being conveyed. Despite these concerns, online researchers recognized the ludic discourse does *something*. As our networked technologies evolved, so too has recognition playfulness as a form of "doing sociability" without which other aspects of online discourse would fall flat.

Researchers have linked the exploration of conflict in Internet-mediated, asynchronous learning environments (IMLEs) specifically to playful and ludic discourse. Holcomb (1997), for example, noted the joking around was a powerful means to create an online sense of community and facilitate the organization of new and distinct social hierarchies (p. 16). Rouzie (2001), in turn, maintained IMLE discourse often combined serious and playful purposes to provoke and mediate conflict and to negotiate power relationships. Early research highlights how scholars have approached the social and relational work of writing in online classroom spaces and notes it does not always work as instructors intend.

THE RESEARCH CONTEXT

My interest in this area was piqued by my work in a pre-MOOC, global, Internet-mediated online project called Sharing Cultures. The project connected students at my university in Chicago, Illinois, with students in Port Elizabeth and Stellenbosch, South Africa, and in Volgograd, Russia. Every northern hemisphere Spring Semester from 2003 to 2011, the project engaged students and instructors in participating courses in networked, asynchronous, written discussions about issues such as culture/community/identity, HIV/AIDS, global politics, and human and constitutional rights. The participants and structure of the project continued to evolve, but the goals remained constant: to use digital technologies to provide international learning experiences for students who did not have the means to participate in traditional exchange programs, and to create an online space where students and teachers from different backgrounds could share perspectives, experiences, and beliefs.

All of the student participants were first-year university students identified as "at-risk" in terms of preparedness for university-level work by their home institutions and enrolled in gateway courses required for their continuation at university. In the online, global classroom, students were asked to do four things with the discussion-focused portions of the global exchange: introduce themselves, respond to other students, continue discussions with their peers over the course of the semester on issues of local and global concern related to the course theme, and, in a nutshell, "share cultures." Students also posted graded, classroom-based writing reading and writing assignments in response to teacher prompts that varied by home-institution course, but were visible to all participants.

To address problems of student access to computers and networks, the project was embedded in courses at each institution. Class time across time zones was used to access the international discussion board, both as a means of keeping it a central component of the course and to ensure access to the technological tools needed for the exchanges. Because the participating institutions had different levels of access to high-speed Internet service (from good, to spotty, to none), the Sharing Cultures discussions were alphabetic text-based, without the addition of images, sound, and video available in many other digital platforms.

THE RESEARCH PARTICIPANTS

This study draws from five years of the Sharing Cultures project discussion board interactions, involving four institutions, 663 students, and 14 different instructors over the five-year period (see Table 6.1).

DATA COLLECTION AND SAMPLING

For data collection and sampling, both data availability and my research questions served as a guide. For data collection, I had access to discussion boards from project years 2006, 2007, 2008, 2010, and 2011. In the five project years of data available for this study, the numbers of students participating fluctuated considerably, and numbers of posts and discussion threads available for analysis also varied.

My research goals included an examination of how students successfully generated response in their introductory posts and an analysis of what happened in student writing in the extended discussions that followed the introductions. I therefore pulled a representative sample of introductory and extended discussion threads from across the five project years. My sample included 300 total discussion threads, with 174 "successful" introductory threads (defined as introductory posts that

Table 6.1. Participating Institutions, Instructors, and Students.

Year	2006	2007	2008	2010	2011	Total
Participating Institutions	1 South Africa	1 South Africa	1 South Africa	1 South Africa	1 South Africa	
	1 U.S.	1 U.S.	1 U.S.	1 U.S.	1 U.S.	
				1 Russia	1 Russia	
# Instructors	10	10	7	3	3	14*
# Students	213	191	184	45	30	663

* Some of the same instructors participated in multiple years.

generated the most responses overall), 72 "unsuccessful" introductory posts (defined as introductory posts that did not generate any response at all), and 54 "extended" discussion threads (defined as threads that took place after the introductions and that engaged the most students over the longest periods of time during the semester).

My selection criteria for "successful" and "unsuccessful" introductions was based on an initial review of which introductory posts generated the most responses and which generated no responses. To rule out the possibility top response-generating posts were simply the first posts on a busy discussion board, I resorted the introductory posts by date and time posted. No pattern of clustered responses by date emerged. Initial sorting framed my inquiry into the role of *ludic-as-phatic* discourse in establishing social connections and guided the development of my coding system for the rhetorical activity that creates social groupings in an IMLE.

DATA CODING AND ANALYSIS

Once I had selected the three hundred sample discussion threads, I developed my analytic coding schemes for the introductions and the extended discussions. My goal was to develop schemes that were "conceptually meaningful but also sensitive to the data" (Bazerman, 2008, p. 312) and that made my theoretical perspective and interpretive stance on the corpus explicit (Smagorinsky, 2008, p. 399). To explore how the student writing functioned as relational (phatic/ social) and transactional (information sharing), I developed a system to overlap coded dimensions in the same segment (see Table 6.2). The overlap allowed for a more nuanced analysis of the posts (e.g., making it possible to analyze a statement that included factual personal information, but also written in a humorous way).

Table 6.2. Analytic Coding Scheme for Introductions.

First Pass—INTRODUCTIONs

Unsuccessful or Successful

me-focused or other-focused

me-focused and other focused

Second Pass—INTRODUCTIONs (4 Dimensions)

Playful/Humorous	Earnest	Paralinguistic cues	Meta-awareness
• joking, word play, jesting directed at GNLE context / "play with frame" • joking, wordplay, jesting directed at self • joking, word play, jesting, "messing with stereotypes" directed at other • joking, word play, jesting general • invocation of pop culture or celebrity affinities • playful response/ play back to someone (getting the joke/playing back)	• description of linguistic/cultural heritage • standard greeting/ goodbye • description of hobbies, likes, activities • description of self/status	• emoticons • excessive punctuation • all caps • lol, jk, just kidding, *off set text*, ha, etc.	• acknowledges what captures attention • expresses understanding of how discussion board works

In a first pass through the total 246 introductory posts in the corpus, I designated 174 introductions as "successful" and 72 as "unsuccessful" based on if they generated significant and sustained response threads, with significant response defined as five or more responses including discussions that extended over eight to twelve weeks of the project. I also coded all of the introductory posts as "me-focused," "other-focused," or both, noting segments where the student poster directed questions to a real or imagined audience or acknowledged a potential respondent or any "other" out there.

In a second pass, I coded the introductions themselves and the sequence of responses for the expressive tone of the writing (playful/ ludic or earnest) and how each segment was written, specifically looking for how paralinguistic emotional cues and "phatic" moves were encoded in each segment. I developed the subcodes for the playful/humorous and earnest codes out of significant patterns that came out of my initial reviews of the corpus.

"HA-HA- HA-HA- HA-HA- HA-HA!!!!!!!!"

My cataloging of the top-all-time-response-generating introduction titles compared to the numerous "no reply at all" introduction titles suggested a connection between playful writing and success and earnest writing and failure in the IMLE context. Indeed, of the 174 top response-generating introductory posts analyzed for this study, 153 (88%) titles are coded as funny/playful in some way. Of the 72 posts that received no responses whatsoever, 70 (97%) of the titles are coded as entirely earnest, while only 2 (3%) unsuccessful introduction titles are coded playful/humorous in some way. The best way, however, to understand the effect of the titles as ludic-as-phatic action is to see actual samples of successful and unsuccessful titles side by side (see Table 6.3).

Titles alone reveal something about how attention is created in online classroom discussions; it is not a typical face-to-face "Hello. How are you?" Instead, it is funny, or quirky, or silly, or exaggerated, or non-sensical, pop-culture related, or provocative. Successful posters use ludic discourse in provocative ways to reach out to readers/responders and invite them in, to make them feel like they have a reason be reading a particular post. In fact, writing with this *ludic-as-phatic* rhetorical strategy is a dominant feature of the successful introductions overall, and it is accomplished in a variety of ways in the introductions.

On the whole, the successful introductions were dominated by writing that included more playful/humorous segments (25%) than earnest (11%), were both me-focused (20%) and other-focused (5%), were heavily infused with written paralinguistic cues (30%), and had some evidence of meta-awareness of the discussion board context (8%). Unsuccessful introductions were overwhelmingly earnest (49%), were more me-focused (38%), and contained far fewer playful segments (1%), inscribed paralinguistic cues (5%) or meta-awareness of the context (3%). Students wrote their playful/humorous moves in several ways throughout the introductions, including: joking/"messing with" stereotypes/assumptions of others (12%), joking/poking fun at self (20%), joking/poking fun at the IMLE/Sharing Cultures context itself (11%), joking and word play in general (16%), playing back to someone else's post (17%), and enthusiastic invocation of pop culture or celebrity affinities (24%).

The playful small talk (*ludic-as-phatic*) served to invite response and convey to readers to the emotional/affective tenor with which readers should interpret the posts. The playfulness of the relational information was interspersed with actual transactional personal information and thoughts. The impact of *ludic-as-phatic* rhetorical strategies was evident in 153 (88%) of the 172 successful introductions, which all had segments

Table 6.3. Example Successful and Unsuccessful Introduction Post Titles.

Examples of Titles Generating Most Response 2006–2011	Examples of Titles Generating No Response 2006–2011
hello there you bunch of U.S. pupetts	me
Huge 50cent fan!!!!!!!!!!!!!!!!!!	The me nobody knows
Smokey McPot	Let us begin.
Young Nubian Queen	"name's" Introduction
ROCK STAR	My other side . . .
Ahoy to da yanks from mother africa	Introduction to me, "name"
Death metal mixed with dance	A quick glance at "name"
HOLLYWOOD HERE I COME!	who is "name"
MELLYMELV IS IN THE BUILDING!!!	Who?
Fascinating isn't it?	All about name . . .
LUCKY LADY FROM THE LAKESIDE	Molweni Nonke (hello everybody)
"IT'S CHATTING TIME SO—O..."	Introducing "name"
straight outta schaumpton	Welcome to the world of me
Even Better Than The Real Thing	It's me . . . "name"
Hey hey hey!!!!	All about "name"
Don't tell me pudding is Pie!	Welcome 2me
I'm not wearing any pants	me myself and I
midterms are so FUN	An introduction about me
They call me Scary Kerry	Me!
Shit is Going to Hit the Fan!!	A very interesting student profile
heyta yall !!!!:-)	"name"
shutter CLICK	hi!
xaxa:-D	Hello, It's Me.
HiP HoP is dead!!!	I'm a lovely person.
A Fun Floridian YO!	Goeiemore almal (Good morning all)
I CUDDLE WITH WILLIAM SHATNER EVERY NIGHT! SHAKE AND BAKE!	Goeie dag (Good day)
I love Big Macs	Hello.
Country Gal YEE HAW	another one from NMMU
Hot Momma	sharing cultures
Peter Pan: To Live would be an awfully big adventure!!!!	Hello, my classmates!

continued on next page

Table 6.3—*continued*

Examples of Titles Generating Most Response 2006–2011	Examples of Titles Generating No Response 2006–2011
Texas Girl	"name" from Minnesota
Appel ... like Apple!	its a gud day
BoooooTyLicious	Just me
UNAPPRECIATED DREAM	All about me
HEY P.I.M.P.S	Mr "name"
2 Dollars Short	another one from NMMU

coded as playful/humorous in some way. Those same 153 introductions also had some segments coded as earnest, with about one third of each post segments on average coded as playful and two thirds coded as some form of earnest self-description. Notably, it was a combination of playful and earnest, usually with some written paralinguistic information that consistently created the social connections necessary for continued conversation and continued learning. The ludic discourse, playful in a variety of ways, served as an important social lubricant, "provoking and mediating" interest and sometimes conflict (Rouzie, 2005, p. 284), allowing for the other, important transactional information to be read in both earnest and playful form.

Ha-ha" "LOL" "Just kidding! Buwhahah:-) ;-) *This is Paralinguistic*

For a segment of an introductory post to be read as playful, fun, joking, poking fun, enthusiastic, or funny by a wide audience, it must be *written* that way. Researchers have found the paralinguistic cues associated with face-to-face communication are represented textually and graphically in online conversations (Haas et al., 2011; Thurlow, 2003; Thurlow & Bell, 2009; Thurlow & Poff, 2012; Androutsopoulos, 2000). In an examination of the frequency of use of the "IM" features, Haas et al. (2011) found that majority of these posts are "*additive* and . . . are related to *paralinguistic inscription* [emphasis original]" (390), rather than simply shortcuts to abbreviate the message, which is a common assumption about writing practices in text messaging and instant messaging (Crystal, 2009; Thurlow, 2003).

I found similar patterns of paralinguistic inscription using IM features in the successful introductions on the Sharing Cultures discussion boards, with all 153 of the 153 (100%) successful introductory posts coded as playful/humorous and earnest. In the IMLE discussion board environment, students were not required to "shorten" posts due to word limits. Instead, the choice to combine these elements was a rhetorical one given the constraints of the crowded text-only digital space of the IMLE.

The following entries representative "successful" introductory posts that highlight the role the written paralinguistic cues played in allowing students to "read" one another, to establish a tone overall, to smooth communication, and to contribute to the phatic creation of a "social fabric" (Coupland, 2003, 5). In these examples, segments coded as playful (including pop culture references and other subcodes) are in bold text, paralinguistic cues are italicized, earnest (including subcodes) are underlined, and meta-awareness (expressing an understanding of the Sharing Cultures and/or how the discussion board works, negative or positive) are strikethrough.

> **I Like 2 Pet Puppies . . . and spanking Monkies should be an Olympic sport**
> So I guess NOW would be a good time for me to do the whole "Hi my name is" . . . (*buwhahah* **this makes me think of m&m**) *anywhoooo.*
> Hi my name is M_____ignon Stokes **and yes I will admit I like to pet Puppies I have been petting puppies since the tender age of 17.**
> Ok basic background Info:
> I'm almost 20 *(*Gives a High 5 to my "Real" imaginary friend*)*
> I study at NMMU **(No More Money University)**
> I'm Currently doing a BA Genral *EXTENDED...*
> **I Dislike eating dead Cow...**aka I'm pasciterean
> I'm quite fond of Reading,writing,photography,art etc. etc.
> And I am so over this Blog...
> **SOoooo** *Drop me a Line or 99!!*
> **Peace Be da Journey**
> M_____ NMMU at 2008–02–18 06:27

If each segment was read alone and out of context from the others, a reader might miss the playfulness of "My name is M___ and yes I will admit I like to pet puppies . . ." M___'s reference to "spanking Monkies" is also clearly a form of transgressive, sexual humor that m_____ extends throughout the post, establishing himself, posturing really, and inviting like-minded folks to reply. In fact, humor related to sex and drugs was a frequent component of the playful/humorous writing on the discussion boards, often serving as a filter for response; those who were offended did not reply, while those who were willing to play picked up the thread and responded along those lines.

In the next posts, the playful, earnest, and paralinguistic elements are combined in similar ways:

I CUDDLE WITH WILLIAM SHATNER EVERY NIGHT! SHAKE AND BAKE!

ALLO ALLO WORLD!

how are you today you beautiful amazing people *?!*

weeeellll if you wanna know i am fabulous!

I currently attend columbia college in chicago studying marketing.

Uhmmmm i'm in a band and we rock socks, I also play golf, and have been for 11 years. *weird?* I love to just hangout and talk, and just have an all around super time! **SHAKE AND BAKE!**

i love puppys, and kittens, and everything soft. i also love to cuddle. i hate lance too.

no seriously though, i'm a good guy and i always look forward to meeting and talking to new people about anything.

so talk to me = *D*

By d_____ CCC at 2008–03–06 17:21

HiP HoP is dead!!!,

'Hey *wassup* everybody!

My name is lb_____ from East London in South Africa.

I\'m currently a student at NMMU doing the BA Ext course, its a foundation course and im hoping to change to LLB next year.

I am a very handsome guy the current Mr NMMU, *(JOKES)!!* **Lets just say Im cute.**

I am a \"*hip hop head*\" and **loving the new Papoos, Game, Jigga and Nasir Jones\'s albums.**

Hip Hop is dead and 50 helped kill it, but I think he is going to try bring it back to life when he drops his new album.

My lecturer will kill me if she sees the slang I\'ve used to write this introduction so, allow me to get serious now.

I am 21 years of age, I am Xhosa

and I enjoy watching Rugby and Top Gear its a motor car show.

When i graduate **I intend to become the Dr's Advocate.**

Jokes aside I will become an Advocate.

Ohh and holla back if you are a \"*Hip Hop Head*\" (**ladies in particular please!**)

lb_____ NMMU at 2008-02-18 06:27

The combination of elements (i.e., playful/humorous, earnest, and written paralinguistic cues) was found across all of the 153 successful introductory posts with playful elements. While the numbers of segments coded in each category varied, the intertwined, entangled nature of the combinations did not change. The pattern that emerged was thus one where all three elements could be present in one sentence or one string of sentences. As such, these posts accomplished the relational and phatic work of the writing while also accomplishing the transactional or informational work of the writing.

Combining ludic and paralinguistic writing to create the relational underpinnings for successful introductions demonstrates a rhetorical savvy showcasing solid understandings of tenets of audience, purpose, available means of communication, *ethos, logos,* and *pathos* in this particular environment. Allowing and even encouraging students to write in this way might be a hard sell in the classroom given the negative reception such writing has received in the popular press and in educational environments. Nevertheless, this type of conversation can create an important social selection mechanism for the participants on the discussion board. Here the small talk invites conversation, but only with a specific group of self-selecting people who were able to find some kind of affinity with one another and those affinities regularly crossed nationalities and ethnicities in the global, intercultural setting. Posting in this way demonstrates participants understood discourse practices in this medium and their own socio-semiotic positions within it. That awareness allowed students to use the tools available to assist in the overall socialization of the group, creating a sense of social connection.

I like to think i'm a funny person . . . (funny looking) haha just kidding

The *ludic-as-phatic* written discourse in the posts was quite often self-referential. Students rarely poked fun at others (and when they did, it was directed at assumptions/stereotypes, not individuals); instead, they poked fun at themselves, exaggerating aspects of their life stories, often noted with a paralinguistic "ha-ha" cue in the text itself, or including fun or quirky tidbits of information about themselves.

The 153 "successful" introductions contained 274 segments coded as playful, with 54 instances (20%) of self-referential/self-deprecating humor conveyed through words and paralinguistic written cues. These self-referential playful segments were not consolidated in just a few of the introductions; rather, they appeared across almost all of the posts with playful/humorous segments. Two examples here demonstrate how students use the self-referential joking coupled with written paralinguistic cues to help their peers "read" them and *want* to read them. The bold text indicates segments that include some kind of self-referential or self-deprecating playful move. The italicized written paralinguistic cues:

Im bringing sexy back . . . heres how

Hello everyone! My name is _____. i am a junior at Columbia college double majoring in broadcast journalism and marketing communication. I am a fun girl who can turn any frown up side down. **I have some pretty funny nicknames including porkchop (apparently when i was a baby i was a little pudgy)** *haha.* **Froglegs is another . . . I got this one basically because my friends think i have noo coordination when it comes to dancing.** I have some normal nicknames too . . . like Barbie and ladybug.

I like to think im a funny person . . . *(funny looking) haha just kidding.* **Here is a joke that describes my life . . . its called blonde driving:**

A blonde was swerving all over the road and driving very badly, so she got pulled over by a cop. The cop walked up to her window and asked, "Miss, why are you driving so recklessly?" The blonde said, "I'm sorry sir, but wherever I go, there's always a tree in front of me and I can't seem to get away from it!" The cop looked at her and said, "Lady, that's your air freshener!"

I love the color pink, in fact my (new apartment) is all pink, from the walls to the furniture. *(think Audry Hepburn in Breakfast at Tiffany's)* I live alone in the city (which sucks...the alone part). One very important thing i should mention is that I'm turning 21 *IN A WEEK* and a half*!!!!!* I'm absolutely positively *sooo* excited about that! I hope you had a fun time reading my little rant/introduction!

By ccc at 2007–03–13 18:06 I Introductions I

The Freaky-Guy

My name is mm_____, **my friends call me Chris Brown** *(ha ha!).* I come from Kimberley(South Africa). I'm old enough to go clubbing. I'm a Law Student at the Nelson Mandela Metropolitan University and I'm enjoying it thus far. I intend on completing the course as soon as possible and then in turn specialise in Commercial Law.

I enjoy watching television and driving on the free-way at night, because that is when all the *"SPEED-FREAKS"* come out to play! I'm crazy about freaky-girls, **mainly because they claim that I'm a freaky-guy** :-). And, i love guitar. It is an awesoem instrument to play **(I tried and I don't expect to exceed very far—my pinkie is too little)** :(

By mm_____ NMMU at 2007-03-02 08:24

As evidenced by the frequent paralinguistic "ha-ha"s or "just joking"s or "lol"s after an exaggeration or personal tidbit, and the instructions for readers to think of a particular movie star or pop culture icon, the students appear to be aware of the emotional tone of the messages they are sending and seem to use on-screen cues to convey that tone. Students combine the self-referential, self-deprecating humor with the paralinguistic written cues as a means of conveying personal information to strangers in a socially acceptable way, of engaging interest, and, ultimately, of provoking some kind of reply.

Lions and Tigers and Bears, Oh My!

The playful written small talk on the discussion boards occasionally played with or made fun of the "other," but not usually directly. This type of "messing with" each other appeared when students were playing with the assumptions and stereotypes they believed the others to have about them and is of particular interest in a globally networked classroom. This type of interaction was *ludic-as-phatic* with a bit of an edge, serving even more as a test or filter than the merely playful, quirky, or transgressive. There were 33 segments of 274 total from the 153 successful "playful/humorous" introductions coded as "joking, word play, jesting, messing with stereotypes directed at other." This form of play with assumptions highlights a whole host of student understandings of the social activity and the layers of the project—the discussion boards and the goals of cultural sharing, the varying cultures and subject positions of the participants, and the existing stereotypes about each other.

The most identifiable examples of this type of *ludic-as-phatic* discourse have always been generated by the South African students and played back by the U.S. students. The South African students often articulated a heightened awareness of the mistaken assumptions that Americans might have had about Africa; they assumed some level of ignorance and played (with an edge) to see whether or not they were right. Those assumptions were also often obvious and primed for the testing (in every year of the project, U.S.-based students in all classes referenced *The Lion King* as a source of information about countries in Africa). The U.S. students, on the other hand, seemed not to consider mistaken assumptions that South Africans might have had of them. Those assumptions typically took much longer to work their way to the surface of the discussions. Awareness or lack of awareness of assumptions reveals a sociocultural layer unique to the power positions of the two countries in the world and, sadly, the arrogance with which many Americans perceive the world.

In the introductory post here, student s___ utilizes *ludic-as-phatic* discourse as discussed above, but also moves into an edgier space when he references a pet lion. The post was not the first or only appearance of lions on the Sharing Cultures discussion board, or of tigers, or bears, or elephants, or monkeys. In each instance, posts like this one initiated some of the most fruitful, "sharing" conversations, all the while filtering out the people who just did not get it. In the two examples below, the South African students very purposefully and very explicitly "mess with" the assumptions of the American students who might be out there. Much as with the other paralinguistic, self-referential joking, and pop culture examples of *ludic-as-phatic* writing in the introductions, they are able to attract attention, generate response, and sustain conversation over the course of the semester.

The GREAT one himself it's FIASCO but not lupe!!

Whats up!!!! My name is S_____ aka fiasco how u guys doing? Im first year student at NMMU im studying Media Studies. Im young Xhosa male just came back frm the UK, I took a two year break, living and working in the UK. It was cool the British are cool people really friendly and quiet open to many cultures. I was born in Cape Town then moved to Bloemfontien at the age of sixteen. after arriving back in SA I was really keen to be back in the country and studying, it's been alright so far I've met lots of cool peeps local and international. I enjoy listen to music, watching movies, chillin with my friends and going out. Im down to earth, ambitous just a normal cool dude. Yo people I got to go can't chat here 4eva hopefully I'll might some of one day and we kick it go out 4 a beer or something, until we chat again **'snap' almost 4got ya i got a pet lion it's called Simba**, anyway tar! tar! asta la vista! peace1! cheers have a good one.

    By s___ NMMU at 2007-03-05 11:17 | Introductions | |

THATS AWSOME

YOUR SO LUCKY TO HAVE A PET LION. I HAVE ALWAYS WANTED AN EXOTIC PET LIKE THAT. EITHER A LION OR A CAPOOCHEN MONKEY OR SOMETHING LIKE THAT. HOW OLD IS YOUR LION? IS IT A MALE OR FEMALE? IS IT NICE, AND IS IT TRAINED? LIKE, CAN YOU GO AND JUST PLAY AROUND WITH IT? I ONLY HAVE DOGS, THREE OF THEM. HOPE TO TALK TO YOU SOON.

    By t_____ CCC at Mon, 2007-03-05 16:23 | reply

Hey whats up!!!!

Hi how are you? im "chillin" , **yo about the lion i was just kiddin I don't really have a lion just wanted to see if anybody fell for it sorry about that I didnt think that anyone was that gullable sorry Im not trying to be rude we (South Africans) are not allowed to tame wild animals unless you have a resort or reserve, but its cool that you want one I think its allowed in the States.** Thanks for the message and I hope it goes well with the pet thing. What are you studing and what do hope to achieve with degree?

    By s_____NMMU at Mon, 2007-03-12 10:55 | reply

yeah!

When I looked at your title I saw Fiasco and I Was like YEAH! I neer really liked any sort of hip hop till I heard Lupe. I read somewhere that he is not considered one of the new pioneers of hip hop, and is one of the only artists that is keeping what he does real. Unlike a lot of the crap that is

played on the radio here. Plus he's from Chicago so its even sweeter. You
into Common or Kanye?
 The name is N_____ by th way.
 By n____ccc at Tue, 2007-03-13 01:01 I reply

In the first example, s___ uses all forms of *ludic-as-phatic* discourse
found in this study, which very successfully generates responses and in
different ways. One student respondent, t___, is so excited by the lion
that s/he responds in all upper case, missing the playing altogether.
Another respondent, n___, skips the lion completely, responding to
the Hip Hop reference instead. S___ then clearly articulates his overall
approach to using the *ludic-as-phatic*, saying "yo about the lion i was just
kiddin I don't really have a lion just wanted to see if anybody fell for it
sorry about that I didnt think that anyone was that gullable sorry Im
not trying to be rude . . . " He makes sure that the misinformed reader
understands that he meant to have fun, not to harm. This demonstrates
an awareness of the overall social goals of the project and the potential
hurt caused by playing with assumptions in this way.

In another example, sv___ warns s/he is playing with assumptions
by titling her/his introduction "stereotype type." Here the students
respond primarily to the music references in his post, but they also
congratulate sv___ on her/his effective play for attention in the introduction, with one exception. sv___ does not gently rebuke the student
who asks if riding bears is safe. It is possible that because in that particular response post, there are no paralinguistic cues from bf___ about
whether or not he or she is joking back. The student does not convey
what he or she hopes the response will be. Whatever the case, sv___
simply ignores the post; the student didn't "get it," so sv___ does not
interact. Instead s/he mentions how much s/he appreciates the fact that
the other students are aware of her/his play. The *ludic-as-phatic* filter,
then, has worked, connecting her/him to people s/he now considers,
and thanks for, being "open minded."

stereotype type

Hey there, my name is _____, from Mthatha. If you have no idea
where that is, go to google and look up 'crime capital of the world' and if
that doesn't work try "universe."I am a first year Law student at NMMU.
**Studying here has made me more tolerant toward animals as we have a
very intelligent elephant in our class. The monkeys are good in practical
exercises but they lack in theory. In between lectures we hangout at the
dining hall, where we share the spoils of the previous days hunt. Coming
to school is a hustle because bears (our official mode of transport) are
in hibernation.** I enjoy listening to hip-hop and neo soul. My favorite

artists are Common,Aesope Rock,Jill Scott,Gaopele and Mos Def.I have to go now

By sv_____ NMMU at 2007-03-09 08:13 | Introductions | blog |

BEARS?

Is riding bears safe? if it is, thats cool, i would like to ride a bear some day then. thats kind of funny, because here in chicago out profesional football team is called the chicago bears, although i have never seen one here. whatever, i find it intresting that you consider Mthatha the murder capital of the world, and i have never herd of it. I know that a lot of people who come to America are afraid because so many peopel think that we have an outrageous amount of crime, and we might, but i never feel like my life is in danger. Do you feel like your life is in danger when you walk arond in your home town?

By bf_____ CCC at Wed, 2007-03-10 01:41 | reply

FOR THE LOVE OF MUSIC

Wud up Sv_____! Your INTRODUCTION caught my attention so i thought i would drop you a comment. ITs was interesting how you used stereotypes to introduce your self. I noticed that we have something in common HIP-HOP! I LOVE HIP-HOP! And i also like common, mizz Scott and MOS DEF! I acually saw Mos Def last year in New York at the Apollo. Well write me back if you want to chit chat!! BYE

By I_____ccc at Tue, 2007-03-13 16:34 | reply

Hello

Haha! That was funny. I do realize that you're joking. But ya made me laugh. I wish we COULD ride bears around, that would be awesome. Imagine a world without cars, but bears! I love Aesope Rock too, have you ever listened to Jurassic 5 or Atmosphere or Michael Franti? You'd like them if you like Aesope. Haha, I'm still laughing. Dude, thanks for making my day. Check out the music.

Peace,

By sb_____ccc at Tue, 2007-03-13 16:31 | reply

The new danger

Ha ha I love this. We should all have intros like this.
I LOVE MOS DEF!

By sa_____ccc at Wed, 2007-03-14 00:33 | reply

What happened to Talib

I'm glad that I'm not the only Mos fan on this site because I'm the only one in my class. Most people, that I know, are into that whole "bling

bling" type of hip hop. Anyway, what ever happene to Talib Kweli? The last time I saw him he was performing a jiggy song with the Black Eyed Peas. Please dont tell me Talib has sold out. If you know what happened keep me posted
> peace
> By sv_____ NMMU at Fri, 2007-03-16 08:29 | reply

Thanks for realising that I

Thanks for realising that I was joking, its not often that foreigners discard that garbage that CNN shoves down your throats. For example, Ludacris came to South Africa last year and asked that we make him chief for a day. I personally thought that was the most ignorant thing I've ever heard. Anyway,thanks for being open-minded and I've Atomsphere but not the other two,I'll check them out. By the way, you should try finding albums by two of the dopest South African cats, Tumi and the Volume, and Hymphatic Thabs.Iam sure you'll love them.
> peace
> By sv_____ NMMU at Fri, 2007-03-16 07:35 | reply

Aesope Rock is so awesome!

FROM LUDIC-AS-PHATIC TO LEARNING

Participants who wrote successful introductions overwhelmingly approached the IMLE with a *ludic-as-phatic* lens, with 88 percent of the introductory posts that generated sustained discussion containing some combination of playful elements with written paralinguistic cues to make connections with other students. Only 1 percent of the unsuccessful introductory posts analyzed, those that generated no response, contained some combination of those elements. Instead, the unsuccessful posts were overwhelmingly earnest and self-focused. They were friendly and perfectly nice, but they did not give their readers any reason to give back; they did not contain the phatic discourse that enables open channels of communication.

The introductory phase of the IMLE activity might easily be characterized in a disparaging way, as small talk often is, as focused on the "social nonsense" or even on "transgressive" material. My analysis of the discussion board activity across five years of the Sharing Cultures project, however, suggests this initial social, *ludic-as-phatic* phase is key to an IMLE in which global communicators are expected to learn from one another. In a continuation of this study, it became clear engaged, interactive, extended discussions throughout the semester did **not** take place for the participants who had not made connections with peers through the introductory phase. The 66 percent of total students who participated in the discussions that followed the introductory posts in the Sharing Cultures IMLE are nearly identical to the 66 percent of total students that successfully forged discussion board relationships with other students in the introductions. The discussion board activity of these participants was characterized by high numbers of posts and comments across many participant-generated discussions. The remaining 29 percent of student participants, after "unsuccessful" introductions and/or no attempts to reply to the introductory posts of their peers, limited their activity on the discussion board overall to direct responses to teacher assignment prompts. The pattern of activity for these students was characterized by relatively few posts, depending upon how many teacher prompts each student encountered, and no comment activity on other student posts.

In the context of global, online learning environments, initial, social/ phatic, "small-talk" exchanges between student participants should be included as key elements of curricular design. The *ludic-as-phatic* aspects of introductory conversations can and should be explored as powerful rhetorical tools for navigating social activity in IMLEs. Understanding these strategies appears to be of particular importance for getting relationships off the ground in large-scale teaching and learning spaces. Without the *ludic-as-phatic* writing strategies mediating the multiple layers of social network connections, the discussion, the collaboration, the sharing, and therefore the peer-to-peer learning, simply does not happen.

CONCLUSION

As writing teachers, we share an unspoken assumption participation and response drive learning and are responsible for creating a classroom community. In increasingly global, online classrooms, the writing that is generated on a site is often a direct index of level of participation. Since computer-mediated communication was first introduced in the composition classroom, researchers have explored the need for digital networked participation and how students take that participation in their own directions when given the opportunity to do so (Rouzie, 2005; Fleckenstein, 2005; McKee, 2002). While there is agreement on the value of online written interaction and the recognition of significant social, cultural, and technological barriers to equal participation, there has been limited rhetorical investigation of how student writing structures participation.

In this study, I have questioned *how* students write to successfully generate response and create social connections in an IMLE and have uncovered one key, comprehensive answer: they include phatic, relational rhetorical moves to initiate and sustain conversation. The conclusion may seem obvious. However, phatic and relational speech and writing are often discounted as extraneous to the real writing tasks at hand or as nonsense and a waste of time when articulated in negative terms. My research demonstrates such writing is necessary for the other forms of writing and learning to happen in an IMLE.

It is a challenge to recognize the value of this type of discussion board writing. In the project years with large numbers of student participants (2006–2008 with roughly two hundred students each year), it was easy to get lost in what looked like silly, crazy, "nonsense" in the introductory posts and never see how students were using *ludic-as-phatic* relational strategies to make connections and decide with whom they wanted to converse.

Understanding *ludic-as-phatic* relational rhetorical strategies appears to be important for getting relationships off the ground in large-scale teaching and learning spaces where students must work to create social connections with relative strangers. As teachers who create Internet-mediated learning spaces, we need to consider how the underpinnings of social conventions shift and change in global digital networked environments. While no easy solution exists, students and teachers can learn to be aware of how relational rhetorical strategies merge with transactional writing in digital networked writing spaces. In fact, if we do not teach students how to make facilitative connections, we are failing to teach effective communication for global online environments.

Based on the research presented here, I suggest shifting our attitude toward phatic and relational writing and helping our students develop a rich understanding of this rhetorical means of creating social fabric in digital, networked, and intercultural spaces. We can make use of this research in two important ways related to working with the *knowledge practices of academic writing* in online classrooms. First, we can help students recognize the writing they do in online discussion spaces as sophisticated ways of making connection, building argument, and creating alignment and identification with an audience. Second, we can do the analytical work to understand global IMLE writing as situated in a unique and evolving rhetorical situation. Writing is increasingly taking place in digital, networked environments. We should therefore work to understand how this writing works as a process and a product worthy of our scholarly and teacherly attentions.

References

Androutsopoulos, J. K. (2000). Non-standard spelling in media texts: The case of german fanzines. *Journal of Sociolinguistics, 4*(4), 514–533. https://doi.org/10.1111/1467-9481.00128

Androutsopoulos, J. K. (2010). Localizing the global on the participatory web. In N. Coupland (Ed.), *The handbook of language and globalization* (pp. 201–231). Hoboken, NJ: Wiley. https://doi.org/10.1002/9781444324068.ch9

Basharina, O. (2007). An activity theory perspective on student-reported contradictions in international telecollaboration. *Language Learning & Technology, 11*(2), 82–103.

Baym, N. (1993). Interpreting soap operas and creating community: Inside a computer-mediated fan culture. *Journal of Folklore Research, 30*(2/3), 143–176.

Bazerman, C. (2008). Theories of the middle range in historical studies of writing practice. *Written Communication, 25*(3), 298–318. https://doi.org/10.1177/0741088308318025

Belz, J. A. (2002). Social dimensions of telecollaborative foreign language study. *Language Learning & Technology, 6*(1), 60–94.

Brown, P., & Levinson, S. (1987). *Politeness: Some universals in language usage.* Cambridge, MA: MIT Press.

Cogdill, S. (1996). @go tuesday. *Kairos: A journal of rhetoric, technology, and pedagogy, 1*(2). Retrieved from http://kairos.technorhetoric.net/1.2/binder2.html?coverweb/Cogdill/gotuesday.html

Coupland, J. (2003). Small talk: Social functions. *Research on Language and Social Interaction, 36*(1), 1–6. https://doi.org/10.1207/S15327973RLSI3601_1

Coupland, J., & Coupland, N. (1992). How are you? Negotiating phatic communion. *Language in Society, 21,* 207–230.

Crystal, D. (2009). *Txtng: The gr8 db8.* New York, NY: Oxford University Press.

Eco, U. (2000). *Kant and the platypus: Essays on language and cognition* (A. McEwen, Trans.) New York, NY: Harvest Books.

Fernback, J. (2003). Legends on the net: An examination of computer-mediated communication as a locus of oral culture. *New Media & Society, 5*(1), 29–45. https://doi.org/10.1177/1461444803005001902

Fleckenstein, K. (2005). Faceless students, virtual spaces: Emergence and communal accountability in online classrooms. *Computers and Composition, 22*(2), 149–176. https://doi.org/10.1016/j.compcom.2005.02.003

Gumperz, J., & Berenz, N. (1993). Transcribing conversational exchanges. In J. Edwards & M. Lampert (Eds.), *Talking data: Transcription and coding in discourse research* (pp. 91–121). Hilsdale, NJ: Lawrence Erlbaum.

Haas, C., Takayoshi, P., Carr, B., Hudson, K., & Pollock, R. (2011). Young people's everyday literacies: The language features of instant messaging. *Research in the Teaching of English, 45*(4), 378–404.

Holcomb, C. (1997). A class of clowns: Spontaneous joking in computer-assisted discussions. *Computers and Composition, 14*(1), 3–18. https://doi.org/10.1016/S8755-4615(97)90035-9

Holmes, J. (2006). Sharing a laugh: Pragmatic aspects of humor and gender in the workplace. *Journal of Pragmatics, 38,* 26–50.

Holmes, J., & Marra, M. (2004). Relational practice in the workplace: Women's talk or gendered discourse? *Language in Society, 33,* 377–398.

Holmes, J., & Schnurr, S. (2006). Doing femininity at work: More than just practice. *Journal of Sociolinguistics, 10*(1), 31–51.

Jaworski, A. (2000). Silence and small talk. In J. Coupland (Ed.), *Small talk* (pp. 110–132). London, England: Longman Harlow.

Laver, J. (1975). Communicative functions of phatic communion. In A. Kendon, R. Harris, & M. Key (Eds.), *Organization of behavior in face-to-face interaction* (pp. 215–238). The Hague, The Netherlands: Mouton.

Malinowski, B. (1989). The problem of meaning in primitive languages. In C. Ogden & I. Richards (Eds.), *Supplement to the meaning of meaning* (pp. 146–152). San Diego, CA: Harcourt, Brace, Jovanavich.

McCarthy, M. (2003). Talking back: 'Small' interactional response tokens in everyday conversation. *Research on Language in Social Interaction, 36*(1), 33–63.

McKee, H. (2002). 'YOUR VIEWS SHOWED TRUE IGNORANCE!!!': (Mis)communication in an online interracial discussion forum. *Computers and Composition, 19*(4), 411–434. https://doi.org/10.1016/S8755-4615(02)00143-3

Naaman, M., Boase, J., & Lai, C. (2010). Is it really about me? Message content in social awareness streams. *Proceedings of the 2010 ACM Conference on Computer Supported Cooperative Work.* doi:10.1145/1718918.1718953

Ogden, C., & Richards, I. (1989). *The Meaning of Meaning.* San Diego, CA: Harcourt Brace Jovanavich.

Rouzie, A. (2001). Conversation and carrying-on: Play, conflict, and serio-ludic discourse in synchronous computer conferencing. *College Composition and Communication, 53*(2), 251–299. https://doi.org/10.2307/359078

Rouzie, A. (2005). *At play in the fields of writing: a serio-ludic rhetoric.* Cresskill, NJ: Hampton Press.

Schandorf, M. (2012). Mediated gesture: Paralinguistic communication and phatic text. *Convergence (London), 19*(3), 319–344. https://doi.org/10.1177/1354856512439501

Senft, G. (1995). Phatic communion. In J. Verschueren, J. Ostman, & J. Blommaert (Eds.), *Handbook of Pragmatics* (pp. 1–10). Amsterdam, The Netherlands: Benjamins.

Smagorinsky, P. (2008). The method section as conceptual epicenter in constructing social science reports. *Written Communication, 25*(3), 389–411. https://doi.org /10.1177/0741088308317815

Thurlow, C. (2003). Generation txt? The sociolinguistics of young people's text messaging. *Discourse Analysis Online, 1*(1). Retrieved from http://extra.shu.ac.uk/daol/art icles/v1/n1/a3/thurlow2002003-01.html

Thurlow, C., & Bell, K. (2009). Against technologization: Young people's new media discourse as creative cultural practice. *Journal of Computer-Mediated Communication, 14*(4), 1038–1049. https://doi.org/10.1111/j.1083-6101.2009.01480.x

Thurlow, C., & Poff, M. (2012). Text-messaging. In S. Herring, D. Stein, & T. Virtanen (Eds.), *Pragmatics of computer mediated communication* (pp. 163–190). New York, NY: Mouton de Gruyter.

7

THE MOOC AS A SOUK
Writing Instruction, World Englishes, and Writers at Scale

Kaitlin Clinnin, Kay Halasek, Ben McCorkle, Susan Delagrange, Scott Lloyd Dewitt, Jen Michaels, and Cynthia L. Selfe

ABSTRACT

The project investigates the nature of digitally-mediated pedagogies implemented in a writing Massive Open Online Course (MOOC) and how participants leveraged those pedagogies and course content to accommodate their personal learning objectives. Employing concepts of universal and participatory design, we explore ways the MOOC offered a meaningful educational experience for learners in the global context. Analyzing elements of the course illuminates the potential of the MOOC as a site for global learning. We also find the pedagogical experience of teaching a MOOC has implications for teaching composition from a multilingual and multicultural perspective. Beneficial for individuals who identify as English Language Learners and English as First Language Writers, the multilingual, multicultural, universal, and participatory approach employed in the MOOC values the sets of literacy experiences and practices all students bring into the classroom.

Keywords: collaboration, community building, discussion forums, globalization, MOOCs, participatory design, social media, universal design, World Englishes

INTRODUCTION: MOOCS, UNIVERSAL DESIGN FOR LEARNING AND PARTICIPATORY DESIGN

Nearly everyone in academia has an opinion about MOOCs—Massive Open Online Courses—and professors are more likely than not to disapprove of them (Jaschik & Lederman, 2013). Despite the reservations expressed by faculty regarding the quality, pedagogical effectiveness, educational legitimacy, and ethics of MOOCs, the number of MOOCs being offered and the number of institutions offering MOOCs continue

DOI: 10.7330/9781607326649.c007

to increase. The platforms (e.g., Coursera, edX, and Udacity) accommodate tens of thousands of learners by granting access to seemingly endless learning assets: captured lectures, multimedia presentations and demonstrations, open-source videos, and online texts. Learners then apply what they've learned to assignments, activities, quizzes, and course assessments often without direct feedback from instructors.

The MOOC pedagogical model diverges dramatically from the model of face-to-face higher education familiar to most of us: faculty meet with students in a set, physical location one to four times per week for a ten- to sixteen-week semester. We believe this significant departure from the traditional model drives many concerns about MOOCs—especially among writing teachers. For decades, the discipline of composition studies has worked through professional organizations (e.g., the Conference on College Composition and Communication, the National Council of Teachers of English, and the Modern Language Association) to keep the teaching of writing small: small class sizes, small loads for instructors. MOOCs, the argument goes, potentially compromise those years of political and educational advocacy for keeping the teaching of writing intimate and to sustain the working lives of instructors.

In the midst of these and other raging debates about MOOCs, our team at Ohio State University (OSU) conceived, developed, and offered a MOOC (from inception to the last class session) in eight months between November 2012 and June 2014. The course, "Writing II: Rhetorical Composing," shared many learning outcomes and course objectives with the second-level writing course at OSU (English 2367), but was not intended to duplicate that course or stand as proxy for it. Rather, we conceived of "Rhetorical Composing" as an opportunity to open and extend our teaching to learners around the world.

In this chapter, we consider how two particular elements—universal design for learning (UDL) and participatory design (PD)—shaped our approach to "Rhetorical Composing" and how these elements of course design and participants' engagement have influenced our research and future instantiations of the MOOC and writing classes generally. Specifically, we discuss how we employed the concepts of universal design (McTighe & Wiggins, 2004), participatory design (Robertson & Simonsen, 2012), and the principles that inform them to evaluate the pedagogical decisions we made in the "Rhetorical Composing" MOOC, especially as related to the global, multilingual population (Clinnin, 2014). We will reflect on the decisions made as instructional staff and explore how participants responded to these elements of the course design. Drawing upon participatory design principles, we will consider how participant feedback and productions have changed our pedagogical approaches and course design for the next iteration of the MOOC and our other face-to-face and hybrid writing courses.

FRAMING THE MOOC: LEARNING AS A GLOBAL COLLABORATION

Writing II: Rhetorical Composing, a ten-week course offered between April and June 2013, was advertised as an advanced writing course. Similar in its focus to the second-year writing course offered in the Department of English at Ohio State, "Rhetorical Composing" emphasized critical reading and writing, rhetorical analysis, multimodal composing, and research-based inquiry. In the months leading up to the debut of the "Rhetorical Composing" MOOC, we began thinking about the challenges of teaching English composition on a massive, global scale. The scope became clear in early February 2013, when we received Google Analytics data showing 26,002 visits to our course enrollment page between January 5 and February 4, 2013. These early indicators of the global nature of the course were confirmed by responses from our demographic survey of enrolled participants. Nearly 39,000 individuals enrolled in the course, with some 3,076 completing at least one writing assignment. Of the 7,030 participants who provided demographic data, 63 percent were L2 learners (English was not their primary or "first" language).

When we saw visitors hailed from seventy-five countries, we knew our prospective course participants would speak and write a variety of Englishes with varying fluency. For example, our page received 1,698 visits from India, 970 visits from the United Kingdom, and 49 visits from Nigeria. These are all countries where English is an official spoken language, yet the variations of Indian, British, and Nigerian Englishes are quite distinct, as are the histories and complex cultures of these countries. At a more granular level, every individual speaker of English is unique—influenced by unique local circumstances, language influences, and life experiences. We recognized attending carefully to UDL and PD would be critical to the success of the course for these learners in particular as navigating a course platform informed by U.S. educational practices and approaches to writing instruction might be foreign to them. With this context in mind, the team began thinking about how to facilitate a positive, enriching course experience for speakers who would use many varieties of English and a range of cultural and historical experiences influencing their language-use patterns.

One of the challenges in teaching a writing MOOC to a global audience was determining which concepts and skills were most vital and could be most effectively conveyed across cultures, languages, rhetorical contexts, and genres (Barratt, 2014; Mahboob & Dutcher, 2014). To address this challenge, the instructional team opted to build course objectives, content, and the assignment sequence around principles of composing from a rhetorical perspective. Rather than focus on conventions of alphabetic academic English, the team focused attention on rhetorical principles intended to engage all participants and enable them to develop their communicative abilities to emphasize "enduring understanding" (Sample, 2011b): When informed by knowledge of and ethical use of rhetorical principles and practices, texts will serve authors' audiences and purposes more mindfully and persuasively.

By focusing course objectives on standard rhetorical concepts such as audience and purpose, we believed the course content would be open to adoption and adaptation by participants for their own personal, professional, and cultural contexts. The conceptual shift was reflected in how we referred to the course. Initially we had shortened the MOOC title "Writing II: Rhetorical Composing" to simply "Writing II," which emphasized the composing component. However, as we realized the global scope of the class and the differing experiences of the enrolled participants, we began referring to the course as "Rhetorical Composing" as a way to demonstrate the openness of the course and its emphasis on rhetoric.

To model UDL principles and open intellectual engagement, we developed a statement of philosophy that encouraged a respectful learning environment characterized by an open attitude toward a wide range of world Englishes. The statement reflected insights from Canagarajah (2007) and in later iterations of the MOOC the work of Barratt (2014); Canagarajah (2013a; 2013b); Mahboob and Dutcher (2014); and McCorkle, Halasek, Clinnin, and Selfe (2016). The statement evolved into a "Global Englishes" section of our Coursera MOOC, and it encouraged participants to be generous readers and users of global Englishes.

On that page, we asked participants to recognize and respect the Englishes spoken by class members. We also encouraged them to "Talk with other course participants about the variety of English that they are using, where they learned it, and the history of the place that shaped their language use" and "Share strategies for learning and using English, and share tactics for overcoming the difficulties you encounter." To facilitate comprehension and interest from participants, we included a text transcript of our philosophy statement and a video we produced on Global Englishes. We also consulted Paul Kei Matsuda, who specializes in second language learning, to gain insight on the tasks ahead of us.

At the bottom of the Global Englishes page, we asked participants to consider producing their own text or video responses as an optional "Level Up Challenge." In the spirit of participatory design, we seeded the page with short videos from two talented graduate students at The Ohio State University, and in these videos, the students discussed their relationship with global Englishes. In them, Sang Hee Ryu (originally from Korea) and David Wandera (originally from Kenya) offer personal perspectives, advice, and strategies for learning English in global contexts.

Convinced a generous and open approach to world Englishes informed by UDL could help *all* writers, we also added clarifying remarks to the Global Englishes page and invited "*all* course participants, including fluent speakers of English, to think about how best to use this course to meet their personal goals and contribute to a vibrant learning community."

It wasn't long before the "Writing and Learning in a Global Context" forum began filling up with personal stories about learning English and composing in different Englishes; incisive debates about how global Englishes vary and how to comment most productively on peers' writing in this global context; and valuable links to writers' Level-Up responses, many of which were posted on YouTube. We were intrigued, for instance, by a video from Russian participant Alina Mia, who noted previous teachers had given her a limited understanding of English language practice, suggesting British English and U.S. English comprised the two primary "kinds" of English. Alina disagreed with this reductive linguistic mapping. She noted:

> Talking and communicating with people who speaks English [. . .] all over the world, watching movies, and series, and so on, I also discovered, with happiness actually, that I'm not the only one who thinks there are not just *two* kinds of English, but *more*, these Englishes how you call it here World Englishes. (Siluyanova, 2013)

When the team asked Alina if she'd consider adding her video to the Digital Archive of Literacy Narratives at http://daln.osu.edu so it could be re-posted on the Global Englishes page, Alina replied, "It was my first experience in making video and in using youtube.com. Your letter gave me courage and energy to continue my journey in the World of Rhetoric!" (personal communication, 2013). Alina's video is one example of how willing participants were to collaborate with us in designing the course and how their contributions enriched their experiences and the experiences of their peers.

For our team the experience of thinking from a world-Englishes perspective proved one of the most valuable learning experiences associated with the "Rhetorical Composing" MOOC. Certainly, we learned a great deal about the pragmatic challenges of teaching in a globalized environment and came to admire those writers in our MOOC who readily embraced the challenges inherent in communicating with different varieties of English. We also learned how valuable the perspectives of global Englishes speakers could be. These writers contributed in rich and generous ways to our own and others' understandings of what it means to communicate effectively in international online environments. They exhibited the courage needed to learn new languages and to practice writing skills in public spaces. They reminded us—in Paulo Freire's (2003) words—about the rich benefits all teachers gain when they enter into dialogue with students:

> Through dialogue, the teacher-of-the-students and the students-of-the teachers cease to exist and a new term emerges: teacher-student with students-teachers. The teacher is no longer merely the-one-who-teaches, but one who is himself taught in dialogue with students, who in turn while being taught also teaches. They become jointly responsible for a process in which all grow. (p. 80)

FRAMING ENGAGEMENT: PARTICIPATION AND INTERACTION IN COURSE DESIGN

One frequent critique of MOOCs is the lack of interaction among participants and faculty. In addition, many MOOCs have relied on video lectures to distribute information asynchronously. Heavy use of lecture-based instruction has led some educators to characterize MOOCs as massive content delivery systems rather than spaces for massive teaching and learning opportunities (Krause, 2013). It was from this awareness of the assumed limitations of MOOCs that our conceptions of peer reviews and discussion forums were conceived and evolved.

Based upon previous experiences with discussion forums, the "Rhetorical Composing" team valued the possibilities for interaction and collaborative learning that the forums facilitated. The distributed nature of the course meant discussion forums were spaces where participants could interact with others, and the global distribution of participants resulted in discussion forums that were active constantly. In addition to the community formation objectives, the instructional team conceived of the forums as an opportunity for active learning. We were concerned MOOCs were more effective as content delivery machines than authentic learning opportunities. The discussion forums were a component already included in the Coursera platform, and almost all MOOCs hosted on Coursera made use of discussion forums as a location for participant (and faculty) interaction.

Previous MOOC discussion forums functioned as a space for participants to comment on lectures, ask questions about course materials, and share work. As a way to include more active learning opportunities and more forms of action and engagement in the course, we enacted a "flipped classroom" learning process. It began with course objectives (Sample, 2011a, 2011c), proceeded through the video lectures, and ended with an optional activity posted to the discussion forums. The activities were opportunities that enabled participants to engage the video concepts, but put them into practice according to their own interest.

The discussion forums were one of the earliest parts of the course to go live in April 2013. By the end of the first weekend, participants from all over the globe had participated in the "World Englishes" forum intended to open conversation regarding multiple forms of English and to set the expectation all languages and experiences were valuable. Many of the posts were responses to the Global Englishes instructional video (discussed earlier), but the threads quickly took on lives of their own. By the end of the course, over 2,500 individuals had posted in the discussion forums and created over 20,700 posts in over 6,500 threads.

As an example of the active learning and engagement, at the end of one video on the rhetorical concept audience, participants were asked to pick a topic of interest in their local community and create a message about their topic for multiple audiences. Participants were encouraged to post these practice activities to the discussion forums and to respond to one another by providing feedback on the messages. The team hoped that by encouraging participation in the discussion forums, more individuals would participate in the course experiences in ways that were most effective and convenient for their own learning style and personal goals.

In fact, peer review was at the heart of the course from its inception. Like many writing teachers, we employed peer review in face-to-face courses, creating workshops, designing peer review methods, and modeling of the collaborative engagement we ourselves practiced in our own writing (Bruffee, 1984; DeWitt, 1988; Trimbur, 1989; Wiener, 1986). Like many writing teachers, researchers, and students themselves, we were struck by the uneven quality of peer review in our courses and students' abilities to provide meaningful, substantive, constructive commentary to one another (Flynn, 1984; Karegianes, Pascarella, & Pflaum, 1980; Kastra, Tollefson, & Gilbert 1987; Mangelsdorf, 1992; Matsuno,

2009). We also recognized the need to provide structured, systematic instructional support for peer review (Mangelsdorf, 1992; Zhu, 1995) and the affordances and constraints of the online context for peer review (Flynn, 2011). The MOOC gave us the opportunity to test our assumptions about peer review. If it was a less than satisfactory activity for students, why did we continue to include it in our courses? One answer is disciplinary habit. Peer review has long been a customary and staunchly defended practice in composition.

Conducting peer review at scale with composition students was not entirely new practice for the MOOC teaching team. Our re-imagining of peer review in the MOOC was partially informed by the Commonplace curriculum, developed by Scott Lloyd DeWitt, Michael Harker, and Aaron McKain in the First-Year Writing Program at The Ohio State University (2007–2012; Harker, 2009). In this curriculum, students were asked to produce writing for the readership of an online journal of undergraduate writing, *Commonplace* (http://www.commonplaceuniversity.com).

We also recognized, given the online nature of the MOOC, that substantive and detailed instruction; attention to UDL principles of multiple forms of representation, action, and engagement; and opportunities for modeling and practice would be critical to creating a productive context for peer review. To meet these goals and needs, we created *The WEx Guide to Peer Review*, an online instructional manual designed to introduce participants to our peer review process facilitated through the Writers Exchange (WEx), an in-house peer-review platform. Because participants engaged in peer review had also submitted their own writing for review, they received extensive explanation of the assignment prompt and assignment outcomes used to create an assessment rubric. Participants were asked to rate the writing numerically based on rubric items and then provide a written explication of that rating using WEx's three-step method that asks participants to "Describe-Assess-Suggest":

Describe
In your own words, describe the part of the writing that you are responding to. This is helpful to writers because it allows them to understand how you are reading their writing.

Assess
After you describe the part of the writing you are responding to, assess what you are reading by pointing out both strengths and weaknesses. This is helpful to writers because it points out where their writing succeeds and where it falls short of succeeding.

Suggest

After you describe and assess the part of the writing you are responding to, suggest how the writer might make changes if he or she were to revise or how the writer might think differently about writing in future assignments. After every major assignment in this class, writers will complete reflections that address the revisions suggested by their peer reviewers and their own re-reading of the submission. Additionally, the final assignment will ask writers to revise an assignment of their choice. Your suggestions for revisions help your classmates at multiple points throughout the writing process. Not only are you helping them become better writers, but you are also helping them with the course assignments.

In our early team discussions about the MOOC, we considered creating a gateway mechanism participants needed to pass through and which would confirm they had completed the training module before they could submit and review writing to the MOOC. Doing so would increase the likelihood they would understand the assignment, the assessment rubric, and the "Describe~Assess~Suggest" scheme repeated throughout the class. We also anticipated these steps would help define the process and expectations, mitigating to some degree the challenges we faced in conveying a pedagogy of peer review.

As we grew closer to the opening of our course, we decided against various gatekeeping mechanisms in the course design after more fully understanding why participants were enrolling in the MOOC and further reflecting on the "open," universal, and participatory attributes of this new course format. As we came to learn, some participants were less than satisfied with the reviews they received in WEx. Many participants were legitimately justified in their dissatisfaction. Their reviewers had apparently either not read *The WEx Guide* or not completed the training module, or they had rushed through their reviews, providing little to no substantive feedback with which the writer could work. Dissatisfaction prompted them to employ the forums as an "alt-site" for engaging one another as writers.

Participants voiced their concerns and comments on peer review in a discussion forum entitled "Disappointing reviews on Assignment 2." This public, participant-created and participant-directed forum raised a number of meaningful issues, including the need for additional instruction in conducting peer review. *The WEx Guide* did not go far enough, as one participant noted when he wrote that "[s]imply expecting that people would read a training guide and apply the concepts right away is far too unrealistic."

The sentiments expressed by participants in the "Disappointing reviews" forum often turned on the notion of a learning curve for peer review, reminding one another, as Vivian did, "many of your reviewers are just like you . . . learning," something that was likely the "biggest driver for reviews that don't seem to ring true or seem off base." Sheryl echoed Vivian's perspective, recognizing that "we're all really being required to do peer review that we've never done" but also acknowledging that the WEx criterion-based review "does force us to slow down and really think about what we're reading." As a remedy to disappointing reviews, Vivian invites her MOOCmate to employ the discussion forums to collaborate with trusted peers, a recommendation that she suggests "might give you a more rounded idea of what you need to focus on when writing. You might want to tag your trusted reviewers and let them know when your piece is in the forum so that they can visit and give you feedback."

Participants in effect redesigned the discussion forums as alt-sites for peer review, extending and enriching our pedagogical intentions for the space. They resisted, in some ways, our "formulaic design strategies" (DiSalvo, Clement, & Pipek, 2012, p. 182) embedded in the WEx platform, employing the discussion forums, Facebook, and a Google+ community as additional platforms for peer review.

One of the unexpected aspects of the discussion forums was the development of the socio-emotional relationships (Rovai, 2007). The instructional team had thought of the discussion forums as primarily task-based and content-oriented spaces; participants would respond to the course content in the discussion forums as a way to practice the course concepts. It was expected participants would interact and learn collaboratively as they responded to each other's postings. The interpersonal relationships and community formation, however, were not initially considered to be primary goals of the discussion forums. Yet it rapidly became clear participants were using the discussion forums more often for the socio-emotional payoff and personal responses to their work rather than as a repository for their classroom activities.

This socio-emotional orientation continued through many of the discussion forums as participants began to share their course assignments and engage in more peer reviews than those required through WEx. In fact, it could be argued that the discussion forums functioned successfully as informal collaborative spaces for participants to exchange their writing and ideas, as opportunities to work through points of misunderstanding they sometimes encountered in conveying their ideas to others. In an optional forum related to Assignment 2, participants shared their assignment submissions as a way to crowd-source more peer feedback and encouragement.

After Felma posted her synthesis essay, she received feedback from other participants that complimented her writing style and suggested improvements to the title and the conclusion. But more important than the feedback on writing is the sense of community and personal attachment. Felma notes "my friends in coursera [sic] became my inspiration," and she thanks several participants including Kareen and Deusilene, who "patiently guided me in posting this stuff" and provided direction for her essay (Aguilan, 2013). Other participants chime in and offer their thanks to Felma for sharing her work and subsequently provide additional affirmation for her writing choices and elements of her assignment. The discussion is markedly different from the mandated peer reviews. Whereas the peer reviews through WEx rely on anonymous peers responding to a rubric, the submissions shared through the discussion forums emphasize the identity of the writer and provide more affirmation as opposed to critique. As Donna writes, "being part of this thread is like being part of a family" (Alexander, "Cut from the same cloth").

Throughout the course, we were surprised by the volume of the discussion forum posts and the rate at which participants produced thoughtful responses to their peers. However, the most surprising discovery was how participants took the discussion forums initially conceived as task-based learning opportunities and transformed them into fleshed out dialogues about the nature of peer review and anonymity that contained substantial socio-emotional investment. The participants desired more interpersonal contact, which was limited due to the massive course size and the online distribution, so they re-designed one of the common spaces in order to facilitate this personal experience. We also learned that, although as academics we privilege anonymous peer review, this is not necessarily the case for participants. In contrast to our experiences as writers and reviewers, the participants in "Rhetorical Composing" valued additional avenues for peer review that included personal identification. The desire for identification stemmed from a desire to make more connections; in a massive open online course, it's the moments of connection with another writer that participants valued as transformative learning experiences.

FRAMING ENGAGEMENT: DEVELOPING SKILLS, BUILDING COMMUNITIES

One noteworthy area impacted by the central tenets of participatory and universal design was the constellation of social media sites that orbited the MOOC. As we began to plan and build our inaugural run of "Rhetorical Composing," our impulse was to offer participants a variety of spaces where they could discuss problems, engage in knowledge exchange, and organically extend the lessons of the MOOC into their own conversations and writing processes. In addition to the discussion forums already mentioned, we established one officially sanctioned Google+ group ("Rhetorical Composing") for distributing information about office hours via Hangouts and other housekeeping matters and one designated Twitter hashtag (#WExMOOC) to pass along updates and promote course-related events. However, in spontaneous acts of participatory design, it was the learners themselves who set up and ran their own social media spaces.

In addition to additional private Google+ groups, many of our enrollees established Facebook groups and participated on Twitter, and several even kept their own blogs during their MOOC experience. Early in the course, learner-generated content began to emerge; the first participant post in "Rhetorical Composing" was a Google Map that plotted enrollees' locations all across the globe, and Russian participant Alina posted an encouraging video message to the rest of the enrollees that recounted her experience learning World Englishes. Far from a "If you build it, they will come" moment, it was clear our job was to let our learners do the building.

This fecundity of organic social media activity bore out the predictions made early on by Thomas Evans, our team's senior instructional designer and open courses coordinator, who advised us against over-building these sorts of spaces and instead allowing the learners to take the initiative. His advice was helpful because it enabled certain participatory design and universal design strategies that helped galvanize the group. Here, we heeded Robertson and Simonsen's advice to allow the people using particular technologies to shape them to their needs, thus empowering them to create a more durable sense of community, and ultimately to develop the spaces where learning best happens for the greatest number of people (Robertson & Simonsen, 2012, p. 2). Furthermore, making this move early helped set the tone for duration of the course.

The capacity for social media to empower learners through participatory and universal design principles was especially evident in the visual Public Service Announcement (PSA) assignment, one of three main composing assignments for the course. For this assignment, participants were asked to compose a PSA addressing a pressing social issue of their choice; participants could also choose from several suggested forms—posters, postcards, or thirty-second video/photo stories—or select other media and formats for their PSAs. As we designed the PSA assignment, we intentionally worked to incorporate UDL and PD practices by

BIKE TO WORK

Cycling is one of the most **cost efficient** modes up to five kilometres in urban transport.

The most **dominant** mode of passenger **transport** in the European Union is by **car.**

CAR TO WORK

Figure 7.1. Visual Public Service Announcement on Biking to Work, Produced by "Rhetorical Composing" MOOC Participant.

suggesting a range of media and genres for production, and a variety of methods/sites for sharing and discussing that work, moves that to some degree address all three UDL principles. Final products included a postcard urging people to ride bicycles to work (Figure 7.1), a poster promoting adoption, and short videos denouncing gun violence or warning viewers of the impact of ocean pollution.

These assignments were varied in terms of topic, purpose, and form, and presented conceptual and technical challenges for the learners. In addition, given several technical limitations on our end, participants had to store their PSAs off site at some designated hosting service— Dropbox, YouTube, Imgur, etc.—and provide a link to them in their WEx submissions. While we had initially established threads within the discussion forum to encourage more reflective talk about brainstorming, building concepts, sharing technical advice, and revising initial designs, a good bit of this activity spilled out into the various social media outlets, where the character of the conversations took on a decidedly different tone that reflected the potential of universal design.

Our expectation had been participants would use our Google+ and Twitter sites like they used the discussion forums. For the PSA assignment, the discussion forums became an adaptable space for participants to collaboratively solve the technical problems described earlier. "Can't get your video to show up in Dropbox? Here's how." "URL in WEx doesn't work? Send your PSA to me and I'll give you feedback."

The ways in which participants used social media tools developed a decidedly different tone. Over time, participants created their own social media sites connected to their participation in the course. For example, soon after we launched our Google+ group "Rhetorical Composing," a participant created her own Google+ group called "Rhetorically Inclined," a private site with only forty-five participants (Rhetorical Composing has 1275 members). Social networking through these sites facilitated technical problem solving; it also allowed writers to extend activities associated with the PSA assignment (brainstorming, critiquing, working on revision strategies, and so on) into more intimate spaces than the official discussion forums, thus facilitating greater degrees of engagement while allowing them more control in managing those conversations. In the "Rhetorical Composing" community, for instance, Craig Yager shared his video PSA on the importance of curtailing online activity (http://youtu.be/RS69hubXmHM), soliciting feedback from the community members (Figure 7.2).

Several comments on the piece complimented Craig on his approach to the topic, remarked on the effectiveness on the overall message, and also suggested technical revisions to the video. The comment thread supplemented what Craig would have received in the more formal WEx peer review platform, with the added benefits of being more relaxed in tone, and inviting more interaction between composer and reviewer.

In some cases, participants reinforced the philosophical underpinnings of our MOOC. Consider Marco Antonio's "The Unofficial WEx Victim's Guide to Peer Review" (Silva, 2013b): an animated short hosted on Vimeo and shared in our discussion forum and on several social media sites (http://vimeo.com/66921440). The tongue-in-cheek explanation of the peer review process actually explains the value of the process in much the same way that we envision it: peer review is a skill to be developed over time, and much of the value of the process lies in giving feedback as well as getting it. Marco's video presents this information in a more vernacular, playful, in-joke-laden manner than our "official" content, intentionally satirizing rhetorical concepts covered in the course (for instance, the "homeless guy" character's *ethos* is undercut by his consistently excellent advice to the viewer). Ultimately, user-generated content such as this extends the

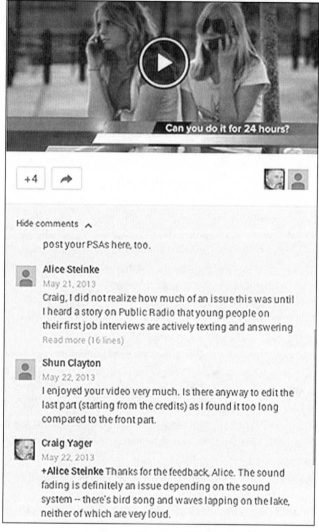

Figure 7.2. "Rhetorical Composing" MOOC Participants Share and Respond to Peers' Work in the Google+ Community.

"sanctioned" conversation of the MOOC by recasting core arguments about the importance of audience, context, and overall rhetorical awareness in the composing process.

Participants also produced projects that adopted the course as their subject in order to provide user feedback outside of the course sanctioned methods. The instructional team built the assignments intentionally open so that participants could adopt them to whatever their purpose or interest was. It was hoped that participants could make use of the general assignment requirements to produce a project that would be useful for their work or personal life. Most of the participants chose this option and created research-based projects on topics ranging from conservation efforts to the effects of social media. However, some participants chose to focus their assignment on the "Rhetorical Composing" MOOC itself and adopt the instructional team as its audience. Through this meta-level approach to the assignment, participants made a space for their thoughts and opinions to be heard in ways that would normally not fit in typical end-of-course evaluations.

In one assignment entitled "Week 7: Content Management Systems— The Good, The Bad, and the Ugly," Herbert identifies himself as a technical writer interested in Content Management Systems (CMS) and how they can be improved from the perspective of students, users, and designers. He analyzes what he considers the relative strengths, weaknesses, opportunities, and challenges of online CMS by focusing specifically on the OSU "Rhetorical Composing" MOOC. He values CMS such as "Rhetorical Composing" for its ability to bring "large bodies of the world's people [to] learn, [to] express themselves, and [to] share different cultural exchanges that a classroom could not provide; and [to] grow as human beings in a global environment" (Vaughn, 2013). Herbert then addresses the major issues with the MOOC experience: users will become frustrated by the oversights that are probably inevitable when designing an entirely online, immersive experience. He provides evidence for this frustration by quoting from other participant posts in the discussion forum—those noting unclear course requirements for certificates and the difficulty navigating through various links and modules in the course interface. Although Herbert does not provide any solutions for the design flaws, the value of his assignment to the instructional staff is immense. Essentially, Herbert's assignment functions as an unsolicited individual usability test. By pointing out specific issues with how the user interface prevented the overall goal of facilitating user interaction and learning experience, Herbert provided direct feedback to instructors about the functionality of the site usability, a topic not part of a typical end-of-course evaluation.

Another participant submission for Assignment Four responded to the central course concept of peer review. In the assignment "To the Rhetorical Composing Team, on to better peer reviews," Marco Antonio provides an analysis of the current flaws with the peer review system and offers research on ways to improve it. As a software engineer, Marco Antonio explicitly states the importance of listening to user response in his field and the desire to use this assignment as a way to help improve the system. He uses evidence from the discussion forums to suggest the complaints about the peer review system are perhaps surprisingly unrelated to technical issues, but focus more on the low quality of received peer reviews (Silva, 2013a).

Through an analysis of the posts, Marco Antonio concludes participants are frustrated not by peer reviews that demonstrate lack of effort, but rather the lack of consistency among received peer reviews. He offers calibration as a way to decrease the variance of the peer reviews. He also suggests improving *The WEx Guide* with more examples and feedback regarding the peer review process would help other participants provide more consistent results. As with the author of "Content Management Systems," Marco Antonio has identified a problem from the participant-user perspective—a problem the instructional team might not initially see as a cause of concern.

These two assignments stand out because of their effort to identify a problem with the "Rhetorical Composing" course and offer a solution to the instructors. By submitting these assignments to the discussion forums, the writers initiated participatory design of the assignments. The instructional team might have identified the peer review system and the user interface as areas in need of improvement for subsequent iterations of the MOOC. The participant-driven identification of and response to these issues, however, enables the instructional team to more effectively focus on providing meaningful solutions.

By the end of the course, it became clear providing our MOOC participants the leeway to problem solve, coordinate, and coalesce as a learning cohort using social media was the right course of action. The Freirean notion of joint responsibility in the pedagogical process thus ensures the types of engagement we hope to create in learning experiences. The participants' urge to find multiple outlets to promote and exercise the central goals of the course experience is strong, and one that we would do well to cultivate rather than suppress. Also, one interesting observation is the group's apparent willingness to engage in peer review of one another's work in social media groups without the safety afforded by anonymity. In these instances, there is a demonstrated need to want to connect on a personal level with fellow writers in some way, which raises important questions about the ethics of a blind, random review structure (George, 1984). Ultimately, these observations can help educators imagine ways of better using technologies that encourage robust back-channel activity.

CONCLUSION: (RE)FRAMING OUR UNDERSTANDING

Throughout our experience developing and teaching the "Rhetorical Composing" MOOC, we have come to a greater appreciation of how principles of Universal Design and Participatory Design can be applied to develop courses and enhance learning. Although we considered UDL principles as we developed the content for Rhetorical Composing, the participants showed us other arenas in which UDL principles can be effectively applied for the good of all. In addition, the participants' willingness to engage with the course content and design made them effective partners in how the course was run during the first and future iterations. Here are a few realizations that have been particularly noteworthy as we consider not only how we design and teach MOOCs but other distributions of courses including face-to-face and hybrid classes.

In terms of global Englishes, we have gained a deep appreciation of how much we needed to learn about teaching in instructional contexts characterized by world Englishes and how our insights from this study could improve our own courses, and our interactions with all writers whether we taught (Halasek et al., 2014). Rather than *tolerating* others who speak English as a second, third, or fourth language, we can *seek out* their first-hand expertise on specific English language-learning tactics that work well for contemporary learners—both online and, increasingly, in our classrooms. We can, further, develop our own willingness to model the open attitude toward linguistic experimentation and risk-taking, speaking specifically about the courage it takes to learn a new language and to practice it in public. And we can take the time, in every class, to speak about the different varieties of English that exist in the world and that are practiced daily. If we have English-language learners in our classes, these discussions will signal our appreciation of their efforts. If we have no such students in our classes, these discussions will serve to educate native English speakers about the necessity for an open and accepting attitude toward language learning in increasingly globalized, and often digital, communication contexts.

Although our research into the data on peer review is still in its infancy, we have affirmed our commitment to it as a pedagogical method. Participants came to value the anonymous peer review system because it fostered their own critical reading and reviewing skills. It allowed them a space to actively demonstrate their understanding of rhetorical concepts. In other words, the MOOC comprises for participants a kind of experimental rhetorical laboratory, a space wherein the often-hidden difficulties associated with conveying ideas to one another are made more transparent. However, we take the criticisms and suggestions of the participants seriously. We have also taken into account the partici-pants' responses to WEx and our approach to peer review. For example, we have added to the peer review process a "Reflection" on the peer reviews, a short (200–300 words) synthesis and revision plan that pre-cedes the assigning of "Helpfulness" scores. Slowing down the process at this point, we anticipate, will create more opportunities for authors to consider the value of individual reviews before assigning them scores. We are also revamping *The WEx Guide* and peer review content in order to provide more training on how to best engage in peer review. We still maintain the value of blind peer review. However, we shall also encour-age participants to use the discussion forums and social media as spaces for them to engage in personalized peer review in order to foster more socio-emotional connections. It is these lessons the participants in the "Rhetorical Composing" MOOC have challenged us to learn.

The experience of participant engagement with the course design and elements has also made the team desire continued feedback from participants. Subsequent iterations of the MOOC will include Com-munity Teaching Assistants (TA). These TAs will be former "Rhetorical Composing" participants involved in the design and implementation of the MOOC. The TAs will take an active part in the discussion forums by helping to foster the socio-emotional investment that so many of the participants searched for in the MOOC. They will also help us as the instructional team develop more effective activities and user inter-faces especially as related to peer review. We believe fostering ongoing conversations about pedagogy, course design, and rhetorical principles with former participants will benefit participants as we produce more accessible course materials and learning practices. And we as instructors will learn more about how to more effectively teach writing at both the massive, global and less-massive, local scale for all students.

Ultimately, designing and teaching the "Rhetorical Composing" MOOC has reaffirmed our commitment as an instructional team and individual teachers to universal design and participatory design prin-ciples. At nearly every turn during the MOOC, we found ourselves learning that "ideal of 'mutual learning', between 'users' [participants] and 'developers' [teachers] through common experiences" (DiSalvo et al., 2012, p. 189). Engaging UDL principles to make the course accessible for diverse modes of learning makes the course better for all participants and instructors—and engaging participatory design creates opportunities for dynamic redesign and learning for all.

Although we identified our pedagogy as student-centered, using participatory design principles has transformed our pedagogy from student-centered to student-built. We now recognize the value of engaging participants in continued dialogue regarding their experiences to create better learning experiences. By combining universal design and participatory design, by recognizing the ways in which our students are our best teachers, we believe that our changing pedagogy will be more effective, engaging, and transforming for all.

References

Aguilan, F. G. (2013, April). Cut from the same cloth. Message posted to https://class.co ursera.org/writing2-001/forum/thread?thread_id=2289

Barratt, L. (2014). Teaching the expanding universe of Englishes. In A. Mahboob & L. Barratt (Eds.), *Englishes in multilingual contexts* (pp. 99–113). Dordrecht, The Netherlands: Springer.

Bruffee, K. A. (1984). Collaborative learning and the 'conversation of mankind.' *College English, 46*(7), 635–652.

Canagarajah, A. S. (2007). The ecology of global English. *International Multilingual Research Journal, 1*(2), 89–100.

Canagarajah, A. S. (2013a). *Literacy as translingual practice: Between communities and classrooms.* London, England: Routledge.

Canagarajah, A. S. (2013b). *Translingual practice: Global Englishes and cosmopolitan relations.* London, England: Routledge.

Clinnin, K. (2014). Redefining the MOOC: Examining the multilingual and community potential of massive online courses. *Journal of Global Literacies, Technologies, and Emerging Pedagogies, 2*(3). Retrieved from http://joglep.com/index.php/archives/vo ulme-2-issue

DeWitt, S. L. (1988). Using teacher modeling to create good peer responders (Master's thesis). Normal, IL: Illinois State University.

DiSalvo, C., Clement, A., & Pipek, V. (2012). Participatory design for, with and by communities. In T. Robertson & J. Simonsen (Eds.), *Routledge international handbook of participatory design* (pp. 182–209). London, England: Routledge.

Flynn, E. A. (1984). Students as readers of their classmates' writing: Some implication for peer critiquing. *Writing Instructor, 3*(3), 120–128.

Flynn, E. A. (2011). Re-viewing peer review. *The Writing Instructor. Academic OneFile.* Retrieved from proxy.lib.ohio-state.edu/login?url=http://go.galegroup.com/ps/i.do ?p=AONE&sw=w&u=colu44332&v=2.1&id=GALE%7CA291179447&it=r&asid=edbd44 077cd41cd159002b925ad4cd40

Freire, P. (2003). *Pedagogy of the oppressed.* New York, NY: Continuum.

George, D. (1984). Working with peer groups in the composition classroom. *College Composition and Communication, 35*(3), 320–326.

Halasek, K., McCorkle, B., Selfe, C. L., DeWitt, S. L., Delagrange, S., Michaels, J., & Clinnin, K. (2014). A MOOC with a view: How MOOCs encourage us to reexamine pedagogical doxa. In S. D. Krause & C. Lowe (Eds.), *Invasion of the MOOCs: The promises and perils of massive open online courses* (pp. 156–166). Anderson, SC: Parlor Press.

Harker, M. (2009). *Common place: A citizen's guide to persuasion for an age that desperately needs one.* With S. L. Dewitt, & A. McKain. New York, NY: McGraw-Hill.

Jaschik, S., & Lederman, D. (Eds.). (2013). *The 2013 inside higher ed survey of faculty attitudes on technology.* Washington, DC: Inside Higher Ed and Gallup.

Karegianes, M. L., Pascarella, E. T., & Pflaum, S. W. (1980). The effects of peer editing on the writing proficiency of low achieving tenth grade students. *Journal of Educational Research, 73*(4), 203–207.

Kastra, J., Tollefson, N., & Gilbert, E. (1987). The effects of peer evaluation on attitude toward writing and writing fluency of ninth grade students. *Journal of Educational Research, 80*(3), 168–172.

Krause, S. (2013). MOOCs and webinars. Retrieved from http://stevendkrause.com /2013/01/26/moocs-and-webinars

Mahboob, A., & Barratt, L. (Eds.). (2014). *Englishes in multilingual contexts.* Dordrecht, The Netherlands: Springer.

Mahboob, A., & Dutcher, L. (2014). Dynamic approach to language proficiency—a model. In A. Mahboob & L. Barratt (Eds.), *Englishes in multilingual contexts* (pp. 117–136). Dordrecht, The Netherlands: Springer.

Mangelsdorf, K. (1992). Peer reviews in the ESL composition classroom: What do the students think? *English Language Teachers Journal, 46*(3), 274–284.

Matsuno, S. (2009). Self-, peer-, and teacher-assessments in japanese university EFL writing classrooms. *Language Testing, 26*(1), 75–100.

McCorkle, B., Halasek, K., Clinnin, K., & Selfe, C. L. (2016). Negotiating world Englishes in a writing-based MOOC. *Composition Studies, 44*(1), 53–71.

McTighe, J., & Wiggins, G. (2004). *Understanding by design: Professional development workbook.* Alexandria, VA: Association for Supervision and Curriculum Development.

Robertson, T., & Simonsen, J. (2012). Participatory design: An introduction. In J. Simonsen & T. Robertson (Eds.), *Routledge international handbook of participatory design* (pp. 1–14). London, England: Routledge.

Rovai, A. P. (2007). Facilitating online discussions effectively. *Internet and Higher Education, 10*(1), 77–88.

Sample, M. (2011a). Planning a class with backward design. *The Chronicle of Higher Education.* Retrieved from http://chronicle.com/blogs/profhacker/planning-a-class -with-backward-design/33625

Sample, M. (2011b). Teaching for enduring understanding. *The Chronicle of Higher Education.* Retrieved from http://chronicle.com/blogs/profhacker/teaching-for -enduring-understanding/35243

Sample, M. (2011c). Teaching for uncoverage rather than coverage. *The Chronicle of Higher Education.* Retrieved from http://chronicle.com/blogs/profhacker/teaching -for-uncoverage-rather-than-coverage/35459

Siluyanova, A. (2013, April 22). Englishes, Alina, Russia. *YouTube.* Retrieved from https://www.youtube.com/watch?v=lThuD1Ox0p8

Silva, M. A. A. (2013a, April). Brainstorming: A call to our instructors, on to better peer reviews. Message posted to https://class.coursera.org/writing2-001/forum/search ?q=Brainstorming%3A+A+call+to+our+instructors%2C+on+to+better+peer+reviews#20-s tate-query=Brainstorming%3A+A+call+to+our+instructors,+on+to+better+peer+reviews

Silva, M. A. A. (2013b, April). The unofficial WEx victim's guide to peer review. Retrieved from http://vimeo.com/66921440

Trimbur, J. (1989). Consensus and difference in collaborative learning. *College English, 51*(6), 602–616.

Vaughn, H. (2013, April). Week 7: Content management systems—The good, the bad, and the ugly. Message posted to https://class.coursera.org/writing2-001/forum/thr ead?thread_id=6310

Wiener, H. S. (1986). Collaborative learning in the classroom: A guide to evaluation. *College English, 42*(1), 52–61.

Zhu, W. (1995). Effects of training for peer response on students' comments and interaction. *Written Communication, 12*(4), 492–528.

8

"RESOURCES ARE POWER"
Writing across the Global Information Divide

Amber Engelson

ABSTRACT

The chapter explores how Indonesian scholars access written academic resources when confronted with the digital divide and increasing demands they publish in internationally indexed journals. The chapter highlights how these individuals negotiate the information divide through strategic literacy sponsorships and personal networking. In the process, they bring hard-to-access digital written resources to their Indonesian academic communities and help share Indonesian knowledge with non-Indonesian audiences. Despite this success, the author contends creating a global academic conversation where digital written information truly flows, we must examine how the information divide affects *all* written scholarship. The chapter therefore closes with ways the author approaches the politics of global academic writing in her U.S.-based classroom by reframing access as a digital and linguistic issue.

Keywords: digital divide, information divide, global literacies, access, open access, academic publishing, Indonesia, literacy sponsorship, global pedagogy

INTRODUCTION

The Internet and the English language have been lauded as great equalizers in our increasingly globally-connected world (Castells, 1996; Fishman, 1998; Fishman, Conrad, & Rubal-Lopez, 1996; Crystal, 2001). The argument claims as the Internet and a "neutral" global language helps information "flow" across national borders, the world becomes more equitable. In global written communication, these tools seem to present the possibility more voices might enter academic conversations. However, my ethnographic research at the English-medium Indonesian Consortium for Religious Studies (ICRS) shows publishing

DOI: 10.7330/9781607326649.c008

internationally in a developing country like Indonesia remains difficult because of economic inequality.

Equal access to English-language resources through online databases and even reliable Internet sources are privileges many writers in Indonesia do not have. Both, however, are both virtual pre-requisites to getting published by reputable "international" publishing houses. Tensions caused by this digital divide have been exacerbated by a governmental mandate Indonesian scholars publish in internationally indexed journals, most of which are in English (Canagarajah, 2002; Lillis & Curry, 2010)—a language many Indonesians have yet to master. The combined digital and linguistic divide[1] form what I term an "information divide," where written resources do not flow as freely as needed for global academic writing.

This information divide did not stop the scholars at ICRS from participating in global academic writing. The Indonesian writers with whom I worked engaged in informal and institutional networking to access digital academic resources. Such networking brought individual and systemic benefits to Indonesia: individually, it helped writers at ICRS enter the global digital academic conversation; systemically, it allowed ICRS to share access to digital written resources within Indonesia and beyond.

Raising awareness of the global information divide via "on-the-ground" research in the Global South[2] is an important first step in creating a more equitable digital written conversation; however, there are also pedagogical interventions instructors in the Global North might exercise to further raise awareness of the issue and even the playing field. Therefore, this chapter concludes with ways I foster an increased understanding of the politics of global written communication in my U.S. classrooms. By framing the global information divide as a phenomenon affecting *all* writers globally, I hope to cultivate writers who engage in academic writing in global contexts in effective and equitable ways. By linking global networks to local conversations through research and pedagogy, we can create a digital written conversation where academic resources more freely flow between the Global North and the Global South.

THEORIZING THE INFORMATION DIVIDE

Scholars such as Appadurai (1996), Ferguson (2006), Pennycook (2007), and Trimbur (2009) establish globalization as an unequal process. Globalization is, in Trimbur's words, a "contradictory and uneven process operating through transcultural localizations" (p. 113).[3] Thus, when one looks to the local, it becomes clear the notion of equitable global "flow" is problematic, for not everyone has equal social or economic footing within a society or across borders. In Ferguson's words,

As [. . .] contemporary [Africa] shows so vividly, the "global" does not flow, thereby connecting and watering contiguous spaces; it hops instead, efficiently connecting the enclaved points in the network, while excluding (with equal efficiency), the spaces that lie between the points. (Ferguson, 2006, p. 47)

Resources thus "hop" from one privileged enclave, or "technological gateway" (Hawisher, Selfe, Guo, & Liu, 2006), to another, leaving vast areas without access to the global information network. If one closely examines how the Internet and English are used—and by whom—the notion these resources are "neutral" tools available to all writers is challenged. Although some scholars have benefited, uneven access to digital and linguistic resources creates an information divide posing problems for many in terms of writing and publishing globally.

Locating the Digital Divide

Indeed, Grabill (2003), Pandey (2006), Ford (2007), and Ruecker (2012) have highlighted the "digital divide" operates within and between communities in developed and developing worlds. The digital divide—a "stratification in the access and use of the internet" (Ragnedda & Muschert, 2013, p. 1)—is caused by and can perpetuate existing inequalities "by giving increased prestige to those in position to use new technologies of communication." These *digital literati* can move "to create new opportunities to realize their goals in social, political, or economic spheres" (4). Digital access cannot be separated from existing power relations, and such factors have implications for writing practices and processes in these environments.

As my research highlights, to understand the role digital literati might play in perpetuating or challenging digital inequality, one must consider stratifications across national borders and within a country. For example, although over 53 million Indonesians have Internet access, this represents only 20.4 percent of the population, vs. the 88.5 percent reported to have online access in the United States ("Internet Live Stats," 2016). Given the role the Internet plays in disseminating academic knowledge, this inequality favors scholars in the Global North in academic publishing.

In Indonesia, Internet access is largely through mobile phones rather than traditional computer technology: as of 2011, ownership of mobile phones with Internet capability in Indonesia outnumbered desktop or laptop ownership by two to one ("Nielsen Report," 2011, p. 5). The number of Indonesians who can afford cell phones far outnumbers those who can afford computers. Yet accessing and reading web-based academic texts via cell phone is more difficult than on a computer, forcing less-privileged Indonesians to rely on Internet cafes, photocopy shops, or, for some, universities. The costs of academic databases, however, make full access to internationally indexed academic resources difficult (Canagarajah, 2002). These factors all have important implications for who can write and publish online and how.

Locating the Linguistic Divide

The increasing expectation scholars access contribute to international academic conversations via their writing exacerbates tensions caused by the digital divide. As Canagarajah (2002), Pedersen (2010), and Lillis and Curry (2010, 2015) have shown, and as Indonesian research indicates, to be considered credible academics, global scholars are increasingly required to publish in internationally indexed journals, most of which are in English. As Lillis and Curry (2010) explain:

> Because these high-status "international" journals are predominantly produced in Anglophone-center countries and are mainly published in the linguistic medium of English, in many academic disciplines English has become naturalized, that is, unquestioningly accepted as the primary language of publishing. (p. 3)

English's link to academic publishing reflects the Anglophone center's long monopoly on global publishing, and on what constitutes "publishable" knowledge and "good academic writing." Such linguistic imperialism, in conjunction with the digital divide, makes it more difficult for scholars in developing countries to enter the global academic conversation—creating what I term a global information divide.

Locating Agency

Despite the global information divide, scholars are quite savvy at maneuvering within this system to gain access. Hawisher, Selfe, Guo, and Liu (2006) apply the Chinese notion of *guanxi*, a Chinese term denoting a "complex set of social networks operating through personal connections" (p. 620), to highlight such agency. By exploring the literacy lives of a graduate student from Taiwan and one from China, they show these women's ability to navigate the "interdependent relationships between learning English(es) and learning digital literacies" (p. 620). Despite the "hegemonic" and "overlapping formations of globalization, informatization, and U.S. culture" that influence these women's literacy lives, the academic connections of their Taiwanese and Chinese parents and friends, or guanxi, helped both students study abroad and increase their digital literacy (p. 634). And with this digital literacy, they were able to "design and redesign" the literacy practices of the web (p. 632).

In addition to personal networking, Hawisher, Selfe, Guo, and Liu (2006) and Ruecker (2012) show how writers rely on more formal institutionalized networking—what Brandt (1998) terms *literacy sponsors*—to access resources. Literacy sponsors, according to Brandt, are "agents, local or distant, concrete or abstract, who enable, support, teach, model, as well as recruit, regulate, suppress, or withhold literacy—and gain advantage by it in some way" (p. 166). Literacy sponsorships are often in the economic best interests of the sponsor, but Brandt is careful to acknowledge the agency of those sponsored to "reroute" the sponsor's resources to forward "self-development and social change" (p. 166). She argues today's multiple and intersecting literacy sites and the complicated sponsoring networks that come with them, whether "secular, religious, bureaucratic, commercial [or] technological," open up avenues for the appropriation of resources for purposes sponsors might not originally intend (p. 166). Those with the economic means may have the power to implement their interests, but those sponsored can also appropriate the resources offered to benefit their own communities.

Such agency and the important role both guanxi and literacy sponsors play in helping scholars access resources was evident in the Indonesian literacy context where I conducted my research. When the digital literati there engaged in such networking, they were able to design and re-design global publishing practices to benefit their Indonesian community.

METHODS

An ethnographic approach, which involves moving "back-and-forth among historical, comparative, and current fieldwork sources" (Heath & Street, 2008, p. 33), was particularly suited to understanding this situated agency. Central to the scholarship outlined here is the notion one must understand literate acts as existing within a nexus of other activities, a literacy "ecology." In the words of Hawisher, Selfe, Guo, and Liu (2006):

> In both global and local contexts, the relationships among digital technologies, language, literacy, and an array of opportunities are complexly

structured and articulated within a constellation of existing social, cultural, economic, historical, and ideological factors that constitute a cultural ecology of literacy. (p. 619)

This ecological understanding of literacy requires a research approach that acknowledges the broader sociocultural context where writing acts are situated. An ethnographic orientation allowed me to do that.

Although only a portion of my research is presented here, my larger project involved a year of data collection during 2009–2010[4] and a subsequent follow-up study in 2014. In my initial project, I took an ethnographic approach to explore student writing practices as connected to their broader institutional and sociopolitical contexts. In the follow-up study I drew from this ethnographic data to focus more specifically on issues of access at ICRS—a process that lent itself to the specific case study data presented in this chapter. Overall, the following methods were used to gather the material presented here:

- *Text-based research:* on Indonesia's history and its sociolinguistic context, past and present
- *Observational research:* of sociolinguistic practices both at ICRS and in Yogyakarta
- *Program-related document collection:* of faculty handbooks, promotional brochures and other hard copy materials only available on-site
- *Semi-structured interviews with faculty and graduate research assistants:* about institutional history and global literacy sponsorships
- *Semi-structured interviews with Ph.D. students:* about students' individual literacy histories and writing practices, both in English and Indonesian
- *Teacher research:* on classroom conversations that happened as students took part in a year-long academic writing course I developed and taught
- *Analysis of students' written work:* from texts written in the course I developed and taught[5]

The mixed-method approach was an effective mechanism for studying global online writing practices. It helped me understand how global digital communication is mediated by real-world material circumstances and inequity. It also made visible how individual and institutional actors took agency and negotiated across the information divide to access digital written resources.

MAINTAINING "INTERNATIONAL STANDARDS OF ACADEMIC EXCELLENCE"

On my first day of teaching in Yogyakarta, Indonesia, I found myself negotiating numerous temporary street stalls lining the sidewalk. As I jumped back and forth between officially-sanctioned foot paths and the speeding traffic, twenty-four-hour "fotocopy" shop signs indicated I was getting close to the Indonesian Consortium for Religious Studies (ICRS), where I would be researching and teaching Ph.D.-level English writing. The signs pointed to numerous services, and were mostly in English: "Free Wi-fi," "Copy," "Print," "Scan," "Laminate," "E-book." As I peeked into these well-lit shops, I saw lines of Indonesian students waiting patiently for the giant photocopy machines to create their hardcopy and e-book academic texts—for a price much cheaper than the "official" versions available through publishing houses and bookstores.

This ethnographic anecdote is to emphasize the tactics many individuals in the developing world employ to engage in scholarly activities. Just as material circumstances forced me to move back and forth between where I was *supposed* to be as a pedestrian and where I *needed* to be to move forward, so too do material circumstances force Indonesians to negotiate between what they *should* do and what they *must* do to procure the written resources necessary to take part in global digital conversations. When it came to ICRS, this negotiation involved both informal guanxi networking and more formal engagements with literacy sponsors. Such networking was necessary to maintain ICRS's global programmatic identity and to negotiate a governmental policy requiring Indonesian scholars to publish in internationally indexed journals.

Maintaining Programmatic Standards

Bridging the information divide to engage in digital written communication across national borders is crucial to maintaining ICRS's programmatic identity. In their Mission Statement, ICRS self-identifies as an "Indonesian, International, Inter-Religious Studies Ph.D. program," a local-global institutional identity reflected in programmatic goals:

- To provide a setting for Ph.D. research on religions that is rooted in Indonesian culture and religious beliefs, but in dialog with the international community.
- To produce a Ph.D. program in Religious Studies that maintains international standards of academic excellence but is controlled and directed by Indonesian scholars.
- To promote North-South and South-South exchanges with good

universities in different parts of the world. ("Introducing ICRS-Yogya," 2009, p. 7)

These goals show a clear desire for ICRS to be rooted in Indonesia and run by Indonesians, but also connected to international academic conversations, a complicated identity when confronted with economic inequality and English's hegemony as global lingua franca.

Because of English's dominance, ICRS's founders chose to adopt it as its official language, a decision not without controversy, as evidenced in the program's Language Policy: "The decision to use English" the document explicitly states, "was painful to decide since we are aware of the imperialism of English" ("Language Policy," 2009). Painful or not, the majority of internationally indexed academic writing circulating globally in digital form *is* in English. As ICRS's director Siti Syamsiatun explained, "Most Religious Studies scholarship that takes an anthropological view of religion is published in English" (personal communication, July 11, 2014), a testament, as discussed previously, to the language's links to the economic power of the United States and Great Britain. In order to "maintain international standards of academic excellence," English is a must, particularly for those wishing to access internationally indexed written resources.

Maintaining Governmental Standards

Complicating matters, the Indonesian government also recently became interested in "maintaining international standards" in academic publishing. In 2012, the Indonesian Director General of Higher Education issued a mandate requiring all undergraduates, graduates, and faculty to publish their research before receiving their degrees or promotion (Sugiharto, 2012). Though undergraduate and M.A. students can submit their work to Indonesian-medium journals, both Ph.D. students and current faculty must publish in internationally indexed journals to receive their diplomas or to advance from lecturer to full professor positions (McAdams, 2012). The mandate caused a stir in academic communities across Indonesia, for it assumes all Indonesian scholars have the linguistic fluency to publish in internationally indexed journals—again, most of which are in English—and that Indonesians have the same access to academic resources that those working from more privileged countries do (McAdams, 2012).

Siti Syamsiatun, explained the linguistic pressure this mandate puts on her fellow faculty members in this way:

It's a big issue. Because many lecturers have already been serving in academia for 10–15 years, and they should have entered the rank of professor. But no, the government now makes the requirement that to become a professor, you have to hold a Ph.D. and to publish in international journals, which are mostly in English. Even though these lecturers have published a lot in Indonesian and are well-known locally. It's stressful, because many lecturers from my generation completed all their studies in Indonesian. And at the time there were few international programs in English so they were not reading and writing in English. (personal communication, July 7, 2014)

The majority of Indonesian faculty, however, do most of their research, writing, and thinking in Indonesian, which, as Sugiharto (2012) argues, puts them at a disadvantage when the government wants more of its universities to be labeled "world-class" by international (read: Western) standards. Returning to Ferguson's argument that global resources hop from one privileged enclave to the next, scholars at ICRS can be considered "privileged" when compared to other Indonesians because of ICRS's English-medium focus. However, given the digital divide, such privilege does not place them on equal footing with scholars writing in literacy contexts situated in the Global North.

Confrontations with the Global Information Divide

Even with linguistic access to global academic conversations, access to *recently* published resources remains uneven in Indonesia. The Ph.D. students with whom I worked were explicit about the role such material inequality played in their writing lives and how possibilities to publish in English were limited by available resources.

In a post-semester interview, one Ph.D. student, Roma, pointed to the limited number of current hard-copy English-medium texts available to him:

[I]n Indonesia many reference are 20 years old [. . .] Sometimes when Indonesians have new reference, they tend not to show it to colleagues, but for me myself, I take books from 2005 to 2009 to photocopy center to share [. . .] But some reject that idea. Because resources are power. And in higher education, if they hold the power for such a long time, it will give them power. So we can't add to a *real* Western academic conversation. (personal communication, May 14, 2010)

If resources are power, Roma sometimes feels powerless when faced with the global information divide. He is quite aware that citing new research is necessary when writing for a "real" academic conversation.

Even if recent hardcopy texts are not readily available, some might argue digital texts offer a solution. Another student's testimony, however, challenges the notion that digital access necessarily means equal access to academic scholarship. In a literacy narrative I assigned, Ninik drew from her experiences studying in Hawaii to explain how much easier "maintaining international standards" was in Hawaii because of better digital access. She explains: "Students in Hawaii are free to access library from anywhere as long as they have Internet access. Online journals can be downloaded freely by using students' ID [. . .] Internet is an essential tool that students are able to use anywhere with high speed." Ninik continues, writing that ICRS, despite "using international standards" and expecting students to "study the same as in the U.S." does not give her the "same opportunities" because of its "poor internet resources," which has made it "hard to adjust."

These students were not alone; others came to my office hours frustrated there were too few resources—digital or not—to engage in the type of research and writing they wanted to do. For example, one student wanted to research the role religion plays in the humane treatment of animals, but the only books she could find were through Amazon and the cost of buying and shipping them was prohibitive for someone who had a family and made $350 a month.

The stress involved with accessing resources was further complicated by the notion that more easily accessible scholarship written in Indonesian was less "credible" than sources in English. My students and I had multiple conversations about how such a belief was symptomatic of linguistic imperialism, but most student texts still ended up with a majority of English citations—a testament to the fact most Religious Studies scholarship is in English and to the power English-using scholars from the Global North have in defining "credible" research.

Resources *are* power; they dictate who can add to current global written conversations and what they can write about. When it comes to "maintaining international standards" in academic writing, scholars in the Global South are still subject to an information divide. Such inequity, however, did not stop the Indonesian scholars at ICRS from writing and researching. Rather, by cultivating individual and institutional relationships, scholars at ICRS successfully negotiated the global information divide, to the benefit of their own scholarship and their wider Indonesian community.

BRIDGING THE INFORMATION DIVIDE FROM THE GLOBAL SOUTH

Gaining access to global written conversations at ICRS involved multiple types of networking. Students were quite savvy at navigating more informal guanxi networks, but these networks were also made more readily available by institutional engagement with literacy sponsorships. Although a truly democratic digital written conversation is far from a reality, there *are* ways that scholars in the Global South can successfully access and spread global academic information to their local communities and vice versa.

Engaging with Guanxi Networks

One way students engaged with guanxi networking was by sharing university library logins garnered from Indonesian friends who had studied abroad or from international students or lecturers visiting from the Global North. Students repeatedly came to my office hours to get help accessing the *content* they would use in their texts. Together we would navigate my U.S. university's library website, locating and downloading peer-reviewed articles and e-books that might contribute to their scholarly work, not just for current assignments, but for the dissertation they anticipated writing in the future. These moments highlighted the luxury of easy, immediate access I had taken for granted in my own graduate studies.

That this sharing of the Global North's resources was technically "illegal" did not escape students' notice. During a literature review assignment, one student offered to share a university password he had received on a fellowship to the U.S. Rather than immediately accepting his offer, his peers first cautioned him against sharing it with too many people, fearing he might lose his privileges. After further discussion, they set up a spreadsheet where students chose a time they would use his password so simultaneous Indonesian logins wouldn't trigger the university's security system. These moments show the lengths to which students in the Global South will go to access information more readily available to students elsewhere.

For some, getting digital access to scholarly databases is a privilege requiring careful, tactical networking, among close peer groups. The fact the password sharing I observed at ICRS most often occurred in-person and between close acquaintances highlights the importance of guanxi networking in Indonesia; students seemed more comfortable doing something technically illegal when it could be construed as collaborative research among peers, as opposed to the type of anonymous illegal downloading sites like Sci-Hub offer.

Engaging with Literacy Sponsors

Such peer networking would have been difficult or not possible without institutional strategizing on ICRS's part. In fact, one of the reasons the program chose English as its official language was to connect to literacy sponsors in the Global North. The program was initially funded by a five-year $1 million grant from the U.S.-based Ford Foundation. Syamsiatun explained that the founders used the money to provide student tuition scholarships for "Indonesian, and other students from Asia and Africa" and to connect the program "to international student exchange programs" (personal communication, July 11, 2014). Initial funding has since been supplemented by the U.S.-based Henry Luce Foundation, which helps foster student exchanges. These exchanges are one way scholars working at ICRS can access the university passwords and current academic texts necessary to contribute to global written conversations.

ICRS does more than foster in-person knowledge-sharing; it has also begun building partnerships that make written resources digitally—and legally—available to Indonesians. In 2009, ICRS became part of an open-access project, Globethics.net: a legal, open-access, multilingual online library focused on sharing global research in ethics across the information divide. As their website explains, "the founding conviction of Globethics.net was that more equal access to knowledge resources in the field of applied ethics will enable persons and institutions from developing and transition economies to become more visible and audible in the global discourse on ethics" ("Portrait of Globethics.net," n.d.).

With funding help from sponsors in the Global North,[6] Globethics developed partnerships with academic institutions in Switzerland, China, India, East and Francophone Africa, Russia, Argentina, Turkey, and Indonesia, where ICRS directs its open-source Islamic Ethics library ("Annual report," 2015). These partners reach out to universities and libraries in their respective countries to gather resources to share across borders. A promotional brochure from the organization (notably, in English) explains: "*GIVE* your articles and books for *their* studies, research, teaching, decision-making, action; *TAKE their* articles and books for *your* studies, research, teaching, decision-making, action" (original emphasis, Your Offer; Your Benefit 2014). The free give-and-take has been successful. From 2012 to 2013, there was a growth of 32 percent in registered participants, from 71,411 to 94,322, and Indonesia had the second largest number of registered users, after India, with 15,034 participants ("Annual report," 2013, p. 4). Since 2013, Indonesia has taken the lead with 20, 875 registered users, with the total number of registered users jumping to 162,747. As of 2015, Globethics had made legally available, free-of-charge, 1,777,847 full-text articles and books; 41 special collections; 428 journals; and 478 reference works. Furthermore, each month an average of 30,000 written documents are downloaded from their database, up from 5,100 in 2013 ("Annual Report," 2013, p. 4; "Annual Report," 2015, pp. 4, 6).

With its involvement in Globethics, ICRS opens up legal digital access for Indonesians and for non-Indonesians who may not have access to published information written by Indonesians. Nina, the current program executive for ICRS's branch of Globethics, explains:

> The purpose of Globethics is to link South and North. To give free access to library for countries in the South. Because you know we have some difficulties to get resources. We don't have money, so that's why Globethics was started. And also so the North knows what's happening in the South. (personal communication, July 10, 2014)

She went on to explain how Globethics gives Indonesian scholars the chance to engage in digital writing practices meant to spread Indonesian knowledge abroad: "Every year, we have a peer-reviewed essay competition for Indonesian scholars to get published, so we hope that some [submissions] are in English, so the wider world knows more about Indonesia and Islamic ethics from an Indonesian perspective" (personal communication, July 10, 2014). Globethics has also funded and distributed two English-medium books with the help of ICRS: *Dealing with Diversity: Religion, Globalization, Violence, Gender and Disaster in Indonesia* (Adeney-Risokotta, 2014) and *Religion and Television in Indonesia: The Ethics Surrounding Dakwahtainment* (Sofjan & Hidayati, 2013). In these cases, the use of a global academic *lingua franca* creates bridges across the information divide, to the benefit of scholarship in the Global South *and* the Global North.

But submissions do not *need* to be written in English. Nina explained in the database, "Some of the articles are in English, but some also in Indonesian. It's multilingual, so many languages." Part of her job, in fact, is to contact researchers around the world to gather "resources related to Islamic ethics, whether in Indonesian, English or Arabic." She then "approaches small universities in rural areas far from Yogyakarta or Jakarta [more privileged educational epicenters] so they will post our link in their website. And they give information to their students that it's a free, online library that they can access at any time, anywhere you go. And many resources are [written] in Indonesian." The fact Globethics is multilingual is important to Nina because it allows non-English using Indonesians access to knowledge written in their home language: "so for Indonesians who don't understand English, they can just open the website in Indonesian language" (personal communication, July 10, 2014). Global access to academic resources is an economic and linguistic issue. By creating a multilingual website, Globethics encourages "flow": opening up digital access within Indonesia to institutions and scholars without the cultural capital English bestows.

Language is not the only impediment to full access within Indonesia; the digital divide still exists. As mentioned, the majority of Indonesians access the Internet through cell phones, a medium that does not allow for the easy reading of academic articles, whatever the language. According to Nina: "If we are lucky to have computer, maybe we don't need fast connection—so even if it's not a good connection, we still can download the document easily. But on the cell phone it is still a bit slow." Unequal access to the right technology, then, impedes the full and open exchange of knowledge. However, Globethics is working on this issue and, according to Nina, it should be "fixed" in the "next two years": "They are improving [the website] so you can open it through smart phones, because not many people have computers here. But smart phones, yes" (personal communication, July 10, 2014). Such local-global collaborations hold promise for bridging the information divide and revising digital interfaces to allow for more equal access.

It would be naive to argue multilingual open-access databases are the only answer to equalizing an academic publishing conversation connected to the economic interests of the Global North. However, the work these scholars are performing to bridge the global information divide is a step in the right direction. As my research shows, despite material disadvantages, the Indonesian scholars with whom I worked are capable of accessing knowledge withheld from the developing world through both personal and institutional networking.

BRIDGING THE INFORMATION DIVIDE FROM THE GLOBAL NORTH

One way to render obsolete the information divide affecting international writing is to make U.S. students aware of the politics involved with academic writing and publishing and with that, aware of how their own writing practices are subject to and implicated in the global information divide. To do so, I encourage monolingual American students to see themselves as implicated in this divide by defining "access" in both economic and linguistic terms.

From a global perspective, many U.S. students are subject to the linguistic divide because they are incapable of accessing resources in languages other than English. Though economic circumstances might privilege these "mainstream" students, when it comes to accessing written information across languages and national borders, they too are at a deficit. After all, as future scholars, business-people, editors at publishing houses, and so forth, the more information they can access from as many sources and languages as possible, the better—particularly in a world that is so rapidly globalizing. Reframing "access" as an issue affecting *all* scholars (to varying degrees) is one way to encourage a more equitable and open flow of resources from local to global and back again. I bring this belief to a first-year writing course I call "Writing Locally, Researching Globally."

Contextualizing the Global Information Divide

Because of its global focus, this first-year writing course attracts a mix of international and domestic, primarily monolingual students. Though some of the activities outlined here draw from the linguistic assets international and multilingual students bring to the conversation, I have found the sequence is just as beneficial to classes of mostly monolingual domestic students. To get students thinking globally about research and writing, we begin with an Edward Said video, "On Orientalism," where Said discusses the historical role that Western research practices have played in imperialist projects (Jhally, 2012). After discussing ways Orientalist "research" worked to justify colonization and the subjugation of people who had few official channels to "speak back," I assign students a chapter called "Uneven Internationalization" (2010) from UNESCO's *World Social Science Report: Knowledge Divides* (pp. 141–162). The chapter contemporizes Said's video with statistical data outlining the monopoly scholars in the Global North have in the academic publishing industry and the imperialist role English plays in maintaining that monopoly, often at the expense of other languages and perspectives from the Global South.

These texts give students a glimpse into issues highlighted by my Indonesian research: namely, academic research and publishing has long been tied to economic power and access, and thus privilege. The theoretical context prepares students to participate in activities that highlight the information divide more concretely.

Experiencing the Global Information Divide

To make economic resources and access related to writing more "real" to students—and to help introduce them to library-based research—we do an activity sequence that first removes and then restores students' privilege. After discussing research questions, we develop a sample question for the class to research at the library, where, in groups, they must find at least five pertinent sources. But there's one catch; they cannot use any digital resources.

What initially seems like a scavenger hunt becomes a chance for students to learn to navigate the research process using many of the same tactics my Indonesian students used. Encountering this temporary "digital divide," they are forced to physically move toward the sources they need in the library stacks. To do this successfully, they must draw on the embodied expertise of librarians. Through this human networking, they learn the library and they experience firsthand—in an admittedly small way—some of the challenges researchers and writers in the Global South experience on a daily basis. After this experience, we discuss their tactics for finding sources, the setbacks they faced, and what they think they missed out on because of the digital divide. We then return to "Uneven Internationalization" to connect the activity to global issues of access.

This activity helps frame a visit from the librarian, who introduces students to Academic Search Complete and the Directory of Open Access Journals (DOAJ), a database of peer-reviewed, multilingual journals indexed by country, language, and discipline, with 8,811 journals from 129 countries available.[7] To familiarize students with these databases—and to emphasize the differing perspectives they might gain from different resources and languages—we do a comparative activity. Where students are asked to devise another class research question and to do a search for relevant peer-reviewed articles, first with Academic Search Complete and then with DOAJ. (If there are fluent multilingual writers in the class, I ask they do the same search in their home languages if they feel comfortable doing so.)[8]

We then compare the top five results from each database, analyzing what disciplines sources come from, the languages they're in, and what country the researchers hail from. In the ensuing discussion, we note whose voices are most privileged in each database, upon ways students' own research might benefit from a global perspective, and importantly, upon the limitations of monolingualism. When confronted with the diverse linguistic resources their multilingual peers can access, monolingual American students face the reality they too are subject to the information divide because of linguistic limitations. After a final reflective writing activity that asks students to connect these hands-on activities to the issues of access discussed in Said's video and their assigned reading, students are prepared to begin planning their own local-global projects.

Bridging Local and Global

Students begin this planning process by drafting a research question on a topic of interest to them, and they use their new-found library abilities to create an Annotated Bibliography with ten to twelve peer-reviewed sources. In keeping with the "Writing Locally, Researching Globally" theme, four of these sources must be non-Western, either in English or another language, and taken from DOAJ to ensure that they're peer-reviewed. The requirement encourages students to draw from all of their linguistic resources and to imagine the academic conversations they're entering as truly global.

Once they've gathered this global research conversation, we do one more framing activity—a research proposal that satisfies moves typically seen in the genre. However, in keeping with the focus of the course, I also ask students to think globally about audience and rhetorical choices. To begin their proposal, I ask students to summarize the research conversation they've collected and explain how they plan to add their own ideas to this conversation. Then, I ask students to imagine writing for at least two academic audiences: to one in the United States and to one non-U.S. audience who might benefit from their research. After deciding on audiences, I ask students to answer the following questions for each:

- Why might you share your research with this audience?
- What sources will be most compelling to this audience, and why?
- What information about your topic can you assume they know, and thus can be excluded?
- What information do they need to know, and thus must be included?

After they've considered their options, I ask students to reflect on which audience they plan to write to, and why.

Not surprisingly, American students, whether multilingual or monolingual, often choose to write to an American audience because they are most comfortable with this context; at least they've imagined how they might share their research with non-American audiences in the future. If there are international students in the class, usually half choose to write to an American audience so they might add research they've translated from their home country's research articles to the research conversation here; for the same reasons, the other half chooses to share knowledge they've garnered from their American research with English-using audiences in their home countries.

Overall, this assignment encourages students to imagine research as a global endeavor—to think rhetorically and to link our discussions of open access and the politics of online global publishing to their own "local" projects. Armed with this global rhetorical awareness, an understanding of the politics of international publishing, and the secondary research they've done, students are prepared, in my mind, to write their local-global research papers.

CONCLUSION

These pedagogical activities highlight my belief all research should be framed as a translingual, global endeavor. As Canagarajah (2012), and Horner, NeCamp, and Donahue (2011) argue, we must encourage a fluid back-and-forth between languages in our classrooms and scholarship. Such translingual fluidity between languages suggests resources "flow" equally to all who choose to participate in global academic conversations. Research and writing must also be framed as a process tied to power relations privileging some scholars over others. As my Indonesian data shows, digital and linguistic divides still exist, prohibiting the full and free "flow" of information promised by the digital revolution and those who laud English as the great equalizer.

To bridge this divide, we in the Global North must help students examine their privilege and question assumptions about "credible research," where it comes from, and in what language(s). In a global information economy, the more voices spreading knowledge, the more knowledgeable we might become. And the more languages writers can access, the more information they can share across the language divide. Though classroom activities might seem a paltry way to challenge systemic academic inequality, they help. Indeed, many of the students with whom we work will go on to become the knowledge-creators of the future.

Perhaps our conversations about the global information divide will encourage these knowledge-creators to contribute their scholarship to open access journals. Perhaps our conversations about the benefits of multilingual research will help them challenge monolingualist educational policies in the future—or even encourage them to become multilingual English-users themselves (if they aren't already). And perhaps, with their understanding of the global politics of academic publishing, some of them, as future journal editors, will look with new eyes at the manuscripts submitted by scholars working in the Global South and see not "lazy scholarship" but a lack of resources if literature reviews don't mention the "newest" English-medium sources available. In short, I believe discussing the politics of publishing with our students can make a difference in helping global online written conversations truly "flow."

Notes

1. The term "linguistic divide" should not be equated with linguistic deficit. There are 418 distinct languages within the country, and most Indonesians speak Bahasa Indonesia, the national language, in addition to at least one local language, making the majority of the population multilingual (Lowenberg, 1992). The term "linguistic divide" merely refers to English access, or, in the case of many U.S.-based scholars, the monolingualism that puts them at a deficit when it comes to accessing global information in languages other than English.

2. In this chapter, the term "Global North" describes those regions that hold much of the world's socio-economic and political capital—namely, North America, Western Europe, and developed parts of East Asia. The term "Global South" is used to describe developing countries, most of which are located in the Southern Hemisphere.

3. Trimbur (2009) critiques both Pennycook and Appadurai for their continued use of the word "flow"; despite their use of this term, their *theoretical* frameworks do work to challenge the idea that with globalization resources flow equally to all.

4. I initially traveled to Indonesia in 2009 as a member of the U.S. Department of State English Language Fellows program, where I was asked to teach and develop curriculum at ICRS and to conduct English language teacher training throughout Indonesia; although my ethnographic research happened simultaneous to my duties as an English Language Fellow, it was in no way sponsored by the U.S. government.

5. Overall, nine Indonesian Ph.D. students and three faculty members chose to participate in my larger project. Given the power differentials inherent in teacher research—for instance, the possibility students' grades would be affected by their (non)participation in my research—obtaining informed consent for my 2009–2010 project was a multiple-step process. Obtaining permission to do teacher research involved the office manager distributing informed consent forms and keeping them locked away until final grades were submitted to ensure I was unaware of who had agreed to participate. Although still allowed to take notes, only information from those students who chose to participate could be included in my project. Obtaining consent for student writing activities was similar to that of the teacher journal. Although I could read student texts *as a teacher* throughout the course, *as a researcher,* I had to wait until the course was done before analyzing students' complete portfolios. And finally, all interviews were conducted after grades were posted to ensure students' participation (or non-participation) did not affect my assessment of their work in my class. Separate informed consent was obtained for the 2014 follow-up project and the process was much less involved because participants were no longer my students.s

6. The program partners with over two hundred sponsors. Some of their library partners include IFLA, Sage, Gale/Cengage Learning and others; some institutional partners include UNESCO, the World Council of Churches, the Swiss-based Linsi Foundation, and the UN Research Institute for Social Development.

7. I draw students' attention to http://Globethics.net as well, but given its focus on ethics and religion (something my first-year students rarely choose to write about), DOAJ is often more useful because of its broad journal base.

8. To avoid "othering" multilingual and/or international students, it is important to make this multilingual research optional.

References

Adeney-Risokotta, B. (Ed.). (2014). *Dealing with diversity: Religion globalization, violence, gender and disaster in Indonesia*. Geneva, Switzerland: Globethics.net.

Annual report. 2013. (2013). Brochure. Geneva, Switzerland: Globethics.net.

Annual report. 2015. (2015). Brochure. Geneva, Switzerland: Globethics.net.

Appadurai, A. (1996). *Modernity at large: Cultural dimensions of globalization*. Minneapolis, MN: University of Minnesota Press.

Brandt, D. (1998). Sponsors of literacy. *College Composition and Communication, 49*(2), 165–185. https://doi.org/10.2307/358929

Canagarajah, A. S. (2002). *A geopolitics of academic writing*. Pittsburgh, PA: University of Pittsburgh Press. https://doi.org/10.2307/j.ctt5hjn6c

Canagarajah, A. S. (2012). *Translingual practice: Global Englishes and cosmopolitan relations*. London, England: Taylor & Francis.

Castells, M. (1996). *The rise of the network society*. Malden, MA: Blackwell.

Crystal, D. (2001). *Language and the Internet*. Cambridge, England: Cambridge University Press. https://doi.org/10.1017/CBO9781139164771

Jhally, S. (Ed.). (2012, October 28). *Edward Said on orientalism*. Retrieved from https://www.youtube.com/watch?v=fVC8EYd_Z_g

Ferguson, J. (2006). *Global shadows: Africa in the neoliberal world order*. Durham, NC: Duke University Press. https://doi.org/10.1215/9780822387640

Fishman, J. (1998) The new linguistic order. *Foreign Policy, 113*, 26–40. https://doi.org/10.2307/1149230

Fishman, J., Conrad, A., & Rubal-Lopez, A. (Eds.). (1996). *Post-imperial English: Status change in former British and American colonies, 1940–1990*. New York, NY: Mouton de Gruyter. https://doi.org/10.1515/9783110872187

Ford, D. (2007). Technologizing Africa: On the bumpy information highway. *Computers and Composition, 24*(3), 302–316. https://doi.org/10.1016/j.compcom.2007.05.005

Grabill, J. (2003). On divides and interfaces: Access, class, and computers. *Computers and Composition, 20*(4), 455–472. https://doi.org/10.1016/j.compcom.2003.08.017

Hawisher, G., Selfe, C., Guo, Y., & Liu, L. (2006). Globalization and agency: Designing and redesigning the literacies of cyberspace. *College English, 68*(6), 619–636. https://doi.org/10.2307/25472179

Heath, S. B., & Street, B. V. (2008). *On ethnography: Approaches to language and literacy research*. New York, NY: Teachers College Press.

Horner, B., NeCamp, S., & Donahue, C. (2011). Toward a multilingual composition scholarship: From English only to a translingual norm. *College Composition and Communication, 63*(2), 269–300.

Internet Live Stats. (2016). *Real time statistics project*. Retrieved from http://www.inter netlivestats.com

Introducing ICRS-yogya: A portrait of an international graduate program in inter-religious studies. (2009). Brochure. Yogyakarta, Indonesia: Indonesian Consortium for Religious Studies.

Language Policy. (2009). *Faculty handbook: ICRS yogya*. Yogyakarta, Indonesia: Indonesian Consortium for Religious Studies.

Lillis, T., & Curry, M. J. (2010). *Academic writing in a global context: The politics and practices of publishing in English*. London, England: Routledge.

Lillis, T., & Curry, M. J. (2015). The politics of English, language and uptake: The case of international academic journal article reviews. *Association Internationale de Linguistique Appliquée Review, 28*(1), 127–150. DOI:10.1075/aila.28.06lil

Lowenberg, P. (1992). Language policy and language identity in Indonesia. *Journal of Asian Pacific Communication, 3*(1), 59–77.

McAdams, M. (2012, February 18). Quality in scholarly research in Indonesian universities. *Jakarta Post.* Retrieved from http://www.thejarkartapost.com

Neilsen Report. (2011). *The digital media habits and attitudes of southeast Asian consumers.* New York, NY: Nielsen.

Pandey, I. (2006). Literate lives across the digital divide. *Computers and Composition, 23*(2), 246–257. https://doi.org/10.1016/j.compcom.2006.02.004

Pedersen, A. (2010). Negotiating cultural identities through language: Academic English in Jordan. *College Composition and Communication, 62*(2), 283–310.

Pennycook, A. (2007). *Global Englishes and transcultural flows.* London, England: Routledge.

Portrait of Globethics.net. (n.d.). *Globethics.net.* Retrieved from http://www.globethics .net/web/ge/about-us/portrait

Ragnedda, M., & Muschert, G. W. (2013). *The digital divide: The Internet and social inequality in international perspective.* Retrieved from http://www.eblib.com

Ruecker, T. (2012). Exploring the digital divide on the U.S.-Mexico border through literacy narratives. *Computers and Composition, 29*(3), 239–253. https://doi.org/10.1016/j .compcom.2012.06.002

Sofjan, D., & Hidayati, M. (2013). *Religion and television in Indonesia: Ethics surrounding dakwahtainment.* Geneva, Switzerland: Globethics.net. Retrieved from http://www.glo bethics.net/documents/4289936/13403252/Focus_15_online.pdf/463705d0-c057 -435e-aeea-aab65ebd8488

Sugiharto, S. (2012, February 25). Imposing a publish or perish policy. *The Jakarta Post.* Retrieved from http://www.thejakartapost.com/news/2012/02/25/imposing-a-pub lish-or-perish-policy.html

Trimbur, J. (2009). English in a splintered metropolis: South Africa after apartheid. *Journal of Advanced Composition, 29*(1–2), 107–137.

Uneven Internationalization. (2010). *World social science report: Knowledge divides,* 143–162. Paris, France: UNESCO.

Your Offer; Your Benefit. (2014). Brochure. *Globethics.net.* Geneva, Switzerland: Globethics.net.

9

ACTIVITY THEORY, ACTOR-NETWORK THEORY, AND CULTURE IN THE TWENTY-FIRST CENTURY

Beau S. Pihlaja

ABSTRACT

The chapter examines how activity theory and actor-network theory can serve as analytical frameworks for researching culture and international communication. In this chapter, I demonstrate how to apply these frameworks to the intercultural encounter, and how instructors can use them as tools for teaching students to compose in intercultural contexts. Reflecting on the dynamics of online composition and technologically mediated knowledge work, these theories can be used in composition, analysis, and instruction.

Keywords: activity theory, actor-network theory, intercultural communication, intercultural competence, professional communication, technological mediation

INTRODUCTION

Contemporary knowledge work often involves technologically mediated, regular contact including sending verbal and written messages to people from other cultures (Cummings, 2011; Bridget Rabotin, 2014; Manning, Larsen, & Bharati, 2015; Manning, Larsen, & Kannothra, 2017; Society for Human Resource Management, 2012). From the intercultural encounter of call centers to an email sent between colleagues across borders and time zones, we are increasingly conveying information, intentions, arguments, etc. in interculturally networked environments. Those researching, writing, or preparing others to write in technologically mediated intercultural contexts need to manage a range of issues in this globally networked reality. Activity theory (AT) and actor-network theory (ANT) can serve as bases for addressing this new reality. Applied as frameworks for analyzing and tools for engaging

DOI: 10.7330/9781607326649.c009

technologically mediated interculturally networked situations, AT and ANT stabilize complex intercultural situations while accounting for the often unspoken cultural differences in such encounters.

After overviewing AT and ANT's approaches to conceptualizing activity, the chapter reflects on the difficulties of defining culture in terms of "operationalizing" each. These difficulties are illustrated by two comparable but discrete approaches to studying intercultural encounters: intercultural communication and intercultural communication competence. The chapter will then highlight how AT and ANT might be used to analyze the situation more fully and guide intercultural engagement. Finally, the chapter will present recommendations for how practitioners, theorists, and teachers of professional and technical writing in intercultural contexts might apply AT and ANT in these rhetorical encounters. The chapter then ends with suggestions for future research, pedagogy, and study of global communication.

LITERATURE REVIEW

Activity Theory/Actor-Network Theory[1]

AT, supplemented by ANT, can be an effective framework for analyzing written intercultural encounters. By accounting for the nexus of acting subject, tool, and object/objective in activity (AT) and by tracing the network of actors (sometimes inanimate) that constitute the context of many intercultural encounters (ANT) both approaches account for the complexity of such encounters while giving participants concrete and relatively stable points of focus amid that complexity. These points of focus help forestall the stereotyping of cultural others by directing focus away from mysterious, "internal" motivations of others and on the organizing function of the activities, goals, mediating tools, rules, etc. The focus both on the object/objective (AT) and on the "enrolling" function of actors (ANT) can set the groundwork for navigating a technologically mediated intercultural encounter. With these points of comparison in place AT and ANT's concrete application to writing in the intercultural encounter will be clearer.

Vygotsky (1978) proposed learning occurred in the interaction of the acting "subject" with tools and "mediating objects." These tools and mediating objects could be instruments or concepts, most significantly language. Imagine two individuals (Maria and Fatima) emailing one another at their company ProductCorp. Maria may be using a specific email software program on a particular computer or mobile device to compose the email and send it over a companywide intranet or across international or global telecommunications networks (tools) to Fatima. Both use genres of communication and that company's language of business (tools) that enable and constrain what can be said.

A. N. Leontev (2009) expanded AT by focusing on action and activity and by drawing attention to the object being created in activity and the objective toward which activity is conducted as a component of learning. In the previous example, Maria might be emailing Fatima about an issue with a circuit board, the product (the object/objective) they are both involved in creating. The circuit board about which the email is being written governs what can be said and how. Thus, what Maria and Fatima can say in their email is intimately bound up with the nature of the circuit board, their shared "object." Yrjö Engeström (1987, 1999, 2009) later combined the theories of Vygotsky and Leontev by expanding the "triangle" created by the concept of a subject in relation to tools (Vygotsky, 1978) and an object/ive (Leontev, 2009). The expansion included the "rules and norms" governing an activity, the "community" where the subject(s) find themselves when engaged in an activity, and a "division of labor" within the activity. The expansion of elements gave a fuller picture of an activity's context.

In our example, Maria and Fatima might have rules and norms for composing emails both handed down by ProductCorp (which might change over time) and their own training before or outside the company. There might also be rules and norms for ensuring a secure transmission of the information in the email that enable and constrain what Maria and Fatima write to one another. There might be a distinct division of labor determining how the individuals engage in the email itself and the object they are both part of developing. Perhaps, Maria is a supervisor and Fatima an engineer in a particular department. Finally, the "community" might be the same or different for both persons. They might be in a division of research and development. Or one might be in sales and another in production. Or they might inhabit distinct national, racial/ethnic, and linguistic communities. (Suppose Maria grew up speaking Spanish in Buenos Aires and Fatima Arabic in Yemen.) Both are women—a factor that brings a set of cultural expectations based in their communities, now also shaped by their role as knowledge workers for a global corporation. These dynamics will shape how they communicate about their shared object, the circuit board.

For AT to serve as a tool of analysis and to account for learning over time, one identifies "contradictions" in the AT system. Contradictions might occur in any of the mutual relationships established by the system. There might be a breakdown in how the subject uses a tool or how a tool impacts the subject's relationship to the community's rules. Identifying these contradictions enables the subject to learn and develop and, potentially, overcome these contradictions to complete the development of the object or meet the objective. In the example, perhaps Maria needs to show Fatima a schematic of the circuit board indicating precisely where the design is flawed, but is constrained by company-determined limits on what can be sent using the network. Security rules and norms might prevent individuals from sending confidential company designs on personal/mobile devices. Perhaps Maria is a supervisor in a different department and lacks the authority to make demands of Fatima.

Significant is the balance between simplicity and complexity in this conception of activity. AT orients focus on the goal-directed nature of activity and places at the fore the "object" and "objective" of that activity. Its concern with development over time might also account for culture change and increased cultural competence in an activity. Finally, its emphasis on the place in the system for the "tool" (both instrument and instrumental concept) is significant. The impact of tools (e.g., communication technologies) we call upon to act (e.g., write/compose) is often minimized/erased in intercultural encounters. On this point, ANT accounts for how tools might affect an acting subject and not simply serve as the instrument *of* the subject.

Bruno Latour (1993) argues, in the modern period, an entirely artificial conceptual split developed between "Nature" and "Society." Latour argues this split attempts to provide clean conceptual categories for addressing a complex and radically connected world where politics (which concerns society) and science (which concerns nature) do not play nicely methodologically. Rather, science is deeply implicated in our political life and vice versa. Latour's name for this connected-ness is "networked." Given this methodological approach, Latour's notion of the "network" encompasses "culture," and it can be analyzed in a similar fashion.

For Latour (2005), humans and non-human objects "enroll" one another in "assemblages," clusters of people and objects where "actors" or "actants" (themselves acting assemblages) use power and persuasion to do things. There are "mediators" who help actors transition and enact while transforming the action and the actor in the process. In addition, "intermediaries" help transition and enact things without changing the things they are transporting in and of themselves. Latour calls for sociology researchers to "follow the actors themselves" as they move through (what we used to call the "social") and track how they use mediators and intermediaries to build the social. This differs from AT as there is no assumption the "object" will organize any actor's activity. Indeed, it seemingly expands Leontev suggestion the object first "subordinates" the activity to itself and is not simply the goal toward which the "subject" the "real" actors are moving. It is itself a full-fledged "actor."

Rhetoric and writing studies and technical and professional communication have used AT and ANT as mechanisms for examining oral and written rhetorical activity such as analyze genres, student's writing practices and collaborative composition in online environments (Russell, 1997, 2009; Bazerman & Russell, 2003; Bazerman, 2003; Spinuzzi, 2003, 2008, 2011, 2014). Yet the precise relationship of AT and ANT remains a point of contention (see Spinuzzi, 2008). They overlap and concern themselves with similar dynamics. Moreover, there are several "generations" of AT. The third is the most fully theorized and useful, but some attention must be given to the emerging "fourth" generation that attempts to account for how multiple "organizations" (activity systems themselves) interact. According to Spinuzzi (2012) this fourth generation of AT "understands internetworked activities by examining the interorganizational collaborations to which they contribute" (p. 404). Given the complexity of multinational (and thereby intercultural) companies with their multiple divisions and hierarchies perhaps relying on other organizations (e.g., suppliers, responsive manufacturing providers, etc.) this fourth generation might prove promising for analyzing and intervening in technologically mediated intercultural encounters.

Defining and Operationalizing "Culture"

Ingrid Pillar (2009) notes a theoretical and definitional indeterminacy makes scholars hesitant to deploy the concept of "culture," and the conceptual muddiness at the outset hobbles studies of intercultural encounters. Even with clarity in defining culture, problems applying (i.e., "operationalizing") those definitions in concrete situations persists. Determining whether one is even in an "intercultural" encounter can be difficult as can which rhetorical choices to make when communicating with individuals from other cultures. Moreover, the research on culture and intercultural interaction can appear limitless.

Edward T. Hall's conception of "high-" and "low-" context cultures has been particularly significant for those studying communication and rhetoric. Hall (1976) conceived of cultural communication on a continuum from "high" to "low." Cultures that rely on implicit methods of sharing information (e.g., indirectness) are "high" on the continuum. Cultures that require a great deal of information to be stated explicitly are "low" on the continuum. Difficulty to apply in all situations, Hall's model of context can be particularly problematic in technologically mediated situations. While "silence" might communicate a great deal in a high context culture, it may not be possible to determine whether failure to reply to an email is a silence-that-communicates or the result of a disruption in the telecommunication network. Hall's conceptions of cultural communication is thus difficult to put "into practice" when technology mediates an encounter.

Geert Hofstede's (2001, 2010) work and the GLOBE study (House and Global Leadership and Organizational Behavior Effectiveness Research Program, 2004), which extended his work, are represent other influential approaches to culture. Hofstede's cultural "dimension" indices represent a tool for thinking through cultural difference and navigating intercultural encounters. The Power Distance index establishes the extent to which those with little power in a culture tolerate and accept the unequal distribution of power. The Uncertainty Avoidance index determines the extent to which a culture can tolerate ambiguity. Individualism vs. collectivism indicates whether people in a culture see themselves as independent individuals or as members of a group. Masculinity vs. femininity traces the extent to which a culture exhibits characteristic stereotypically ascribed to men (e.g., "competitiveness") or women (e.g., "caring"). Long-term orientation vs. short-term orientation describes whether a culture orients itself to traditions by honoring and keeping them (short-term) or by adapting pragmatically to circumstance when solving problems. Indulgence vs. restraint indicates whether on the whole a culture restrains the expression of human desires or is more tolerant toward their expression. Despite such specifics, it is unclear what steps individuals should take in an intercultural encounter based on scores in these dimensions.

In comparison to Hall and Hofstede, Clifford Geertz (1973) suggests "culture" includes "webs of significance [humans themselves have] spun" (p. 5). The notion of a culture as a "web" we "spin" adds a sense of agency and subjectivity. However unconsciously, we are participants in creating the meaning we convey in our culture. These complex and interconnecting significations can only be approached "interpretively" or "hermeneutically." Geertz's work is that of an anthropologist, carefully and consistently engaged in the search for cultural meaning making from both insider and outsider perspectives. But like Hofstede, Geertz's definition is difficult to operationalize. Workers have neither the time nor wherewithal to necessarily engage in deep ethnographic study in order to communicate, troubleshoot, and plan thoroughly with cultural others.

Instead, many people understand culture only in terms of difference. "Culture" is a boundary-defining concept, something that is intrinsically *not* something else. Arjun Appadurai (1996) suggests that the "cultural" be thought of as "only those differences that either express, or set the groundwork for, the mobilization of group identities" (p. 13). Appadurai focuses on interaction, the interplay of groups and individuals acting differently, and pinpoints specific sites of encounter between cultures. Like Hofstede, he is concerned with "dimensions" vs. static, conceptual "substances" (1996, pp. 12–13), and he concentrates on action and movement, what he calls "global cultural flows" (1996, p. 37). It is not, however, obvious how to convert Appadurai's conceptions into discrete actions, for like Geertz, he takes the stance of and calls upon the tools of an anthropologist, reflecting deeply and broadly on the "flow" of cultural signification, its meaning, its complex dynamics, and his approach provides no real framework(s) for analyzing individual intercultural encounters complicated by technological mediation.

Hall, Hofstede, Geertz, and Appadurai illustrate the expanding foci of studying culture and the intercultural encounter. They focus on the individual thinking cultural subject acting in probabilistic ways (Hall, Hofstede), the cultural subject's role in "weaving" a "web of meaning" (Geertz), and the significance of "difference" (correlated to group identity and activity) as the site of culture all while recognizing the broad powerful "flows" that circulate globally and shape/reshape any set of cultural practices (Appadurai). However, the difficulty in "operationalizing" these conceptions persists. Other approaches (e.g., intercultural communication and intercultural competence) take a different approach to addressing such issues, but they too have their limitations in comparison to what AT and ANT can offer.

Communication and Competence

The literature on intercultural encounters by rhetoricians and researchers in communication studies and in writing studies has flourished recently. Intercultural communication and intercultural competence as fields of academic study provide useful comparative frameworks for analyzing writing in the new globalized, networked context (Herrington, 2010; Rice & Hausrath, 2014). Writing is both communication and an activity in which we are seeking competence or effectiveness. Thus, both approaches serve as useful comparison points for AT and ANT (introduced above and discussed further below) as tools for researching and analyzing writing in the intercultural context.

Surveying the history of intercultural communication (IC) studies, Judith Martin, Thomas K. Nakayama, and Donal Carbaugh (2012) recognize two broad tendencies: an early "aparadigmatic" (transitioning to "functionalist") perspective in culture and a more "critical" or "interpretive" approach to the topic. They identify five modes of inquiry in the study of the intercultural: theoretical, descriptive, interpretive, comparative, and critical (Martin, Nakayama, & Carbaugh, 2012, pp. 25–26). These modes are concerned with practice (vs. abstractions) in culture (even in "theoretical inquiry," p. 25). IC studies thus tend to take a functionalist or practical approach to communicating between cultures. Communication is a matter of finding the right "codes" for transmitting what is already thought to be believed by the communication subjects. The persistence of "sophisticated stereotypes" in IC training (Sorrells, 2012) reveals even cautious approaches risk ossifying the perspective of cultural insiders while attempting to stabilize a cultural other to convey meaning to them.

Intercultural *competence* studies focus on measurable and teachable practices related to intercultural interaction. Brian Spitzberg and Gabrielle Changnon, acknowledging the complexity of the term "competence," cite core components as "motivation," "knowledge," and "skills," which also attend to "context" and "outcomes" (Spitzberg & Changnon, 2009, p. 7). They proceed to categorize models according to types (e.g., compositional, co-orientational, developmental, etc.). Whereas IC researchers are pre-occupied with discursive action in an intercultural encounter, intercultural competence models expand relevant components to include specific skills like "listening," "responsiveness," and dispositions such as "attentiveness" (see Spitzberg & Changnon, 2009, pp. 37–42). Most models are concerned with outcomes, goals for competencies achieved, and practiced in an intercultural encounter (e.g., "cohesion," "goal attainment," "appropriateness," etc.; see Spitzberg & Changnon, 2009, pp. 42–43). The concern distinguishes intercultural competence research from IC research with more focus on observable action and outcomes.

Intercultural competence theorists recognize part of success in an intercultural encounter is "positional awareness." Stella Ting-Toomey (2012) proposes one of the most significant components of "conflict competence" is "mindfulness" (p. 288). Other scholars note the importance of cultivating an awareness of our "global position" (Bennett, 2009; Pusch, 2009) and refining one's sensitivity to cultural difference (Pusch, 2009, pp. 73–74). Such awareness is crucial to achieving intercultural competence. Without a sense of one's "position" culturally and globally, making these competent rhetorical choices can prove impossible.

Despite explicit and sustained focus on action and outcomes in inter-cultural competence research/modeling, the action and desired outcomes are conceived very generally and independent of the action in the encoun-ter. "Effectiveness" and "adaptation" are non-specific. It is instructive that in the edited volumes that survey issues in both fields, abstract conceptual-izations of culture and "communication" and "competence" are addressed first with a separate section applying the concepts to particular contexts; see, for instance, *The Routledge Handbook of Language and Intercultural Communication* (Jackson, 2012), and *The Sage Handbook of Intercultural Competence* (Deardorff, 2009). The *Sage Handbook*, for example, has nine chapters dedicated to the application of intercultural competence theory to specific contexts. These include training in human resources (Storti, 2009), business (Moran, Youngdahl, & Moran, 2009), and social work (Fong, 2009). The *Routledge Handbook* takes a similar approach.

For all the increased concern to account for complexity in intercul-tural encounters and avoid stereotypes, the central metaphors of "com-munication" and "competence" are rather static. Models or theories rarely account concretely for the goals of an encounter. Rarely do they address the material circumstances in which goal-oriented activity is tak-ing place in an intercultural encounter. Therefore, "culture" could never be anything but an abstract concept precisely because what subjects are trying to do is also abstracted, encoded in metaphors for activity.

Culture, Writing Pedagogy, and Technological Mediation

Researchers are only beginning to address writing in technologically mediated intercultural encounters. Scholars who do often adapt previ-ous scholarship to the new situation. For example, R. Peter Hunsinger (2011) relies heavily upon Appadurai's (1996) five "-scapes" to guide technical communicators in the process of "localizing" their communi-cation for different contexts. In another example, Carol Barnum (2011) utilizes Hofstede's dimensions to analyze email communications.

Yet, researchers and educators in the fields of communication and rhetoric are still calling for and proposing methods for teaching stu-dents to cope in the new global environment (e.g., St.Amant, 2005; Davis, Chen, Peng, & Blewchamp, 2011; Rice & Hausrath, 2014). A relatively recent volume edited by Barry Thatcher and Kirk St.Amant curates the issues facing technical communication instructors from an intercultural rhetorical perspective and proposes "pedagogies and prac-tices" (Thatcher & St.Amant, 2011). A volume like this immediately clar-ifies whether a theoretical perspective (on culture, IC, or intercultural competence, for example) can be productively operationalized. In some cases, contributions assume definitions of culture in their pedagogical approach or are sidetracked by the definitional complexities of defining and concretizing the "cultural" and "intercultural." Charles Kostelnick (2011), for example, focuses on the broad theoretical potential of images to generally mean different things in different cultures. Others propose a comparative approach (e.g., by focusing on differences in rhetorical practice, see Padmanabhan, 2011). These examples, however, do not offer students, workers, or teachers a concrete framework for written engagement in a particular situation. The problem dovetails with the concern for how research is even supposed to be conducted.

Going Forward

To be fair, more "heuristic" notions of culture are also subject to critiques that having so expanded the definition, such heuristics encapsulate everything and thus nothing (recall Pillar's complaint). This is no less true when the concept of the "network" is applied to the concept of the socio-cultural (Thompson, 2003; Holton, 2005; Lynch & Rivers, 2015). While intercultural communication and competence studies struggle to provide sufficiently complex and active steps to evaluating and engaging the intercultural "other," one might argue AT and ANT render the technologically mediated intercultural encounter so complex as to make it equally difficult to engage and evaluate. Here it is the focus on *tool-mediated activity* that makes AT and ANT so valuable. The material conditions of communication and the study of contradictions and development over time in activity as well as regulating ANT to a supplementary role may prevent the approach from succumbing to the everything-and-therefore-nothing-is-cultural approach.

Given the proliferation of telecommunications technologies and the fact the "contact zones" (Pratt, 1991) in the modern world now happen online, IC and intercultural competence research must account for and contend with the material conditions in which any intercultural encounter is happening. Until recently there had been little discussion of tools or technologies shaping intercultural communication—other than to assume that they facilitate the intercultural encounter without changing it substantially. Scholars perceive this as an issue to address (Sorrells, 2012) and a site for expanding "competence" in IC (O'Dowd, 2012). In this context, AT and ANT can be applied to the technologically mediated written *intercultural* encounter in ways that avoid stereotyping, and focus on activity in productive ways for working in intercultural contexts.

THEORETICAL APPROACH
At/Ant and the Written Intercultural Encounter

Those who regularly study, encounter, or teach others to write in intercultural environments can use AT (supplemented by ANT) to "stabilize" intercultural encounters sufficiently to better navigate the encounter. AT and ANT are in the first instance tools of analysis. Tracing the elements identified in the systems (tools, objects, communities, etc.) stabilizes a complex activity where writing/composition occurs. Identifying contradictions in the system lays the groundwork for using the framework given by the system to negotiate solutions. Having introduced AT and ANT and provided a point of contrast between previous conceptions of culture and proposals for intercultural communication/competence skills, ways AT and ANT can serve as both modes of analysis and tool of engagement can be clearly stated.

Focus On "Activity" (Object, Objective)

Unique to AT is the organizing function of "activity." People interacting to do knowledge work across cultures are trying to *do* things, and writing is a crucial part of that activity. Foregrounding what we (individually or collectively) do is important when analyzing and making rhetorical writing choices in intercultural encounters. Failure to keep this in mind can cause confusion and frustration.

The first step in using AT to study and engage the intercultural encounter is identifying the subject(s) and the object/objective in the activity. Beginning with the observable activity of a perceived cultural other and attempting to identify the shared object and objective helps qualify a perpetual concern in human affairs with others' "intentions" (e.g., in written communication). We too often see the actions of others (e.g., word choices or sentence constructions in emails/IMs) as motivated by who they "are" based on some quality that is purportedly tells us why they do what they do ("people from group x" are y, etc.). Seeing action (e.g., choices in writing) as *within* a system of activity and not simply the product of an internal, cognitive "subject" resists stereotyping in a concrete way.

Running our analysis of any intercultural encounter through this framework allows us to conceive of the subject as making rational choices within activity. Applying this model moves the student of the intercultural encounter away from static binaries ("culture A" vs. "culture B") foregrounding the qualifications attached to Hofstede's theorization (i.e., no cultural dynamic score of a country necessarily applies to any individual from that country) or Geertz's notion of culture as a "web" (here provided more specific "content"). While any student of the intercultural encounter would concede the reality of individual differences within a "culture," AT keeps that individual-collective complex unified in the act of analysis. Analysis of this sort will aid those writing in technologically mediated intercultural environments (or those teaching them to do so) make effective rhetorical choices based on observations vs. guessing who their interlocutor "is."

Community, Division of Labor, Tools, and Rules

With the object and objective in view, those writing in intercultural digital spaces also look to the other components in the complex system in which all actors are embedded. A perpetual problem in an intercultural environment is how to relate the individual and the particular situation ("micro" perspective) to larger "cultural" ("macro") dynamics that shape individuals' action in a given situation. AT accounts for both in a single system. AT's subject is already situated in the larger "community" and "division of labor" within the system—preventing the encounter from reducing to two individuals simply "interacting" or "communicating."

Crucial to understand in an intercultural encounter is any subject can belong to multiple "communities." One is not just an "Indian" or "an employee at Microsoft." Different rules (implicit and explicit) govern our work than those that govern our family interactions. Yet either may impinge on the other in often invisible ways. Identifying who is expected to do what in an activity is thus useful for stabilizing an activity long enough to determine where expectations might not match or where exactly one might act in "culturally competent" ways.

Given the concern with tools in the system it is important to remember "tools" can be instruments we use to complete a task (e.g., a hammer to build a house, a computer to send an email). They can also be instrumental "concepts" that help us act in ways appropriate or beneficial to accomplishing our task or engaging our activity. A genre might be a conceptual used in an activity to accomplish goals. We know we have to adopt different writing conventions when conversing with a boss, a friend, a lover. The rules governing the use of these genres (conceptual tools) might change for any activity and depending on the community and division of labor. Identifying these components will be crucial for anyone engaged in an activity involving intercultural subjects.

The AT system strikes a balance between the multifaceted nature of human activity and simplifying any activity or encounter long enough to engage it critically and efficiently. Those attempting to make composition decisions (or teach others to do so) when writing in technologically mediated intercultural environments can use AT to stabilize their "rhetorical situation" and make more precise communicative choices. The next question becomes: What does one look for when plotting the intercultural encounter using AT?

AT and "Contradictions" (i.e., "Difference")

Tracing the AT system lays the groundwork for pinpointing contradictions, places where one element of the activity disrupts another due to a mismatch. For activities successfully accomplished over time despite contradictions, identifying contradictions can also reveal how they have been overcome historically. The wisdom of subjects is rendered visible by showing how they have coped, providing the basis for changing the rules, division of labor, tools, etc. to more effectively accomplish the activity. Here lies a potential use-value of AT for analysis and teaching composition in intercultural contexts.

In applying AT (and even ANT) we rely on prior perceptions of subjects in an intercultural encounter as a cultural other (whether or not these are "stereotypical"). Having identified the elements of an objective-directed activity, we can begin testing each element (through study or direct questioning) to determine where the breakdowns occur in the activity, testing if and what the "cultural differences" (perceived or actual) are. Here Appadurai's (1996) definition of the "cultural" helps analyze differences. Differences consistently used to "mobilize group identity" over time might be considered "cultural" (vs. the result of personality). Those writing and composing in digital spaces must remember everyone is embedded in multiple "communities" governed by various rules and hierarchies/divisions in labor impacting individual writing/communicative choices.

AT's awareness of communities, rules and norms, and the division of labor is one of its strengths that helps us coordinate the more "functional" approaches to culture (i.e., figuring out what people do differently so we can act or react "competently") and more "critical" approaches (i.e., recognizing the disparate and complex political, social, and economic forces that shape our activity and that cannot be ascribed to ideal conceptions of "culture"). Identifying the communities and different rules potentially at play gives writers in intercultural contexts concrete points of focus in complex and sometimes emotionally fraught circumstances. Indeed, one can use AT to focus "mindfulness" and cultivate an awareness of our "global position" when writing in an online environment.

ANT as Analytic Supplement

Latour's conception of ANT also illuminates the intercultural encounter. Recalling Spinuzzi's (2008) point ANT cannot really cope with "development" (p. 205), ANT will not necessarily help writers "accumulate" skills for engaging cultural others through time and amid changes to cultures themselves. Yet ANT might contribute in a supplementary way to analyzing the encounter with a cultural other.

Inanimate Objects as Actors

The main concern for ANT is "actors" engaged in a process of "enrolling" one another in "assemblages" of activity whose objects might not necessarily be shared. The conception is more anarchic than AT. Latour's dictum for ANT is "follow the actors." Whatever they do is what establishes a "network" of activity. What is most controversial about the theory is the ascription of "actor" status to non-humans, the principle of "symmetry." This attempt to make visible what is often rendered invisible in analysis of activity (or culture for that matter) is also what makes ANT potentially valuable.

While AT acknowledges a tool along with subject and other "nodes" constitutes an activity, ANT makes mutual impact a basic principle of the network of relations. One can start literally anywhere and trace how anything is essentially a "subject." As we attempt to cope with writing in a progressively more technologically mediated intercultural world, we need to ask questions about how the communication technologies are "acting" on us in determinative ways. The reduction of much "communication" to text, distributed across time zones (and therefore asynchronous) might be having a powerful impact, creating pressures on "cultures" in ways we have only begun to question. The reduction minimizes non-verbal cues, diminishes silence as a mode of communication, complicates informal elements of communication, etc.

While tools have always been a part of human interaction, they are becoming more significant as they shape global communication. Accounting for how the material conditions of writing (e.g., software interfaces, email/IM client interfaces, etc.) in the intercultural encounter shapes how we enroll and conscript one another by constraining compositional possibilities or providing unique affordances for composition is ever more important. If the telecom infrastructure for either actor is weak (e.g., in "underdeveloped" locales), this "acts" on the network, shaping when and how written messages (emails, texts) are received. Such messages, already distributed by time and space, are hard to compose and interpret. Any attempt to analyze or teach others to cope in such an encounter will need to account for these dynamics (see Walton, 2013). ANT serves as a means of drawing attention to the inanimate objects shaping intercultural interactions. As Spinuzzi (2015) suggests, adopting the perspective of "symmetry" is fundamentally a "methodological move" and even with things we think of as very "human—cognition and persuasion—it sometimes makes sense to take a symmetrical viewpoint in one's methods" (29). By opening our perspective to the non-human as actor, instructors of writing/composition can help render these inanimate objects visible to students as they prepare to write in networked intercultural contexts.

ANT and Rhetorical Power ("Enrolling")

This leads to ANT's second significant contribution: the emphasis it places on how actors are "enrolling"—"rhetorically persuading"—one another in a network. ANT reminds us we are not simply actors who pass messages back and forth ("communicate") or actors who simply perform appropriately (demonstrate "competence"). We are constantly attempting to get people to work in accordance with our desires. It is not enough to talk about "communication" or "competence" without reference to this persuasive dynamic. In discussions of intercultural communication or competence theory, it is often assumed people will want to "understand" or "learn from" or "behave appropriately with" their cultural other. ANT asks us to consider how we are doing more than this.

To draw the two concepts (inanimate "actors" and "enrolling") together, consider an email from a western academic to a potential project collaborator at a university in south Asia. The intention of sending the email is not simply to "communicate" (though certainly not less than that) or even compose in a way that demonstrates "competency" in western or south Asian email etiquette. It is to collaborate on a particular project, the parameters of which both actors might only vaguely understand as they send and receive emails. The goal of the sender is to "enroll" her colleague into the project that meets larger objectives (educational, professional, personal, etc.) that might not overlap for both parties. She seeks to convince her colleague to contribute and to go along with the project as she conceives of it; the colleague does the same with her. Studying the encounter requires more than an analysis of the messages sent back and forth in terms of "politeness" or language proficiency. Any analysis must account for the attempt to convince and convince within the material conditions that enframe the attempt. "Silence" in this exchange cannot be easily interpreted. Is it due to a misunderstanding? A failure in the communication infrastructure? As what is acting on these attempts to convince cannot be decided in advance, ANT, with its call to trace associations, should enter the "toolkit" of globally networked writers.

AT/ANT as Supplemented by Other ICC and Competence Models

AT and ANT are not self-sufficient tools for analyzing intercultural encounters. Together, they provide a way of describing, interpreting, comparing, and evaluating encounters. But the content of the dynamics to which AT and ANT draw our attention cannot be pre-defined, only observed in action over time. Thus, AT and ANT together provide a site for negotiating universal and particular cultural perspectives. Activity defined in these frameworks has elements that are universal, yet individuals will approach each element differently and thus constitute "culture."

AT and ANT therefore serve as tools allowing individuals to understand a situation by looking for dynamics and to pinpoint where contradictions appear. Accordingly, other tools of cultural analysis should be used to pinpoint the specifics of a culture-based contradiction. While individuals can map their own perspective of an activity and can articulate where the contradictions seem to happen, no one can move forward with a deeper analysis without specific knowledge and skills related to the particular context of their cultural other. The organizing structure of AT and ANT, however, help prevent reductive stereotyping tendencies to which we are all susceptible.

AT and ANT might function as a tool for supervisors and instructors for assessing intercultural competence in their technologically mediated written communication. These frameworks provide a vocabulary for assessing students' ability to identify and adapt to contradictions appearing in writing across cultures. Such ability is observable and might be a useful signal of an individual's intercultural competence related to composing online.

APPLICATION OF IDEAS

The ideas presented here are provisional and require further research. Here, I provide suggestions for further work and ways in which practitioners, theorists, and teachers of professional and technical communication might use AT and ANT in their writing, study, and teaching.

AT/ANT as Analytical Tools

Practitioners of professional and technical communication in intercultural environments can trace their compositional activity through the "nodes" of the AT framework. What is the object of the composition? What is the object's relationship to the larger objective, the institutional (or personal) purpose for which it is being composed? What rules govern this particular composition? Once the composition has been situated, individuals should notice contradictions in the system. For example, are responses to questions posed to other individuals in the community (departments, work teams, etc.) not making sense? Are colleagues perceived to be from "other cultures" responding in unexpected ways in relation to your perceived division of labor (e.g., acting above or below your understanding of the company hierarchy)?

Those professional and technical communicators whose composition is heavily mediated by technology (emails, IM, web designers, etc.) should step back from the framework and identify any component of their composing process—specifically the technological tools they use (laptops, phones, software programs, etc.) and trace how that element impacts the process. Specifically, look at how these tools influence, direct, and constrain the process of composing. If some rupture is occurring, identifying how the technology is contributing to that disruption should be clearly articulated. Having identified where contradictions occur and how actors and objects influence the process, composers in intercultural environments might call upon intercultural communication skills or competencies learned and begin probing what potential cultural values, practices, and beliefs might be causing them (e.g., are differing beliefs about power distance (Hofstede) shaping the encounter in the division of labor?). The AT and ANT frameworks can help stabilize the context in which these questions are asked and help prevent leaping to conclusions based on simplistic ideas about the other's culture.

AT/ANT as Research and Pedagogical Frameworks

Theorists of intercultural professional and technical communication can use AT and ANT frameworks to analyze activity, mapping the actions of subjects they are studying. They may ask: what can we understand about an act of composition when in this framework? Tracing contradictions within the different relationships will be the most helpful for stabilizing and framing intercultural encounters.

Teachers of professional and technical communication can use these frameworks as a pedagogical tool to help students stabilize the activity of composing in intercultural environments. Asking what the object and objective are comports well with rhetorical concerns for audience and exigency. Thinking about the tools they use and the ways tools shape the process can help students see where contradictions arise and how they might be overcome. The rules/norms, communities, and division of labor components of the AT framework are a good way to organize and qualify the usual training about cultures (perspectives on time, power, politeness, etc.). Here AT and ANT must not be considered replacements for IC and intercultural competence approaches in the writing classroom (e.g., St.Amant, 2005; Rice & Hausrath, 2014). Rather individuals might use AT and ANT to coordinate and organize those skills within a more explicit focus on activity as laid out by them.

The AT framework can also help develop rubrics for evaluating the intercultural competence of students in their composing. How well do students understand the purpose of their composition (e.g., its relationship to the objective of the activity)? How well are they able to see the ways telecommunications tools in particular are shaping and guiding their writing activity whether they realize it or not? In this way, AT and ANT can be especially helpful to instructors in professional and technical communication.

CONCLUSION

The chapter proposes two theoretical frames, Activity Theory (AT) and Actor-Network Theory (ANT), should be used as tools to study and learn in the international digital ecosystem. In this chapter, I proposed these theories be used as frameworks of analysis for researchers of culture and international communication. I demonstrate how they might be applied to the intercultural encounter and how they could serve as tools for instructors teaching students to compose in intercultural contexts. I also illustrated how these theories can be used in analysis, research, and instruction.

There are several ways in which the ideas proposed here might be extended:

- Theorists of intercultural encounters might explore how AT and ANT can be used as frameworks for studying encounters and engaging cultural others in those encounters. "Locating" culture in the AT system is difficult, while ANT works to productively complicate the notion of "culture" as stable category of analysis. Continuing to refine how we might talk about "culture" with these systems will improve their value for theorists and practitioners.

- Researchers must continue to explore how these frameworks of analysis and practice impact the technologically mediated composition process for knowledge workers who regularly communicate internationally. Specifically, the ANT notion of actors "enrolling" other actors, creating new and unpredictable (and unmanageable) networks, needs to be explored and expanded. Studying the role of inanimate objects in "acting" (per ANT) is also important. Further clarifying when and where such objects serve as intermediaries vs. mediators in intercultural encounters specifically will be especially important.

- Instructors of intercultural communication and competence should test the AT/ANT frameworks to see if they are useful for helping students to grasp the complexity of intercultural interaction. These theories also need to be tested to determine if they are easier to "operationalize" than the other models and theories.

We are still in the infancy of writing and composing within globally networked knowledge work. It is difficult to see precisely what will emerge in this new world of work. Activity theory and actor-network theory provide fruitful ways of coping with the emerging reality. Both offer concrete ways to cope with the tension between the universal and particular in intercultural encounters. Both draw into view the inanimate objects which facilitate our conveyance of ideas, arguments, and messages with cultural others in global context. And both theories account for change in systems over time (especially valuable given the constant change in cultures and technologies). As we move from our globally networked infancy to adulthood, these approaches provide technical and professional writers a way to grow.

Note

1.   I am grateful to my colleague Consuelo Salas who collaborated with me on a project completed for a seminar exploring AT/ANT in Fall 2013. Much of this section is drawn and summarized from that collaboration.

References

Appadurai, A. (1996). *Modernity at large: Cultural dimensions of globalization*. Minneapolis, MN: University of Minnesota Press.

Barnum, C. (2011). What we have here is a failure to communicate: How cultural factors affect online communication between east and west. In K. St.Amant & F. Sapienza (Eds.), *Culture, communication, and cyberspace: Rethinking technical communication for international online environments* (pp. 131–156). Amityville, NY: Baywood. https://doi.org/10.2190/CULC6

Bazerman, C. (2003). What is not institutionally visible does not count: The problem of making activity assessable, accountable, and plannable. In C. Bazerman & D. R. Russell (Eds.), *Writing selves, writing societies: Research from activity perspectives* (pp. 428–482). Fort Collins, CO: The WAC Clearinghouse.

Bazerman, C., & Russell, D. R. (Eds.). (2003). *Writing selves, writing societies: Research from activity perspectives*. Fort Collins, CO: The WAC Clearinghouse.

Bennett, J. M. (2009). Cultivating intercultural competence: A process perspective. In D. K. Deardorff (Eds.), *The sage handbook of intercultural competence* (pp. 121–140). Thousand Oaks, CA: Sage.

Bridget Rabotin, M. (2014). The intricate web connecting virtual teams. *T+D, 68*(4), 32–35.

Cummings, J. N. (2011). Geography is alive and well in virtual teams. *Communications of the ACM, 54*(8), 24–26. https://doi.org/10.1145/1978542.1978551

Davis, B., Chen, T., Peng, H., & Blewchamp, P. (2011). Meeting each other online: Corpus-based insights on preparing professional writers for international settings. In K. St.Amant & F. Sapienza (Eds.), *Culture, communication, and cyberspace: Rethinking technical communication for international online environments* (pp. 157–182). Amityville, NY: Baywood. https://doi.org/10.2190/CULC7

Deardorff, D. K. (Ed.). (2009). *The sage handbook of intercultural competence*. Thousand Oaks, CA: Sage.

Engeström, Y. (1987). *Learning by expanding: An activity-theoretical approach to developmental research*. Helsinki, Finland: Orienta-Konsultit Oy.

Engeström, Y. (1999). Activity theory and individual and social transformation. In Y. Engeström, R. Miettinen, & R.-L. Punamäki (Eds.), *Perspectives on activity theory* (pp. 19–38). New York, NY: Cambridge University Press. https://doi.org/10.1017/CBO 9780511812774.003

Engeström, Y. (2009). The future of activity theory: A rough draft. In A. Sannino, H. Daniels, & K. D. Gutiérrez (Eds.), *Learning and expanding with activity theory* (pp. 303–328). New York, NY: Cambridge University Press. https://doi.org/10.1017/CBO 9780511809989.020

Fong, R. (2009). Intercultural competence in social work: Culturally competent practice in social work. In D. K. Deardorff (Eds.), *The sage handbook of intercultural competence* (pp. 350–361). Thousand Oaks, CA: Sage.

Geertz, C. (1973). *The interpretation of cultures: Selected essays*. New York, NY: Basic Books.

Hall, E. T. (1976). *Beyond culture* (1st ed.). Garden City, NY: Anchor Press.

Herrington, T. K. (2010). Crossing global boundaries: Beyond intercultural communication. *Journal of Business and Technical Communication, 24*(4), 516–539. https://doi.org /10.1177/1050651910371303

Hofstede, G. H. (2001). *Culture's consequences: Comparing values, behaviors, institutions, and organizations across nations* (2nd ed.). Thousand Oaks, CA: Sage.

Hofstede, G. H. (2010). *Cultures and organizations: Software of the mind* (3rd ed.). New York, NY: McGraw-Hill.

Holton, R. J. (2005). Network discourses: Proliferation, critique and synthesis. *Global Networks, 5*(2), 209–215. https://doi.org/10.1111/j.1471-0374.2005.00115.x

House, R. J., & Global Leadership and Organizational Behavior Effectiveness Research Program (Eds.). (2004). *Culture, leadership, and organizations: The GLOBE study of 62 societies*. Thousand Oaks, CA: Sage.

Hunsinger, R. P. (2011). Using global contexts to localize online content for international audiences. In K. St.Amant & F. Sapienza (Eds.), *Culture, communication, and cyberspace: Rethinking technical communication for international online environments* (pp. 13–37). Amityville, NY: Baywood.

Jackson, J. (Ed.). (2012). *The Routledge handbook of language and intercultural communication*. New York, NY: Routledge.

Kostelnick, C. (2011). Seeing difference: Teaching intercultural communication through visual rhetoric. In B. Thatcher & K. St.Amant (Eds.), *Teaching intercultural rhetoric and technical communication: Theories, curriculum, pedagogies and practices* (pp. 31–48). Amityville, NY: Baywood. https://doi.org/10.2190/TIRC2

Latour, B. (1993). *We have never been modern* (C. Porter, Trans.) Cambridge, MA: Harvard University Press.

Latour, B. (2005). *Reassembling the social: An introduction to actor-network-theory.* Oxford, England: Oxford University Press.

Leontev, A. N. (2009). *Activity and consciousness.* Pacifica, CA: Marxist Internet Archive. Retrieved from https://marxistsfr.org/archive/leontev/works/activity-consciousness.pdf

Lynch, P., & Rivers, N. (2015). Introduction: Do you believe in rhetoric and composition? In P. Lynch & N. Rivers (Eds.), *Thinking with Bruno Latour in rhetoric and composition* (pp. 1–19). Carbondale, IL: Southern Illinois University Press.

Manning, S., Larsen, M. M., & Bharati, P. (2015). Global delivery models: The role of talent, speed and time zones in the global outsourcing industry. *Journal of International Business Studies, 46*(7), 850–877. https://doi.org/10.1057/jibs.2015.14

Manning, S., Larsen, M. M., & Kannothra, C. G. (2017). Global sourcing of business processes: History, effects, and future trends. In G. L. Clark , M. P. Feldman, M. S. Gertler, & D. Wojcik (Eds.), *The new Oxford handbook of economic geography.* Oxford, England: Oxford University Press.

Martin, J. N., Nakayama, T. K., & Carbaugh, D. (2012). The history and development of the study of intercultural communication and applied linguistics. In J. Jackson (Ed.), *The Routledge handbook of language and intercultural communication* (pp. 17–36). New York, NY: Routledge.

Moran, R. T., Youngdahl, W. E., & Moran, S. V. (2009). Intercultural competence in business: Leading global projects; Bridging the cultural and functional divide. In D. K. Deardorff (Eds.), *The Sage handbook of intercultural competence* (pp. 287–303). Thousand Oaks, CA: Sage.

O'Dowd, R. (2012). Intercultural communicative competence through telecollaboration. In J. Jackson (Ed.), *The Routledge handbook of language and intercultural communication* (pp. 340–356). New York, NY: Routledge.

Padmanabhan, P. (2011). Technical communication in India: Through the lens of intercultural rhetoric. In B. Thatcher & K. St.Amant (Eds.), *Teaching intercultural rhetoric and technical communication: Theories, curriculum, pedagogies and practices* (pp. 49–63). Amityville, NY: Baywood. https://doi.org/10.2190/TIRC3

Pillar, I. (2009). Intercultural communication: An overview. In D. K. Deardorff (Ed.), *The Sage handbook of intercultural competence* (pp. 3–18). Thousand Oaks, CA: Sage.

Pratt, M. L. (1991). Arts of the contact zone. *Profession, 33*–40.

Pusch, M. D. (2009). The interculturally competent global leader. In D. K. Deardorff (Ed.), *The Sage handbook of intercultural competence* (pp. 66–84). Thousand Oaks, CA: Sage.

Rice, R., & Hausrath, Z. (2014). The necessity of teaching intercultural communication competence in literacy classes. *Journal of College Literacy and Learning, 40,* 19–34.

Russell, D. R. (1997). Rethinking genre in school and society: An activity theory analysis. *Written Communication, 14*(4), 504–554. https://doi.org/10.1177/0741088397014004004

Russell, D. R. (2009). Uses of activity theory in written communication research. In A. Sannino, H. Daniels, & K. D. Gutiérrez (Eds.), *Learning and expanding with activity theory* (pp. 40–52). New York, NY: Cambridge University Press. https://doi.org/10.1017/CBO9780511809989.004

Society for Human Resource Management. (2012). *Virtual teams.* Retrieved from https://www.shrm.org/research/surveyfindings/articles/pages/virtualteams.aspx

Sorrells, K. (2012). Intercultural training in the global context. In J. Jackson (Ed.), *The Routledge handbook of language and intercultural communication* (pp. 372–389). New York, NY: Routledge.

Spinuzzi, C. (2003). *Tracing genres through organizations: A sociocultural approach to information design.* Cambridge, MA: The MIT Press.

Spinuzzi, C. (2008). *Network: Theorizing knowledge work in telecommunications* (1ˢᵗ ed.). Cambridge, England: Cambridge University Press. https://doi.org/10.1017/CBO978 0511509605

Spinuzzi, C. (2011). Losing by expanding: Corralling the runaway object. *Journal of Business and Technical Communication, 25*(4), 449–486. https://doi.org/10.1177 /1050651911411040

Spinuzzi, C. (2012). Working alone together: Coworking as emergent collaborative activity. *Journal of Business and Technical Communication, 26*(4), 399–441. https://doi.org /10.1177/1050651912444070

Spinuzzi, C. (2014). How nonemployer firms stage-manage ad hoc collaboration: An activity theory analysis. *Technical Communication Quarterly, 23*(2), 88–114. https://doi .org/10.1080/10572252.2013.797334

Spinuzzi, C. (2015). Symmetry as a methodological move. In P. Lynch & N. Rivers (Eds.), *Thinking with Bruno Latour in rhetoric and composition* (pp. 23–39). Carbondale, IL: Southern Illinois University Press.

Spitzberg, B. H., & Changnon, G. (2009). Conceptualizing intercultural competence. In D. K. Deardorff (Ed.), *The Sage handbook of intercultural competence* (pp. 2–52). Thousand Oaks, CA: Sage.

St.Amant, K. (2005). An online approach to teaching international outsourcing in technical communication classes. *Journal of Technical Writing and Communication, 35*(2), 191–201. https://doi.org/10.2190/H7MP-GJJH-1MHG-KPH6

Storti, C. (2009). Intercultural competence in human resources: Passing it on. In D. K. Deardorff (Eds.), *The Sage handbook of intercultural competence* (pp. 272–286). Thousand Oaks, CA: Sage.

Thatcher, B., & St.Amant, K. (Eds.). (2011). *Teaching intercultural rhetoric and technical communication: Theories, curriculum, pedagogies, and practices.* Amityville, NY: Baywood.

Thompson, G. (2003). *Between hierarchies and markets: The logic and limits of network forms of organization.* New York, NY: Oxford University Press. https://doi.org/10.1093/acprof :oso/9780198775270.001.0001

Ting-Toomey, S. (2012). Understanding intercultural conflict competence: Multiple theoretical insights. In J. Jackson (Ed.), *The Routledge handbook of language and intercultural communication* (pp. 279–295). New York, NY: Routledge.

Vygotsky, L. S. (1978). *Mind in society: The development of higher psychological processes.* M. Cole, V. John-Steiner, S. Scribner, & E. Souberman (Eds.). Cambridge, MA: Harvard University Press.

Walton, R. (2013) Bridges and barriers to development: Communication modes, media, and devices. *Kairos: A Journal of Rhetoric, Technology, and Pedagogy, 17*(3). Retrieved from http://kairos.technorhetoric.net/17.3/topoi/walton

10

EXAMINING DIGITAL COMPOSING PRACTICES IN AN INTERCULTURAL WRITING CLASS IN TURKEY
Empirical Data on Student Negotiations

Mª Pilar Milagros

ABSTRACT

The chapter presents part of a study on how intercultural students in an undergraduate "Writing for Social Sciences" course in Turkey use technology to compose multimodal assignments. To this end, the chapter reviews three types of materials: papers, presentations of multimodal assignment, and an exit interview with students. By examining these items, the author reveals how students position themselves in various identities (e.g., good student, assertive writer, or resisting-negotiating student) to secure different roles in the classroom context.

Keywords: borders, identity and power negotiations, intercultural writing, online communication technologies, resistance, rhetorical strategies

INTRODUCTION

In a world of continually emerging technologies, English communication and writing instructors must constantly reinvent their technological skills. As educators in second-language (L2) intercultural contexts, we—in turn—need to create classroom spaces where students can compose texts that engage in negotiations among personal and local identities while also acquiring certain global identity traits. Furthermore, such spaces must bridge connections between what students learn in the classroom and how they learn outside the classroom. As such, students need to learn how to balance between acquired knowledge and prior life experiences and knowledge when composing in such contexts (Greenhow, Robelia, & Hughes, 2009).

The chapter examines a border context between Europe and Asia with various cultures and ways of seeing the world. "Borders" in this

DOI: 10.7330/9781607326649.c010

chapter are not only geopolitical markers, but also metaphoric borders inside the classroom (Selfe & Selfe, 1994). Thus, this chapter addresses how to reexamine classroom borders and reconfigure them into more usable spaces, and it concludes that writing, to accomplish that, we should examine Pratt's (1991) concept of "contact zones," which she described as "social spaces where cultures meet, clash, and grapple with each other, often in contexts of highly asymmetrical relations of power" (p. 33). Pratt's concept is crucial because writing classrooms in intercultural contexts can become spaces in which negotiations and resistance may coexist with imitation and mimicry as writers attempt to learn how to communicate with global audiences while retaining some of their local identity traits.As such, the topics and ideas covered in this chapter are of significance to educators in writing studies because a review of such factors can provide a model writing instructors can use to help writers with intercultural backgrounds learn to communicate in our global community and negotiate border spaces in various ways.

In essence, the author of this chapter argues students in L2 composition contexts engage in negotiations of identities and power whenever provided within educational spaces that embody those opportunities. By advocating this point, the author first outlines online writing practices in the particular context of her research (the study presented here). Next, the author summarizes theories and frameworks that informed her research/this study. In so doing, the author identifies the methods she used to explore such relationships. The chapter then concludes with the author's presentation of the results of this project and a discussion of what these results mean for educators in writing studies.

EDUCATIONAL CONTEXTS

Much U.S.-based research in composition studies is focuses on models of instruction that expect students to be participatory in their own learning (Faigley, 1985; Bruffee, 1986; Brodkey, 1987; Guba & Lincoln, 1989; Bizzell, 1992; Eaton & Pougiales, 1993; Trimbur, 1994; Dann, 2002). In fact, current pedagogies in Rhetoric and Composition and related fields conceive education as "a coaching and enabling process" (Huot, 2002, p. 164), in which, according to McLoughlin and Lee (2010), "we need to "move towards a social and participatory pedagogy rather than one based on the acquisition of pre-packaged facts" (p. 31). Furthermore, with the Web 2.0 platform infiltrating the classroom (Greenhow, Robelia, & Hughes, 2009; Harmandaoglu, 2012; Karakulakoglu & Meric, 2012; Saka, 2015), the word "participatory" has also acquired different connotations. Overall, the idea is that students be viewed as more responsible for and participatory in their own learning "confront established social structures and relationships [and] are more inclusive, more egalitarian, more responsive to human needs, interests and satisfactions, and [are against] the cause of maintaining social arrangements that divide people radically along lines of success, status, wealth, and privilege" (Lankshear & Knobel, 2011, p. 86). Such a perspective is quite different from the educational context one encounters in Turkey (the location in which the reported on study takes place). For this reason, it is important readers understand theories based on social constructivism, although clearly valuable in Western contexts, may not be so pervasive in other contexts—as is the case in Turkey.

Turkey and the L2 Context

Turkey is often perceived as a traditional country with a teacher-centered educational system (Altun & Büyükduman, 2007). Here, the teacher is conceived as an authoritative figure who passes knowledge to passively receiving students, which resonates with Freire's (2000) concept of "banking education" (p. 72). Within this context, composition instructors need to be careful, for students need to feel there are choices they can make; otherwise, students might wrongly believe they have no power, or that they have become "consumers" rather than "producers" (de Certeau, 2002). Rather, as Anderson (2003) poses, we should equip "prosumers" "to participate in new media discourses empowers them to act in a world in which the knowledge currencies are increasingly digital." Our classrooms need to become spaces where borders between concepts and practices, such as written and visual texts (Trimbur, 2002), and notions of consumer and producer, among others, must be constantly negotiated and blurred.

To address such factors, second-language (L2) writing instructors could design courses choosing local content topics and incorporating activities that offer spaces where intercultural learners can incorporate their prior knowledge. Furthermore, by incorporating activities that use Web 2.0 as a platform, writing classroom might become spaces where "knowledge is decentralized, accessible, and co-constructed by and among a broad base of users" (Greenhow, Robelia, & Hughes, 2009, p. 247). Ultimately, L2 writing classrooms will become a place in which negotiations and resistance can happen. Resistance emerges as a crucial theme in this project and is informed by postcolonial feminist theorist Chandra Talpade Mohanty (2003), who defines it as "self-conscious engagement with dominant, normative discourses and representations and in the active creation of oppositional analytic and cultural spaces" (p. 148). If L2 writing classrooms truly welcome student negotiations, they can become places in which multiliteracies and intercultural identities are truly valued and pondered, and where students do not perceive that certain discourses, which may be at odds with some of their own cultural practices (Fox, 1994; Villanueva, 1993, 2001), are imposed on them.

Multiplicity in Educational Contexts
Researchers such as Şahin (2001) and Tezci and Gürol (2002) find a range of classes—including those with a more social-constructivist instructional design—are perceived quite positively by both instructors and students in Turkey (as reported by Altun & Büyükduman, 2007). When working in international contexts, rhetoric and composition instructors must therefore think in terms of multiplicity. In sum, even if students share cultural backgrounds or constitute heterogeneous groups, they might still present distinct differences that should be considered when teaching writing (Uysal, 2008, p. 193).

Such differences can result from a variety of factors. In a country like Turkey, where individuals must pass highly competitive university entrance exams, some students might consider "constructivist instructional design as "time consuming," "boring," "unnecessary," and "irrational" because they should devote most of their class time learning what they need to know to pass their exams (Altun & Büyükduman, 2007, p. 35). Conversely, students might think that instructors who deviate from practices associated with these objectives might be trying to assign more work to them (Sener, 2007, p. 7). Thus, understanding how students who have passed examinations value social-constructivist environments can benefit L2 writing educators, their students, and the local educational context. In such cases, to promote multicultural and intercultural educational contexts that value students' prior knowledge and experiences, "understanding how [L2 writers] participate in their new academic communities and acquire academic discourses in their second language (L2) has become critical" (Morita, 2004, p. 573). Thus, various pedagogical practices can be employed to accomplish that purpose.

Respecting and promoting multiliteracies and multiple identities is important in terms of whose knowledge counts as valid in educational settings. To help students in their academic lives and also in our global community, teachers should prompt them to acquire new academic discourse vocabularies (Faigley, 1985; Bruffee, 1986; Brodkey, 1987; Bizzell, 1992). However, as our global community continues to evolve, composition instructors should also try to teach academic discourses as flux rather than focusing on standard practices. They should additionally include discussions of local context and meanings into educational exchanges into such undertakings, for such ideas provide important lesson the field of English as a Lingua Franca (ELF) can teach us.

To this end, Sifakis and Bayyurt (2015) and Nelson (2011) argue educators need to understand and promote the idea there are multiple Englishes and students can learn to attain the social and cultural competence needed to communicate with global audiences. In fact, Nelson (2011) declares "[i]n thinking about [. . .] social and cultural competence, we come much closer to intelligibility, comprehensibility, and interpretability in the world Englishes framework" (p. 91). Likewise, Giroux and McLaren (1994) assert, to create truly liberatory classrooms, we should value students' personal voice and deconstruct the concept of "authoritative voice." Thus, we can help students understand that identity (as a student, a global citizen, a local citizen, etc) means "multiplicity" (Turkle, 1999, p. 647) and is a process vs. a stagnant entity.

RESEARCH METHODS

In truth, relatively little research has been done on how self-assessment and reflection in L2 online writing contexts might lead to student negotiations. To address this gap, I examined students' multimodal papers—artifacts created using all means of online technology available to students. I also conducted semi-structured exit interviews where students provided a self-assessment of their own work. In examining such factors, I sought to understand how students perceived and used technology when composing multimodal assignments and thus to answer two central research questions:

- Rhetorical strategies L2 writers employ to negotiate identity traits?
- Rhetorical strategies L2 writers employ to negotiate prior knowledge?

The answers to these questions could help address the afore-noted research gap.

Negotiations denote certain power dynamics; in fact, Min-Zhan Lu (1990) cautions composition instructors that we need to "remind ourselves and our students that there are both personal and social reasons for contesting and changing the very discourse they are trying to master"

(p. 20). Thus, students' strategies in utilizing technology are examined to understand whether discourse norms are contested and students demand more power and/or various roles in the classroom. Results are compared to Hofstede, Hofstede, and Minkov's (2010) "Cultural Dimensions," wherein Turkey scored a 66-point value under the category of power distance (p. 58), which he describes as "the extent to which the less powerful members of institutions and organizations within a country expect and accept that power is distributed unequally" (p. 61).

Research Site and Participants

In Turkey, students must pass the national university entrance exam (ÖSS in Turkish) to qualify for one of 450,000 available admission spaces available at Turkish universities. In the case of the author's home institution (reported on here), students must also take the TOEFL exam, and students who pass the TOEFL are required to take a course in "writing in the disciplines." For the study reported on here, that class was ACWR 104, "Writing for Social Sciences," and it consists of three parts:

1. A data paper for which students collect some data via surveys or observation and then represent that information visually

2. A remediation project where students propose a more creative mode to re-create their research results

3. A presentation of their "remediation" at the end of the semester

The data reported on in this chapter is from my Spring 2014 ACWR 104 class, which focused on controversial issues in visual communication.

In Spring 2014, I was assigned to teach a section of ACWR 104: Writing in the Social Sciences. In this class, students from across the university's social sciences majors are taught to write a proposal, a literature review, an argumentative essay, and a multimodal project. After obtaining IRB approval to conduct my case study, I introduced my project to the class, provided students with the consent form, and told them they could reread it and return it signed by the next class meeting. Out of the fifteen students registered for the class, seven signed the consent form; of the seven, one of had to cancel her exit interview. As a result, none of the documents written by that student has been included as part of the data because I could not triangulate my interpretations.

The information presented here is thus based upon data obtained from six participants, which attains what Maxwell (2005) would consider a *"purposeful selection"* quota (p. 88). The number of students is representative of the individuals involved in this class not only in terms of gender (there were five men and ten women at the beginning of the semester), but also of major area of study (psychology, media and visual arts, sociology, economics, international relations, history). The six participants are identified as Yoda, Furkan, Pink, Anthony, Selin, and Doğa, which are pseudonyms chosen by the participants.

Materials Collected for Analysis

For this project, the following materials were collected for analysis:

- *Data Paper:* Students had to draft a research paper based on collecting their own data to support a thesis. To this end, students choose to create a survey or conduct observational research associated with creating a multimodal product. For this project, students were required to present their research results in a visual form (table, figures, and so on).
- *Remediation Project:* Using instructor comments on the visual representation in their data papers, students they drafted a one-page proposal to recreate the visual representation via other modes, and this chapter reports on one of these alternatives (i.e., the remediation presentation).[1] This assignment was collected at the end of the semester and is multimodal because it combines aural, oral, and written modes.
- *Exit Interviews:* These included open-ended questions about online communication technologies and included questions asking students to define/interpret technology, asking them if and how technology has improved their writing skills and critical thinking skills, and asking about particular choices related to creating the multimodal assignments.

I analyzed data papers and remediation presentations to understand how technology and visual rhetoric affected students' composing practices. I then used data from exit interviews for triangulation purposes.

Research Models

I used three models to frame this study:

- Speech act theory (Searle, 1997; Searle, Kiefer, & Bierwisch, 1980), and language fundtions, such as "requesting clarification, thanking, evaluating, predicting, complaining, apologizing, and giving directives" (Nassaji & Cumming, 2000, p. 102)
- Ivanič's (1998) theories of writing and identity
- Maguire and Graves's (2001) research on rhetorical conventions, which informed my analysis with concepts such as genre conventions

Specifically, I drew on speech act theory to categorize students' rhetorical strategies while they used technology in general or discussed their choices with me during individual interviews. I then employed Ivanič's (1998) theories to categorize students' identity traits as they practiced reflection and self-assessment in the exit interviews. Finally, Maguire and Graves's (2001) research provided concepts such as "rhetorical conventions" (p. 565), which I applied to classify some of the identity traits inhabited by my ACWR 104 writers, namely that of "aware student" as students showed they knew what specific assignments expected of them.

Data Analysis

The three data sources described here were reviewed at different stages. I conducted a discourse analysis on students' data papers and remediation projects as soon as students completed each of these items. (I chose discourse analysis because language can be used to recreate power relations and discourse analysis can help uncover unequal power relations.) Through this application, I discovered certain, common patterns—namely, rhetorical strategies students used and their choices regarding technology and visual medium. Here, I equate "rhetorical strategies," such as promising, asserting, among others, to Searle, Kiefer, and Bierwisch's (1980) theories about speech acts as performing certain utterances. By using speech act theory to understand what communicative strategies students performed, I was able to understand what they wanted to express.

I then used Ivanič's theories to understand if students positioned themselves in different identity traits, such as self-as-author, or aware writer, in these projects. In so doing, I also observed Canagarajah's (2004) institutional roles, and, thus, identified various identity traits of a student: good student and resisting student/writer, among others. Overall, I found students employed a wide range of rhetorical strategies to inhabit or to perform different identity traits. Then, after analyzing students' documents, I interviewed students to triangulate my interpretations. Once the interviews were transcribed, I employed discourse analysis to identify rhetorical strategies students used to negotiate their own interpretations and various roles in the classroom.

RESULTS

As I analyzed these materials, I realized certain themes or identities kept repeating themselves. This section, in turn, presents my report on the most frequently inhabited identities observed in these L2 writers. These identities included

- Good student
- Resisting and/or negotiating student
- Aware student/writer
- Assertive student/writer

I defined these categories as follows:

- I interpret "good student" as an identity in which students have done what they perceive their instructor expects them to do. Students might inhabit that identity by using technology or explaining their choices as a space in which they inform their instructor that they have followed her advice; they could also thank her for the advice and guidance provided; third, students could also pose a need; finally, students could also show pride in how much they had accomplished in this class.
- At times, my students used technology and reflection spaces to position themselves as "resisting/negotiating student/writers." As such, students resisted or even negotiated certain assignments and genre expectations by either proposing alternatives or talking back to instructor.
- I use "aware student/writer" as a category to describe how students used technology, how they engaged the writing process, if they were aware of their limitations as writers among other issues related to conventions of writing in general and reflection as a genre in particular.
- The "assertive student/writer" identity reports on instances in which students positioned themselves as writers who, in spite of the fact that they sometimes struggled with organizing academic papers and even with English, they were also aware that they knew how to do certain things. Thus, these L2 writers were, at times, very assertive in what knowledge they already had before they registered for this class.

These factor thus serve as the mechanism/framework I use in discussing results in this section.

Data Papers

The first set of data comes from my analysis of data papers. Out of the six students who participated in the study, three conducted a survey and three used an observation protocol to collect data; their choice of a method was determined by their topic and purpose. In this data analysis section, students' experimentation with genre norms is investigated. Moreover, students' use of technology in general is also explored by identifying rhetorical strategies students used to position themselves in various identity traits as they incorporated visuals in their papers.

Results indicate that while students experimented with genre norms, they mostly inhabited the "good student" identity trait as they followed

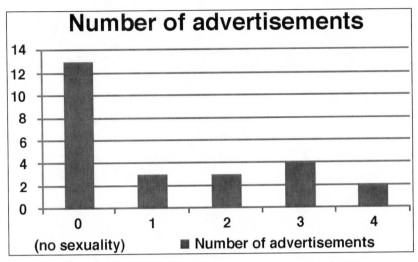

Figure 10.1. Yoda's Bar Graph Indicating Number of Adverts with Sexuality Content.

quite closely the sample paper examined in class. Namely, most of students' data papers had six sections: introduction, background, hypothesis, methodology, results, and conclusion. Two students also included a section on limitations of their study as the sample data paper I had shared in class.

In terms of students' selection of visuals to represent their data, their choices can be categorized in two main groups: some students showed resistance to some parts of the assignment, namely what kinds of visual images they should include, and, as such, the most commonly inhabited identity trait was that of a "resisting student." The second most commonly inhabited identity trait was thus "good student," as students followed the paper sample shared by instructor.

For "resisting" students, some of the figures and/or tables created by students were rather ineffective in terms of fulfilling assignment criteria: summarizing and representing results in visually enticing and clear ways. In Yoda's case (see Figure 10.1), one of her visuals was not very effective because the categories she was trying to represent were the same; namely, both the *x* and *y* axis show numbers, which was unclear to the audience.

Although Yoda attempted to explain the degree of sexuality content in ads at the bottom of the bar graph, she should have indicated that with explanations rather than numbers. Doǧa, who conducted a survey in which she asked participants to identify whether they identified themselves with a "TV famous figure" and the reasons why (see Figure 10.2), also created an ineffective visual in terms of labeling her categories.

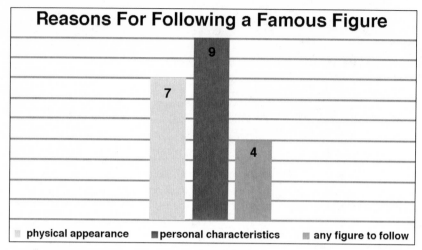

Figure 10.2. Doğa's Figure to Showcase Participant's Reasons for Following a Famous TV Figure.

In her visual, Doğa was trying to show the number of research participants who follow a famous figure on TV under each category. Whereas her first two categories, "due to physical appearance" and "personal characteristics," are clear, the gray category, "any figure to follow," is confusing and not necessarily related to the other categories.

Another category of ineffective visual representation showcases students using tables that are both unclear and too crowded (see Table 10.1). Three out of six students fall in this category.

Selin's data representation resembles the observational protocol she probably used for her fieldwork; however, she should have summarized those results in a more effective and enticing visual. Moreover, Selin does not identify what "data" stands for, and, thus, this visual is rather difficult to comprehend. Along the same lines, Anthony and Furkan also created tables that were congested with information that required too much contextual information to be effective.

There were, however, some students who understood and used technology quite effectively to represent their data visually. As such, those students inhabited the identity trait of "good student" as they followed the model the instructor shared with them. For example, Pink, used a visual (see Figure 10.3) which was clearer, visually speaking, to showcase surveyed women's opinions on Photo shopped images.

Pink's visual is much more effective because she clearly identifies the number of respondents under each clearly labeled category. Doğa also

Table 10.1. Selin's Representation of Instances of Categories in Each Video (Data).

	Passive Gender Role	Dehumanization	Sexual Objectification	Stereotypical Gender Size
Data-1	0	0	0	5
Data-2	0	0	0	5
Data-3	0	5	4	4
Data-4	5	0	5	4
Data-5	0	2	5	0
Data-6	5	0	2	2
Data-7	2	5	5	1
Data-8	5	4	3	3
Data-9	5	0	3	1
Data-10	4	0	5	3

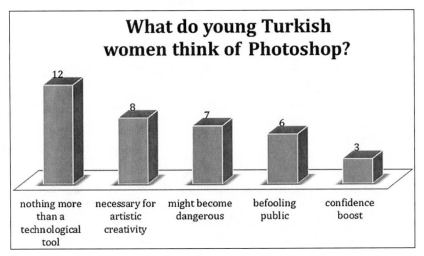

Figure 10.3. Pink's Bar Graph Showing Number of Participants under Each Attitude toward Photoshop.

managed to create a simple but clear table to show her data in terms of participants' perceptions of their own bodies (see Table 10.2). Doğa decided not to take unnecessary risks in that section of her data paper and, thus, she simply represented her data by identifying how many male and female participants spoke of their body satisfaction levels, which was one of the categories she examined in her data paper.

Table 10.2. Doğa's Representation of Participants' Responses in Terms of Relationship to Their Bodies.

	Happy with his/her body	Not happy with his/her body	Thinks his/her body has some defects but happy with it
Female	1	3	7
Male	4	3	2
Total	5	6	9

Remediation of Data Proposal

After receiving feedback from instructor, students wrote a remediation proposal to re-represent/remediate visual data. In that proposal, each student chose a more creative visual medium to represent their data. Out of the six students who participated in this case study, two chose Prezi, and four decided to use PowerPoint.

Yoda and Doğa chose Prezi as the creative mode to recreate/remediate their data paper. Overall, their remediation in general and use of Prezi technology in particular was rather successful, but their choice of medium is categorized under the identity trait of "good student" as students were trying to fit in what they may perceive was expected of them.

As for the students who chose Prezi, they inhabited the identity trait of "resisting student." Yoda's Prezi presentation mostly consisted of using short video clips that showcased the different roles in which women were represented on Turkish TV commercials. All of those video clips were in Turkish, so she had to translate them for me as I do not speak that language. Doğa, the other student who chose Prezi, was not so successful in presenting her ideas in more creative ways. Her data paper surveyed a number of adolescents who identified TV series they watched; then, the subjects rated if and how those series influenced their concept of beauty. Although Doğa included some images from the series her respondents identified, most of her remediation presentation simply regurgitated her paper (not what the assignment entailed). Consequently, these two students used a more creative medium to "resist" some of the assignment's criteria and expectations.

The other four students used PowerPoint presentations that were both visually effective and related to their project and/or topic. Figure 10.4 is an example of a poor choice to represent some visual data, including some typos. Selin was a particularly resisting student throughout the semester: overall, she never spell-checked her work, and in her remediation presentation, she simply repeated most of the information from the data paper (not what was called for in the assignment).

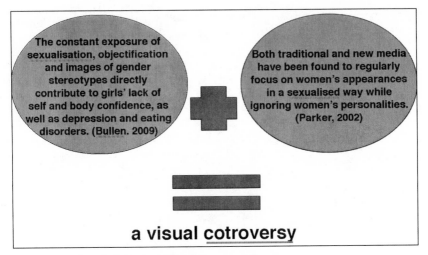

Figure 10.4. Selin's Definitions of "Visual Controversy."

Furkan and Selin used various enticing images, but it was not always clear how those images related to their topic and/or project. For example, Furkan conducted a survey in which he first asked his respondents to choose a definition of propaganda, and then showed them various images to understand whether they could identify those as propaganda. In his remediation, Furkan decided to use snapshots of his survey questions (see Figure 10.5) instead of adding bulleted lists; besides, he did not share any of the pictures from the survey to his audience.

Overall, Furkan insisted on using the same ineffective charts, which were crowded with information and difficult for the audience to understand. Similarly, Selin's PowerPoint presentation included all twenty images she showed her survey participants (see Figure 10.6). Generally, students' rhetorical choices show that students resisted certain practices and assignments.

Interviews

Six interviews were scheduled during the last week of class and after all remediation presentations had been delivered. Overall, the longest interview lasted forty-five minutes, but an average interview ran for thirty-five minutes. Interestingly, the interview with the participant who had the most developed English-language and media-literacy skills only lasted thirty minutes as she did not engage much with my questions. While I asked many questions in the interviews, only responses

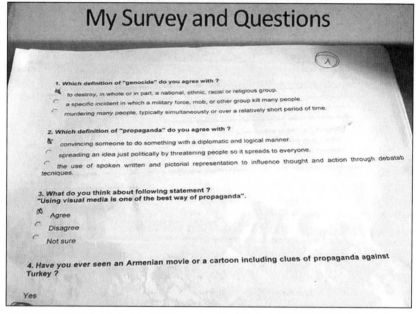

Figure 10.5. One of Furkan's Remediation Project Slides Showing a Snapshot of His Original Survey.

to the questions on specific technology use choices are analyzed in this section.

One key question asked students to identify what part of the multimodal project they were most proud of and to justify their answer. The question aimed to provide students with a space to engage in reflection and self-assessment so I could analyze their metalanguage. Interestingly, Anthony's presentation was not very effective in terms of content, but he disagreed with me, thus inhabiting the identity trait of a "resisting" student, as he refused to accept my interpretation/evaluation and offered plausible counter explanations and interpretations for his choices.

Another common positioning was that of "assertive (self-as-author)" student. Overall, four out of six students positioned themselves in this identity trait by making statements while reflecting on their work. For example, when I asked Anthony what he was most proud of, he used the rhetorical strategy of "making a statement": "It is the presentation of course because I planned it really carefully with the time challenge so, I really enjoyed presenting it because the topic is the only topic that I could talk hours, hours, and hours. It was so hard for me to talk only ten minutes. I planned very carefully and I really enjoyed that presentation" (personal communication, May 13, 2014). Doğa also thought

Figure 10.6. Selin's Remediation Presentation Pictures.

her remediation presentation was very effective because, "I really cared about it and I improved it [. . .] I think that using some videos and pictures from these series that I am examining. It really helped people to understand what I am really want to say" [*sic*] (personal communication,

May 15, 2014). Finally, Pink asserted her presentation was what she was most proud of:

> And I was like trying to give people another point of view about Photoshop and I think I kinda like managed to do it because I showed them what people were thinking like what people think they were thinking was actually different than what they were thinking. My images kinda like proved it because they were saying something and they were showing something else with these images so I was actually proud of that, of how it all came together. (Personal communication, May 15, 2014)

Another identity trait some of the students inhabited was that of a "good student." The most commonly used rhetorical strategy here was thanking instructor for her invaluable advice. Furkan, for example, asserted

> [m]y graph included as you know, only zero and one representation and I changed it into pie charts and I used three pie charts and you advise me that you should use a definition of a propaganda and give the answers to that question. And I showed the questions and with percentage pie, I told the percentage. (Personal communication, May 14, 2014)

When I informed him during his interview the particular pie chart he had referred to was inaccurate, he positioned himself as a good student again; as such, his rhetorical strategies were: apologizing for not having noticed that technical error before, and promising to be more careful in his next assignment. Doğa also inhabited the identity of a good student by asserting that she had followed my advice: "I improved some that you gave me like my graph was not good. I improved them, I changed them" (personal communication, May 15, 2014). Overall, students who positioned themselves as good students did not want to challenge or negotiate my interpretations and observations.

A final identity trait that was inhabited by students was that of "aware writer"; as such, students showed awareness of their limitations, or even genre expectations. The most frequently used rhetorical strategy was making a statement. Selin, for example, asserted "it was very difficult to prepare a data and a graph, doing a maybe a pie chart even maybe a easy pie chart was difficult for me" (personal communication, May 14, 2014). On the other hand, Doğa asserted "[r]acist things . . . I see them in the visuals also, and they are all around us. And I know how to see them in visuals and how to prevent to, not to be influenced by them because I am aware of them" (personal communication, May 15, 2014). Finally, Pink outlined genre expectations in her interview: "I think kind of like managed to sum it all up and to show people what I was trying to mean by choosing the topic and my hypothesis because I was really like convinced that Photoshop is not what people are trying to say it is" (personal communication, May 15, 2014).

DISCUSSION

The study reported on here contributes to current research on students' reflection and self-assessment in intercultural writing and second-language (L2) contexts by providing insights on how intercultural students in Turkey positioned themselves in various identities as they reflected on and negotiated their use of online communication technologies. One of my initial goals for this project was to understand how intercultural writers in an educational context deemed "traditional" use metalanguage to explain how they perceived and used technology to compose multimodal assignments.

From the results reported here, one might conclude this study has investigated how students moved from one identity to (an)other, thus engaging in authentic dialogue with their instructor to negotiate their technology use choices and strategies to compose multimodal assignments. The project has, consequently, explored the intersections between: (1) various identity traits, such as good student, resisting writer/student, assertive student, and aware student; and (2) intercultural writers' understanding and practice of reflection in assessing how successfully they have used technology in general to compose multimodal assignments and the impact of technology on their composing practices. The second intersection has been examined mainly via the exit interview, a space in which students could engage in self-assessment to foster dialogical exchanges with their instructor. Here, I coded students' metalanguage to categorize rhetorical strategies.

Overall, as the results reported here indicate students employ different rhetorical strategies to inhabit various identity traits. In fact, it might initially seem contradictory for the same student to perform the identity of a good student and a resisting student in the same assignment, but as Turkle (1999) asserts

> [t]he self no longer simply plays different roles in different settings [. . .] The windows metaphor suggests a distributed self that exists in many worlds and plays many roles at the same time. The "windows" enabled by a computer operating system support the metaphor, and cyberspace raises the experience to a higher power by translating the metaphor into a life experience of 'cycling through.' (p. 644)

Thus, it is important for rhetoric and composition scholars in L2 contexts to provide students with learning spaces where they can understand that acquiring some global identity traits is not at odds with maintaining their local identities. In a context such as the one described in this study, those spaces are crucial, for Turkish students from upper-middle class backgrounds tend to show acceptance of English as a medium of instruction (Doğançay-Aktuna & Kızıltepe, 2005), but students from different socio-economic classes might show some resistance to this practice.

Rhetorical Strategies and Identity Performance

As I started analyzing students' data papers to examine their use of technology, it was clear to me that students employed various rhetorical strategies to position themselves in various identity traits. To conceptualize this situation, I created a map of identities, which I then cross-analyzed with the interview transcripts. The identities I have identified here are "institutional roles" (Canagarajah, 2004), and focus on student identity features in particular because, after all, this research project focused on intercultural students enrolled in a writing class. Based on the results outlined in the previous section, the two most commonly inhabited identities were "good student," and "resisting/negotiating student," followed by a few instances of "self-as-author," and, at last, the least inhabited identity trait: "assertive writer."

Making statements was, by far, the most widely used rhetorical strategy for various identity positionings, and, thus, this analysis section starts by interpreting the reasons why. Many of the students in my classes have graduated from private high schools, have attended the in-house preparatory school for at least two semesters, and/or have traveled extensively to English-speaking countries. Consequently, they are very familiar with English-only institutions and certain "Western" pedagogical practices. For example, self-assessment and reflection may very well be deemed Western concepts, but, as English has become a lingua franca, many L2 writers from other countries are somehow familiarized with those two concepts as well as with some other academic literacy practices.

In addition to my intercultural writers' prior experience with English-speaking academic contexts, as participation in the discourse of self-assessment increased, students appropriated some of that language to show their instructor that they have learned some lessons they could apply in their writing. Consequently, as students gained more confidence in using metalanguage to describe their abilities, they seemed to shift toward the identity trait of "assertive writer." However, I do not wish to imply a cause-effect relationship between an increasing participation in self-assessment and a rise in writer's awareness. (I consider the relationship between rhetorical strategies usage and identity position-ings rather complex.)

As my intercultural writers made statements, they positioned them-selves as either "assertive writers" by speaking of their prior knowledge, or as "aware writers" by clearly explaining and understanding rhetorical conventions. Besides, during the interview, students also used "making statements" whenever they identified connections between what was being taught in the classroom and their prior experiences outside the classroom, thus exerting critical thinking. That yielded a very fascinat-ing finding in this project: students clearly engaged in conversations on and dialogue of identities. In most of the answers, except those classified under the "good student" identity trait, students seem to move from one identity to (an)other, which resonates with Turkle's (1995) theory of "identity as a set of roles that can be mixed and matched, whose diverse demands need to be negotiated" (p. 180). Providing intercultural writers with opportunities to reflect on their own writing can help them engage in dialogue with their instructor, which grants them opportunities to become intercultural global rhetors who can be prosumers of knowledge.

On the other hand, my intercultural students also used "making assessments" to portray themselves as aware technology users/tech-savvy students. It was fascinating to observe that students' responses were sometimes quite complex and even seemingly contradictory. As a researcher and an educator, it was fascinating to notice how these intercultural writers sometimes talked about themselves as being almost experts, especially in terms of technology use and of understanding the potential of technology. A plausible explanation for that would be that our students "have grown up in a technology saturated and an image-rich culture, questions of communication and composition absolutely will include the visual, not as attendant to the verbal but as complex communication intricately related to the world around them" (George, 2002, p. 32). Therefore, being exposed to and composing texts that combine visual, written, and aural media is second nature to them.

In spite of the fact that most students were rather assertive and even portrayed themselves as experts at times, some of them also portrayed themselves as "good students" during the interview. As such, students used the rhetorical strategies of agreeing with and praising/compli-menting the instructor because, after all, they may consider her the "authority" figure. Students switching from being assertive to compli-menting the instructor could be explained as a cultural influence due to the fact that this research project was conducted in a context that is considered traditional, educationally and culturally speaking. Another possible explanation for this seemingly contradictory finding—namely students did not want to share authority with the instructor while they also portrayed themselves as "aware writers" who knew how to do certain things prior to attending my class: could be that no identity trait is a clearly and distinctly separated from other traits. Quite on the contrary, I would assert that the fact that these L2 writers presented such a range of identity traits shows that our identities as writers are multiple, complex, and interconnected as Turkle, among others, have asserted.

A final compelling finding revolves around technology use. It was interesting to observe that, when given a chance to be creative, only two students used Prezi, which is more dynamic than PowerPoint, to remediate their data papers. A plausible explanation could be that, as an instructor, I used PowerPoint a few times in class, so students were positioning themselves as "good students" by following my model and acknowledging my authority figure. On the other hand, such finding could also be because, according to Said (2000), "[b]orders and barriers, which enclose us within the safety of familiar territory, can also become prisons, and are often defended beyond reason 'or necessity'" (p. 147). Students may not want to take unnecessary risks that may not meet requirement and course expectations.

Rhetorical Strategies, Technology, and Knowledge

Valuable conclusions can be inferred from students' answers during the exit interview as they positioned themselves in "resisting" and "negotiating student" identity traits. One of the most striking findings in this section stresses the fact that many students resisted my interpretations of their technology choices both in their data paper and remediation presentation. At first, I was shocked because I had assumed that, as a somewhat experienced educator, I knew the best learning method and path for my students. However, Furkan, Anthony, and Pink employed giving advice as a rhetorical strategy to position themselves as resisting students who demanded more in-class work on how to create effective multimodal assignments. Notwithstanding my initial reaction, I became a reflective practitioner and understood that students chose to position themselves as resisting students because they had truly embodied critical thinking.

Resistance was mostly practiced by either giving advice to instructor as to what could be improved or changed in the class, or by negotiating my interpretations. For example, many of the interviewed students affirmed they would have like to choose their own data collection research method. In general, I can conclude that resistance was a rhetorical strategy used to engage in negotiations. Thus, providing our students with opportunities to engage in reflection will help them "become prepared for and adapt themselves to the economic challenges of affiliation with globalization, the information society and the knowledge and skills they demand. In other words, they are in the process of negotiation on how to find a proper combination of local and global" (Koç, 2006, p. 41).

Another frequently inhabited identity trait was "assertive writer," which mostly appeared in the exit interview. As such, some students affirmed that technology had not helped them improve their critical thinking skills as they were already aware of its potential, and, thus, could already use technology critically before my class. I have used Bourdieu's concept of *tabula rasa* to make meaning of these intercultural writers' prior experiences and knowledge. I assert that students do not come to our classes as blank slates on which we can inscribe information; they already have certain knowledge that we, as writing instructors, should honor and respect.

In general, it was fascinating to observe that, when given the opportunity, intercultural writers did engage in negotiations of knowledge with their instructors by asserting that they already possess some knowledge that should be valued and incorporated in the classroom. Providing intercultural writers with these opportunities may mean that, at times, those writers may switch roles with their instructor in the sense that they knew what worked best for them. To me, identifying instances in which power dynamics were reversed was very illuminating. Although I am conscious of the fact that students' power may only apply to this particular context, the L2 writing classroom as a "linguistic habitus" (Bourdieu, 1991, p. 37), it was nonetheless inspiring to see how some of these intercultural writers were very assertive about their prior knowledge.

CONCLUSION

Composition and writing educators in intercultural contexts should create spaces in which we help students share their prior knowledge with their peers and their instructors. I believe it is in the creation of those spaces (third spaces, according to Homi Bhabha) that we will be able to accomplish what educational settings that are informed by social constructivism purport to do, which is encouraging students to be more participatory in and responsible for their own learning. Writing instructors working in intercultural environments should be flexible enough to accommodate those social constructivist theories that inform their pedagogies to fit students' needs in a given context. Although some research in Turkey has proven that certain student populations did find social constructivist instructional design useful, we cannot and should not assume that all social identities (different social classes and ethnicities, just to name two) may welcome those practices.

Composition instructors should strive to build spaces that combine two things: first, we should carefully design activities that use technology in general and online communication technologies in particular to engage students in knowledge consumption and production. Second, we should design activities that create spaces that promote reflection and negotiations. We should constantly attempt to equip our students with the tools to use, adopt, and adapt existing genres and conventions. By combining those tools and activities, our classrooms could become those alternative spaces in which our students could practice how to adopt and adapt to new and global literacies (Mills, 2011), and truly and meaningfully participate in ways that are not discriminatory to them and their own individualities. Finally, using online communication technologies in the classroom in ways that invite students to be more creative and critical will contribute to students' lives and life-long learning.

I would like to end with recommendations for future practice and research. The study has collected data from an instructor's class only. In the future, it would be beneficial to conduct a case study that examined different sections offered by various instructors. We could examine how online communication technologies are used across different sections of a class with a core curriculum to understand whether conclusions drawn in this chapter could also apply to other contexts.

Note

1. Per department requirements, students do not submit a written assignment, but are graded on the oral delivery of their remediation and on their use of creative mediums and visuals instead. For the purposes of this chapter, I wanted to utilize students' oral presentations; however, when I asked students if I could film them, most of them were not comfortable with that idea. In the end, I decided to include the actual multimodal product.

References

Altun, S., & Büyükduman, F. I. (2007). Teacher and student beliefs on constructivist instructional design: A case study. *Educational Sciences: Theory and Practice, 7*(1), 30–39. Retrieved from http://www.kuyeb.com/pdf/en/8453e471e716cb8385db98f35b86 1d8001_altun_eng.pdf

Anderson, D. (2003). Prosumer approaches to new media composition: Consumption and production in continuum. *Kairos: A Journal of Rhetoric, Technology, and Pedagogy, 8*(1). Retrieved from http://kairos.technorhetoric.net/8.1

Bizzell, P. (1992). *Academic discourse and critical consciousness.* Pittsburgh, PA: University of Pittsburgh Press.

Bourdieu, P. (1991). *Language and symbolic power.* Cambridge, MA: Harvard University Press.

Brodkey, L. (1987). Academic writing as social practice. Philadelphia, PA: Temple University Press.

Bruffee, K. (1986). Social construction, language, and the authority of knowledge: A bibliographical essay. *College English,* (48), 773–790. http://dx.doi.org/10.2307/376723

Canagarajah, A. S. (2004). Multilingual writers and the struggle for voice: Assessing some approaches. In A. Blackledge & A. Pavlenko (Eds.), *Negotiation of identities in multilingual contexts* (pp. 266–289). Clevedon, England: Multilingual Matters.

Dann, R. (2002). *Promoting assessment as learning.* London, England: Routledge.

de Certeau, M. (2002). *The practice of everyday life* (S. Rendall, Trans.). Berkeley, CA: University of California Press.

Doğançay-Aktuna, S., & Kızıltepe, Z. (2005). English in Turkey. *World Englishes, 24*(2), 253–265. https://doi.org/10.1111/j.1467-971X.2005.00408.x

Eaton, M., & Pougiales, R. (1993). Work, reflection, and community: Conditions that support writing self-evaluations. *New Directions for Teaching and Learning, 56,* 47–63.

Faigley, L. (1985). Nonacademic writing: The social perspective. In L. Odell & D. Goswami (Eds.), *Writing in nonacademic settings* (pp. 231–248). New York, NY: Guilford.

Fox, H. (1994). *Listening to the world: Cultural issues in academic writing.* Urbana, IL: National Council of Teachers of English.

Freire, P. (2000). *Pedagogy of the oppressed* (30th anniversary ed.; M. B. Ramos, Trans.). New York, NY: Continuum.

George, D. (2002). From analysis to design: Visual communication in the teaching of writing. *College Composition and Communication, 54*(1), 11–39. https://doi.org/10.2307/1512100

Giroux, H., & McLaren, P. (1994). *Between borders: Pedagogy and the politics of cultural studies.* New York, NY: Routledge.

Greenhow, C., Robelia, B., & Hughes, J. E. (2009). Learning, teaching, and scholarship in a digital age: Web 2.0 and classroom research: what path should we take now? *Educational Researcher, 38*(4), 246–259. https://doi.org/10.3102/0013189X09336671

Guba, E., & Lincoln, Y. S. (1989). *Fourth generation evaluation.* Thousand Oaks, CA: Sage.

Harmandaoglu, E. (2012). The use of Twitter in language learning and teaching. In A. Colibaba, M. Vlad, & C. Colibaba (Eds.), *Proceedings of the 5th edition of the conference "ICT for language learning."* Florence, Italy: Libreria Universitaria.

Hofstede, G., Hofstede, G. J., & Minkov, M. (2010). *Cultures and organizations: Software of the mind* (3rd ed.). New York, NY: McGraw-Hill.

Huot, B. (2002). Toward a new discourse of assessment for the college writing classroom. *College English, 65*(2), 163–180. doi:10.2307/3250761

Ivanič, R. (1998). *Writing and identity: The discoursal construction of identity in academic writing.* Philadelphia, PA: Benjamins. https://doi.org/10.1075/swll.5

Karakulakoglu, S. E., & Meric, O. (2012). How and why do Turkish scholars use social networking platforms? In A. Tokar, M. Beurskens, S. Keuneke, M. Mahrt, I. Peters, C. Puschmann, van Treeck, T., & K. Weller (Eds.), *Science and the Internet* (pp. 31–41). Düsseldorf, Germany: Düsseldorf University Press.

Koç, M. (2006). Cultural identity crisis in the age of globalization and technology. *The Turkish Online Journal of Educational Technology, 5*(1), 37–43.

Lankshear, C., & Knobel, M. (2011). *New literacies* (3rd ed.). New York, NY: Open University Press.

Lu, M. Z. (1990). Writing as repositioning. *Journal of Education, 172*, 18–21.

Maguire, M., & Graves, B. (2001). Speaking personalities in primary school chidren's L2 writing. *TESOL Quarterly, 35*(4), 561–593. doi:10.2307/3588428

Maxwell, J. A. (2005). *Qualitative research design* (2nd ed.). Thousand Oaks, CA: Sage.

McLoughlin, C., & Lee, M. J. W. (2010). Personalised and self-regulated learning in the web 2.0 era: International exemplars of innovative pedagogy using social software. *Australasian Journal of Educational Technology, 26*(1), 28–43. https://doi.org/10.14742/ajet.1100

Mills, N. (2011). Situated learning through social networking communities: The development of joint enterprise, mutual engagement, and a shared repertoire. *CALICO Journal, 28*(2), 345–368. https://doi.org/10.11139/cj.28.2.345-368

Mohanty, C. T. (2003). *Feminism without borders: Decolonizing theory, practicing solidarity.* Durham, NC: Duke University Press. https://doi.org/10.1215/9780822384649

Morita, N. (2004). Negotiating participation and identity in second language academic communities. *TESOL Quarterly, 38*(4), 573–603. Retrieved from http://onlinelibrary.wiley.com/jounal/10.1002/(ISSN)1545-7249

Nassaji, H., & Cumming, A. (2000). What's in a ZPD? A case study of a young ESL student and teacher interacting through dialogue journals. *Language Teaching Research, 4*(2), 95–121. https://doi.org/10.1177/136216880000400202

Nelson, E. C. (2011ri). *Intelligibility in world Englishes: Theory and application.* New York, NY: Routledge.

Pratt, M. L. (1991). Arts of the contact zone. *Profession, 91*, 33–40.

Şahin, Y. T. (2001). Yapilandirmaci yaklasimin bilissel ve duyussal ogrenmeye etksi. *Kuram ve Uygulamada Egitim Bilimleri, 1*: 463–482.

Said, E. W. (2000). *Reflections on exile: And other literary and cultural essays.* London, England: Granta Books.

Saka, E. (2015). Integrating new media into higher education: A Turkish case in transmedia, convergence, and gamification. In B. Akdenizi (Ed.), *Digital transformations in Turkey: Current perspectives in communication studies* (pp. 123–139). London, England: Lexington Books.

Searle, J. (1997). *Speech acts: An essay in the philosophy of language.* Cambridge, England: Cambridge University Press.

Searle, J. R., Kiefer, F., & Bierwisch, M. (Eds.). (1980). *Speech act theory and pragmatics.* Dordrecht, Holland: Reidel. https://doi.org/10.1007/978-94-009-8964-1

Selfe, C., & Selfe, R. (1994). The politics of the interface: Power and its exercise in electronic contact zones. *College Composition and Communication, 45*(4), 480–504. https://doi.org/10.2307/358761 http://www.ncte.org/cccc/ccc/online-archive

Sener, J. (2007). In search of student-generated content in online education. *E-mentor, 4*, 1–8. Retrieved from http://www.e-mentor.edu.pl/artykul/index/numer/21/id/467

Sifakis, N., & Bayyurt, Y. (2015). Insights from ELF and WE in teacher training in Greece and Turkey. *World Englishes, 34*(3), 471–484. https://doi.org/10.1111/weng.12150

Tezci, Erdoğan, & Gürol, Aysun. (2002). Yapilandirmaci ogretim tasarimi uygulamasinin yaratici dusuncenin gelisimine etkisi. II. Uluslararasi Egitim Teknolojileri Sempozyumu ve Fuari, Sakarya Universitesi.

Trimbur, J. (1994). Taking the social turn: Teaching writing post-process. *College Composition and Communication, 45*: 108–118.

Trimbur, J. (2002). Delivering the message: Typography and the materiality of writing. In G. Olson (Ed.), *Rhetoric and composition as intellectual work* (pp. 188–202). Carbondale, IL: Southern Illinois University Press.

Turkle, S. (1995). *Life on the screen: Identity in the age of the Internet.* New York, NY: Simon and Schuster.

Turkle, S. (1999). Cyberspace and identity. *Contemporary Sociology, 28*(6), 643–648. https://doi.org/10.2307/2655534

Uysal, H. H. (2008). Tracing the culture behind writing: Rhetorical patterns and bidirectional transfer in L1 and L2 essays of Turkish writers in relation to educational context. *Journal of Second Language Writing, 17*(3), 183–207. https://doi.org/10.1016/j.jslw.2007.11.003

Villanueva, V. (1993). *Bootstraps: From an American academic of color.* Urbana, IL: National Council of Teachers of English.

Villanueva, V. (2001). The politics of literacy across the curriculum. In S. McLeod, E. Miraglia, M. Soven, & C. Thaiss (Eds.), *WAC for the new millennium* (pp. 165–178). Urbana, IL: National Council of Teachers of English.

SECTION III

Connecting

To use online writing to create a system of interaction where author and reader continually shift roles and exchange information in interactive ways that build a continually interacting community around a shared area of interests or common ideas. Chapters in this section work to create dialogue and transactional rhetoric, including topics to prompt dialogue and to generate sustainability.

WE ARE THE FIRST HUMANS TO **CONNECT** WITH EXTRATERRESTRIAL LIFEFORMS KNOWINGLY, WE'RE MAKING HISTORY.

11

WRITING CENTER ASYNCHRONOUS/ SYNCHRONOUS ONLINE FEEDBACK
The Relationship Between E-Feedback and Its Impact on Student Satisfaction, Learning, and Textual Revision

Vassiliki Kourbani

ABSTRACT

This study investigates connections between asynchronous online feedback from writing center (WC) tutors and revision by non-native speakers (NNS). The chapter specifically examines work by students who speak English as a foreign language (EFL) at an American university in Greece. Results indicate the effects of online tutoring are positive. However, e-feedback is sometimes ineffective due to difficulty understanding and applying tutor comments. Further development of quality e-feedback is needed, and a combination of online and onsite visits may yield enhanced results.

Keywords: e-feedback, online tutoring, revision, technological literacy, writing center

INTRODUCTION

Computer-mediated communication (CMC) writing techniques challenge how educators "define, create, and modify writing centers" (Lewis et al., 2009, p. 130), and many writing centers (WC) use online tutoring sessions to assist students. Much professional discussion, however, focuses on CMC techniques vs. exclusively face-to-face (F2F) tutoring. Individuals in writing studies could thus benefit from examinations of online tutoring in order to provide more sound pedagogical approaches.

The chapter presents the results of a study examining writing tutor feedback and resulting student revision delivered in a technologically-enhanced learning environment. The study focuses on a virtual learning space at the Hellenic American University (HAU) Writing Center in Athens, Greece. Such an approach addresses the problem of the

DOI: 10.7330/9781607326649.c011

usefulness and operationalizability of online tutoring practices when compared to F2F tutoring. The chapter also examines connections between online feedback from WC tutors and related revision produced by NNS writers.

STUDY CONTEXTS

Many WC studies (Thonus, 2002; Goodfellow, 2005; Lea, 2007; Gillespie & Lerner, 2008) focus on F2F tutor-tutee interaction and writing center theory and practice. However, few examine effects of tutor feedback on tutees' written texts in subsequent revision (see Williams, 2004; Williams & Severino, 2004) probably because "rarely is writing center assessment connected with assessments of quality or change(s) in students' writing" (Thonus, 2002, p. 112). Less research examines how WC sessions affect way(s) non-native speakers (NNS) revise subsequent drafts. Rather, most research explores dynamics between tutors and tutees in face-to-face tutoring sessions (Lea, 2007; Gillespie & Lerner, 2008). Ritter (2002), for example, explores WC interaction as helping "revision strategy but does not trace these strategies beyond the confines" of the tutorial (Williams, 2004, p. 176). To address this gap, Williams reviews the relationship between WC interaction and revisions by non-native speakers in F2F situations. Although final drafts "did not receive consistently higher holistic evaluations" (p. 173), findings reveal connections between tutorial interaction and revision, especially for small-scale sentence-level problems.

The existing research examines correlations between the activities during WC sessions and how students revise drafts. Although research demonstrates the importance and relevance of feedback, little is known about "the social practice of feedback in the online environment" (Contijoch, Burns, & Candlin, 2012, p. 23). The omission is problematic as feedback is considered a vital component toward "the growth of social learning, social and cognitive development in a collaborative environment, of which online communities of practice are a part of" (Gullett, 2010, p. 3). Accordingly, this study broadens the previous research on F2F WC tutorials by describing online practices in asynchronous tutorials involving NNS at an American university in Greece. In today's "post-modern, multi-cultural, and globalized classroom" (Myatt, 2010, p. 29), culturally diverse students are expected to evaluate critically, select sources wisely, and incorporate awareness of levels of literacy in advanced disciplinary English to succeed (Craig, 2012). These factors are important when writing online because practitioners have to "rethink pedagogical aspects and issues related to teaching, learning and assessment" (Krish, Maros, & Stapa, 2012, p. 202).

By exploring how asynchronous communication provides "social practice" in online environments (Swan & Shea, 2005), this study examines the effects of a tutorial on a single revision process. As such, this study enhances our understanding of online writing practices in global contexts by providing the basis for a technologically and pedagogically challenging e-learning discourse.

THE EVOLUTION OF TECHNOLOGY

The chapter extends scholarship by academic literacy studies and learning in higher education (Lillis, 2001; Thesen & Pletzen, 2006) through examining literacy as enabling students to "project their physical and emotional presence" (Krish, Maros, & Stapa, 2012, p. 202). In essence, the term "literacies" (plural) provides evidence "for the ways literacy practices, reading and writing texts, are contextualized social practices and central to the process of learning in the academy" (Jones & Lea, 2008, p. 208). An academic literacies approach thus views academic writing as a process beyond the mastery of language skills. Rather, academic writing is "learning to acquire a repertoire of linguistic practices that are based on complex sets of discourses, identities, and values" (Paltridge, 2002, p. 18).

Recent approach of learning to write as a social act emphasizes context, for students also "need knowledge of the culture, circumstances, purposes, and motives that prevail in particular academic settings" (Paltridge et al., 2009, p. 6). Writing is an "act of identity" (Ivanič, 1998, p. 15) where people combine various socio-cultural practices to make their own contribution to challenge dominant practices and discourses. These factors are important to writing in international contexts (Zawacki & Habib, 2014) because students might have "different organizational preferences, different approaches to incorporating material from text into writing, different perspectives on reader orientation, different uses of cohesion markers" (Grabe & Kaplan, 1996, p. 239).

Digital Literacies and Learning

Electronic communication technologies alter how people write in relation to genres, writer identities, and reader engagement (Hyland, 2002). New media have contributed to the teaching of writing through the cognitive era in the 1980s and the sociocognitive era in the 1990s (Warschauer, 2010). Learning paradigms have thus "evolved beyond traditional face-to-face approaches, especially in institutions in higher learning" (Kelsey & St.Amant, 2008; Krish, Maros, & Stapa, 2012, p. 202).

Over the last decade, automated writing evaluation and open-source netbook computers have brought "a shift in learner-centered approaches in teaching and learning" (Krish, Maros, & Stapa, 2012, p. 202). Today, the so-called digital natives (Rosen, Carrier, & Cheever, 2010) learn in a different manner, creating pressures to use newer technologies (e.g., mobile media) in university programs. Many researchers note this Internet generation processes information differently than others, for they have always been connected through networks (Hay, 2000; Zheng, & Ferris, 2008; Jones et al., 2010). Hence, to incorporate technology in the transmission of knowledge, practitioners must "rethink pedagogical aspects and issues related to teaching, learning and assessment" (Krish, Maros, & Stapa, 2012, p. 202). Therefore, the goal is to create a cutting-edge e-learning discourse. In fact, digital pedagogy is a term that might carry different meanings for various audiences; for this study, it will mean more than pedagogy "that uses digital technology and media" (Myatt, 2010, p. 29). Rather, it indicates a pedagogy that "seeks to incorporate an awareness of the different levels of digital literacy that students bring into the post-modern, multi-cultural, and globalized classroom" (Myatt, 2010, p. 29; Canagarajah, 2013). Accordingly, technology is not only a tool, but also "represents a new culture that demands a new practice" (Beebe & Bonevelle, 2000, p. 42).

One fundamental principle of constructionist pedagogy is "it fosters the conversation about technology" of great importance if tutors want to converse with writers about their writing "in ways that support writers as they move with increased confidence into their own discourse communities" (Myatt, 2010, p. 27). Therefore, tutors need to feel comfortable communicating in an online environment and be sensitive to student needs. From an international perspective, this perspective opens a new frontier for learner identity formation, expression, and development as well as cultural inclusivity (Goodfellow & Lamy, 2009).

METHODS

This study examined WC asynchronous online feedback and its impact on student learning and textual revision. The purpose of the study was to establish if improvement occurred from the first to the second draft of a paper and to identify to what extent the feedback provided to students influenced their revisions.

Project Overview

To access students' learning with asynchronous online writing conferences, this research project sought to address the following questions:

- Do undergraduate students make changes to a revised draft following online consultations with WC tutors? If so, are the revisions mainly of higher-order (global problems i.e., expression of ideas) or lower-order concerns (sentence-level problems i.e., grammar, spelling, and punctuation)? Does online tutoring work effectively with higher-order revisions?

- Does the feedback provided to students on their discourse, sociolinguistic, and linguistic competence influence their revisions? If so, which type of feedback do students address more effectively in their revisions?

The research reported here was conducted at The Hellenic American University (HAU) Writing Center in the city of Athens, Greece, during Fall 2010.

Subject Selection

The project involved a writing class (Writing II) at The Hellenic American University and consisted of first-year undergraduate students in the second semester of their studies. All students were enrolled in the basic writing class required of all undergraduates. Moreover, students were informed participation in the study was voluntary. They were also reminded their choosing not to participate would not affect their current or future relation with the university, the professor, or the researcher. Students were working toward undergraduate degrees in a range of fields; five students were business majors, one was a psychology major, and four were English majors. Most were native Greek speakers, and of the ten, nine were Greek and one was Polish.

The specific research project was conducted under the assumption students had been practicing academic writing skills as well as editing and revising their texts for prior studies. It was also assumed students had achieved an introductory level of competence with the necessary technological means to improve their writing in an interactive and collaborative learning environment (e.g., Blackboard, Moodle). Therefore, subjects chosen for this particular study were selected because they constituted "critical cases" and conformed to a "criterion" of a critical moment of interaction in a "crucial site of engagement" (Scollon & Scollon, 2004, p. 28). Students were informed of the purpose of the research and were reassured about the anonymity and confidentiality of their responses.

Data Collection Procedures

A detailed research plan was submitted to and approved by the Institutional Review Board (IRB), and data were collected once approval was received. After being informed about the purpose of the research and reassured about the anonymity and confidentiality of their responses, students were given a form to complete indicating their consent to participate in the particular study. Two NES WC tutors also participated in the study and identifying certain errors in texts reviewed. These tutors also read and completed an informed consent form and were assured that their identities would not be made public without their permission.

Student Essay Topic

Of the essays written by students in Writing II, only one had to be submitted to the WC for feedback—an informative essay on "The News Coverage of the Haiti Earthquake." Students were given ten days to write the first draft and submit it to the WC for feedback, and WC tutors returned assignments within seventy-two hours. The instructor then gave students one week to revise their first drafts and submit final drafts to tutors for feedback and comments were returned within seventy-two hours. Students' typed first and second drafts were kept on electronic files identified by assigned numbers for each individual.

Data Classification: Taxonomy of Error Marking Categories

Tutors used a table (see Table 11.1) to provide guidelines for giving students with consistent feedback based on categories used in rhetoric books for writing (Glenn & Gray, 2007).

The particular classification draws on a number of models of competence and proficiency that reflect the linguistic, sociolinguistic, pragmatic, and discourse-level knowledge types of communicative language ability (Bachman, 1990; Bachman & Palmer, 1996; Kastman Breuch, 2005; North, 1996) and on reviews of current practice (Bhatia, 2004; Burnapp, 2006). In this context, writing is a complex, co-constructed endeavor defined by social and discursive practices (Breen, 2001) and as a "social practice, embedded in the cultural and institutional context in which it is produced and the particular uses that are made of it" (Hyland, 2002, p. 48). The following classification was adapted to include the components of communicative language ability relevant to writing as a rhetorical process, namely (see Table 11.1):

Table 11.1. Error Categories Used in WC Marking and Analysis.

Error Categories	Description
Discourse Competence/Textual Knowledge (DC)	*Rhetorical Organization* introduction-controlling and supporting ideas, conclusion *Coherence* thematic unity *Cohesion* contextual links marked by grammatical and semantic links
Sociolinguistic Competence/ Social-Pragmatic Knowledge (SC)	*Diction* word choice *Audience Awareness* *Purpose Awareness* rhetorical styles *Citation Practices* Integrating Sources (paraphrase, summary, quotations, avoiding plagiarism) Accurate citation/documentation of sources
Linguistic Competence/ Grammatical Knowledge (LC)	*Grammar-Sentence structure* verb tense, verb form, articles, word form, number, prepositions, word order, fragments, comma splices *Mechanics* spelling, capitalization, punctuation

- Linguistic knowledge: morphology, syntax, semantics (Glenn & Gray, 2007)
- Sociolinguistic knowledge: functional uses of writing, register, situational practices, procedures, and conventions (Connor, 2002; Bhatia, 2004)
- Discourse knowledge: cohesion (Halliday & Hasan, 1976), coherence, genre (Bhatia, 2004)

These categories were used because of their traditional validity in WC tutor feedback (Gillespie & Lerner, 2008) and because they have been the focus of studies about foreign and second language writing (Cohen & Cavalcanti, 1990; Hedgcock & Lefkowitz, 1996).

Data Coding

The tutors involved in the study collected and coded essays independently for both sets of drafts (first and revised, total forty essays), according to the error category classification system used in the HAU WC marking and analysis (see Table 11.1). Upon completing the coding, the tutors and researcher met to discuss the ratings. In cases where tutors disagreed, the researcher intervened so a consensus could be reached.

The reported inter-rater reliability was 0.90, and the agreed-upon coding was included in the data analysis. (Accidental oversights of errors were not treated as disagreements.) After the error coding was agreed upon, corrections in the form of actual comments appeared in the right-hand margin of students' papers. Tutors then drafted an email summarizing their comments, attached the student's paper with inserted comments, and email both to students' accounts. After collecting both drafts, the following coding procedures were established to capture aspects of the revision process (Williams, 2004).

First/Second Draft Coding

First and second draft coding began at the level of T-units used often in the analysis of spoken and written discourse (Young, 1995; Sachs & Polio, 2007). Accordingly, first and second drafts were divided into T-units, and errors were counted based on the error category classification system used in the HAU WC marking and analysis (see Table 11.1). In addition, revisions were coded for changes in linguistic accuracy and revision patterns were classified into five categories (see Table 11.2).

RESULTS

Quantitative Analysis

The results revealed most students' drafts improved after the online exchange (Tables 11.3 and 11.4), and of the total 308 T-units, 121 (39%) were correct and 187 (61%) erroneous. The total number of errors resulted to 254 indicating there were T-units containing more than one error. One-hundred and three (40.6%) existing errors were related to students' grammatical knowledge (LC), 112 (44%) to their sociolinguistic knowledge (SC), and 39 (15.4%) to their discourse knowledge (DC). The reduction in lower-order (e.g., grammar and mechanics) concerns (LC) was significant, followed by a reduction in higher-order (global problems such as expression of ideas) concerns (DC). The reduction in addressing socio-pragmatic knowledge (SC) (research skills, audience awareness) was much lower.

Table 11.4 summarizes student revision behavior between the first and second drafts. Specifically, of the total 321 T-units, 214 (67%) were

Table 11.2. Student Revision Analysis Categories.

Category	Description
1. Partially corrected (PC)	Corrected original error(s) but introduced new error(s) in the revised T-unit.
2. Completely corrected (CC)	All errors from original T-unit were successfully corrected.
3. New Additions (NA)	New T-units were introduced which were either:
A. Error Free (NA-EF)	• Error Free (NA-EF)
B. Erroneous (NA-ERR)	• Erroneous (NA-ERR)
4. Deletions (DL)	Original T-units were deleted.
5. Completely unchanged (CU)	No response to the correction was apparent following tutors' feedback.

Table 11.3. First Draft Summary of Students' Errors.

Students	T-units	LC	SC	DC	Total[1]	EF[2]	ERR[3]
1	32	4	11	4	19	15	17
2	31	9	7	1	17	19	12
3	31	4	29	1	34	8	23
4	30	10	3	8	21	11	19
5	37	6	16	9	31	13	24
6	27	16	8	3	27	9	18
7	28	8	17	4	29	9	19
8	32	19	8	7	34	9	23
9	36	21	4	1	26	18	18
10	24	6	9	1	16	10	14
Total	308	103	112	39	254	121	187

1. Total number of errors
2. Error free T-units
3. Erroneous T-units

correct and the remaining 107 (33%) erroneous. The total number of errors resulted in 126, indicating certain T-units contained more than one error. Thirty-seven error classifications (29.4%) involved students' grammatical knowledge (LC), seventy-two (57.1%) involved sociolinguistic knowledge (SC), and seventeen (13.5%) encompassed discourse knowledge (DC). These factors mean students faced more problems addressing issues of expression, sentence structure and vocabulary. Therefore, it proved difficult for students to follow tutors' comments

Table 11.4. Second Draft Summary of Students' Short-Term Revision Behavior.

Students	T-units	LC	SC	DC	Total[1]	EF[2]	ERR[3]
1	32	1	6	0	7	26	6
2	32	1	3	0	4	29	3
3	28	1	24	1	26	8	20
4	34	6	3	3	12	23	11
5	41	2	13	10	25	18	23
6	30	8	2	1	11	19	11
7	28	3	1	0	4	25	3
8	31	5	5	2	12	23	8
9	36	6	7	0	13	25	11
10	29	4	8	0	12	18	11
Total	321	37	72	17	126	214	107

1. Total number of errors
2. Error free T-units
3. Erroneous T-units

trying to explain lexical nuances (SC) due to their poor command of vocabulary and syntax.

Table 11.5 depicts the codification of student errors according to the error category classification system used in the HAU WC marking and analysis procedure (Table 11.1). Results show students improved their drafts substantially, following the comments provided by WC tutors. Out of the first draft 187 erroneous T-units, 87 (46.5%) were completely corrected (CC), 57 (30.5%) partially corrected (PC), 32 (17.1%) were left the same (CU), while the remaining 11 (5.9%) erroneous T-units were deleted (DL). There were also twenty-five new additions (NA); seven error-free (NA-EF) and eighteen erroneous (NA-ERR) T-units.

The analysis of student revision behaviors between first and second drafts suggests in most cases students successfully addressed errors pinpointed by WC tutors. The reduction in lower-order (grammar and mechanics) concerns (LC) was significant (64%), followed by a reduction in higher-order (expression of ideas) concerns (DC) (56.4%). The reduction in addressing socio-pragmatic knowledge (SC) (research skills, audience awareness) was much lower (35.7%).

1. First Draft Erroneous T-units

Overall, students made significant progress as a result of the online exchange, and the comparison of drafts showed students made significant reductions in their total amount of errors in the three major

Table 11.5. Types of Student Revision.

Students	ERR T-units(1)	CC	PC	CU	DL	NA-EF	NA-ERR
1	17	10	6		1	1	
2	12	9	2		1	1	1
3	23	1	13	7	2		
4	19	8	3	3	5	4	5
5	24	4	5	15		1	3
6	18	10	8				3
7	19	16	1	1	1		1
8	23	14	3	5	1		
9	18	7	11				
10	14	8	5	1			5
Total	187	87	57	32	11	7	18

Table 11.6. Students' Revision Behavior Outcome.

Errors	First draft	Revision (second draft)	Reduction (%)
Linguistic Competence (LC)	103	37	64.0
Sociolinguistic Competence (SC)	112	72	35.7
Discourse Competence (DC)	39	17	56.4
Total/Average	254	126	50.4

categories (50.4%) (Table 11.6). Specifically, the reduction in lower-order (grammar and mechanics) concerns (LC) was significant (64%) following by a reduction in higher-order (expression of ideas) concerns (DC) (56.4%). However, results for the remaining category requiring mastery of rhetorical styles, academic discourses, and research skills were not significant (35.7%) (Table 11.6).

Finally, Table 11.7 summarizes individual student results related to second draft revision within each category, and Table 11.8 highlights students' results regarding types of revision. These results indicate

- For partially corrected (PC) T-units, most errors reflected students' inability to incorporate in-text references
- The same results also applied to the category of completely unchanged T-units
- For the category of new additions, most errors reflected students' lack of linguistic competence.

Table 11.7. Second Draft/Summary of Individual Student Results.

Students	PC			CU			NA-ERR		
	LC	SC	DC	LC	SC	DC	LC	SC	DC
1	1	6							
2		2					1	1	
3		15		1	9	1			
4	3		1		1	2	3	2	
5		5	1	1	8	7	1		2
6	5	2	1				3		
7	1			1			1	1	
8	3	2		2	3	2			
9	6	7							
10	2	4					2	4	
Total	21	43	3	5	21	12	11	8	2

Table 11.8. Second Draft/Types of Student Revision.

Errors	Partially changed (PC)	Completely unchanged (CU)	New additions / erroneous (NA-ERR)
Linguistic competence (LC)	21 (31%)	5 (13%)	11 (52%)
Sociolinguistic competence (SC)	43 (64%)	21 (55%)	8 (38%)
Discourse competence (DC)	3 (5%)	12 (32%)	2 (10%)
Total	67 (100%)	38 (100%)	21 (100%)

Qualitative Analysis

Qualitative analysis identified certain themes:

Finding 1: Students make changes to their revised draft following online consultations with WC tutors. The analysis suggests students often successfully address errors pinpointed by WC tutors. Results indicate when changes (whether minimal or substantial) are made, they overwhelmingly tend to improve students' papers. The comparison of ten pairs of student papers (Table 11.6) shows students make significant reduction (50%) in their total number of errors in all five major categories. The reduction in lower-order (sentence-level) concerns (LC) is highly significant (64%) followed by a quite significant reduction (56.4%) in text-based problems (such as cohesion and coherence) (DC).

Results for the remaining category (SC) that require mastery of various rhetorical styles, academic discourses and research skills, however, are not significant (35.7%). Also, the writing skills of many HAU students reveal English as second language concerns including poor command of vocabulary and syntax, confusing rhetorical patterns, and lack of knowledge of rhetorical features of genres and conventions of research-based writing, similar to other second language research (Williams, 2006).

Regarding source-based writing, students reveal "they were not only not discouraged from plagiarizing in secondary school but also encouraged to engage in inadvertent plagiarism by schoolteachers who provided them essay models to memorize and repeat in order to facilitate standardization in grading" (Ronesi, 2009, p. 88). It is also worth mentioning notable individual variation exists in the progress among the ten student participants (Tables 11.3 and 11.4). The observation is supported by earlier L2 writer research noting "there is a tremendous variability in students' ability to benefit from grammar instruction and feedback" (Ferris & Hedgcock, 1998, p. 201; Goldstein, 2006). However, individual variation regarding students' ability to use and process teacher as well as tutor feedback effectively "has been a largely unexplored question in error question research" (Ferris, 2006, p. 91). Therefore, educators are called to address the "challenges of global communications" ("CCCC Committee on Globalization," n.d.) for L2 students to acquire knowledge of "the culture, circumstances, purposes, and motives that prevail in particular academic settings" (Paltridge et al., 2009, p. 6).

Finding 2: Lower-order features (sentence-level problems/grammar and mechanics) are more likely to be revised than higher-order problems. Results show surface-level problems are more likely to get revised than text-based problems, and students seem able to correct errors they consider easy to address (e.g., grammar mistakes). Following tutors' feedback, students seemingly found it easier to note a missing verb and make the appropriate change vs. rearrange sections of text (see Rounsaville, 2015).

This finding is supported by research on revision by L2 writers (see, for instance, Williams, 2004). Indeed, students successfully revise easy-to-address surface problems. Fathman and Whalley (1990) show when students receive grammar feedback indicating the place but not the type of errors, they significantly improve their grammar scores in revised drafts. Conversely, complex problems involving further explanation and analysis are revised with less success or not at all. However, complex problems related to students' discourse knowledge (paragraph order, coherence, cohesion) are often addressed successfully because the feedback is more straightforward or the nature of errors is less complex vs. problems involving source-based writing.

The last finding suggests some errors could be "treatable" because they "occur in a patterned rule-governed way"; whereas, others could be "untreatable" because "as students cannot consult a handbook or set of rules to avoid or fix those errors" (Ferris, 1999, p. 6). In this study, students seem able to address "treatable" errors (e.g., subject-verb agreement) whereas they have more difficulty correcting content and appropriate organizational related concerns like integrating in-text references, which could be considered "untreatable." This finding suggests "different categories represent separate areas of knowledge which may be acquired through distinct processes and cannot be treated as if they were equivalent" (Campillo & Arnandiz, 2010, p. 212). Students seem more confident revising more treatable, rule-governed errors, but seem to have difficulty addressing untreatable, idiosyncratic errors requiring acquired language knowledge (Parrish & Linder-VanBerschot, 2010).

Finding 3: Different types and categories of errors were affected differently by error commentary. Results show successful student revisions are high, and the percentage of successful revisions in most of the individual error categories is significant (Table 11.6). However, in both categories of partially corrected (PC) and completely unchanged (CU) instances, remaining errors are lexical categories (e.g., word choice and idioms) and errors regarding source integration and accurate citation. In fact, students have a good deal of difficulty with the use of the APA style in formatting, citations, and in-text references. Apart from their low L2 proficiency, students' difficulty in addressing specific error categories may be due to their inability to understand the actual terminology in some of the tutors' comments (Hutchings, 2006).

Previous research shows there are instances where e-feedback is ineffective due to difficulty understanding and applying tutors' comments. Students at lower levels of L2 proficiency might not possess the linguistic competence to self-edit (Ritter, 2002; Williams, 2005). Particular areas of difficulty involve content- and organizational-related concerns (global problems) (i.e., expression of ideas and vocabulary) rather than comments addressing grammar (sentence-level problems), which are probably easier to address and correct (Blau & Hall, 2002). According to Leki (1991), when students receive written feedback, they may either not read it, read it but not understand it, or understand it but not know how to respond to it. That might also be the case with the students at Hellenic American University. In fact, it seems students find it easier to understand written feedback on sentence-level problems instead of organizational related problems due to their lack of the "receiving culture and its communicative values [. . .] and genre conventions" in the L2 (Magistro, 2007, para. 12, 14). As Magistro explains (2007), only when students learn to conform to "rhetorical themes" can they "critically decide and take responsibility" for understanding and selecting the appropriate discourse choices to indicate "agency in discourse" (Canagarajah, 2004, p. 267).

DISCUSSION

Results reveal the positive effects of WC online feedback on students' revised drafts as related to areas for improvement. Through qualitative and quantitative analysis, various themes and implications for future courses of action emerged.

Theme 1: Usefulness/Convenience of E-Feedback

Findings confirm research suggesting online tutoring "befitted students' eagerness to work online, attracted shy students who hesitated to visit in person, and catered to non-traditional students' 'hectic lifestyles'" (Soven, 2006, p. 448). Results also show when revisions are attempted, they overwhelmingly improve students' papers, especially for small-scale revision of sentence-level problems. Second drafts highly improve, indicating the continued need for first draft input and an opportunity to revise in this area.

Students mostly revise their papers correctly (CC). There are also cases falling in the middle of the revision rating scale in which students introduce new errors in their effort to revise already pinpointed problems (PC). For tutors who want to help students to improve as writers and critical thinkers, the findings of this small-scale study are to be taken as encouraging. Not only do student writers follow tutors' commentary; they also, in most cases, address errors pinpointed by WC tutors. However, it seems some students are unable to address certain errors (especially higher-order concerns,) either due to low L2 proficiency or to the difficulty stemming from the terminology in some of the tutors' comments (Hutchings, 2006).

The previous observations suggest two contradictory yet coexisting conclusions: most students pay attention to tutor suggestions that help improve their essays, yet some ignore, avoid, or become confused with the tutor commentary due to the lack of visual communication cues (see Yergeau, Wozniak, & Vandenberg, 2008). It appears students have difficulty incorporating material in their original discourse—probably because paraphrasing and summarizing skills are complex activities entailing an overwhelmingly cognitive load on students. External constraints may include factors like the assignment itself, discourse conventions, cultural assumptions and the nature of the material. Internal factors may consist of "L2 proficiency, cognitive schemata, cognitive skills, and metacognitive skills" (Kirkland & Saunders, 1991, p. 105). A possible solution is for students to receive more analytical and detailed feedback with more alternatives to address problematic areas involving higher-order concerns.

Theme 2: Type and Thematic Content of E-Feedback

A second theme involves the thematic content of e-feedback comments involving a "disconnect between student expectations and tutors' diagnosis which is hard to negotiate in an online environment" (Remington, 2006, p. 3). Some suggest students have difficulties understanding and applying certain comments and note errors might require different treatment, or what Powers (2001) calls "an attitude adjustment" on behalf of tutors to "lead writers to the solution of their own problems" (p. 369). In fact, the asynchronous online faceless nature does not allow tutees to ask questions, respond to comments, raise issues, and actively work with tutors toward the revisions (Hobson, 1998).

Students' need for explanation and guidance is not easily accomplished during the asynchronous online interactions offering "less chance for the back-and-fourth hashing out of such issues that an in-person meeting allows" (Remington, 2006, p. 2), to determine what factors "shape the textual interactions which constitute the 'visible' community in these environments" (Goodfellow, 2004, p. 380). Moreover, students might be in need of more time that would allow them to be in real-time contact with WC tutors, to revise in their effort to improve language, and to tackle writing skills. In fact, many writing experts agree "ESL writers need more of everything: more time, more opportunity to talk, listen, read, and write in order to marshal the vocabulary they need to make their own background knowledge accessible to them in their L2" (Raimes, 2003, p. 55).

True, online tutoring through synchronous software would give tutors the chance to arrange and host discussions in real-time in order to address students' questions about writing issues or specific confusing comments difficult to understand and apply. In addition, F2F tutorials could provide students with needed individualized attention given varying educational, cultural, and language learning backgrounds. In fact, research suggests asynchronous online tutoring cannot deal and cope effectively with affective concerns such as emotional instability or writing stress that also constitute an important part of tutors' work (Boquet, 2002). The synchronous online tutoring mode could enable students to establish a supportive, interpersonal relationship in a "faceless environment" (Hewett, 2006).

Theme 3: Pedagogical and Research Issues

The study highlight pedagogical and research issues and emphasized the significance of the tutor variable, the variation in each student achievement and the effects of various tutor editing strategies on students' improvement of their writing skills. Therefore, various research areas appear worth exploring further:

- Examining what students do when receiving error commentary by tutors
- Identifying and accommodating individual student variability when responding to error feedback
- Understanding different types of errors on student progress in terms of accuracy and appropriateness

The findings presented here suggest approaches for tutors in order to enhance WC asynchronous online practices:

- Vary commentary for treatable and untreatable errors
- Employ a standard set of clear and direct comments
- Provide detailed responses to awkward, syntactically incorrect sentences
- Use facilitation strategies to help students acquire a deeper understanding of their writing

Perhaps the most useful conclusion is NNS students have a diversity of concerns different nature than compared to native speakers of English. Learning to write effectively in a foreign language is complex, for it is not an "isolated activity, but a social and cultural experience" (Xing, Wang, & Spencer, 2008, p. 73).

Students often come to Hellenic American University with no skills when confronted with specific academic tasks. Therefore, when addressing NNS, the academic community needs to remember not to assume anything. Tutors should not assume Greek students know what a thesis statement is or that they understand the basic idea of a paragraph, or the rules governing plagiarism. Accordingly, writing instructors must remember writing and prewriting strategies are often foreign to NNS.

With NNS, none of these principles can be assumed. Students simply follow and use diverse principles underlining similar or dissimilar rhetorical practices in their native language. The rhetorical conventions familiar to native speakers (e.g., writing, structure, and intellectual property) are not universally understood or accepted. Rather, they differ across cultures, making writing a paper for an American academic audience confusing for non-native speakers/writers (Zawacki & Cox, 2011). Consequently, tutors should focus on the questions, cultural presuppositions, writing processes, and learning experiences of those students so as to "help in transferring these skills to the target language and adjusting them to a different academic environment" (Xing, Wang, & Spencer, 2008, p. 72).

CONCLUSION

This entry explored relationships involving asynchronous electronic feedback on students' revisions of their written assignment. While limited, this study highlights an important role for online tutoring in improving writing skills and helping students develop a sense of autonomy (Sinclair, 2009) as "members of a learning community" (Falloon, 2012, p. 121). These findings outline the potential asynchronous online tutoring has when implemented appropriately.

Recommendations for Institutional Courses of Action

Students have difficulties understanding and applying specific comments involving lexical errors and complex global concerns with sentence structure. Thus, for the effective implementation of asynchronous online tutorial sessions, there is a need to develop and follow clear procedures for responding online in appreciating "text-only" environments and for creating appropriate roles for online tutoring (Gullett, 2010). Studies show tutors need different skills—particularly, attitudes, when working with EFL students. Specifically, WC tutors should use standard, clear, and direct comments to familiarize students with comments that seem vague, obscure, or difficult to understand. Tutors can use questions to start a dialogue and get students thinking about their own papers. They can offer praise, highlight words to show "error" patterns, direct students to resources, model revisions, and explain idioms and technical grammar errors like comma splices and run-ons.

The findings here suggest systematic research is needed to better understand this topic. The research should center on how online tutoring can maximize learning, particularly "in terms of cognitive and achievement outcomes" (Johnson, 2006, p. 51) resulting from the revision process. Due to differences between tutorials with NS and NNS, one needs to understand there is no "panacea-like solution" (Howard, 2009, p. 686) to accommodate diverse learners, serve the multiple NNS learning needs and create a functional learning environment that meets learning styles. Therefore, further investigation needs to be done to establish whether and to what extent, WCs ought to use a combination of synchronous and asynchronous online communication along in a more systematic way. Further experimentation is needed for "filling all the potential pedagogical gaps and situations" (Howard, 2009, p. 686), to accommodate a diversity of learners, creating a community of learning.

While acknowledging not every tutoring session are perfect, the most productive sessions offer a blending of instructional methods, writing pedagogy, and different modalities. No longer seen as a threat to the existence of WCs, "online tutoring should be viewed as a viable outgrowth of tutoring" (Arzt, Barnett, & Scoppetta, 2009, para. 38).

Recommendations and Implications for WC Theory and Practice

The findings from this study make several contributions to the current literature and provide additional evidence with respect to the online tutoring modality. Following the trend of using new technologies in teaching university students, offering online tutoring in WCs is not just an option or an alternative. Online tutoring has rather has become rather a necessity since the technological evolution and the proliferation of social media have "permanently changed the environment for writing in post-secondary education" (Harris, 2000, p. 193; Falloon, 2012). Responding to the present and future competitive requirements, WCs ought to work toward creating a cutting-edge tutoring service, both in regard to technology as well as pedagogy in order to develop "the multifaceted perspective necessary to improve our understanding of literacy in online and other digital spaces" (Coiro et al., 2008, p. xii).

Literacy learning is no longer a part of one set of skills or competences; rather, it is a constant "effort to navigate a multiplicity of discourses" (Grimm, 2009, p. 20). Therefore, there is a need for further research when designing an online pedagogy to address tutees' needs in regard to what they need to know about "writing processes as they are affected by technology" (Harris, 2000, p. 194). Writing center practitioners thus need to carefully assess what students need to know in order to develop and improve their writing "on a case-by-case, problem-centered basis" (Hewett, 2010, p. xviii). The best option would be the "mixing and matching" (Hewett, 2010, p. 35) of modalities to better serve tutees' diverse educational, cultural, and language learning backgrounds in promoting "deeper cognitive engagement" (Falloon, 2012, p. 110), "deeper learning and interaction" (Aksal, 2009, p. 34) as well as making students understand and reflect on "epistemologies, power relations, identities, and ideologies that circulate in different discourses" (Grimm, 2009, p. 15; Cope & Kalantzis, 2012).

While the data collected in this study clearly indicate the usefulness of online tutoring (Soven, 2006; Aksal, 2009; Arzt, Barnett, & Scoppetta, 2009; Falloon, 2011), the need to gather further data, with a larger student population over an extended period of time, in support of the findings, is of paramount importance to the growing body of literature concerning writing center studies. For WC practitioners who are interested in exploring the nature of asynchronous electronic feedback regarding the impact on students' revisions, the study provides valuable information. It also sheds light on online tutoring practices that not only offer F2F tutorial sessions but also wish to extend their services due to the constantly evolving social and technological context of communication and learning.

References

Aksal, F. (2009). Action plan on communication practices: Roles of tutors at EMU distance education institute to overcome social barriers in constructing knowledge. *Turkish Online Journal of Educational Technology, 8*(2), 33–47.

Arzt, J., Barnett, K., & Scoppetta, J. (2009, January). Online tutoring: A symbiotic relationship with writing across the curriculum initiatives. Special issue on writing technologies and writing across the curriculum. *Across the Disciplines, 6*(January). Retrieved from https://wac.colostate.edu/atd/technologies/arztetal.cfm

Bachman, L. (1990) *Fundamental considerations in language testing.* Oxford, England: Oxford University Press.

Bachman, L., & Palmer, A. (1996). *Language testing in practice.* Oxford, England: Oxford University Press.

Beebe, R., & Bonevelle, M. (2000). The culture of technology in the writing center: Reinvigorating the theory practice. In J. A. Inman & D. N. Sewell (Eds.), *Taking flight with OWLs: Examining electronic writing center work* (pp. 41–51). Mahwah, NJ: Lawrence Erlbaum.

Bhatia, V. (2004). *Worlds of written discourse.* New York, NY: Continuum.

Blau, S., & Hall, J. (2002). Guilt-free tutoring: Rethinking how we tutor non-native-English speaking students. *Writing Center Journal, 23,* 23–44.

Boquet, E. (2002). *Noise from the writing center.* Logan, UT: Utah State University Press.

Breen, P. (Ed.). (2001). *Learner contributions to language learning: New directions in research.* New York, NY: Pearson.

Burnapp, D. (2006). Trajectories of adjustment of international students: U-curve, learning curve, or third space. *Intercultural Education, 17*(1), 82–93. https://doi.org/10.1080/14675980500502412

Campillo, P., & Arnandiz, O. (2010). Corrective feedback: The case of treatable and untreatable errors. In M. Caballlero Rodríguez & M. Pinar Sanz (Eds.), *Modos y formas de la communication humana, 2* (pp. 211–218). Cuenca, Spain: University of Castilla–La Mancha.

Canagarajah, A. S. (2004). Multilingual writers and the struggle for voice: Assessing some approaches. In A. Blackledge & A. Pavelenko (Eds.), *Negotiation of identities in multilingual contexts* (pp. 266–289). Clevedon, England: Multilingual Matters.

Canagarajah, A. S. (2013). Agency and power in intercultural communication: Negotiating English in translocal spaces. *Language and Intercultural Communication, 13*(2), 202–224. https://doi.org/10.1080/14708477.2013.770867

CCCC Committee on Globalization of Postsecondary Writing Instruction and Research. (n.d.). Retrieved from http://www.ncte.org/CCCC/committees/globalization

Cohen, A., & Cavalcanti, M. (1990). Feedback on written compositions: Teacher and student verbal reports. In B. Kroll (Ed.), *Second language writing: Research insights for the classroom* (pp. 155–177). Cambridge, England: Cambridge University Press.

Coiro, J., Knobel, M., Lankshear, C., & Leu, D. (Eds.). (2008). *Handbook of research on new literacies.* New York, NY: Routledge.

Connor, U. (2002). New directions in contrastive rhetoric. *TESOL Quarterly, 36,* 493–510.

Contijoch, C., Burns, A., & Candlinm C. (2012). Feedback in the mediation of learning in online language teacher education. In L. England (Ed.), *Online language teacher education: TESOL perspectives* (pp. 22–38). London, England: Routledge.

Cope, B., & Kalantzis, M. (2012). *Literacies.* Cambridge, England: Cambridge University Press.

Craig, J. (2012). Teaching writing in a globally networked learning environment (GNLE): Diverse students at a distance. Presentation at Conference on College Composition and Communication, St. Louis, MO.

Falloon, G. (2011). Exploring the virtual classroom: What students need to know (and teachers should consider). *Journal of Online Learning and Teaching / MERLOT, 7*(4), 439–451.

Falloon, G. (2012). Inside the virtual classroom: Student perspectives on affordances and limitation. *Journal of Open, Flexible and Distance Learning, 16*(1), 108–126.

Fathman, A., & Whalley, E. (1990). Teacher response to student writing: Focus on form versus content. In B. Kroll (Ed.), *Second language writing: Research insights for the classroom* (pp. 178–190). Cambridge, England: Cambridge University Press. https://doi.org/10.1017/CBO9781139524551.016

Ferris, D. (1999). The case for grammar correction in L2 writing classes: A response to Truscott (1996). *Journal of Second Language Writing, 8*(1), 1–11. https://doi.org/10.1016/S1060-3743(99)80110-6

Ferris, D. (2006). Does error feedback help student writers? New evidence on the short and long-term effects of written error correction. In K. Hyland & F. Hyland (Eds.), *Feedback in second language writing: Contexts and issues* (pp. 81–104). New York, NY: Cambridge University Press. https://doi.org/10.1017/CBO9781139524742.007

Ferris, D., & Hedgcock, J. S. (1998). *Teaching ESL composition: Purpose, process and practice.* Mahwah, NJ: Lawrence Erlbaum.

Gillespie, P., & Lerner, N. (2008). *The Longman guide to peer tutoring* (2nd ed.). Boston, MA: Allyn & Bacon.

Glenn, C., & Gray, L. (2007). *The writer's harbrace handbook, brief edition* (3rd ed.). Belmont, CA: Thomson.

Goldstein, L. (2006). Feedback and revision in second language writing: Contextual, teacher and student variables. In K. Hyland & F. Hyland (Eds.), *Feedback in second language writing: Contexts and issues* (pp. 185–205). New York, NY: Cambridge University Press. https://doi.org/10.1017/CBO9781139524742.012

Goodfellow, R. (2004). Online literacies and learning: Operational, cultural and critical dimensions. *Language and Education, 18*(5), 379–399. https://doi.org/10.1080/095 00780408666890

Goodfellow, R. (2005). Academic literacies and e-learning: A critical approach to writing in the online university. *International Journal of Educational Research, 43*(7–8), 481–494.

Goodfellow, R., & Lamy, M. N. (2009). A frame for the discussion of learning cultures. In R. Goodfellow & M. N. Lamy (Eds.), *Learning cultures in online education* (pp. 1–14). London, England: Continuum.

Grabe, W., & Kaplan, R. (1996). *Theory and practice of writing: An applied linguistic perspective*. London, England: Longman.

Grimm, N. (2009). New conceptual frameworks for writing center work. *Writing Center Journal, 29*(2), 11–27.

Gullett, E. (2010). The impact of quality e-feedback as an element of social learning theory applied in the context of e-learning communities of practice. In N. Karacapilidis (Ed.), *Web-based learning solutions for communities of practice: Developing virtual environments for social and pedagogical advancement* (pp. 1–12). Hershey, PA: IGI Global. https://doi.org/10.4018/978-1-60566-711-9.ch001

Halliday, M. A. K., & Hasan, R. (1976). *Cohesion in English.* London, England: Longman.

Harris, M. (2000). Making up tomorrow's agenda and shopping lists today: Preparing for future technologies in writing centers. In J. Inman & D. Sewell (Eds.), *Taking flight with OWLs* (pp. 193–202). Mahwah, NJ: Lawrence Erlbaum.

Hay, L. E. (2000). Educating the net generation. *The Social Administrator, 57*(54), 6–10.

Hedgcock, J. S., & Lefkowitz, N. (1996). Some input on input: Two analyses of student response to expert feedback in L2 writing. *The Modern Language Journal, 80*(3), 287–308.

Hewett, B. (2006). Synchronous online conference-based instruction: A study of whiteboard interactions and student writing. *Computers and Composition, 23*(1), 4–31. https://doi.org/10.1016/j.compcom.2005.12.004

Hewett, B. (2010). *The online writing conference: A guide for teachers and tutors.* Portsmouth, NJ: Boynton/Cook Heinemann.

Hobson, E. (1998). *Wiring the writing center.* Logan, UT: Utah State University Press. https://doi.org/10.2307/j.ctt46nzf8

Howard, S. (2009). The benefits of face-to-face interaction in the online freshman composition course. *Journal of Online Learning and Teaching / MERLOT, 5*(4), 685–697.

Hutchings, C. (2006). Reaching students: Lessons from a writing centre. *Higher Education Research & Development, 25*(3), 247–261. https://doi.org/10.1080/07294360600793002

Hyland, K. (2002). *Teaching and researching writing.* London, England: Longman.

Ivanič, R. (1998). *Writing and identity: The discoursal construction of identity in academic writing.* Amsterdam, The Netherlands: John Benjamins. https://doi.org/10.1075/swll.5

Johnson, M. (2006). Synchronous and asynchronous text-based CMC in educational contexts: A review of recent research. *TechTrends, 50*(4), 46–53. https://doi.org/10.1007/s11528-006-0046-9

Jones, C., Ramanau, R., Cross, S., & Healing, G. (2010). Net generation or digital natives: Is there a distinct new generation entering university? *Computers & Education, 54*(3), 722–732. https://doi.org/10.1016/j.compedu.2009.09.022

Jones, S. G., & Lea, M. R. (2008). Digital literacies in the lives of undergraduate students: Exploring personal and curricular spheres of practice. *Electronic Journal of E-Learning, 6*(3), 207–216.

Kastman Breuch, L. A. (2005). The idea(s) of an online writing center: In search of a conceptual model. *Writing Center Journal, 25*(2), 21–38.

Kelsey, A., & St.Amant, K. (Eds.). (2008). *Handbook of research in computer mediated communication.* Hershey, PA: Idea Group Reference. https://doi.org/10.4018/978-1-59904-863-5

Kirkland, M., & Saunders, M. (1991). Maximizing student performance in summary writing: Managing cognitive load. *TESOL Quarterly, 25*(1), 105–121. https://doi.org/10.2307/3587030

Krish, P., Maros, M., & Stapa, S. (2012). Sociocultural factors and social presence in an online learning environment. *GEMA: Online Journal of Language Studies, 12*(1), 201–213.

Lea, M. R. (2007). Emerging literacies in online learning. *Journal of Applied Linguistics, 4*(1), 79–100.

Leki, I. (1991). The preferences of ESL students for error correction in college-level writing classes. *Foreign Language Annals, 24*(3), 203–218. https://doi.org/10.1111/j.1944-9720.1991.tb00464.x

Lewis, B., Pueschner, G., Gaffney, K., & Weyandt, C. (2009). Changing the landscape of writing centers in the two-year college through online discussion boards. *Minnesota English Journal, 45*, 130–143.

Lillis, T. (2001). *Student writing: Access, regulation, desire.* London, England: Routledge.

Magistro, E. (2007, Spring) The multilingual classroom: New Rhetorical frontiers in L2 writing. *College Quarterly, 10*(2), 1–12.

Myatt, A. J. (2010). Human-computer interface design for online tutoring: Visual rhetoric, pedagogy, and writing center websites (Doctoral dissertation). Atlanta, GA: Georgia State University, Paper 65. Retrieved from http://scholarworks.gsu.edu/english_diss/65

North, B. (1996). The development of a common framework scale of descriptors of language proficiency based on a theory of measurement (Unpublished doctoral dissertation). London, England: Thames Valley University.

Paltridge, B. (2002). Academic literacies and changing university communities. *Revista Canaria de Estudios Ingleses, 44*, 15–28.

Paltridge, B., Woodrow, L., Harbon, L., Phakiti, A., & Shen, H. (2009). *Teaching academic writing: An introduction for the second language classroom.* Ann Arbor, MI: University of Michigan Press. https://doi.org/10.3998/mpub.300562

Parrish, P., & Linder-VanBerschot, J. (2010). Cultural dimensions of learning: Addressing the challenges of multicultural instruction. *International Review of Research in Open and Distance Learning, 11*(2), 1–19. https://doi.org/10.19173/irrodl.v11i2.809

Powers, J. (2001). Rethinking writing center conferencing strategies for the ESL writer. In W. Barnett & J. Bulmer (Eds.), *The Allyn and Bacon guide to writing center theory and practice* (pp. 368–375). Boston, MA: Allyn & Bacon.

Raimes, A. (2003). What unskilled ESL students do as they write: A classroom study of composing. In T. Silva & P. Matsuda (Eds.), *Landmark essays on ESL writing* (pp. 37–61). Mahwah, NJ: Lawrence Erlbaum.

Remington, T. (2006). Reading, writing, and the role of the online tutor. *Writing Lab Newsletter, 30*(5), 1–5.

Ritter, J. (2002). Negotiating the Center: An Analysis of Writing Center Tutorial Interactions between ESL Learners and Native-English Speaking Writing Center Tutors (Doctoral dissertation). Indiana, PA: Indiana University of Pennsylvania. *Dissertation Abstracts International, 63*(06A), 2224.

Ronesi, L. (2009). Theory in/to practice: Multilingual tutors supporting multilingual peers: A peer-tutor training course in the arabian gulf. *Writing Center Journal, 29*(2), 75–94.

Rosen, L. D., Carrier, L. M., & Cheever, N. A. (2010). *Rewired: Understanding the iGeneration and the way they learn.* New York, NY: Palgrave Macmillan.

Rounsaville, A. (2015). Taking hold of global Englishes: Intensive English programs as brokers of transnational literacy. *Journal of Literacy and Composition Studies, 3*(3), 67–85. https://doi.org/10.21623/1.3.3.5

Sachs, R., & Polio, C. (2007). Learners' use of two types of written feedback on an L2 writing revision task. *Studies in Second Language Acquisition, 29*(1), 67–100. https://doi.org/10.1017/S0272263107070039

Scollon, R., & Scollon, S. W. (2004). *Nexus analysis: Discourse and the emerging Internet.* New York, NY: Routledge.

Sinclair, B. (2009). The teacher as learner: Developing autonomy in an interactive learning environment. In R. Pemberton, S. Toogood, & A. Barfield (Eds.), *Maintaining control: Autonomy and language learning* (pp. 175–198). Hong Kong, China: Hong Kong University Press. https://doi.org/10.5790/hongkong/9789622099234.003.0010

Soven, M. (2006). *What the writer tutor has to know.* Boston, MA: Thomson Wadsworth.

Swan, K., & Shea, P. (2005). The development of virtual learning communities. In S. R. Hiltz & R. Goldman (Ed)., *Asynchronous learning networks: The research frontier* (pp. 239–260). New York, NY: Hampton Press.

Thesen, L., & Pletzen, V. E. (2006). *Academic literacy and the languages of change.* London, England: Continuum.

Thonus, T. (2002). Tutor and student assessments of academic writing tutorials: What is 'success'? *Assessing Writing, 8*(2), 110–134. https://doi.org/10.1016/S1075-2935(03)00002-3

Warschauer, M. (2010). Invited commentary: New tools for teaching writing. *Language Learning & Technology, 14*(1), 3–8.

Williams, J. (2004). Tutoring and revision: Second language writers in the writing center. *Journal of Second Language Writing, 13*(3), 173–201. https://doi.org/10.1016/j.jslw.2004.04.009

Williams, J. (2005). Writing center interaction: Institutional discourse and the role of peer tutors. In K. Bardovi-Harlig & B. Hartford (Eds.), *Interlanguage pragmatics: Exploring institutional talk* (pp. 37–65). Mahwah, NJ: Lawrence Erlbaum.

Williams, J. (2006). The role(s) of writing centers in second language writing instruction. In P. Matsuda (Ed.), *Politics of second language writing: In search of the promised land* (pp. 109–126). Anderson, SC: Parlor Press.

Williams, J., & Severino, C. (2004). Second language writers and the writing center. Introduction to special issue of *Journal of Second Language Writing, 13*, 165–172. https://doi.org/10.1016/j.jslw.2004.04.010

Xing, M., Wang, J., & Spencer, K. (2008). Raising students' awareness of cross-cultural contrastive rhetoric in english writing via an e-learning course. *Language Learning & Technology, 12*(2), 71–93.

Yergeau, M., Wozniak, K., & Vandenberg, P. (2008). Expanding the space of f2f: Writing centers audio-visual-textual conferencing. *Kairos: A Journal of Rhetoric, Technology, and Pedagogy, 13*(1). Retrieved from http://technorhetoric.net/13.1

Young, R. (1995). Conversational styles in language proficiency interviews. *Language Learning, 45*(1), 3–42. https://doi.org/10.1111/j.1467-1770.1995.tb00961.x

Zawacki, T., & Cox, M. (2011). Introduction to WAC and second language writing. *Across the Disciplines, 8*(4). Retrieved from https://wac.colostate.edu/atd/ell/zawacki-cox.cfm

Zawacki, T., & Habib, A. S. (2014). Internationalization, English L2 writers, and the writing classroom: Implications for teaching and learning. *College Composition and Communication, 65*(4), 650–658.

Zheng, R., & Ferris, S. P. (2008). *Online instructional modeling.* Hershey, PA: IGI Global. https://doi.org/10.4018/978-1-59904-723-2

12

CLICKS, TWEETS, LINKS, AND OTHER GLOBAL ACTIONS
The Nature of Distributed Agency in Digital Environments

Lavinia Hirsu

ABSTRACT

The chapter explores distributed agency in global contexts through building on scholarship from rhetoric, composition, and intercultural communication. *Kony 2012* is a viral campaign initiated by Invisible Children, and it serves as a productive case study. To draw global support in their efforts to apprehend African warlord Joseph Kony, Invisible Children relied on a plan that encouraged users to enact the Fourth Estate, a distributed form of agency beyond cultural borders. While successful, Invisible Children struggled to channel the global conversation toward their mission. The chapter uses Henry Jenkins's (2009, 2012) concepts of spreadability and drillability to describe and problematize what took place in terms of tensions between the local and the global in systems of social media. As the Kony campaign illustrates, successful writers know how to move from the agency of one to the agency of many and stay attuned to an always-connected public sphere.

Keywords: agency, digital literacy, digital participation, global action, global circulation, intercultural communication, public sphere, social media, spreadability

INTRODUCTION

Over the past ten years, viral campaigns have significantly reshaped the public sphere. Today, activists or citizens who accidentally find out about the next viral campaign from their Facebook friends are often invited to be part of a collective effort to change the world, regardless of their cultural background or media. To be a global citizen means focusing on the new viral phenomenon to (re)circulate and respond to events located near and far. Individual participation is entangled in

DOI: 10.7330/9781607326649.c012

"networked communities" that are "fluid and unpredictable" (Limbu, 2014, p. 141). To explore agency in such online environments, I relate findings from a case study of a viral campaign, *Kony 2012*, led by Invisible Children (IC).

Founded in 2004, IC has largely been coordinated by Bobby Bailey, Laren Poole, and Jason Russell. With the help of an international team of American activists, IC has led numerous activities to improve the living conditions of children in Uganda (Zuckerman, 2012). In their 2012 campaign, IC wanted to gather global support to stop the illegal practices of Joseph Kony, the African leader of the Lord's Resistance Army (LRA). The IC campaign is significant in examining the afore-noted issues for two reasons: first, it provides an in-depth understanding into the nature of distributed agency in global contexts; second, it offers important pedagogical guidelines that can help students and teachers alike. When the *agency of one* is always part of the *agency of many*, online participation and rhetorical action need careful consideration.

DISTRIBUTED AGENCY IN GLOBAL CONTEXTS

Scholars in intercultural communication note the complexity and messiness of digital spaces. Volumes such as *Computer-Mediated Communication Across Cultures* (St.Amant & Kelsey, 2012) and *Digital Rhetoric and Global Literacies* (Verhulsdonck & Limbu, 2014) challenge long-held assumptions about intercultural competence in a digital world. Damien S. Pfister and Jordan Soliz have remarked that current online interactions are complicated phenomena because they operate on a different scale of many-to-many. Pfister and Soliz (2011) therefore suggest we examine how users engage simultaneously in a semantic web with many other virtual groups and communities. To be competent communicators, students need to develop skills that enable them to work collaboratively across different platforms and to negotiate cross-cultural exchanges (Brewer & St.Amant, 2015). Digital environments call for continuous worldwide participation, and models of intercultural communication need to capture dynamic exchanges that reduce the distance between cultural experiences and multiply the sites of agency and rhetorical action (Pfister & Soliz, 2011, p. 249). According to Rich Rice and Zachary Hausrath, cultural proximity is enabled by "our global interactive age" (Rice and Hausrath 2014, p. 19). "Interactive experiences" facilitate the formation of "collective competence" that does more than recognize cultural difference. Digital environments facilitate and trouble the intersection of multiple cultures and online practices.

The scale of many-to-many is one dimension affecting global action and agency. Rhetorical production is the result of multiple users, as well as the outcome of material agents: the technologies used and the physical conditions under which users compose their texts (Gries, 2012, p. 80; Sheridan, Ridolfo, & Michel, 2012, p. 103). In Jessica Reyman's (2013) words, "with every click and path followed, every status update and tweet entered, every photo and post contributed, every comment, every item tagged, users are collectively producing both the visible and the invisible social Web" (p. 514). The generative force of writing in global contexts comes not only from the *interaction* of multiple elements. According to Gries (2012), the *intra-action* of "human and non-human entities" change dynamic relationships between various actors (p. 69). Individual agents do more than respond or adapt to the platforms they use. They act with and within the spaces they inhabit. YouTube videos are linked to Facebook pages that take readers to news articles to which commentators add their critique. Distributed agency is thus about the acts of rhetorical production and their dynamic interconnections.

An ecological framework better describes how texts come into being in the virtual world. As Jenny Edbauer (2005) suggests, an ecology of "effects, enactments, and events" redefines the notion of rhetorical situation (p. 5). In digital spaces, we no longer work within a particular set of coordinates that determine a predictable outcome. An ecology of online artifacts is open to variable responses, evolves in light of new users and texts, and is always subject to change depending on the production of new materials. An ecological model of distributed agency emphasizes the process rather than the product (p. 13). The process depends on the existence of products (e.g., images, texts, videos), but it is also sensitive to other rhetorical components, such as the actual and potential networks of active participants, the technological infrastructures that connect users, and the nodes and links that help circulate digital artifacts. Finally, an ecological model expands our definition of intercultural communication and makes possible new forms of cultural exchanges and habits.

Rich Rice and Benjamin Lauren state that writing in a globally networked world is "an enormously complex, context-driven, and ongoing process" (Rice and Lauren 2014, p. 155). To join global conversations, one must understand "knowledge is a community generated and community maintained phenomenon" (Verhulsdonck & Limbu, 2014, p. 146). Distributed knowledge builds on cultural and collective sensitivity and on technological versatility. Agency emerges out of the interaction among users in various cultural locations and their ongoing digital practices, platforms, and devices. This creates a fascinating global scene, "elliptical, immersive in diverse environments, dispersed, ordinary (not rarified), mediated, ongoing, and coexistent with other activities" (Micciche, 2014, p. 493). Under these conditions, how can composers enter this scene and effectively transmit their messages? How is collective agency deployed in contexts that cut across media and cultural contexts? An analysis of the *Kony 2012* campaign can help answer these questions and provide lessons for a globally informed pedagogy.

CALLING FOR THE FOURTH ESTATE

To understand how the IC managed their global campaign, I first present the strategies employed by Joseph Kony and the Lord's Resistance Army (LRA). Kony and his soldiers used less conventional tactics to accomplish their goals. In turn, the Ugandan officials and other organizations committed to arresting Kony had a difficult time stopping him. To identify an alternative approach that could bring Kony to justice, the IC came up with a four-part action plan, a model of global outreach both on the ground, in Uganda, and in other neighboring countries. The IC's plan used the interconnected nature of communication and can provide an example of how to deploy agency more effectively in online spaces.

With the intent of removing Yoweri Museveni from the Ugandan leadership, Joseph Kony gathered an army of rebels, attacked villages, stole food, and abducted children to train them as LRA fighters (Cline, 2013, p. 58). The LRA trained these children in the spirit of the group, teaching them how to embrace cruelty and violence toward the enemy, respect and obey leaders, and remain in camps rather than fleeing. Kony seemed to take children indiscriminately away from their families, forcing them to become soldiers, sex slaves, and porters (Le Sage, 2011, p. 1).

In the first years of LRA operations, Kony was primarily active in Uganda, which lacked stable means of communication and a solid infrastructure in many of its rural areas. Because Kony could make his own rules, international organizations attempted to come to a peaceful agreement to avoid losing too much ground. In 2006, Kony showed willingness to discuss terms of agreement; however, the Juba Peace Talks ended with no significant outcomes (Cline, 2013, p. 109). Kony benefited from supplies and money he received during the period of negotiations, only to return to his aggressive military actions with an invigorated group of soldiers. Gradually, he expanded his attacks in other countries, such as Central African Republic, South Sudan, and the Democratic Republic of Congo. International intervention became even more critical as Kony and his army became a global threat. The dispersed nature of his actions crossed national borders and called for a comprehensive approach that could address the cultural values of the LRA and the global implications of their attacks.

The IC argued only this approach could match and beat Kony at his own game. In the face of global violence, people needed everyone's support to catch and give proper trial to Kony and his fighters. As stated on the IC website (see https://invisiblechildren.com), the organization adopted a long-term plan operating at multiple levels. First, IC made a continuous effort to trigger as much public attention as possible beyond the borders of Uganda. Second, media coverage had to be doubled by real action anyone could engage in. To accomplish this goal, IC needed more than publicity. It had to encourage people in different countries to participate in a global search for Kony. However, before Ugandans could benefit from these actions, they needed protection and a coherent system of communication. Kony's army often took advantage of the lack of infrastructure in villages they raided. As a way to counteract these moves, the IC put in place a radio communication system that made the identification of Kony's movement easier and more precise. To connect people in Uganda with a global audience, the IC linked the local radio system with an online tracking tool that enabled viewers to follow the attacks, location, and number of victims registered (see http://tinyurl .com/q5pl6ml). The near real-time connection between the Ugandan villagers and their global audience was expected to increase the urgency of immediate action. Finally, the IC hoped no humanitarian action could be complete without providing continuous support for the displaced families, the victims who endured Kony's abuses, and the young people who had little to no education as a result.

The four-part plan serves as a model of glocal participation in the public sphere and distributed action in multiple locations. The IC recognizes its programs and goals cannot be successful unless citizens of the world contribute to the rescue and reconstruction mission. The activists believe "that a worldview bound by borders is outdated and that stopping injustice anywhere is the responsibility of humanity everywhere" (see http://tinyurl.com/noyc2dj). The IC identifies this engagement as the Fourth Estate, the expression of a distributed form of agency and ethical responsibility. Instead of waiting for national governments to act in the regions where the LRA continue to be active, IC reminds all citizens everyone has the duty and power to positively impact others whose rights have been infringed upon. Instead of relying on macro-structures (established communities, cultures, or inter/national organizations), the IC appeals to every individual to understand their global impact.[1] Indeed, participation in media-rich environments marks an epistemological shift in the current public sphere that both synthesizes and distributes collective agency (Rice, 2013, p. 249).

Many of the IC's strategies also involve enacting distributed agency on the ground. For instance, to convince fighters to disobey Kony and leave their camps, the IC distributed "come home" fliers. The activists could not directly reach out to the rebel units; therefore, they simply dropped fliers from helicopters in areas where they assumed the LRA was conducting its operations. Each flier contained information about safety measures and methods on how to defect. The instructions came with local maps, photographs depicting former soldiers surrounded by their families, and cartoon-like images that illustrated the steps for returning home.

Interestingly, the IC treats these fliers as an opportunity to "plant a seed of hope." Besides being a powerful analogy, the phrase is important because it uncovers attitudes about the rhetorical impact the fliers are expected to have. The IC knows a flier is not a means of persuasion (i.e., a directed message that will lead to a predictable outcome). While this may be the desired goal, the activists admit the complexity of the problem. A leaflet coming from the sky may have minimal effects on the LRA soldiers if considered separately. The rhetorical power of these fliers is contingent on other factors, including the circulation of oral stories about former soldiers who safely returned home, material and psychological conditions within the LRA, personal commitment to rebel groups, etc. The flier cannot persuade by itself, but it can help create the conditions for future persuasion. It is merely one component in an ecology of artifacts that may result in a positive outcome. Therefore, planting the seeds of a global conversation is a more productive and desirable approach. Current communicative practices are more likely to succeed when active and continuous engagement replaces a more linear form of persuasion. In pedagogical terms, the new framework requires teachers to help students initiate and sustain fluid exchanges with their audience. The IC's campaign demonstrates the effectiveness of this approach, as well as its possible limitations.

AND THE WORLD RESPONDED . . .

On March 5, 2012, the IC published on YouTube a video entitled *Kony 2012* (see http://tinyurl.com/6unkq5k; "Invisible Children," 2012a). Its purpose was to make Kony's face an iconic image everyone could recognize worldwide. The video portrayed Jason Russell, one of the IC founders, explaining to his son, Gavin, how he needs to stop Kony. Jacob, Russell's friend, is an African boy who witnessed his brother's death by the hands of the LRA and appears in the video as the representative of all Ugandan children-victims waiting to be rescued. The major challenge with capturing Kony, the video suggests, is that he is not famous: "Joseph Kony is invisible." This is, in fact, the direct call for distributed agency that the video is making. Russell urges everyone to spread and make Kony's face visible to the world. If people started to share images of Kony and speak about the IC mission, policy makers would be more likely to take military action against him. The success of the IC campaign required this important change in Kony's public visibility.

As long as Kony did not exist for people in other corners of the world, Ugandans could not hope to win the fight against the LRA. While some information about Kony's militaristic actions did circulate online, these pieces were not trending on social media or on high-profile sites. Russell encouraged all viewers to change Kony's degree of visibility and hoped that audiences would tune in to the search campaign promptly. Indeed, as Kirk St.Amant (2011) argues in "Globalization and the Digital Divide," one of the challenges of cyberspace is the issue of presence. As more and more people across the globe have access to the Internet, cultural groups gain more opportunities to share their struggles and stories. However, to do so, a community needs to increase its virtual presence and to maintain its visibility (p. 8). Similarly, readers who see these stories from afar on their digital screens need to understand physical distance can be overcome through virtual participation. These actions require skills that can be deployed for active global engagement.

Russell's call was met with immediate response. Viewers shared the video on multiple platforms, such as Twitter, Facebook, blogs, and other websites. Within a week the clip gathered some 100 million views and 5 million tweets, an unprecedented success unmatched by no other long video posted on YouTube (Kanczula, 2012). Users were not just recirculating the video; they were becoming rhetorical agents who committed to different writing acts: tagging, linking, commenting, and sharing. The production of *Kony 2012* morphed into a process of distributed production where everyone could participate. People found out about Kony because their friends, families, and local groups voluntarily made Kony visible and spread the news about his actions.

Some might argue the phenomenon of distributed agency happens automatically because many people are captivated by a digital artifact and want to respond or share it with others. Indeed, at a first glance, this seems to have been the case with *Kony 2012*. However, if we analyze these events, we discover collective agency in Kony's case went through two stages: an *orchestrated phase* where distribution was somewhat administrated by the IC activists, and a *free-determined phase* where distributed agency happened organically and spontaneously. Both forms demonstrate the dynamic, interconnected, and fluid nature of global interactions.

In the first stage, distributed agency was influenced by the IC followers and the communicative infrastructure they had in place. The viral nature of *Kony 2012* was not a total surprise to them. Rather, IC believed in the rhetorical potential of their fans and used it advantageously. The organization had a wide network of people who connected with one another, shared materials online, and kept reporting back to IC about their local activities (Jenkins, 2012). *YouTube* statistics reveal a base of young people (e.g., thirteen- to seventeen-year-old females and eighteen- to twenty-four-year-old males) who contributed to the initial circulation of the clip. The IC made use of distributed agency because they could anticipate the potential outcome of their followers' actions. Even if they could not control what others would say about Kony, the IC had "a self-organising connective action network" that supported their goals (Chazal & Pocrnic, 2016, p. 101).

IC followers took it upon themselves to further appeal to their own networks. Many turned to Facebook, Twitter, and email profiles of twenty culture-makers (e.g., influential celebrities, athletes, and billionaires who could draw attention to the cause). Ellen DeGeneres, Bono, Mark Zuckerberg, Condoleezza Rice, Bill Clinton, and John Kerry are among the individuals who had the power to draw further global interest in Kony's story. In a matter of days, the cascading effect of distributed agency moved from one group of people to another, from the IC fans to celebrities and onward, to the celebrities' followers.

QUESTIONABLE SUCCESS

IC's plan seemed to work. The first three strategies were implemented: (1) they drew the world's attention to their cause, (2) they involved users at a global scale, and (3) they connected local to global by making people spread the word about the plight of Ugandan children. Their last strategy involved sustaining these efforts until officials and international organizations could apprehend Kony. Despite the immediate spread of *Kony 2012*, the campaign failed to trigger concrete sanctions for the LRA. The problem of Uganda's children became visible and present on social media; however, the global conversation seemed to have fewer concrete results than initially thought. Even if people wrote about the Ugandan children or posted tags and comments for the video, local government entities and international political bodies delayed the mobilization of military forces against Kony. Did social media facilitate a furious global conversation that died out as quickly as it started? Were people connecting with each other just because this was a "spectacular" story (Hesford, 2011) and a "grievable cause" that crossed cultural boundaries (Butler, 2010)?

The IC captivated people's attention, but actions that led to its viral circulation did not make people engage more seriously in the social problems brought up by Russell and his followers. Scholars such as Scott and Welch (2014) find little evidence that "inquiry into the 'bigger questions' ever took place" (p. 564). The debates on the fate of the children of Uganda did not target the real conditions of these children on the ground, their material circumstances, and the geo-political conditions of the LRA attacks. Instead, priority was given to the new "technological *form* of the video's launch, the *speed* and *mass reach* of its reception, and the *idea* that the metaphor of global discussion was being made real" (Scott & Welch, 2014, p. 564). Thus, users who responded to the video seemed to conduct rhetorical analyses of the form and circulation methods of the video, instead of exploring the real causes and nature of the social problems in Uganda. Global media rather than local problems became the primary object of attention, and their power to reach people became the topic of debate in itself. As Scott and Welch note, "the *idea* of public conversation *becomes* the conversation," while other more important issues remain unaddressed (p. 564).

Scott and Welch note the responses post-*Kony 2012* demonstrate a fascination with the power of digital technologies. The IC campaign seems to have had "an agency of its own," and audiences marveled at this achievement (p. 569). Although real people were involved in the production and circulation of the video, users wrote about Kony as if it were an independent artifact. Russell called on people across the globe to take the streets and influence their political organizations to help with Kony's arrest; unfortunately, few actually followed his advice. Commentators *were* interested in how the video became viral, but the focus remained on the video's "means, processes, and styles" (Scott & Welch, 2014, p. 569). The people behind the Twitter and Facebook feeds seemed to be the mere spectators of a global phenomenon.

Increasing Kony's visibility required "clicktivism," a hard-to-sustain public engagement practice (Waldorf, 2012). Essentially, with a few clicks, anybody could become a member of the IC community. Such clicktivism has the advantage of leading to immediate distributed action; however, because it is a quick form of response, it can also risk turning into "cheap participation." Clicktivism can be a powerful tool of "making noise" for it draws attention and it encourages mass reply. Yet sharing the video with others in this way does not guarantee in-depth understanding of the social issue at hand.

Scott and Welch critique the global response the IC received because it eliminates the bodies and material conditions of those mentioned in the message, and the bodies of those who produce and respond to that message. According to them, "composition's historic tendency has long been toward the dematerializing belief that knowledge, power, and agency are matters of discourse" (p. 567). Rhetoricity, therefore, lies in the textual, imagistic, aural, and multimodal artifacts that depict real lives. The body retains little to no rhetorical influence on composing and the disappearance or ignorance of the body is highly problematic: "Even as public and digital rhetorical theories emphasize global connectivity and the creation of 'convergence cultures' (see Jenkins) that purport to be progressive portals to the world, these theories take shape in corridors cleansed of globalization's most troubling material effects and evidence of struggle by its discontents" (Scott & Welch, 2014, p. 570).

In digital global encounters, it may be easy to miss the physical conditions of those whose lives we think we can touch. In Kony's case, users who shared and liked the video thought this was enough. Acts of composing alone, such as clicktivism, tagging, and blogging canceled the importance of local action (i.e., taking the streets and putting pressure on local administrators to get involved in this global search). Moreover, rhetorical involvement in the popularization of *Kony 2012* replaced direct involvement in Ugandan's social and political struggles. These critiques raise a few important questions for consideration: if we take this viral campaign as a model of current glocal exchanges, is communication at a global scale fated to dissolve because it is too loosely formed and it gets pulled in too many directions? How does the agency of many impact the few that the world set out to represent and help in the first place?

EXPANDABLE AGENCY

T. M. S. Ruge (2012) writes:

> As it always does, the internet exhaled as quickly as it inhaled, and the world returned to its tepid state of being. The normalcy of global injustice;

the calculated, unabated global spread of the cavern between privilege and want; the cries for freedom almost matched in octave with the inanity and fervor for the latest gadgetry. In a heart beat, we are back to the bitter sweet symphony of humanity's march through time and space. Except that this time, there is a wrinkle in the fabric of normalcy. (pp. 176–177)

The world listened, the world talked, but in Uganda things did not seem to lead to Kony's arrest. Critics of the IC declared the mission an epic failure. A deeper analysis of the artifacts composed and produced in conjunction with the video, however, reveals other reasons why the IC may not have accomplished all goals. Understanding the complex nature of this campaign can help identify the potential and limitations of global participation and action.

Many who watched *Kony 2012* might have missed the opportunity to engage in deeper questions about the real lives of children in Uganda. Similarly, we cannot dismiss the active production of responses from African voices. In fact, according to Ruge (2012), IC created one of the most opportune moments for citizens of Uganda and other African countries to speak up (p. 172). Among individuals who tagged and recomposed *Kony 2012* for new audiences were Teju Cole, Rosebell Kagumire, Semhar Araia, and Solome Lemma. They used their own spaces (on Twitter, Facebook, YouTube, and various news channels) to build up a critical commentary against the video and to compose a distinct image of the children-victims.

The IC did not anticipate this rhetorical turn, and local voices started inserting their own narratives in the same posts where they cited, shared, and linked to the YouTube video. *Kony 2012* didn't fail because users missed asking bigger questions related to the social conditions of Ugandan children. In fact, powerful voices intervened and changed the fate of the campaign early on. Rather, IC was unprepared to deal with local voices, and distributed action took an unanticipated direction. Henry Jenkins's (2009) distinction between spreadability and drillability, two processes of circulation that operate on distinct logics, help us understand how agency changed.

Jenkins defines *spreadability* as "the capacity of the public to engage actively in the circulation of media content through social networks and in the process expand its economic value and cultural worth" (2009, para. 12). Jenkins argues, to be effective, a story needs to circulate across media and gain coverage on a variety of digital platforms. Spreadability thus works in tandem with the distributed agency of users who move an artifact from one site to another. By commenting, tagging, and reposting, participants contribute to the composition of a larger coherent narrative. To spread the IC mission, viewers linked the thirty-minute video with their own comments, evaluations, and supplementary information about the organization. These rhetorical actions spread the message about Kony's abuses and drew in more participants.

Unfortunately, IC was not ready to address drillability. *Drillability* is the users' propensity to uncover details around a viral story, to search for complexity, and to unveil new insights. The drive to discover more explains why certain events have a high rhetorical impact and continue to circulate and maintain high audience interest (Jenkins, 2009). Drillability offers depth and allows for diversity to emerge around a particular event or story. Digital technologies expose any narrative not only to a wide audience, but also to the potential of contestation. To be effective, then, a spreadable story needs to orchestrate and allow for diverse voices to emerge while continuing to circulate and draw interest. Therefore, drillability complicates the nature of distributed agency. Those who get involved in the dissemination of an artifact via digital tools help spread and pluralize a narrative; they add nuance to it and diversity; they grow its visibility exponentially, as well as its complexity.

Drillability was IC's weakness that led to the contestation of their video (Gregory, 2012; Swartz, 2012). Despite a comprehensive approach, the activists primarily focused on Kony, and they did not know how to manage a larger ecology of voices that emerged with great authority. As soon as Kony became a recognizable figure worldwide, its success immediately became questionable. In Gregory's (2012) words, *Kony 2012* was "too successful, too early" (p. 464). IC had no viable long-term strategies to manage their visibility after viral exposure. In fact, 66 percent of the Twitter conversation turned anti-Kony between March 5 and March 12, 2012. Very soon after the official launch of the video, local voices started to complicate the global narrative about Kony, questioning its intentions and worldwide effort.

Using the video, African voices enacted their local agency by counteracting. Through tag writing, hyperlinking, and video sharing, Ugandan journalists (e.g., Rosebell Kagumire, Angelo Izama), scholars who research social issues in Africa (e.g., Mahmood Mamdani), and writers (e.g., Dinaw Mengestu) consistently critiqued and pointed to visual inconsistencies in the IC campaign. The clip reproduced the "white savior industrial complex" (Cole, 2012). Both at the narrative and visual levels, the video pitched Russell against Kony, the good white guy with a cute blond child against the bad African guy (Gordon, 2012; Moore, 2012; Seay, 2012). The visual tropes were connected to images of colonial Africa. Nothing has changed from previous portrayals of

African children and Western interventions in Africa. *Kony 2012* offered a simplified version of Uganda and the initial narrative wanted to make visible a figure that had very little relevance in the lives of Ugandans.

While some argue the wave of critical comments failed to have the same rhetorical impact as the video itself, the numbers show us differently. "Drillability on the Kony story and IC," Gregory (2012) notes, "happened organically in the days and weeks following the release of Kony 2012" (p. 466), and it undermined IC's credibility diffusely. For instance, Rosebell Kagumire (2012), a Ugandan journalist, recorded a video strategically entitled, "My Response to Kony2012," which she posted on YouTube two days after the original publication of the IC's clip. Carrying the same "Kony2012" label, Kagumire's video appeared in the top search results whenever users wanted to find out about the campaign. Even though she did not gather the same numbers of visitors as *Kony 2012*, Kagumire's video went viral with more than half a million of visitors (Ruge, 2012, p. 175). Her response offered an alternative to the circulation of Kony's image that made an impact on YouTube and many other digital platforms. Due to her digital presence, Kagumire was invited to make appearances on a variety of media channels (e.g., *CNN*, *Al Jazeera*, and *The New York Times*), which have increased her visibility and credibility.

What kept Kony at the top of online debates was not spreadability, but drillability—the multiplication of local voices, the enactment of counter-agency grafted on the initial success of the campaign. Teju Cole tweeted about the "white man's burden" in a series of brief messages that managed to draw a wide audience. His tweets were disseminated on Tumblr, Facebook, *The Atlantic*, *The New York Times*, and *Fox News*. Teju Cole's Twitter followers may have helped with the distribution of his messages, but this form of collective agency was not orchestrated, directed, and channeled in the same way IC did with their own followers. Cole and other critics consistently spread critical messages and, their collective agency created a diffuse counter-movement that rendered the IC's call problematic and ultimately irrelevant.

As processes of global communication, drillability and spreadability demonstrate the tensions between the local and the global in the context of diffuse systems of social media. In *Modernity at Large*, Arjun Appadurai (1996) prefigured these cultural-technological movements. In the definition of "global flows," he notes new conditions of global communication happen at intersections of "persons, technologies, finance, information, and ideology" (p. 47). To make sense of globalization, Appadurai tried to systematize global flows under five "scapes": ethnoscapes, mediascapes, technoscapes, financescapes, and ideoscapes. He also recognized the importance of chaos over order, movement over static positions, and change over stability (p. 47). Thus, drillability and spreadability are emergent processes that help us understand "global flows" in concrete, yet dynamic, terms. Social media increase the cacophony of voices that can start any conversation anytime, anywhere. Amid this chaos, we need to articulate communicative models that can help us "plant the seeds" for productive cultural dialogue. Drillability and spreadability are just two manifestations of how global communication can be configured. These concepts should become part of the toolkit of our students in global technical communication, rhetoric, and composition classes. The teaching of traditional concepts (e.g., *ethos*, *logos*, *pathos*, enthymeme, and argumentation) needs to be supplemented with a pedagogy attuned to the realities of a global world in flux where different composing processes exist and follow media-driven logics.

DISTRIBUTED AGENCY AND MISSED OPPORTUNITIES

The IC gathered worldwide support after the launch of *Kony 2012*; yet, spreadability turned into drillability, and the organization lost any control over the public debate around Kony's fate. Loss of agency came with the active participation of critics in various digital spaces and the IC's incapacity to remain relevant among competing voices. The IC lost the opportune moment to speak persuasively about their goals, and they managed to regain worldwide attention only with new artifacts that worked against them.

Posted on YouTube (March 5, 2012), *Kony 2012* was meant to raise awareness about the IC's mission. According to a follow-up video published on the same site on April 20, activists hoped to move the digital movement from the screen to the streets (see http://tinyurl.com/q2nl8ex). As part of the operation "Cover the night," IC supporters were invited to go out in their own towns and cover public spaces with posters, signs, and billboards, demanding Kony's arrest ("Invisible Children," 2012c). Because *Kony 2012* spread out of control so quickly and widely, by April 20 the rhetorical moment that the initial video was supposed to create had been consumed before the set deadline. Meeting on this day in the streets to make Kony's atrocities known was no longer necessary because everyone knew about Kony in early March. The viral nature of the video along with the many artifacts that accompanied the clip raised global awareness better than any other campaign would have done it in a public place.

To regain some control over the campaign, IC created responses to the criticism waged against the organization. Despite this effort to engage in a public debate where meaning is co-constructed, the IC's materials had not been further circulated. Even the twenty-minute follow-up video, "Kony 2012: Part II-Beyond Famous," did not manage to refocus users' attention ("Invisible Children," 2012b). The video gave more space to African supporters, featuring activists in Uganda and the Republic of Congo. The second video did not find its worldwide audience because it was confronted with the issue of timing: the IC posted the material on April 5, too far apart from the first one that traveled at high speed across multiple platforms.

The IC learned the lesson on distributed agency only after the opportune moment passed them. Although they started with a solid four-action plan, they could not accomplish the last phase: to sustain global attention and engagement in order to fulfill their ultimate goal. Without recognizing the role of alternative voices (*drillability*), they defended themselves and corrected their mistakes too late. On March 15, Jason Russell fell under public pressure and had a nervous breakdown. He was recorded on camera, walking naked in San Diego, close to his home, throwing his arms in the air and talking to himself. The clip became viral as well. A second compromising artifact, a photograph of Bobby Bailey, Laren Poole, and Jason Russell showed the three IC leaders in the company of rebels of the Sudan People's Liberation Army. The image had an important rhetorical effect because it contributed to an ecology of materials that systematically questioned the IC's true intentions.

The artifacts influenced the direction of the IC campaign. Distracted by the gossip and scandal created around Russell's images, the power of the campaign diluted, and the agency of many failed to converge toward the primary goal. The IC could not orchestrate an ecology of images that would positively contribute to the organization and got caught in the middle of a rhetorical context created for them by vigilant users. Viewers were not only watching, but they were actually watching with a very critical eye.

Scholars studying online activism have noted digital engagement has changed drastically. In Jeffrey Swift's (2013) study, "Resisting the robust: The Internet Defense League and the Potential of Networked Kairos," composers need to advocate for social issues by acknowledging the importance of distractions, drop-in participants, and distributed agency without immediate and directed outcomes. The "antifragile" model seems to work better in a world where there are too many activist organizations and humanitarian crises to follow. Instead of aiming for composing the best text fit for the right moment (the fragile model), Swift argues that, according to an antifragile approach, an organization or group of participants are less concerned about exploiting the best opportunity for conveying the right message. Rhetorical success depends on the long-term commitment of a network of people who sustain the organization. The network rather than an artifact, mission, or goal is the ultimate achievement; while failure, distractions, and missed opportunities define the mode of being and acting within that group.

IC initially valued and adopted an antifragile model of activism; they recognized the importance of distributed agency that could only be built in time. The leaders tried to establish a network of people willing to spread the message at the right moment (i.e., the launch of *Kony 2012*). The organization's efforts seemed to reach an impasse only when the activists could no longer keep a hand on the trajectory of their artifacts and the meanings they were being attributed. The organization's leadership seemed impatient about failure and turned against the critics. When Russell's images and video seemed to have an agency of their own, the activists didn't immediately recognize the exigencies of the new rhetorical situation and, in time, the world forgot about their call.

TOWARD AN ANTIFRAGILE MODEL OF GLOBAL COMMUNICATION

Tuning in and out of viral campaigns has become a very easy task: a click, a share, or a tweet draws us into a global phenomenon. From a pedagogical perspective, these online exchanges and interventions are important because they teach us how to engage with the world, how to meet people from other cultural spaces, and how to critically respond to their calls. The IC campaign shows us agency in digital environments is effective only when shared with users worldwide. IC's four-action plan worked only insofar as it acknowledged that people enjoy the interactive and connective power of social media (see St.Amant & Rice, 2015, p. vii). According to Rice and Hausrath (2014), these "glocal interactions" facilitate collective competence.

How can we teach distributed action? Is diffuse agency teachable at all? I argue that current technological and communicative conditions demand that we help our students understand and contribute to an "antifragile" model of global communication (see Swift, 2013). First, by analyzing the mechanisms of viral campaigns, students can come to deeper realizations about the nature of global exchanges. As complex phenomena of scale and depth, viral campaigns are models for observing the dynamics among people from different cultural backgrounds.

Teachers in multicultural courses can ask students to trace how world-wide conversations emerge and die out around different topics. The same exercise can also become a civic practice that everyone can attune to. Reading world news is becoming, for instance, a practice of following the most recent viral trends. This is how new digital opportunities for cultural learning open up in the public sphere (Desai, 2013). Carried by an impetus to know more about the true life of Ugandans, many online readers moved from the IC posts to new local and global voices that added depth to Kony's initial narrative. By looking at the multitude of responses, users could continually reformulate their ideas about the mission of the organization and the actual conditions of children in Uganda.

Second, as students analyze and participate in global events, they can identify new processes of communication. Spreadability and drillability represent only two examples that capture global interactions online. To channel their messages, users often experiment with new ways of turning digital content from mere data into information, and then into usable knowledge (Potts, 2014). Emergent digital spaces create conditions for new types of engagement: different practices of active reading, writing, listening, and viewing. As scholars of global communication and as practitioners of writing instruction, we need to keep a critical eye on emergent habits and trends while testing alternative practices ourselves. As we continue to define and describe digitally-born literate practices, we should also invent new modes of connecting to the world in order to build rather than always critique the networks we are part of. When the goal is no longer persuasion but the process of "planting seeds" for a global conversation, teachers and students have the opportunity to watch, learn, and act upon the unfolding transformations of social media and cultural paradigms. As many of our students are already actively involved in their networks, the classroom space can become an invention laboratory, the testing ground for new strategies of participation.

Third, students should explore the cultural consequences of what might seem simple digital actions. Rhetorical moves such as tagging, linking, liking, commenting, and sharing have the power to mobilize people across cultural boundaries; yet, a moment of global attention can easily be just that—a moment. The failure is not when a community or group cannot convince the world of their worthy cause. The failure comes when that group does not fully recognize the power of the network and its most common practices. As the IC campaign proves, cultivating a web of relations becomes more important than a single persuasive narrative that fits a particular cultural mold. To be culturally competent means to understand the potential of digital technologies to weave connections across cultural differences. To do so, we need to find cultural power in "new modes of representation" (Pfister & Soliz, 2011, p. 250), and in the most banal digital acts. A click or a tweet can be a mere gesture; however, each represents a rhetorical action with potential local and global impact. The effectiveness of global communication may not always be visible or quantifiable; instead, it can be traced in the durability of networks and the persistence of connections among users.

Invisible Children has learned these lessons the hard way, although the organization is very proud of its achievements. Since 2012, three LRA members have surrendered and two commanders have been captured. The African Union, European Union, United Nations, and United States have renewed their commitment to international social justice. A rehabilitation center founded by the IC works at its full capacity, and local partners continue to help LRA fighters return safely to their homes (see http://tinyurl.com/p5ffcbb). Now, the IC is ready to move in new directions not before launching a last call: "We Still Need You." In the "Final Video," viewers are informed that strategies and operations to rebuild communities affected by the LRA will be handed over to local organizations (see http://tinyurl.com/p4s493l). Participants in the *Kony* movement can still contribute and exercise their power as *Citizen*(s) (the name of the IC's political advocacy network). In fact, acting as a citizen of the world is an ethical condition that belongs to everyone regardless of cultural affiliations, national commitments, or political interests. In the meantime, IC activists are stepping out of the spotlight but continue to provide updates from the region on their blog. As for Kony, his story remains unfinished, waiting to be changed, challenged, rewritten or forgotten with the next click, tweet, flyer, or breaking news.

Notes

1. William Dutton (2009), and Stephen J. A. Ward and Herman Wasserman (2010) identify this type of global digital participation as the Fifth Estate. New media have enabled the emergence of networks of citizens who establish new parameters of democratic engagement, launch viral campaigns to address social issues, and connect with one another across social networks. While the IC's Fourth Estate fits with this description, the activists behind *Kony 2012* also make an argument for the material consequences that worldwide involvement can have on certain communities around the globe. IC's commitment to global ethics can be seen both in their digital strategies as well as their actions on the ground.

References

Appadurai, A. (1996). *Modernity at large*. Minneapolis, MN: University of Minnesota Press.

Brewer, P. E., & St.Amant, K. (2015). Education and training for globally-distributed virtual teams. *Connexions: International Professional Communication Journal, 3*(1), 3–7.

Butler, J. (2010). *Frames of war: When is life grievable?* Brooklyn, NY: Verso.

Chazal, N., & Pocrnic, A. (2016). Kony 2012: Intervention narratives and the saviour subject. *International Journal for Crime, Justice, and Social Democracy, 5*(1), 98–112. https://doi.org/10.5204/ijcjsd.v5i1.216

Cline, L. E. (2013). *The lord's resistance army*. Santa Barbara, CA: Praeger.

Cole, T. (2012, March 21). The white-savior industrial complex. *The Atlantic*. http://www.theatlantic.com/international/archive/2012/03/the-white-savior-industrial-complex/254843

Desai, G. (2013). *The virtual transformation of the public sphere: Knowledge, politics, identity.* New Delhi, India: Routledge.

Dutton, W. H. (2009). The fifth estate emerging through the network of networks. *Prometheus, 27*(1), 1–15. https://doi.org/10.1080/08109020802657453

Edbauer, J. (2005). Unframing models of public distribution: From rhetorical situation to rhetorical ecologies. *Rhetoric Society Quarterly, 35*(4), 5–24. https://doi.org/10.1080/02773940509391320

Gordon, G. (2012). The power of images: Who gets made visible. In A. Taub (Ed.), *Beyond #Kony2012: Atrocity, awareness and activism in the Internet age* (pp. 103–116). Retrieved from https://leanpub.com/beyondkony2012

Gregory, S. (2012). Kony 2012 through a prism of video advocacy practices and trends. *Journal of Human Rights Practice, 4*(3), 463–468. https://doi.org/10.1093/jhuman/hus024

Gries, L. (2012). Agential matters: Tumbleweed, women-pens, citizen-hope, and rhetorical actancy. In S. Dobrin (Ed.), *Ecology, writing, theory, and new media: Writing ecology* (pp. 67–91). New York, NY: Routledge.

Hesford, W. (2011). *Spectacular rhetorics: Human rights visions, recognitions, feminisms.* Durham, NC: Duke University Press. https://doi.org/10.1215/9780822393818

Invisible Children. (2012a, March 5). Kony 2012. *YouTube*. Retrieved from http://tinyurl.com/6unkq5k

Invisible Children. (2012b, April 5). Kony 2012: Part II-beyond famous. *YouTube*. Retrieved from http://tinyurl.com/njku9fa

Invisible Children. (2012c). Cover the night. *YouTube*. Retrieved from http://tinyurl.com/q2nl8ex

Jenkins, H. (2009). The revenge of the origami unicorn: Seven principles of transmedia storytelling. *Aca-fan: The official weblog of Henry Jenkins*. Retrieved from http://henryjenkins.org/2009/12/the_revenge_of_the_origami_uni.html

Jenkins, H. (2012). Contextualizing #Kony2012: Invisible children, spreadable media, and transmedia activism. *Confessions of an aca-fan: The official blog of Henry Jenkins*. Retrieved from http://henryjenkins.org/2012/03/contextualizing_kony2012_invis.html

Kagumire, R. (2012). My Response to KONY2012. *YouTube*. Retrieved from https://www.youtube.com/watch?v=KLVY5jBnD-E

Kanczula, A. (2012). Kony 2012 in Numbers. *The Guardian*. Retrieved from https://www.theguardian.com/news/datablog/2012/apr/20/kony-2012-facts-numbers

Le Sage, A. (2011). Countering the Lord's resistance army in Central Africa. *Institute for National Strategic Studies* (pp. 1–16). Retrieved from http://ndupress.ndu.edu/Portals/68/Documents/stratforum/SF-270.pdf

Limbu, M. (2014). Digital and global literacies in networked communities: Epistemic shifts and communication practices in the cloud era. In G. Verhulsdonck & M. Limbu (Eds.), *Digital rhetoric and global literacies: Communication modes and digital practices in the networked world* (pp. 131–153). Hershey, PA: IGI Global. https://doi.org/10.4018/978 -1-4666-4916-3.ch007

Micciche, L. R. (2014). Writing material. *College English, 76*(6), 488–505.

Moore, J. (2012). Ethical or exploitative? Stories, advocacy, and suffering. In A. Taub (Ed.), *Beyond #Kony2012: Atrocity, awareness and activism in the Internet age* (pp. 87–102). Retrieved from https://leanpub.com/beyondkony2012

Pfister, D. S., & Soliz, J. (2011). (Re)conceptualizing intercultural communication in a networked society. *Journal of International and Intercultural Communication, 4*(4), 246– 251. https://doi.org/10.1080/17513057.2011.598043

Potts, L. (2014). *Social media in disaster response: How experience architects can build for participation.* New York, NY: Routledge.

Reyman, J. (2013). User data on the social web: Authorship, agency, and appropriation. *College English, 75*(5), 513–533.

Rice, R. (2013). Constructing new mediated knowledge in the process of writing for life. In G. Desai (Ed.), *The virtual transformation of the public sphere: Knowledge, politics, identity* (pp. 246–257). New Delhi, India: Routledge.

Rice, R., & Hausrath, Z. (2014). The necessity of teaching intercultural communication competence in literacy classes. *Journal of College Literacy and Learning, 40,* 19–34.

Rice, R., & Lauren, B. (2014). Developing intercultural competence through glocal activity theory using the connect-exchange study abroad app. In G. Verhulsdonck & M. Limbu (Eds.), *Digital rhetoric and global literacies: Communication modes and digital practices in the networked world* (pp. 154–173). Hershey, PA: IGI Global. https://doi.org /10.4018/978-1-4666-4916-3.ch008

Ruge, T. M. S. (2012). Africa's new status quo: Connected, bold and vocal. In A. Taub (Ed.), *Beyond #Kony2012: Atrocity, awareness and activism in the Internet age* (pp. 172– 177). Vancouver, B.C.: LeanPub.

Scott, T., & Welch, N. (2014). One train can hide another: Critical materialism for public composition. *College English, 76*(6), 562–586.

Seay, L. (2012). Avoiding 'badvocacy': How to do no harm while doing good. In A. Taub (Ed.), *Beyond #Kony2012: Atrocity, awareness and activism in the Internet age* (pp. 126– 135). Retrieved from https://leanpub.com/beyondkony2012

Sheridan, D. M., Ridolfo, J., & Michel, A. J. (2012). *The available means of persuasion: Mapping a theory and pedagogy of multimodal public rhetoric.* Anderson, SC: Parlor Press.

St.Amant, K. (2011). Globalization and the digital divide: Understanding the connections between technology and communication in a global context. In K. St.Amant & B. A. Olaniran (Eds.), *Globalization and the digital divide* (pp. 1–12). Amherst, NY: Cambria Press.

St.Amant, K., & Kelsey, S., (Eds.). (2012). *Computer-mediated communication across cultures: International interactions in online environments.* Hershey, PA: IGI Global. https://doi .org/10.4018/978-1-60960-833-0

St.Amant, K., & Rice, R. (2015). Online writing in global contexts: Rethinking the nature of connections and communication in the age of international online media. *Computers and Composition, 38*(B), v–x. https://doi.org/10.1016/S8755-4615(15)00104-8

Swartz, L. (2012). Invisible children: Transmedia, storytelling, mobilization. *Civic paths.* Retrieved from http://civicpaths.uscannenberg.org/wp-content/uploads/2012/03 /Swartz_InvisibleChildren_WorkingPaper.pdf

Swift, J. (2013). Resisting the robust: The Internet defense league and the potential of networked *kairos. Currents in Electronic Literacy,* 16. Retrieved from https://currents.dw rl.utexas.edu/2013/resisting-the-robust-the-internet-defense-league-and-the-potential -of-networked-kairos.html

Verhulsdonck, G., & Limbu, M. (Eds.). (2014). *Digital rhetoric and global literacies: Communication modes and digital practices in the networked world.* Hershey, PA: IGI Global. https://doi.org/10.4018/978-1-4666-4916-3

Waldorf, L. (2012). White noise: Hearing the disaster. *Journal of Human Rights Practice,* *4*(3), 469–474. https://doi.org/10.1093/jhuman/hus025

Ward, S. J. A., & Wasserman, H. (2010). Towards an open ethics: Implications of new media platforms for global ethics discourse. *Journal of Mass Media Ethics: Exploring Questions of Media Morality, 25*(4), 275–292. https://doi.org/10.1080/08900523.2010 .512825

Zuckerman, E. (2012, March 8). Unpacking Kony 2012. *My heart's in Accra.* Retrieved from http://www.ethanzuckerman.com/blog/2012/03/08/unpacking-kony-2012

13

CONNECTING THE LOCAL AND THE GLOBAL
Digital Interfaces and Hybrid Embodiment in Transnational Activism

Katherine Bridgman

ABSTRACT

This chapter explores activists' work to create continuity between the local and global during what has become known as the Egyptian Revolution of 2011. The hybrid embodiments through which protestors simultaneously worked across both the digital and physical spaces of their activism were key facets of their global communication. This chapter examines the hybrid embodiment of protestor Gigi Ibrahim and how her hybrid embodiment enabled her to provide leadership and to garner resources throughout the revolution. Ibrahim's use of social media during the revolution highlights a powerful facet of global communication that we can incorporate into our classrooms as we prepare students to become agentive global communicators.

Keywords: embodiment, social media, activism, interface, transnationalism

INTRODUCTION

In 2009, Kathleen Blake Yancey challenged us to help students "become the citizen writers of our country, the citizen writers of our world, and the writers of our future" (Yancey, 2009, p. 1). This chapter responds to her call by examining the communication practices of Gigi Ibrahim, who used Twitter to build connections with local and global audiences during what has become known as the Egyptian Revolution of 2011 (January 25 to February 11). Ibrahim's activities reveal a powerful facet of the composing processes of global communicators who—through their *hybrid embodiments* across digital interfaces—are becoming the writers of our future. (I define hybrid embodiment as the simultaneous presence of an author across digital and physical spaces.) Activists such

DOI: 10.7330/9781607326649.c013

as Ibrahim formed their hybrid embodiments by coordinating action and accessing resources locally and globally. As individuals form hybrid embodiments, they can work across digital interfaces as conduits of action in the digital and physical spaces around them.

This chapter opens with a discussion of how to teach global communication strategies. Next, the chapter addresses uses of social media during the Egyptian Revolution and ways protestors' work across social media contributed to the revolution's success. Finally, the chapter examines hybrid embodiment as a facet of Ibrahim's global communication—and how it enabled her to provide leadership and maintain her visibility across the digital and physical spaces of the revolution. By exploring such factors, we can understand the work of digital activists as global communicators and how their work builds connections with local and global audiences. Such analyses reveal the role of digital interfaces as conduits for diverse action across a variety of spaces.

TEACHING HYBRID EMBODIMENT

Strategies of hybrid embodiment enable global activists to overcome two challenges to communal accountability in online spaces: the erroneous belief that actions have "no real world consequences" and the problem posed by "remote linkage" among individuals that blinds them to the impact their words and actions have on others (Fleckenstein, 2005, pp. 151–152). Rather than seeing themselves as disembodied in these online spaces that exist in and outside of our classrooms, our students, as future global communicators, must develop an awareness of their embodied participation in "symbiotic knot[s] of bodies" through which their corporeal presence is returned to the relationship it shares with "vision, language, and places" (Fleckenstein, 2010, pp. 80, 83). As students become aware of the symbiotic knot of bodies they are part of, it becomes clear that the "virtualization" of global communication such as Gigi Ibrahim's across Twitter "does not imply disembodiment" (Fleckenstein, 2010, p. 163). Instead, it requires the development of hybrid embodiments through which global communicators can grapple with the transnational "symbiotic knot of bodies" connecting them to international audiences. Hybrid embodiment enables protestors to reach broader audiences while facilitating a sense of immediacy with local and global audiences. Two hybrid embodiment tactics employed by Ibrahim were: (1) simultaneous action that takes place in digital and physical spaces and (2) the use of resources not isolated to either digital or physical spaces of the revolution. Such hybrid embodiment strategies allowed Ibrahim to provide leadership and secure local and global visibilities during the revolution.

Mubarak's corrupt and brutal police force was one reason among many that protestors took to the streets on January 25, 2011—a national holiday celebrating the Egyptian police force (Khalil, 2011, p. 122). While Egyptians had protested against Mubarak before, their protests had not been so large or well sustained. Eighteen days after they took to the streets, protestors forced Mubarak to step down on February 11, 2011. While multiple factors contributed to Mubarak's removal, protestors' use of social media is one clear contributing factor.

The contribution of social media comes into focus when we consider that only 0.001 percent of Egypt's population was on Twitter at the time of the uprisings in 2011 (Wilson & Dunn, 2011, p. 1250). A report from the Dubai School of Government estimates that in the first quarter of 2011 Egypt only had an average of 131,204 active Twitter users (2011). Despite this relatively small number, protestors garnered remarkably large transnational audiences across Twitter including followers in Egypt and around the world. While examinations of social media offer powerful insight into how individuals use such technologies, they also provide powerful strategies instructors can introduce into classrooms to teach students to be effective global communicators.

Many students are already composing in digital environments shared with global communicators like Gigi Ibrahim. For example, a 2015 Pew study found that 92 percent of teens are going online daily with 71 percent reporting they use more than one social networking site (Lenhart, 2015). However, as we work with our students, we cannot assume they possess expert knowledge of the *practices* necessary to successfully use these tools as global communicators (Daer & Potts, 2014). How can we facilitate this knowledge?

In their introduction to a 2008 *College English* special issue on transnational feminist rhetorics, Wendy Hesford and Eileen Schell suggest that one way to facilitate our students' development into global communicators is to emphasize *practices* over *products* of global communication (Hesford & Schell, 2008). In other words, while students might encounter texts produced by global communicators, they need to understand the processes, or practices of production, through which these texts are created. Hesford and Schell point to Gloria Anzaldúa's work to highlight how our roots in literary analysis often prompt us to focus on the products of global communication rather than the rich practices through which these products were created. Such approaches to Anzaldúa tokenize her as an individual writer "over and above a contextual and geopolitical analysis of [her] alternative rhetorical practices" (p. 462) and elide Anzaldúa's process of negotiating intercultural borderlands as fluid spaces for global communication. As our students develop into global communicators, so too must they develop these rich practices of text production.

These rhetorical practices engage global communicators with the "complex of relationships between a maker's identity, her interactions with others, and the things she makes" (Prins, 2012, p. 145). As students delve into this "complex of relationships," they become participants in the shaping of a global network. Beyond "checking Facebook or using their smart phones to access their fantasy sports standings" (Daer & Potts, 2014, p. 23), these students participate in networks that "foreground the role connectivity plays in content management, information organization, and information production in implicit and explicit ways" (Rice, 2006, p. 128). These networks span physical and digital spaces of global communication and are shaped by global communicators who manage, organize, and produce information across them.

SOCIAL MEDIA IN GLOBAL COMMUNICATION

Connectivity resulting from the management, organization, and production of information by users is not a given outcome of social media use. Rather, this connectivity is situated within cultural practices shaping technology use. Kirk St.Amant (2015) demonstrates this through a heuristic for using social media in global contexts. Highlighting the specificity of social media use, St.Amant argues that cross-cultural connectivity requires communicators "to understand a range of factors from the geopolitical to the cultural" (p. 16). He notes "doing so is no easy task," for social media platforms are used differently across cultures.

One trend emerging among protestors is the use of Twitter to attract a global, and frequently largely Western, audience. For example, as our students in North America use social media, they are likely to find themselves in the company of protestors like Ibrahim. In 2014 and 2015, users of social media found themselves using Twitter alongside activists around the globe including pro-democracy protestors in Hong Kong's #UmbrellaRevolution and protestors in Mexico tweeting with the hasthag #TodoSomosAyotzinapa as they demanded the return of teacher trainees who were abducted and later killed. These and other uses of social media by protestors illustrate the Internet's ability to provide "social movements with a cheap and fast means of international communication" (Della Porta & Mosca, 2005, p. 168). As such, social media platforms frequently become key technologies used by "resource poor" activists to access expansive audiences (Della Porta & Mosca, 2005; Eltantawy & Wiest, 2011).

In addition to expanding protestors' audiences locally and globally, social media platforms provide a sense of immediacy for audiences as they "collapse multiple contexts and bring together commonly distinct audiences," allowing global communicators to form relationships with a variety of audiences around the globe (boyd & Marwick, 2011, p. 15). That is, social media can increase the proximity of global audiences to global communicators. Courtenay Honeycutt and Susan Herring explain that one way this intimacy unfolds across Twitter's interface is through the @user syntax (2009). The @user syntax enables the "relating [of] one tweet to another and, indeed, for making coherent exchanges possible" in the "noisy" environment of Twitter (Honeycutt & Herring, 2009, p. 3). Twitter reiterates this immediacy among users through an interface design centering on the newsfeed, bringing the texts of often disparate audiences into proximity with each other—a proximity that can belie the physical distance separating authors. The visual design of newsfeeds reiterates the proximity articulated by the @user syntax by visually threading together tweets to invite new connections among users (Arola, 2010, p. 8). These and other features of social media platforms, "help to instantiate moments of social connectedness and interaction in which identities and interests, rights and responsibilities, can become recognized and performed and even produce new templates for the conduct of civil society beyond the virtual world" (Cottle, 2011, p. 297). In other words, these moments of "social connectedness" enable individuals to recognize their membership in a movement and become a predictor of participation in collective action (Lim, 2012).

As physical and virtual contexts of activists and audiences converged during the Egyptian Revolution, more specific questions emerged about the contribution of social media platforms to the successes of the revolution. Sentiments of the press were reflected through headlines such as "Social Media Sparked, Accelerated Egypt's Revolutionary Fire" from the *Wired* blog *Epicenter* on February 11, 2011 (Gustin, 2011) and "Egypt's Revolution by Social Media: Facebook and Twitter Let the People Keep Ahead of the Regime" from *The Wall Street Journal* online three days later (Crovitz, 2011). Authors Nadia Idle and Alex Nunns suggest Twitter was primarily "used as an alternative press," as a "means for those on the ground to report what was happening for the benefit of their fellow Egyptians and the outside world" (Idle & Nunns, 2011, Introduction). Elsewhere, Sean Aday, Director of the Institute for Public Policy and Global Administration at George Washington University, and a team of researchers (Aday et al., 2010) expand on this account suggesting that activists were aware of the global audience watching from afar as they communicated with each other (p. 3). Researchers Wilson and Dunn (2011) build on Aday et al.'s observation, writing: "Twitter was widely viewed, moreover as a key resource for getting information to the outside world, perpetuating the feeling that the world was watching, which was an important factor for morale and coordination on the ground" (p. 1252). Central to these observations is protestors' awareness of the media they were using and the audiences to whom they were communicating, an awareness St.Amant (2015) reminds us is key for successful global communication.

The use of social media during the Egyptian Revolution illustrates a connection between activists' use of social media platforms and the potential audiences of support that were mobilized as a result. As a result of this connection,

> [t]he transnational, as ethico-political imaginary (of what should be) and as collective political action (the struggle to bring this about), becomes *instantiated* within and through the communicative enactments of protest and demonstration—if only momentarily or imperfectly. (Cottle & Lester, 2011, p. 5)

The transnational scope of such efforts "fundamentally inheres within how [protests and demonstrations] become communicated and mediated around the globe" (p. 4). We must therefore pay attention to the texts produced by these communicators and to the processes through which these texts are created and circulated.

An examination of how protestors used Twitter to harness the affordances of the Internet highlights how educators must introduce students to both the *processes* and the *products* of global communication. Rebecca Tarsa (2015) argues that interfaces accompanying "the proliferation of digital participatory spaces" (p. 12) can ease students' "transition from consumption to production" (p. 13). Tarsa draws from the work of Teena Carnegie (2009) who argues that digital interfaces function as a new media *exordium* enabling authors to "experience higher levels of connection in terms of both social and spatial relationships: they meet, communicate, and build relationships with others, and they explore and encounter new spaces and environments while sitting alone in a single place" (p. 171).

As protestors during the Egyptian Revolution worked across social media interfaces, they harnessed these affordances of social media interfaces to form hybrid embodiments through which they worked in the digital and physical spaces of the revolution. Their hybrid embodiments enabled them to weave their local contexts into a broader global setting that increased protest visibility and garnered the support of audiences around the world. It is through this process of translocal[1] weaving that activists formed hybrid embodiments enabling them to effect change in both the digital and physical spaces of their work. While protestors worked across social media interfaces to do this, their embodied practices as global communicators responded to the world around them in the digital and physical spaces of their activism.

EMBODIMENT ACROSS THE INTERFACE

Central to Ibrahim's work across the interface was her ability to blur distinctions between the material[2] and the corporeal.[3] Deep-seated beliefs about this distinction frequently inform our conversations about technology. Challenging this distinction enables us to understand how local corporeal bodies such as Ibrahim's act globally through their hybrid embodiment across digital interfaces. Hybrid embodiment describes more than how corporeal bodies instrumentally work across digital interfaces. Examining the hybrid embodiment of global communicators enables us to better understand how corporeal bodies form and transform the digital and physical spaces they engage through work across social media interfaces. Ibrahim's hybrid embodiment enabled her to embed her corporeal body as a transformative facet of the variety of spaces she engaged through the interface. In addition to transforming the spaces of her activism, Ibrahim's hybrid embodiment also influenced the capacities of the corporeal body she brought to these spaces.

Fleckenstein (1999) explores this facet of embodiments in "Writing Bodies: Somatic Mind in Composition Studies" when introducing the concept of the somatic mind. She writes: "The concept of somatic mind—mind and body as a permeable, intertextual territory that is continually made and remade—offers one means of embodying our discourse and our knowledge without totalizing either" (p. 281). This relationship between mind and body means that, as we compose, the mind and body are reconstituting both each other and their immediate material surroundings. The relationship between the somatic mind—the embodied mind—and the materials that surround it are central to the somatic mind's "being-in-material-place" (p. 282). As the somatic mind is bound to its material surroundings and its corporeal body, it "[t]urns back on its own constituting system to (re)constitute the context that creates it," thus blurring distinctions between mind and body and between the body and the material realities that surround it (p. 289). Fleckenstein's argument highlights the fluid relationships among mind, body, and material context that are capitalized on by activists through their hybrid embodiment across digital interfaces. Turning our attention to the somatic mind in global communication highlights intercultural communication as a material practice connecting bodies and interfaces to global contexts and enacting change in these contexts.

The blurring between the corporeal and the material is central to our understanding of hybrid embodiment as a process engaged by global communicators. Johanna Drucker (2013) describes this blurring as the "gooey," "constitutive boundary space" of the digital interface. Drucker reminds us of the negotiation that occurs across interfaces ranging from the earliest ENIAC computers to Twitter writing that interfaces are "not just a place of mechanistic negotiation and exchange among elements" (p. 216). Instead, interfaces should "be understood ecologically, as a border zone between cultural systems, with all the complexity and emergent relations that suggests" (p. 216). As we teach our students to engage these complexities through composing as global communicators, we must teach them to see the "gooeyness" of the interface. This is particularly true for interfaces such as Twitter that often become "so familiar [to both us and our students] that we tend to overlook the 'gooeyness' of it—the mutable, mediating activity—and take interface for a thing, static, stable, and fixed. Or we take it as a representation of computational processes, a convenient translation of what is 'really going on' inside. Neither could be further from actuality" (p. 213). Drucker thus reiterates how the intentional process of the somatic mind builds on an already occurring phenomenon of the interface's mutability through which bodies and interfaces are mutually constitutive of each other and their contexts. Jason Farman (2011) reiterates this observation writing that interfaces such as Twitter's "work in tandem with bodies and locales in a process of inscribing meaning into our contemporary social and spatial interactions" (p. 2). Ibrahim's communication practices capitalized on this facet as she used her hybrid embodiment to link the local and global, providing leadership across these spaces and drawing critical resources from each that enabled protestors to maintain their visibilities despite Mubarak's efforts to silence them.

Ibrahim's hybrid embodiment highlights the porous boundaries between the corporeal and the material, the physical and digital, as well as the local and global that our students must negotiate as they develop into global communicators. The analysis that follows traces Ibrahim's strategies of hybrid embodiment that enabled her to work across Twitter's interface as a conduit across which she was able to weave the local and global into a single, broader arena of action during the revolution. Ibrahim's strategies of hybrid embodiment enabled her to provide leadership across the digital interface in both the digital and physical spaces of the revolution at the same time she was struggling to maintain her presence and visibility in both of these spaces. Ibrahim's hybrid embodiment entwined her corporeal body with the material realities she was presented with through both the digital screen and the physical streets of Egypt that surrounded her. As a result, her corporeal body became constitutive of and constituted by the materialities she sought to reshape through her activism. Studying Ibrahim's hybrid embodiment and the factors contributing to it allows us to learn about the material practices of global communicators as they work across physical and digital spaces. In particular, we see how the material practices of global communicators are critical in their success connecting to audiences and implementing their goals.

IBRAHIM'S HYBRID EMBODIMENT ACROSS TWITTER

Ibrahim hybridized her embodiment through coordinating action and accessing resources across the digital and physical spaces of her activism during the Egyptian Revolution of 2011. Ibrahim's strategies of hybrid embodiment challenge us to move beyond seeing her physical presence in the streets of Egypt and her digital presence across Twitter as two discrete phenomena. Instead, her hybrid embodiment allowed Ibrahim to simultaneously work across both of these spaces as one larger space of the revolution. In this space of the revolution, Ibrahim's strategies of hybrid embodiment enabled her to work across Twitter's digital interface to

- Provide leadership across street and screen. Ibrahim provided leadership by choreographing action in both the digital and physical spaces of the revolution. This means that Ibrahim communicated with local and global audiences about ways to participate in the revolution across both digital and physical spaces.
- Maintain visibility across street and screen. Many forms of activism rely on visibility for their success. Visibility frequently relies on access to resources that support the presence of protestors in digital and physical spaces. As Ibrahim struggled to maintain her visibility and her fellow protestors' visibility, she needed access to resources across both the digital and physical spaces of the revolution.

These manifestations of Ibrahim's hybrid embodiment were critical to her success as a global communicator during the Egyptian Revolution because they enabled her to communicate with local and global audiences in the digital and physical spaces of the revolution. Such communication invited reciprocal connections with global audiences that frequently enlisted their support of the revolution and became a key contributing factor in the removal of Mubarak.

HYBRID EMBODIMENT TO PROVIDE LEADERSHIP

Ibrahim's hybrid embodiment enabled her to provide leadership in the digital and physical spaces of the revolution. Her success emerged through the products of her global communication and the processes that sustained this communication. These processes were also carried out by audiences who eventually created their own hybrid embodiments while moving from screen to street and back again. Thus, as Ibrahim was forming her hybrid embodiment, so too was she encouraging others to employ this strategy and carry their online dissent to the streets of Cairo and other cities across Egypt.

Worried the digital manifestations of Egyptians' dissent wouldn't be carried over to the streets of Egypt, Ibrahim used her hybrid embodiment to make her concern known and to remind readers of how important their presence in the streets would be throughout the protests that began on January 25, 2011. For example, on January 15, Ibrahim encouraged Egyptians to move from words to action writing: "we need to stop venting about 'poor us' 'we the repressed people'. . . . GO TO THE STREETS don't just write about it! #Egypt." Five days before the protests were planned, Ibrahim issued a similar reminder of how important protestors' physical presence across Egypt was when she tweeted: "#Jan25 I hope we can get over the logistics and just take to the streets in masses all over #Egypt." Just four minutes later, she tweeted again reminding her readers that their digital cries for protest wouldn't be enough to spark a revolution: "Only when the masses took to the streets in #Tunisia did the 23-yr-old #dictatorship of #BenAli fall . . . I hope #Mubarak is next in #Egypt." In these tweets, Ibrahim challenged readers to engage the interface as a conduit of hybrid embodiment that facilitated their work across both the digital and physical spaces of the revolution.

In addition to reminding her audiences about how important their physical presence across the streets of Egypt would be, Ibrahim also used her hybrid embodiment to share information about how to participate in the protests. We see her doing this in a dialogue initiated with other potential protestors on January 22: "I am not comfortable with all this talk on #jan25 on social networks, it better show on the streets. I will be there, will u?" One response she received to this tweet came from @Bazramit who wrote: "I'll be there with a few friends in Mohandessin. Where will you be?" In the conversation that follows,

Ibrahim and @Bazramit discuss how Ibrahim decided not to attend the marches starting in Mohandessin because there were going to be such large crowds there. She wanted to help with a smaller march needing more people to attend it. While this exchange publicly confirmed and affirmed @Bazramit's participation in the protests, it was also important as it publicly displayed these plans to others who were "eavesdropping" (Messina, 2011) on protestors' Twitter conversations. This exchange illustrates how important Ibrahim's hybrid embodiment was as she made preparations for the revolution public in a forum that would be seen by those already planning to participate in the protests and those perhaps still contemplating if they would join.

Among the Egyptians eavesdropping on these discussions was @Msabrika, who saw Ibrahim's tweets and contacted her about joining the protests. @Msabrika responded to Ibrahim tweeting: "@Gsquare86 what are the options please and when it will start and for how long? #jan25." These responses highlight the importance of Ibrahim's visibility across the physical and digital spaces of the revolution. The hybrid embodiment she formed as she wove these visibilities together made her accessible to Egyptians who had already committed to marching across Egypt and those who were perhaps just turning to Twitter for more information about how to join the protests. Ibrahim immediately responded to @Msabrika with a list of the "main options" where protestors were going to gather: "shubra, imbaba, gam3at el dawal, dar el kada2 el 3ali, el matarya, et7ad el 3omal." A few minutes later, Ibrahim followed up by inviting @Msabrika to send her a personal message.

A little over a week later, we see evidence @Msabrika's eventual participation in the protests when this user tweeted about going to Tahrir Square. Like Ibrahim, @Msabrika looks to have formed a hybrid embodiment through which this user was able to work across both Twitter and the streets of Egypt to change the material realities that surrounded protestors. As Ibrahim and others hybridized their embodiments, they were not only expanding their presence in the local context of the revolution, but they were also expanding their presence into a global context of the revolution.

While Ibrahim was encouraging local audiences to join the protests, she was also providing leadership for transnational audiences catching glimpses of the revolution across Twitter and beginning to show their support. The complex layering of Ibrahim's audiences through her hybrid embodiment highlights what Gail Hawisher and Cynthia Selfe describe as "[t]he dynamic tension between localness and globalness" (Hawisher & Selfe, 2000, p. 277). Rather than choosing between the local and the global, global communicators such as Ibrahim negotiate both through communication practices that give rise to their hybrid embodiments across spaces they share with audiences locally and globally. For example, on February 2, Ibrahim tweeted: "We want the world to revolt with Egyptians . . . international solidarity is more pressure!" This tweet alludes to the solidarity protests that took place around the world and invited global audiences to hybridize their embodiment in much the same way as @Msabrika.

Among the international responses Ibrahim received was a reply from @dawnandluc: "There are Americans who are standing with you over here and encouraging our leaders to stand up!" Many others physically embodied their support in cities around the world as they participated in solidarity marches. For example, on January 21, 2011 @Cer recirculated a post about one such protest in Toronto: "A protest in Toronto, Canada on #Jan25 in solidarity with Egyptians protests." This transnational support illustrates the power of protestors' global communication as their hybrid embodiments enabled them to provide leadership for local and global audiences participating in both the digital and physical spaces of the revolution.

HYBRID EMBODIMENT TO MAINTAIN VISIBILITY

While Ibrahim used her hybrid embodiment to provide leadership securing the presence of protestors across the streets and interfaces of the revolution, her hybrid embodiment also enabled Ibrahim to take critical steps in assuring their visibility across these spaces. Ibrahim worked to maintain this visibility by identifying and using resources across both digital and physical spaces of the revolution. These resources became increasingly urgent as Mubarak fought to maintain control by disconnecting protestors from each other and from the rest of the world. Reporting on January 28, 2011, Matt Richtel, writing for *The New York Times*, wrote that although "autocratic governments often limit phone and Internet access," "the Internet has never faced anything like what happened in Egypt on Friday, when the government of a country with 80 million people and a modernizing economy cut off nearly all access to the network and shut down cell phone service" (Richtel, 2011).

Blogger and activist Ramy Raoof (2011) described the blackouts by Mubarak on his blog writing: "Activists mobile lines and hotlines number were shutdown, social websites (including twitter.com, facebook.com, bambuser.com) and other newspapers websites were blocked, short message service (SMS) was shutdown, mobile phone-calls service was shutdown on different intervals, landlines didn't work in sue areas in Cairo and internet connection shutdown." This effort to isolate protestors illustrates how interfaces are designed to be seen "forgetfully," as ostensibly immaterial (Wysocki & Jasken, 2004, p. 30). When Ibrahim and others struggled to secure Internet connections, the often invisible material infrastructures of the Internet were brought into focus for Ibrahim and her audiences.

Confronted with material limitations that threatened to curtail her visibility during the protests, Ibrahim maintained visibility by accessing resources across the digital and physical spaces of the revolution. Her resulting hybrid embodiment enabled Ibrahim to ensure her presence in these spaces remained visible to others. For example, Ibrahim's digital visibility was frequently challenged by weak connections to the Internet. In a tweet from January 26, she commented on the slow Internet connection over her laptop: "My internet on my phone is working faster than my laptop..sooo fuckin frustrating !! I need to upload so much, and I can't:(..sooo slowww." In this tweet, Ibrahim reveals what happens when the material requirements of Twitter clashed with the local material realities of the revolution during which she had access to neither consistent nor fast Internet connections.

As Ibrahim formed her hybrid embodiment across Twitter's interface, she also negotiated her visibilities in the digital and physical spaces of the revolution. The decisions Ibrahim had to make between these visibilities highlight the "messy complexity" and "oftentimes contradictory nature" (Hawisher & Selfe, 2000, p. 277) of global communication. For example, as Ibrahim maintained her hybrid embodiment, her global visibility across the interface often seems to have come at the expense of her local visibility across the streets of Cairo. We catch a glimpse of this complex dynamic in tweets sent on January 29. These tweets appear to be posted from a location where Ibrahim could access Twitter, but did not have the connection needed to upload images and videos.

After sending a handful of text-only tweets from this undisclosed location, Ibrahim informed audiences she was returning to Tahrir square and would not be tweeting for a while: "i will go now, and i might be back, going back to Tahrir . . . when internet is back i have amazing pics and videos for u all." The next tweets from Ibrahim were sent nearly thirteen hours later. The cost of Ibrahim's brief digital visibility in these tweets is reiterated when she alludes to how secret many of the locations where she accessed the Internet were. For example, in the midst of the tweets above, Ibrahim posted: "NO I DON'T HAVE INTERNET, this is just a happy moment at a 'location' where they have internet, i can't say where." These tweets reiterate how Ibrahim's digital presence across Twitter frequently came at the expense of her physical presence across the streets of Egypt during the protests.

As we read the public tweets circulated by protestors, we must remember that we are only seeing the most public layer of their hybrid embodiment during the revolution. Ibrahim highlighted this in a Skype interview with *New York Times* blogger Robert Mackey (2011) on January 27 when she said: "I also call people and message people just trying to coordinate with you know, I also receive information." We see evidence of this layered visibility and how it intersected with her (in)visibilities across the digital and physical spaces of the revolution in her public tweets when, after sending out some tweets following a brief absence from Twitter due to one of Mubarak's media blackouts, Ibrahim was contacted by another protestor, @monasosh, who tweeted: "@Gsquare86 yaaaaaay GG is back :)" Two minutes later, Ibrahim replied with an inquiry about @monasosh's location. Instead of sharing her location, @ monasosh addressed Ibrahim's question saying she had been there since the first day of the revolution. Ibrahim quickly responded: "@monasosh no seriously i need to upload some shit, where and how do u have internet?" Although @monasosh does not appear to have publicly replied to Ibrahim's question about her location, we cannot assume that @monasosh did not share this information. She may have done so privately. Making such information public risked (a) alerting the authorities to individuals who were rerouting access around the government, and (b) pulling more people to a connection point than could be handled.

While Ibrahim was forming her hybrid embodiment using Twitter to access resources from local audiences, she also accessed resources from global audiences who contributed to her sustained visibility through the revolution. Ibrahim's use of the digital interface to communicate both locally and globally about the day-to-day struggles of protest underscore the translocal relationships she formed with audiences around the globe. Filip Sapienza (2001) suggests that rather than "linking diverse people into a global community or 'village' in which participants, through increased electronic interaction, discover common interests and concerns that transcend specific cultural and national ideologies," global digital communication frequently reiterates how, "far from extinction, cultural specificity exists on the Web as much as global cultural ideas" (p. 435). These cultural specificities were highlighted as Ibrahim repeatedly gestured to the lack of resources protestors struggled to overcome and reached out to audiences who were potentially able to help her overcome this lack of resources. Through Ibrahim's hybrid embodiment, she highlighted the disparity between the "local" she was trying to survive within and the "locals" that surrounded many of her transnational audiences. She also provided these audiences with a way to reach across this gap and help activists connect to resources critical for maintaining their visibilities.

These transnational audiences responded by contributing resources that helped many protestors form the hybrid embodiments that sustained their visibility throughout the revolution. For example, a number of these audience members were part of larger organizations such as Telecomix, a loosely organized collective of web activists, who came forward to help. In addition to receiving and redistributing communications from activists using Morse code and ham radios, Telecomix assembled a list of international Internet Service Providers (ISPs) activists could access via dial-up (Kanalley & Bialer, 2011; Madlena, 2011). These ISP addresses were distributed through means including Facebook and Twitter posts such as one that appeared on Ibrahim's Facebook page on January 29, 2011: "To bypass government blocking of websites, use numerical IP addresses: Twitter '128.242.240.52' Fb '69.63.189.34' Google '172.14.204.99'. A French ISP offers free dial up internet access ~+33 1 72 89 01 50 password: toto. Please pass this on and share." As protestors formed their hybrid embodiments by garnering these resources across Twitter, we see a powerful example of how this global communication practice enabled protestors to blur the boundaries of the digital and physical, expanding a local quest for freedom into a visible transnational movement.

LESSONS FOR THE CLASSROOM

A takeaway for teachers is the need for students to develop frameworks for engaging both the products and processes of global communication. That is to say, students need to develop critical frameworks for both consuming and producing global communication. These frameworks foster students' understandings of how to simultaneously build connections with audiences across physical and digital spaces. This approach to global communication underscores how social media platforms are not simply static conduits enabling the transmission of messages. Rather, these digital spaces are actively shaped by students inviting action across them and the communication strategies that wed our students to distant contexts. Strategies for facilitating students' development into global communicators include experiences with both analysis and production.

ANALYSIS

The ability to analyze texts as well as the interfaces and intersecting contexts they circulate through is a critical skill for global communicators. In particular, this skill enables global communicators to continually adapt to the ever-shifting ecosystems of global communication.

Invite students to analyze digital interfaces and how these interfaces invite or inhibit a variety of embodied interactions. Teena Carnegie (2009) suggests some questions that students might be asked.

> Is the user given knowledge of other participants? If the communication is textual, how much time flexibility does the user have to create and send messages and thereby build connections with others? Does the interface provide visual and audio information about other users? If so, what are the backgrounds and characteristics of the other users? Does the interface itself have a character or agency? If so, to whom would this character or agency appeal? What schemas are being invoked by the interface? What cultural, political, economic backgrounds and interests do these schemas reflect? Who would be familiar with the schemas needed to interact with the interface? Who would be excluded? How accurately does the interface map to the user's experience and potential responses? How reflexive is the interface? Does the interface enable the user to map and follow alternate paths? Is the user asked to remain within a given schema or can he or she draw from other schemas and his or her own knowledge? (p. 172)

Asking questions such as these can facilitate students' awareness that online spaces are not simply disembodied. Instead, online spaces are embodied through dynamic interactions between physical bodies and the material design of interfaces. As global communicators are able to understand these dynamics, the body emerges a key resource enabling communicators to work across both digital and physical spaces simultaneously and invite others to do the same.

Invite students to analyze the texts of global communicators and examine what reciprocal action is being invited and how. This type of assignment might take shape as a case study of a global communicator. In this case study, students would pay particular attention to the choices made by this author. In particular, this assignment turns students' attention to the global communication strategies employed across digital interfaces, the technologies involved in conducting this communication, the time and location of this communication, and the thorough processes behind the decisions made by global communicators. A case study like this highlights the series of decisions that preface successful global communication and allows students to analyze how these decisions enable global communicators to form hybrid embodiments.

Such analysis prepares students to be lifelong global communicators able to engage current contexts and quickly adapt their strategies of production as contexts and practices of global communicators continue to change.

PRODUCTION

In addition to facilitating students' understanding of hybrid embodiment as a facet of global communication through analysis, we can begin inviting students to participate in the process of global communication, something we may find that many of them are already doing.

- Invite students to experiment with forming hybrid embodiments through a public service announcement (PSA) campaign assignment. This assignment invites students to develop PSA campaigns that invite action from a variety of overlapping audiences across a variety of media. By inviting community action, such as picking up litter or doing random acts of kindness, a PSA campaign prompts students to form hybrid embodiments through their own work across digital and physical spaces. Components of this assignment would include inviting students to incorporate multiple media into their PSA. For example, invite students to create posters that are hung up around campus for local audiences and create a Twitter account through which they begin connecting to more global audiences. In reflections on their work, students can be asked to describe how they provided leadership as initiators of this PSA and how they established their visibilities both locally and globally. Students can also then be prompted to think about the different connections that are enabled across digital interfaces as opposed to the print poster.

A PSA assignment invites students to engage Ibrahim's hybrid embodiment strategies discussed here: choreographing corresponding action on and offline and accessing resources from both spaces to maintain visibility.

CONCLUSION

Rather than unfolding as a series of *products*, the tweets examined in this chapter demonstrate that Ibrahim's global communication during the Egyptian Revolution of 2011 was a dynamic *process* through which she developed her hybrid embodiment. Such hybrid embodiment stands out as we examine the leadership Ibrahim was able to provide and the visibility she was able to sustain in both the physical and digital spaces of the Egyptian Revolution of 2011. Teaching students about this hybrid embodiment and raising their awareness of their own practices of hybrid embodiment continues the intellectual work

Christina Haas (1996) initiated when she called for us to hone our abilities to look at and through technology: "I argue that the technology itself is vitally important and that one should look at, as well as through, the technologies of writing, if one is to fully understand, and ultimately wisely use, the technologies of writing" (p. xii). Looking at and through technology enables us to see the symbiotic relationship between cultural tools and cognitive activities that Haas points out are rooted in the "embodied actions of human beings" (p. 44). Such perspective also enables us to see the power of the somatic mind at work as it "[t]urns back on its own constituting system to (re)constitute the context that creates it" (Fleckenstein, 1999, p. 289).

As we embrace this connectivity alongside our students, Rice (2006) reminds us that in 1964 William Burroughs observed that when we are working within a network, we are either participating in the extension of its functions or resisting its functions (p. 130). As we facilitate our students' development into responsive and agentive participants in the network who choose whether to extend or resist it, Rice encourages us to do so by learning the network's methodology of "associations, connections, and juxtapositions" (p. 130). Facilitating students' development of the practices of hybrid embodiment engages them in one facet of this methodology that can be incorporated into our classrooms. As students develop this facet of their global communication practices, the "associations, connections, and juxtapositions" of the network become key factors that frequently hinge on the relationships composers develop with the tools they use and the audiences with whom they connect and move to action locally and globally.

Notes

1. Leppanen et al. underscore two key facets of "new media practice" with their use of translocality. First, referring to the translocal underscores the connectivity among locales. While locales are important, their connections to other locales are often just as important. Second, the term translocal highlights the degree to which "culture is seen as outward-looking, exogenous, focused on hybridity, translation, and identification" (Leppanen et al., 2009, pp. 1081–1082).

2. Here I am using material to refer to the physical attributes of interfaces and the locations engaged through them. This use of material captures one facet of materiality more generally. N. Katherine Hayles (2002) defines materiality as the emergent capacities that emerge from the "nearly infinite physical attributes constituting any physical artifact," "the user's interactions with a work," and the "interpretive strategies" employed that include both physical manipulations and conceptual frameworks (p. 32). She writes: "In its broadest sense, materiality emerges from the dynamic interplay between the richness of a physically robust world and human intelligence as it crafts this physicality to create meaning" (p. 33).

3.   Here I am using corporeal to refer to what Don Ihde (2001) refers to as "body one," the phenomenological "being-in-the-world" (p. xi), the body that is spatially oriented and tangibly present in the world. Failing to account for the social and cultural systems that surround it, "body one" captures only one facet of embodiment.

References

Aday, S., Farrell, H., Lynch, M., Sides, J., Kelly, J., & Zuckerman, E. (2010). *Blogs and bullets: New media in contentious politics.* Washington, DC: Institute of Peace. Retrieved from https://www.usip.org/publications/blogs-and-bullets-new-media-in-contentious -politics

Arola, K. (2010). The design of Web 2.0: The rise of the template, the fall of design. *Computers and Composition, 27*(1), 4–14. doi:10.1016/j.compcom.2009.11.004

boyd, d., & Marwick, A. (2011). I tweet honestly, I tweet passionately: Twitter users, context collapse, and the imagined audience. *New Media Society, 13*(1), 114–133.

Carnegie, T. (2009). Interface as exordium: The rhetoric of interactivity. *Computers and Composition, 26*(3), 164–173. https://doi.org/10.1016/j.compcom.2009.05.005

Cottle, S. (2011). Afterward: Media and the Arab uprisings of 2011. In S. Cottle & L. Lester (Eds.), *Transnational protests and the media* (pp. 293–304). New York, NY: Peter Lang.

Cottle, S., & Lester, L. (2011). *Transnational protests and the media.* New York, NY: Peter Lang.

Crovitz, G. (2011, February 14). Egypt's revolution by social media. *The Wall Street Journal.* Retrieved from https://www.wsj.com/articles/SB10001424052748703786804576137980252177072.

Daer, A., & Potts, L. (2014). Teaching and learning with social media: Tools, cultures, and best practices. *Programmatic Perspectives, 6*(2), 21–40.

Della Porta, D., & Mosca, L. (2005). Global-net for global movements? A network of networks for a movement of movements. *Journal of Public Policy, 25*(1), 165–190. https://doi.org/10.1017/S0143814X05000255

Drucker, J. (2013). Reading interface. *Publications of the Modern Language Association, 128*(1), 213–220. https://doi.org/10.1632/pmla.2013.128.1.213

Eltantawy, N., & Wiest, J. B. (2011). Social media and the egyptian revolution: Reconsidering resource mobilization theory. *International Journal of Communication, 5*(1), 1207–1224.

Farman, J. (2011). *Mobile interface theory: Embodied space and locative media.* New York, NY: Routledge.

Fleckenstein, K. S. (1999). Writing bodies: Somatic mind in composition studies. *College English, 61*(3), 281–306. https://doi.org/10.2307/379070

Fleckenstein, K. S. (2005). Faceless students, virtual places: Emergence and communal accountability in online classrooms. *Computers and Composition, 22*(2), 149–176. https://doi.org/10.1016/j.compcom.2005.02.003

Fleckenstein, K. S. (2010). *Vision, rhetoric, and social action in the composition classroom.* Carbondale, IL: Southern Illinois University Press.

Gustin, S. (2011, February 11). Social media sparked, accelerated Egypt's revolutionary fire. *Wired.* Retrieved from https://www.wired.com/2011/02/egypts-revolutionary-fire.

Haas, C. (1996). *Writing technology.* Mahwah, NJ: Lawrence Erlbaum.

Hawisher, G., & Selfe, C. (2000). *Global literacies and the world-wide web.* New York, NY: Routledge.

Hayles, N. K. (2002). *Writing machines.* Boston, MA: MIT Press.

Hesford, W., & Schell, E. (2008). Introduction: Configurations of transnationality: Locating feminist rhetorics. *College English, 70*(5), 461–470.

Honeycutt, C., & Herring, S. (2009). *Proceedings of the forty-second Hawai'i international conference on system sciences.* Los Alamitos, CA: IEEE Press. Retrieved from http://ella.slis .indiana.edu/~herring/honeycutt.herring.2009.pdf

Idle, N., & Nunns, A. (2011). *Tweets from Tahrir.* New York, NY: OR Books.

Ihde, D. (2001). *Bodies in technology.* Minneapolis, MN: University of Minnesota Press.

Kanalley, C., & Bialer, J. (2011, January 29). Anonymous Internet users team up to provide communication tools for egyptian people. *The Huffington Post.* Retrieved from http://www.huffingtonpost.com/2011/01/29/anonymous-internet-egypt_n_815889 .html

Khalil, A. (2011). *Liberation square.* New York, NY: St. Martin's Press.

Lenhart, A. (2015). *Teens, social media and technology overview 2015.* Retrieved from http://www.pewinternet.org/2015/04/09/teens-social-media-technology-2015

Leppanen, S., Pitkanen-Huhta, A., Piirainen-Marsh, A., Nikula, T., & Peuronen, S. (2009). Young people's translocal new media uses: A multiperspective analysis of language choice and heteroglossia. *Journal of Computer-Mediated Communication, 14*(4), 1080–1107. https://doi.org/10.1111/j.1083-6101.2009.01482.x

Lim, M. (2012). Clicks, cabs, and coffee houses: Social media and oppositional movements in Egypt, 2004–2011. *Journal of Communication, 62*(2), 231–248. https://doi.org /10.1111/j.1460-2466.2012.01628.x

Mackey, R. (2011). Social media accounts of violence in cairo challenge official narrative. *The Lede.* Retrieved from https://thelede.blogs.nytimes.com/2011/10/10/social-media -accounts-of-violence-in-cairo-challenge-official-narrative/?_php=true&_type=blogs&_r=0

Madlena, C. (2011). Telecomix: Tech support for the Arab spring. *The Guardian.* Retrieved from https://www.theguardian.com/technology/2011/jul/07/telecomix-arab-spring

Messina, C. (2011). Groups for Twitter; or a proposal for Twitter tag channels. *Factory City.* Retrieved from https://factoryjoe.com/blog/2007/08/25/groups-for-twitter-or -a-proposal-for-twitter-tag-channels

Prins, K. (2012). Crafting new approaches to composition. In K. Arola & A. Wysocki (Eds.), *composing(media)=composing(embodiment)* (pp. 145–161). Logan, UT: Utah State University Press.

Raoof, R. (2011). Jan25 revolution and content of Egyptian cyberspace. Blog post. Retrieved from http://ebfhr.blogspot.com/2011/06/jan25-revolution-and-online -content_23.html

Rice, J. (2006). Networks and new media. *College English, 69*(2), 127–133. https://doi.org /10.2307/25472197 http://jstor.org

Richtel, M. (2011). Egypt cuts off most Internet and cell service. *The New York Times.* Retrieved from http://www.nytimes.com/2011/01/29/technology/internet/29cutoff .html

Sapienza, F. (2001). Nurturing translocal communication: Russian immigrants on the world wide web. *Technical Communication (Washington), 48*(4), 435–448.

St.Amant, K. (2015). Reconsidering social media in global contexts. *Intercom, 62*(4), 15–17.

Tarsa, R. (2015). Upvoting the exordium: Literacy practices of the digital interface. *College English, 78*(1), 12–33.

Wilson, C., & Dunn, A. (2011). Digital media in the Egyptian revolution: Descriptive analyses from the Tahrir data set. *International Journal of Communication, 5*, 1248–1272.

Wysocki, A., & Jasken, J. (2004). "What should be an unforgettable face . . ." *Computers and Composition, 21*(1), 29–48. doi:10.1016/j.compcom.2003.08.004

Yancey, K. B. (2009). Writing in the 21st century. *NCTE.* Retrieved from http://www.ncte .org.proxy.lib.fsu.edu/library/NCTEFiles/Press/Yancey_final.pdf

14

GLOBALLY DIGITAL, DIGITALLY GLOBAL
Multimodal Literacies among Bhutanese Refugees in the United States

Tika Lamsal

ABSTRACT

The chapter relates how Bhutanese refugee youth create cross-cultural and multilingual identity through new media literacies in the globalized contexts. Such practices enable individuals to foster knowledge by engaging in multimodal learning practices in U.S. schools, involving them in literacy activities within the new context, maintaining global affiliations and identities, and participating in community activities to improve the literacy and cultural environment of their families and communities. Their digital literacies have eased processes of integration and knowledge making inschool settings and helped them join a community that recognizes the importance of social relations and new geopolitical and transnational differences.

Keywords: cross-cultural communication, digital literacies, global Englishes, multilingual writing, multimodal composition, refugee literacies, transnational writing

INTRODUCTION

As means of writing and communication have become more widespread, visuals (both still and moving images) have become popular modes of composition and interpretation. Digital media are "more and more the site of appearance and distribution of learning resources, and writing is being displaced by image as the central mode for representation" (Bezemer & Kress, 2008, p. 166). Within this context, the chapter examines the role of multimodal literacies in shaping academic and cultural identities of the Bhutanese refugee youth in the United States—particularly by explaining how technology has changed the nature of writing and

DOI: 10.7330/9781607326649.c014

uses of digital technology inside and outside of school classrooms. Such examination helps us understand how students' learning practices cross-over from communities to classrooms. Examining digital learning practices of these youth further demonstrates considering composition only as a mode of writing across digital spaces is an understanding of modes or visuals as autonomous. Moreover, use of multiple modalities for writing and community participation becomes part of the culture that exists outside academe, whereby minority communities form their experiences and identities. Use of visuals as autonomous modes, however, under-mines what Appadurai (1990) calls "fluidities of transnational communication" with reference to cultural dimensions (p. 18). Such a practice is akin to moving from one mode to the other rather than understanding the fluid, changing nature of digital configurations through practice; if we extend the idea, only proliferating multiple modalities as discrete modes of communication simply replicates the traditional autonomous models (see Street, 1984, 1993). An analysis of digital literacy practices of the Bhutanese refugee youth encourages teachers and researchers to see, instead, modalities as fluid and emergent.

Based on a two-year-long ethnographic study among Bhutanese refugees in a Midwestern U.S. city (which I call Panorama City), I problematize this notion of autonomous modality. The study places significant focus on the nature of participation to improve participants' abilities to develop new knowledge, create change, and empower themselves (Reason, 2004); it also reveals how marginalized people are situated in social and material relations and how their disempowerment is manifested in cultural arrangements (Quantz, 1992). The study provides a forum for refugees to share and reflect on their knowledge and concerns about their situations and to raise awareness about the social, political, religious, and cultural issues undergirding their quality of life in a new home. Such modality is informed by the assumption multimodality primarily belongs to other disciplines (e.g., communication and information technologies). The study, in turn, offers insight into adopting a more fluid understanding of modality by showing how writing is related to other multimodal forms.

As composition studies and technical communication scholars, we must see the use of technology in writing through ideological models and fulfill our obligation of "trying to understand and make sense of, to *pay attention* to, how technology is now inextricably linked to literacy and literacy education in this country" (Selfe, 1999, p. 414). Doing so helps us acknowledge writing practice is messy, so to evaluate writing practices only through autonomous model risks reifying technology in writing because we only take major characteristics of autonomous model and generalize them. Consider a multimodal composition entitled "Where Home Doesn't Belong" (https://www.youtube.com/watch?v=L7MHEUHlwYg). Narratives woven through images, aural, and visual rhetorical design, this creation relates struggles of Bhutanese refugees in the United States and abroad, in terms of political, economic, cultural, and language issues during adjustment processes.

Stressing the values of diverse students' resources based on prior cultural, linguistic, and overall academic experiences, Matsuda (2002) contends "we need to recognize that when multilingual and multicultural writers enter the U.S. academy, they are not the only ones who need to learn the conventions and assumptions of U.S. academic discourse practices; everyone in the U.S. academy needs to reassess their assumptions about discourse practices in the academy as they come in contact with unfamiliar discourses" (p. 194). Such discourses are always in the making by adopting and extending the literacy practices multilingual and multicultural students from immigrant and refugee communities bring to the United States as resources from their home countries. It is, therefore, our responsibility as teachers and researchers to recognize and promote such resources for meaningful writing and communication in U.S. schools and colleges. Because U.S. students write using English mostly inflected by home rhetorical structures, refugee students feel they are penalized for their "different English"; and refugee students have started using specific multimodal forms of composing because such forms help showcase their multilingual and multicultural repertoires to develop academic skills and cultural identity to succeed in U.S. schools.

Through a combination of participant observation, interpretation of participant interviews and cultural artifacts, and fieldnotes, this study explores how language and literacy can shape social identities and cultural practices of Bhutanese refugees, and how an understanding of their literacy practices contributes to new conceptualizations of language and literacies research. This two-year-long ethnographic study highlights linguistic and cultural resources Bhutanese refugees use at key literacy sites, such as an Elderly Care Center, mandatory ESL classes, weekly cultural and musical gatherings, men's and women's *Kirtan* (religious singing) groups, and youth online forums. It shows how the participants use their learning skills for creating, preserving, and sustaining their linguistic, cultural, musical, and literacy traditions. Of prime significance are ways this study examines these sites as platforms for cultural resistance and for the reproduction and transformation of cultural and literacy practices.

Specifically, the study explores the following research questions: How does literacy develop in minority cultures like refugees? What are some of the forces that constitute literacy experiences of such cultures while in the United States today? How do their multilingual and multimodal literacy practices contribute or hinder immigrants' learning processes? Answers to such questions identify learning patterns in multilingual students, which helps educators offer them more effective support to succeed academically. The development of digital communication technologies and their more accessible affordances have helped these participants express their transnational and transcultural identities across digital spaces through literacy practices that take place beyond their school classrooms.

Street's (1984) ideas on the ethnographic research perspective help us understand the knowledge and values of community members involved in the research process. His ethnographic research with Iranian farmers in a remote village of Cheshmeh engages community members in a dialogic way to co-construct knowledge, involving both researcher and community members. During his observation of community meetings, Street invited participants to share their voices on various issues of immediate cultural and religious significance. He also participated in the discussion by bringing his own Western-shaped ideas on religious and social issues, making his position clear in relation to the local cultural values. It was through such active engagement and participation Street could gain an understanding of the community principles in his research. Gaining an insight from Street's study, the chapter examines local cultural values of the participants, highlighting the significance of such values in promoting literacy and learning among immigrant communities in the United States.

An ethnographic perspective in research, according to Rowsell, Kress, and Street (2013), helps draw out "larger implications pertaining to cultural and social practice" (p. 2). The perspective allows researchers to become a part of a community of research and helps them place an understanding of literacy within a wider understanding of people's everyday lived experiences. Ethnography also allows researchers to explore hidden literacy skills in the society, showing their differences from "explicit technical or 'cognitive' processes" (Street, 1984, p. 222), and makes such skills explicit in a way to challenge policy makers to recognize the significance of learners' engagement and participation in the research.

Because researchers often fail to make explicit implications of individual measures of literacy from an emic perspective, this situation creates an "ivory tower distancing" (Street, 2006, p. 24) between practical and contextual work and individual and cognitive processes. Ethnographic research identifies this problem and works at the local level to address issues local people face daily. Such an approach makes "visible the complexity of local, everyday, community literacy practices and challenge[s] dominant stereotypes and myopia" (p. 22), focusing on everyday meanings and uses of literacy in specific social, economic, multimodal, and cultural contexts. Thus, the approach used in this study can provide greater cultural understanding that can be applied cross-culturally.

MULTIMODAL LITERACIES

Across Cultures

Aural and visual modes have become dominant modes of communication, necessitating writing teachers to "pay attention to *both* writing *and* aurality, and other composing modalities, as well" (Selfe, 2009, p. 618). Moreover, writing is visual, and modes are shaped by historical, social, linguistic, material, and cultural changes. Recent decades have witnessed an increase in the research of minority community literacy practices beyond school classrooms. Street's (1984) ideological model of literacy through ethnographies of different meanings out of people's lived experiences has been useful in examining literacy practices of peripheral and marginalized groups in society, leading to direct implications for school literacy. Barton and Hamilton's (1998) study of "vernacular" literacies of Lancaster communities demonstrates how literacies develop among immigrants across cultures and languages. Similarly, Gregory and Williams's (2000) research on two communities in Spitalfields and London presents an intergenerational study of living, learning, and reading throughout the twentieth century in homes, clubs, churches, synagogues, mosques, theaters, and classrooms.

While studies on literacy practices focus on reading and writing activities within local communities and as located in immediate social, political, and cultural contexts, more recent studies of language and literacy (Pahl & Rowsell, 2006; Baynham & Prinsloo, 2009; Cope & Kalantzis, 2009; Warriner, 2009) have moved toward examining literacy practices within intersecting local and global contexts and in relation to changing communication technologies. As such, the challenge of studying new media in the context of "transnational family relationships is that the technologies themselves are constantly changing and research often seems to be chasing a moving target of technological developments and innovative appropriations on the part of the users" (Madianou & Miller, 2012, p. 7). At a local level, such innovative practices and appropriations of new media by the community members contribute to rich learning experiences across social domains, such as community gatherings and religious institutions in the globalized context, whereby "individuals and groups seek to annex the global into their own practices of the modern" (Appadurai, 1996, p. 4).

Much of the work on transdisciplinary globalization conducted within various disciplines agree on the need to recognize the multiplicities of identities and geographies brought forth by transnational migration. Globalized context thus advocates the need to respect the cultural and language resources refugees and recent migrants bring to their new home (see Hannerz, 2002). Globalization theorists and interdisciplinary scholars, such as Appadurai (1996), and Gupta and Ferguson (2002), critique the segregated backdrop of anthropological fieldwork and advocate a more inclusive theoretical tool that accounts for the migrants and refugees and the flows accompanying them across locations of their migration.

Critiquing globalization in terms of cultural imperialism, Inda and Rosaldo (2002) argue globalization refers to the "intensification of global interconnectedness, suggesting a world full of movement and mixture, contact and linkages and persistent cultural interaction and exchange" (p. 2). Refugees and immigrants, thus unhinged from particular localities, openly transcend specific territorial boundaries; as Inda and Rosaldo further claim, "uprooting of culture is only half the story of globalization. The other half is that the deterritorialization of culture is invariably the occasion for the reinsertion of culture in new time-space contexts" (p. 11). Such reinsertion, as Pennycook (2010) would argue, is a recontextualization that helps refugees repurpose their learning experiences in the new context, and this reshapes that context. Such recontextualization of cultural and linguistic resources offers a perspective to interrogate challenges of globalization by repurposing literacy practices to embrace the multiplicities of disciplinary, ethnic, cultural, historical, national, or geographic origins.

Furthermore, learners are more likely to shuttle between home cultural practices and schooled literacy practices in the process of learning, flattening boundaries between schooled and unschooled sets of skills. Academic institutions themselves can become informed and influenced by hidden literacy skills in society as they bring moving image media, performances, and cultural models from outside school walls to use them as teaching resources. Such resources include multimodal forms of learning that contribute to students' learning process sometimes in more effective ways than formal literacy teaching might do. As Cope and Kalantzis (2010) argue, the global spread of the new media has fundamentally changed how people learn: "Control by others has become self-control; compliance has become self-imposed. New media are one part of this broader equation. The move may be primarily a social one, but the technology has helped us head in this general direction" (p. 91). Such specific effects of media practices, as Horner and Selfe (2013) point out, are dependent on training and the user agency rather than as resources in themselves. According to them, "it is the training (in composition, performance, listening) that 'affords' these effects, not the technologies of production as ordinarily defined" (p. 15). That is, more traditional school modalities are not in themselves a barrier but, rather, the orientation students are asked to take toward these. Drawing could, conversely, be just as limiting for drawers if the modes are taught with a disposition that there is only one correct way to draw.

These theoretical perspectives have infused a critical edge to the conceptions of literacy in this study. Literacy practices are not so much rules and cognitive practices measured through universal standards, but are practices embedded in broader social goals and cultural practices. Using social semiotic theory to examine the multimodal literacies of students, Bezemer and Kress (2008) illustrate how "*meaning material* is moved from social site to social site, from medium to medium, from context to context, in each case requiring social, semiotic remaking and often entailing epistemological change" (p. 169). Knowledge of these theories and definitions of literacy make us more aware of the need to see literacy as a culturally situated discourse dealing with learners' social, cultural, historical, political, economic, and multimodal contexts of learning.

Beyond School Classrooms

In addition to schools, community institutions like church and temple play a significant role in enhancing the learning experiences of the Bhutanese refugees in Panorama City. Through their production of videotexts and the use of multiple languages when preparing notes and scripts for performances, refugees demonstrate an agency over their work. During church meetings, for instance, Christian members of Bhutanese community prepared scripts for speech, singing, and any other cultural presentations. Resham and Melina, born in Nepal and

Bhutan respectively, discussed the significance these writings had for their academic writing at school. For example, they learned to respect their audiences and see how they could write something more persuasive. Without formal training on rhetorical situations, they seemed already steeped in communicating across various audiences by using rhetorically effective writing through videos and other relevant images. To support such rhetorical transfer, in their discussion of the significance of visual rhetoric and images in student writing, Lauren and Rice (2013) argue "for instructors teaching rhetoric and style in basic writing composition, exploring multimodal assignments such as photo essays alongside traditional academic discourse is an effective teaching method, and doing so has the potential to prepare students with an agile writing skill set that will prepare them better for the workplace" (para. 20). Encouraging students to use such multimodal resources becomes more effective in helping gain literacy and language learning skills in schools.

However, what Bhutanese refugee youth wrote and created in their own communities only drew negative responses in U.S. classrooms. Bijaya and Binaya, born in Bhutan in 1990 and in Nepal in 1995, respectively, related their experiences of being punished in U.S. schools for "incorrect and messy" use of English in writing. Such responses to school assignments were mostly based on previous academic experiences and their knowledge of technology. Active inside and outside classroom literacy activities from his early school days, Bijaya learned to read and write simultaneously in both Nepali and English. Bijaya remembered his first days in a U.S. high school after his arrival in Panorama City:

> In the beginning, when I responded to my teachers' questions in the class, most of my classmates used to laugh due to my accent because I didn't come from a native speaker of English background, although I had my schooling until grade nine in English medium. I was good in writing and always scored an A in Nepal, but I had a hard time in the beginning, especially in college writing, to receive grades beyond C and B although I had good grades in my high school in the U.S. too. Although I struggled in the beginning in grade ten, I quickly picked up the pace and improved my reading and writing scores later in the high school. Most of my writing in college, however, was graded on the basis of small grammar mistakes rather than other contents, and my grades suffered a lot because of this.

Such beliefs about implementing language correctness approaches to achieve academic and economic mobility often situate students to abandon their cultural and social realities (Canagarajah, 2011). Encouraging students from diverse cultural and language backgrounds to use their homegrown resources helps them assert their social and cultural identities, and "create and use a range of culturally identified languages and literacies to maintain their 'roots' and, in the process, reconstruct their own culture and community" (Pandey, 2015, p. 188).

Both Bijaya and Binaya actively participate in online communication among their community members and friends from high school and college. Sometimes through social networking sites such as Facebook, blogs, and websites that promote Bhutanese literature and music, and their own website, both Bijaya and Binaya communicate to the outside world through poems and music. However, Bijaya talks about his frustrations that community people on those sites "mostly discuss daily chores, and fun activities more than other useful literature, music and promotional events of their culture and language." He uses these sites for learning language and being conscious of the nuances of English as the users negotiate meanings through regular comments across those sites. Bijaya is active in the Music, Literature, and Arts group and helps produce regular programs for *Triveni*, a local organization to promote Bhutanese culture, literature, and music, and posts those programs to the sites, such as Facebook and YouTube. Bijaya also composes lyrics in Nepali and sings them to his own music. He is a good musician and writer.

Binaya discussed his limited access to computers when growing up in Nepal and the United States. The only places he could use computers were the public libraries in Panorama City. Although he had an interest in using computer for writing and learning new things, Binaya could not use them often. He notes:

> When my father first bought a computer long after we arrived in the United States, he made a time schedule for three of us (siblings) to use it. I felt like using it all the time myself, but it was beyond imagination. In addition to learning to type and using social networking sites, such as Facebook, MySpace, I used computer for everything. Even today whenever I struggle with any concept, English vocabulary, geographical knowledge, or math problems, I resort to computer and learn by finding solutions there.

When he could buy his own computer, Binaya developed most of his computer skills independently. He created a website (http://www.kynepal.com) and regularly updated it with links to new releases of Nepali comedy serials, news reports, and literary and cultural events that took place in Bhutanese refugee and Nepali communities inside and outside the United States Binaya explained those links and posts were well received by his refugee community and other Nepali communities because they include mostly comic skits, current news, and other musical and movie events especially popular among the elderly and the youth in Nepal and the United States.

Binaya also recited a poem titled "Exile" that he wrote when he was in grade 10 on the experiences of exile and sufferings in the new place when living as refugees in both Nepal and in the United States. Although he didn't directly encounter the experiences of persecution and sufferings in Bhutan, Binaya based his writing on stories he heard from family and other relatives about their plight as refugees. Binaya also used such themes arising from his family experiences of isolation and living in different places as refugees when writing for his high school English class. Such stories, as Selfe and Hawisher (2014) believe, "provide an interesting set of cultural tracings of how individuals inhabiting transnational contexts learn, take up, and use digital communication technologies to extend their communicative reach, to maintain their social and cultural identities, and to construct their worlds" (p. 192).

Their multimodal literacy learning at home, however, is not accounted for when doing schoolwork. Yet, Bijaya and Binaya believe whatever they design and learn in their home and community transfers to the classroom. For example, when Bijaya wrote scripts or songs and posted videos on YouTube, he engaged in composing several drafts of those writings. When he followed the same methods in writing his essays for school, he did not receive encouraging feedback. He was mostly evaluated based on "small ESL issues that my teacher encountered in my writing." Schools can help these students academically succeed by acknowledging and recognizing the skills students bring to the classroom from community contexts.

According to Rogoff and Correa-Chavez (2004), "literacy learning could be improved in schools with greater recognition of the everyday language and literacy practices that children engage in skillfully at home and in their communities" (p. xiv). Also, as indicated by Heath (1983) and others, to better understand the literacy practices of minority communities like the refugees we need to discover the usage and functions of language, digital and printed, in the community and the classroom. A recent publication by Canagarajah (2013), *Literacy as Translingual Practice: Between Communities and Classrooms*, further establishes this continuity between learning practices in the communities and that in the school classrooms. The processes of language learning and creative use of technology go together in literacy actions of the students like Binaya, demonstrating what Lantolf (2000) calls the reciprocal effect of computers and humans in computer-mediated communication. Drawing on Vygotsky's notion of mediation in learning, Lantolf observes:

> In opposition to the orthodox view of the mind, Vygotsky argued that just as humans do not act directly on the physical world but rely, instead, on

tools and labor activity, which allows us to change the world, and with it, the circumstances under which we live in the world, we also use symbolic tools, or signs, to mediate and regulate our relationships with others and with ourselves and thus change the nature of these relationships. (Lantolf, 2000, p. 1)

As Lantolf's analysis suggests, the job of teachers and researchers investigating literacy practices is to make explicit what is hidden in the society in the form of symbolic tools, and create student awareness about how uses and designs of such tools and skills contribute to people's meaning making practices in relation to schooled literacy. The latter, however, is hyped to be the only recognized model of literacy that helps social improvement and social mobility, and which Harvey Graff claims perpetuates the literacy myth (Graff, as cited in Street, 1984, p. 10). As such, it is necessary to bring into mainstream discourse discussion about multilingual and multimodal literacy practices of immigrant and refuges communities like Bhutanese refugees and develop theoretical perspectives that consider the situated, contextual, and ideological nature of reading and writing in the context of transnational migration.

Among Refugee Youth

The cultural and literacy practices of the Bhutanese refugees are diverse and changing in the context of Panorama City culture, whereby such practices render recognizable differences the refugees bring to the new context as resources rather than threats. For example, in an open Facebook forum they created, Bhutanese refugee youth communicated their ideas about cultures, social gathering, sports, and language learning, and used this platform to explore their potential as refugee among other communities. During an interview, Binaya explained the significance of such a forum in offering the refugee youth a platform for engendering ideas about major events and activities they regularly organize and for helping them improve their language skills. As Binaya explained:

> I have found these online forums to be very creative for younger generation. The people who feel shy and reserved during physical meetings take advantage of such forums like Facebook. They post their interests and immediate reactions about any activities created online. If there are any learning or sports opportunities, they openly interact about such topics in a way to help us reach to a decision sooner. I have been so excited about having more people pipe in the discussion and openly express their views.

Such collective encounters online have functioned as digital spaces for intercultural communication and contribute to learning English by

Figure 14.1. Facebook: Multiple Languages in Action.

including participants' own cultural and language resources. English, thus, becomes fraught with richer resources as the multilingual participants bring newer constructions in English mixed with their own cultural and social nuances.

As shown in Figure 14.1, most of the participants used Nepali, English, and sometimes Hindi constructions of sentences and communicated ideas in a situated way. With an ownership over their writing, they weighed which language expression would better suit the context by positioning themselves as agents of language and culture vs. positioning themselves as "refugees" who passively accept new ways or remain locked in old ways. They found their own ways to create changing cultural and communication patterns to suit these contexts.

Such language constructions help participants learn and improve their intercultural communication in a new context. Expanding what counts as text in the classroom, as scholars such as Kirkland (2004) suggest, has the potential to influence student motivation. The following screen shot of a post on Facebook (Figure 14.2) informing Bhutanese

Figure 14.2. Priya and Her Group on FB.

youth in Panorama City about initiating a youth group indicates how youth become interested in helping out others in need and using discussions as learning practices. More intriguing is school-going teenage girls have taken the initiative to start a youth group online.

During group discussions online, Priya, a high school student from Bhutanese community at Panorama City, proposed starting a new forum to involve a community of youth in various cultural, social, and other learning activities (see Figure 14.2). Raised and educated in an English-medium boarding school in eastern Nepal until eighth grade, Priya considered herself knowledgeable and competent in written and spoken English. However, when she came to the United States and started school in Panorama City, she realized for the first time she didn't know anything about English, and she could never succeed in the new school environment. Priya shared an experience of being marginalized socially and academically in school in the United States. When she spoke, her friends made fun of her:

> I have only a different accent, but I still believe that I speak a good English. However, every time I spoke either in class or outside, my middle school friends made a laughingstock of me. They tried to imitate my speech disparagingly. They didn't only make fun of me but also bullied me all the time just because I came from a different culture and spoke with an accent. The teachers didn't help me either. There were not many non-native speakers of English in the school until then, so the teachers probably weren't prepared how to deal with the students like me. Then I decided to stay shut all the time both inside and outside the class so nobody could make fun of me. I started to open up little bit more when I went to a private high school, where, although the treatment of white American friends and teachers was not that different, there were a couple of friends from minority ethnic communities like Latin America and Middle East, who I could count in as my friends and who helped me a lot with learning and socializing.

Priya initially thought starting a new online forum could help make more friends and stay in touch with girls from her own community. As a girl raised and educated outside the refugee camps in Nepal, she didn't have many friends from the camps in the United States, making her feel isolated and lonely. Priya was creating a different community rather than attempting to preserve a pre-existing community. Given participants' engagement in such activities, it is important to understand the participants use their literacy skills in the new context to produce culture and society, not simply to join or reproduce an existing one.

When asked what motivated her to start such a group, Priya noted the need for the preservation of culture and language. However, Priya and her friends were not merely involved in preserving their language and culture, but also transforming literacy practices to fit the new context and motivate other community members for active participation and learning. For example, Priya explained how she used Facebook and other literacy resources for learning English. Most of the participants in her group read English novels and posted their responses to these novels online by interpreting these books to understand their own cultural and social experiences about ethnic diversity, marriage, and the role of social institutions in promoting women empowerment.

These activities online don't only help Priya and her friends discuss issues on women empowerment and gender equity in relation to the new cultures; they also boost their morale about learning English. One example of such learning Priya provided was how they learn English and transform knowledge making practices through its implications to the larger world. When the participants posted passages or quotes from any novel they read, they needed to be knowledgeable about the vocabulary and rhetorical contexts of those readings so the writers could respond to those queries about such issues clearly and effectively during peer discussions. That way participants were not limiting their learning experiences to what was in the text, but also expanding and transforming their implications to the new contexts of learning language, culture, and other social and political implications in the society. For Priya, such digital learning practices proved instrumental for acclimatizing to new cultural and academic contexts.

Bhutanese youth like Priya use these online forums for developing leadership opportunities and improving their language skills. Writing often both in Nepali and English, and occasionally in Hindi, most participants jump in without solicitation to offer their suggestions and views about any event or learning opportunity posted online. Online participation thus enhances participants' language and communication skills helping them use several modes, such as image, writing, speech, layout, etc. Online communication as a mode therefore becomes socially, culturally, and linguistically engaging.

According to Bezemer and Kress (2008), a mode is "a socially and culturally shaped resource for meaning making," and "image, writing, layout, speech, moving image are examples of modes, all used in learning resources. Meanings are made in a variety of modes and always with more than one mode" (p. 171). Not writing otherwise for any other purposes, participants become more active users of English including other languages in the process of meaning making. Priya told me they had started to improve English and also preserve Nepali and Hindi through their regular discussions online, as shown above in their Facebook interaction (see Figure 14.1). For example, when Priya posted about library resources for learning, her friends chimed in to discuss the benefits to the community and whether they should participate in visiting the library and using these resources. Other participants also joined the conversation by posting similar offers and scholarship opportunities for college-seeking students.

While Priya was excited about the online forums used for meeting friends to rehearse cultural programs and plan and organize them, she became more intrigued by the opportunity to use such forums for learning and improving communication skills. Moreover, such forums offered opportunities for girls to become active participants in the discussion. Community discussions otherwise became mostly boys-dominated, as girls mostly remained silent and away from such public discussions. Priya was glad things were changing with the easier affordances to technology.

As these examples suggest, the refugee youth are creating new communities and cultures (the "Panorama City Bhutanese community" not the "Bhutanese community") and changing language practices through recontextualization. In the words of Bezemer and Kress (2008), recontextualization forges the "re-presentation of the meaning materials in a manner apt for the new context in the light of the available modal resources. Pedagogically, recontextualization involves the moving of curricular texts in line with the pedagogic features of the environment of recontextualization" (p. 184). The learning skills these youth develop in the communities through the recontextualization of prior language and literacy resources can yield better results by helping the multilingual and multicultural students succeed in school environments.

However, few educational institutions recognize and respect such differences in the use of English to help these youth channel such language resources for meaningful communication. The literacy sponsors are concerned only with the prescribed norms in their teaching and learning activities. They are guided by the standard norms prescribed by the dominant institutions without considering the realities of the people learning them. For example, Priya shared her experiences of emotional breakdown and grade inflation in her freshman English writing courses in college. She was a brilliant student who aspired to go to medical school and wanted to maintain perfect scores in all subject. However, her dreams shattered as she received grades in college English classes; they were upper Bs and Cs despite her hard work writing and revising these papers. Her papers were bled with teacher's comments mostly of minor grammar, punctuation, and transition errors. Priya discussed her frustrations:

> When I went to meet with my teacher with questions as to how I could improve the mistakes as marked on my paper, he simply dismissed my desire for learning by saying that it was natural for the ESL students like me to make those mistakes and that he could understand that because I was a refugee coming from a different background. I didn't need any word of sympathy; that merely reinforced the stereotypes that we are incompetent students coming from different culture. That only added an insult to my injury by forcing me to internalize that as a non-native speaker of English, I could never improve my writing. I literally broke down several times by coming to my dorms and felt helpless. I totally stopped visiting my English teacher since then and turned in my papers whatever way I wrote them. I was too scared to visit the teacher next time.

Priya also showed me papers her teacher had marked. (I've included the first page of an essay—Figure 14.3—as an example.) Priya wrote this paper for her freshman English course for an assignment asking students to conduct primary research on the significance of water in our

Water 139A

1. *The summary of The Neolithic Great Goddess of Sky,Earth and Waters And*
Zig-Zag and M signs

The Neolithic great goddess of sky, earth and waters gives us information, beauty, fertility, sexuality, and the patterns of birth and re-birth. All the listed elements is [are] needed to live as ~~life for us~~ human beings. It teaches [Two] you the meaning and importance of life. (The goddess projects the pattern of story telling, shapes, fertility, and beginning of a new life. (The interesting subject about this article was showing the fertile side of goddess and how everyone has a mother even earth.) During the time period, women were known to do house work and agriculture work whereas the men were supposed to be out bringing money in the house. Water is known [often interpreted] as giving a new life. Times is [spirals] eternity; it keeps going, and we keep discovering new things. Water is often used as a metaphor when explaining about ~~women~~ [female] fertility and the womb. (This article gives information on different goddess: such as [as the] : fish goddess and [represents] how the sea is filled with fish, likewise the womb is filled with water; serpent goddess symbolizes ~~which are~~ [the] ~~Zig-Zag,~~ fertility, very powerful birth and re-births; bird goddess are to [the] bring new life, and her shape often compared to ~~women~~ [a female] body. Finally, [beginning & end.] the egg plays a very important part (in all those goddess womb) because egg and egg shaped womb are to bring new life on the earth. The womb is where life begins.)

⟹ During the ~~late~~ [Neolithic] eras, people didn't have containers to grow their seeds, boil, or cook so they craved [carved] vessels and vase to store food, water, and seeds. The vessels were also used as a tomb

Figure 14.3. Priya's Writing Sample.

world and how water is valued in different cultures. This was an expository essay written in response to this assignment.

I noticed most of the comments noted local-level errors, and Priya said she had points deducted for those errors. She explained she was okay with those marks on her paper and she wanted to learn more with clear explanation of why they were problems so she could improve. Those errors, however, are mostly the communicative patterns or language use Priya commonly employed when writing online as seen in Figure 14.2.

Our judgment of student language quality is often based on the quality of writing they produce in class. As illustrated by Priya's example and her response to it in my interview, such a discouraging and belittling attitude toward the writings of refugee students provides a damaging view of a stable refugee community and culture (of "refugees") and denies the possibility of change. We mainly gloss over the matters of agency students like Priya practice by using multiple cultural, social, and linguistic repertoires in their academic writing. Calling this tendency a normative complex, Blommaert (2013) notes that such complex applies "to the total semiotic fact of the 'written language'. We apply this normative complex whenever we 'read' a written text, and even if our overall judgment can be dominated by specific features such as stylistic fluency or the strength of argumentation, we appear to fold such more specific normative judgments into one total judgment of 'the text'" (p. 443). Despite her willingness to learn, Priya couldn't receive any help from her teacher; he simply asked her to revise and improve, as Priya stated, those "problems in order to receive better grades" without offering help. Such apathy on the part of teacher might also have arisen due to his lack of training or strategies for supporting linguistically and culturally diverse students.

The attitude the teacher showed toward Priya reinforces what Lu and Horner (2013) call the ideology of monolingualism that "associates language difference strictly with subordinated groups" (p. 583). The ideology of monolingualism, according to Lu and Horner, sees slight deviations in writing by those identified as belonging to subordinate social groups "as manifestations of the writers' lack of knowledge or fluency with 'the standard,'" while recognizable deviations in writing by those identified as and located in the "mainstream" as creative innovations (p. 583). If, however, the teacher had been prepared to offer extra support and had more training working with diverse students, he could have developed a better perception of those students and found ways to channel their multimodal, multilingual, and multicultural resources into better learning experiences.

Moreover, academic institutions raise the bar for such refugee students higher when making decisions about such students' admissions. Two participants, Chitra and Dibya, were critical of the provisions for admissions local universities set for such students. Chitra was only four years old and Dibya two when their family left Bhutan for the refugee camps in Nepal. Both came from educated family backgrounds and had completed their high school in Nepal. However, when they arrived in the United States, they were placed in grade 10 as students coming from a different cultural and linguistic background so that they could be familiar with the new educational contexts. They had specific interests in social sciences and IT. Chitra wanted to pursue his higher studies in IT, and Dibya in social work. Their learning curve proved to be steep in the beginning due to their difficulty understanding spoken and written "American English." As they continued to work, they could manage their class assignments and other readings. They felt comfortable with other social sciences and IT classes due to their "competent" education back in Nepal. They graduated high schools from Panorama City in good standing in 2010.

Both Chitra and Dibya complained despite their expertise, knowledge, desire to continue their studies, they couldn't join program of interest because they couldn't make the required grades in their ESL classes. In a local community college in Panorama City, Chitra first took an ESL course as a requirement before being qualified for joining the mainstream writing course. He recalled the comments one of his ESL teachers made on his first essay:

> Although my prior experiences helped little bit in coping with English classes, I was so taken back by the teacher's comments in the beginning when I turned in my first essay to ESL teacher. She told me that mine was a D paper, and she couldn't grade it above that. What seemed to matter more for her was small grammar mistakes. I thought I had written pretty well, but after seeing her comments on the paper I became hopeless that my English was so bad. I later started to use YouTube as a resource for learning English and finding instructions on other subjects as well.

As a requirement for college admission, both Chitra and Dibya were asked to attend ESL classes throughout the year and make certain scores before being qualified to take regular courses. These were requirements for them to get associate's degrees before they could be admitted to undergraduate degree programs. However, Chitra and Dibya couldn't do this for several reasons: first, they couldn't afford to pay for the costly ESL classes; second, they didn't believe in the scores, as they thought that the ways tests were designed made them impossible for securing the expected scores; third, they didn't have time to linger on mandatory ESL classes throughout the year when they had to work and sustain their families at the same time.

When I met them later, both Dibya and Chitra told me they decided to give up. Such cases are only the tip of the iceberg we encounter in academic institutions, as rarely do people speak about such frustrations unless they are pushed because, as Chitra and Dibya revealed to me during the interview, if they spoke about such realities, people might think it was their incapability that landed them in their situation. And they didn't want to expose their weaknesses to the outside world.

CONCLUSION

As we continue to face challenges regarding literacy practices beyond the walls of schools, we need to understand how social practices of literacy work; then we will be able to identify the ways hidden social skills implicitly contribute to people's knowledge construction based on their lived experiences. Such hidden literacy skills develop where notions of school literacy, and of literacy more generally conflict. Schooled literacy becomes a particular form of literacy without which people are deemed to be illiterate, despite their reading and writing skills.

The chapter examined how refugee youth used transnational, semiotic, and cultural resources for reading and constructing identity online. The purpose of this study is to understand how refugee students' digital literacy practices outside of school influence their literacy development in the classroom. The increasing production and circulation of digital texts and online community activities by these refugee youth has brought many languages, cultures, and semiotic resources into contact in the United States as never before. As such, it merits our attention as teachers and researchers of writing.

References

Appadurai, A. (1990). Disjuncture and difference in the global cultural economy. *Public Culture, 2*(2), 1–24. https://doi.org/10.1215/08992363-2-2-1

Appadurai, A. (1996). *Modernity at large: Cultural dimensions of globalization.* Minneapolis, MN: University of Minnesota.

Barton, D., & Hamilton, M. (1998). *Local literacies: Reading and writing in one community.* London, England: Routledge. https://doi.org/10.4324/9780203448885

Baynham, M., & Prinsloo, M. (Eds.). (2009). *The future of literacy studies.* New York, NY: Palgrave Macmillan. https://doi.org/10.1057/9780230245693

Bezemer, J., & Kress, G. (2008) Writing in multimodal texts: A social semiotic account of designs for learning. *Written Communication, 25*(2), 166–195. https://doi.org/10.1177/0741088307313177

Blommaert, J. (2013). Writing as a sociolinguistic object. *Journal of Sociolinguistics, 17*(4), 440–459. https://doi.org/10.1111/josl.12042

Canagarajah, A. S. (2011). Translanguaging in the classroom: Emerging issues for research and pedagogy. *Applied Linguistics Review, 2,* 1–28.

Canagarajah, A. S. (Ed.). (2013). *Literacy as translingual practice: Between communities and classrooms.* New York, NY: Routledge.

Cope, B., & Kalantzis, M. (2009). 'Multiliteracies': New literacies, new learning. *Pedagogies, 4*(3), 164–195. https://doi.org/10.1080/15544800903076044

Cope, B., & Kalantzis, M. (2010). New media, new learning. In D. R. Cole & D. R. Pullen (Eds.), *Multiliteracies in motion: Current theory and practice* (pp. 87–104). New York, NY: Routledge.

Gregory, E., & Williams, A. (2000). *City literacies: Learning to read across generations and cultures.* London, England: Routledge.

Gupta, A., & Ferguson, J. (2002). Beyond 'culture': Space, identity and the politics of difference. In J. Inda & R. Rosaldo (Eds.), *The anthropology of globalization: A reader* (pp. 65–80). Oxford, England: Blackwell.

Hannerz, U. (2002). Notes on the global ecumene. In J. Inda & R. Rosaldo (Eds.), *The anthropology of globalization: A reader* (pp. 37–64). Oxford, England: Blackwell.

Heath, S. B. (1983). *Ways with words: Language, life, and work in communities and classrooms.* Cambridge, England: Cambridge University Press.

Horner, B., & Selfe, C. (2013). Translinguality/transmodality relations: Snapshots from a dialogue (working papers on negotiating differences in language and literacy). Retrieved from http://louisville.edu/workingpapers/doc/self-horner-working-papers-version

Inda, J., & Rosaldo, R. (Eds.). (2002). *The anthropology of globalization: A reader.* Oxford, England: Blackwell.

Kirkland, D. (2004). Rewriting school: Critical writing pedagogies for the secondary english classroom. *Journal of Teaching Writing, 21*(1/2), 83–96.

Lantolf, J. (2000). Introducing sociocultural theory. In J. P. Lantolf (Ed.), *Sociocultural theory and second language learning* (pp. 1–26). London, England: Oxford University Press.

Lauren, B., & Rice, R. (2013). Teaching style in basic writing through remediation photo essays. *The Basic Writing E-Journal, 11*(1). Retrieved from https://bwe.ccny.cuny.edu/LaurenandRiceRemediatingPhoto.html

Lu, M., & Horner, B. (2013). Translingual literacy, language difference, and matters of agency. *College English, 75*(6), 582–607.

Madianou, M., & Miller, D. (2012). *Migration and new media: Transnational families and polymedia.* New York, NY: Routledge.

Matsuda, P. K. (2002). Alternative discourses: A synthesis. In C. Schroeder, H. Fox, & P. Bizzell (Eds.), *ALT/DIS: Alternative discourses and the academy* (pp. 191–196). Portsmouth, NH: Boynton/Cook.

Pahl, K., & Rowsell, J. (Eds.). (2006). *Travel notes from the new literacy studies: Instances of practice.* Tonawanda, NY: Multilingual Matters.

Pandey, I. P. (2015). *South Asian in the mid-south: Migrations of literacies.* Pittsburgh, PA: University of Pittsburgh Press. https://doi.org/10.2307/j.ctt18d839z

Pennycook, A. (2010). *Language as a local practice.* New York, NY: Routledge.

Quantz, R. A. (1992) On critical ethnography (with some postmodern considerations). In M. D. LeCompte, W. L. Millroy, & J. Preissle (Eds.), *The handbook of qualitative research in education* (pp. 447–506). San Diego, CA: Academic Press.

Reason, P. (2004). Critical design ethnography as action research. *Anthropology & Education Quarterly, 35*(2), 269–276. https://doi.org/10.1525/aeq.2004.35.2.269

Rogoff, B., & Correa-Chavez, M. (2004). Preface. In E. Gregory, S. Long, & D. Volk (Eds.), *Many pathways to literacy: Young children learning with siblings, grandparents, peers and communities* (pp. xiii–xv). New York, NY: Routledge.

Rowsell, J., Kress, G., & Street, B. (2013). Visual optics: Interpreting body art, three ways. *Visual Communication, 12*(1), 97–122.

Selfe, C. L. (1999). Technology and literacy: A story about the perils of not paying attention. *College Composition and Communication, 50*(3), 411–436. https://doi.org/10.2307/358859

Selfe, C. L. (2009). The movement of air, the breath of meaning: Aurality and multimodal composing. *College Composition and Communication, 60*(4), 616–663.

Selfe, C. L., & Hawisher, G. E. (2014). Beyond *Literate Lives*: Collaboration, literacy narratives, transnational connections, and digital media. In J. Duffy, J. N. Christoph, E. Goldblatt, N. Graff, R. S. Nowacek, & B. Trabold (Eds.), *Literacy, economy, and power: Writing and research after literacy in American lives* (pp. 185–202). Carbondale, IL: Southern Illinois University Press.

Street, B. (1984). *Literacy in theory and practice.* Cambridge, England: Cambridge University Press.

Street, B., (Ed.). (1993). *Cross-cultural approaches to literacy.* Cambridge, England: Cambridge University Press.

Street, B. (2006). New literacies, new times: How do we describe and teach the forms of literacy knowledge, skills, and values people need for new times? In *The Yearbook of National Reading Conference* (pp. 21–42). Oak Creek, WI: National Reading Conference.

Warriner, D. S. (2009). Transnational literacies: Examining global flows through the lens of social practice. In M. Baynham & M. Prinsloo (Eds.), *The future of literacy studies* (pp. 160–180). New York, NY: Palgrave Macmillan. https://doi.org/10.1057/9780230245693_9

15

GLOCALIZING THE COMPOSITION CLASSROOM WITH GOOGLE APPS FOR EDUCATION

Daniel Hocutt and Maury Brown

ABSTRACT

Composing practices in a digitally networked world are inherently intercultural, and situate local needs and constraints within global opportunities and concerns. Global technologies like Google Apps for Education (GAFE)[1] allow students to compose collaboratively across place and time; to do so, students and teachers must navigate a complex local network of institutional policy, learning outcomes, situational needs, and composing practices while also being aware of the global implications of using the interface to compose, review, edit, and share with others. The chapter describes using GAFE in locally situated composition classes. Using such technologies requires a focus on glocalization and an understanding of how networked composing activity affects the communication process, and the institutions, faculty, and students who are interconnected within it.

Keywords: cloud-based computing, cloud pedagogy, computers and writing, digital literacy, digital writing, first-year composition, glocalization, Google Apps for Education (GAFE), Google Docs, Google Drive, ICT, networked individualism, networked knowledge communities

INTRODUCTION

When composing in digital environments, we entangle ourselves in a global web of networks. As Reid (2008) points out, today's composing technologies are "designed, produced, and assembled through a global network of companies and factories," and that in using these technologies we "necessarily hand over some of the creative process and decision-making responsibilities of authorship to the computer" (p. 68). Whether using commercial hardware and software, freeware, learning management

DOI: 10.7330/9781607326649.c015

systems, or open source solutions, teachers, students, and institutions must agree to the terms of service and conditions of use defined by networks of corporate entities. Adoption of these information communication technologies (ICTs) creates an evolving online global context where our identities and our practices are influenced in visible and unseen ways. Institutions, faculty, and staff who use such ICTs must therefore be aware of the global contexts and ideologies inherent in the interface and made manifest through use while seeking to critically examine how such ICTs affect communication, composing practices, and how we teach them.

Global technology giant Google offers services to consumers in exchange for the information they provide. With strongholds in Internet searching, electronic mail, video streaming, and mobile phone industries, Google offers a suite of services free of charge to K–12 and higher educational institutions: Google Apps for Education (GAFE). The suite of cloud-based software and services provides collaborative functionality for the classroom through email and shared drive applications, as well as open source software that mimics the functionality of Microsoft's Office Suite: Word (functions mimicked by Google Docs), Excel (Sheets), PowerPoint (Slides) and Outlook (Gmail, Contacts, and Calendar). Cloud-based services designed for educational use (e.g., GAFE) afford deeply collaborative activities across multiple applications and interfaces. Google Drive and Google Docs provide shared folders for exclusive, password-protected file sharing and free web- or app-based word processing. Google Docs also offers the opportunity for both asynchronous and synchronous exchange.

As scholars have noted, digital technologies are never neutral (Feenberg, 1991; Selfe & Selfe, 1994). GAFE is no exception. Although there are uses of the technology "for good," and there are promises of improved access to education and equalized spaces, as Selber (2004) notes, "computer technologies are aligned with competitive and oppressive formations that tend to shore up rather than address existing social inequalities" (p. 12). DePew (2015) points out that "despite the 'kumbaya rhetoric' of global equality that digital corporations use to sell their wares, at the end of the day these companies need to turn a profit" (p. 446). When higher education institutions adopt these products and instructors use them, instructors and institutions may be complicit in allowing student work and activity to be mined for profile building and targeted advertising. Using these technologies positions instructors as potential agents of enacting or perpetuating inequalities, exploiting students' labor, or compromising their privacy. Yet even in the global network of Google, composing acts are locally mediated and situated.

The chapter frames GAFE in the context of glocalization and networked individualism, and provides heuristics for others to consider when implementing GAFE in the composition classroom. First, we place this study within the context of current digital composing theory and praxis. Then, we discuss the local uses of GAFE in first-year composition (FYC) classes at a public community college and a private university's professional and continuing studies division. We identify global and local implications for decisions made to implement GAFE for composing, revision, and assessment, with regard to both technological and pedagogical affordances and constraints. We demonstrate that the use of GAFE in the composition classroom creates a glocal system of networks within networks, whereby the individual negotiates within and among local and global communities and cultures.

REVIEW OF THE LITERATURE

Networks, as Castells (2010) notes, "have become the predominant organizational form of every domain of human activity" (p. xliv). He introduces one type of network, the "space of places" (p. xxxi), described as "horizontal networks of communication built around people's initiatives, interests, and desires [that] are multimodal and incorporate many kinds of documents" (p. xxviii). When GAFE is implemented, its interface enacts and makes visible this often invisible or implied network of communication and learning. Castells introduces another type of network, the vertical "spaces of flows" (p. xxxii), which he describes as "the material organization of time-sharing social practices that work through flows" (p. 442). The synchronous and asynchronous collaborative activities offered on a global scale as part of Google's multinational networked corporate entity reflect the global environment, or space of flows, which mediates and connects the space of places. Castells depicts the space of places as horizontally contiguous and in tension with, but not in binary opposition to, the vertically networked space of flows (pp. xxxvii, xxxix). Students using GAFE are connected in terms of both "place" (the interface, reconstituted among multiple devices and physical locations) and "time" or "flow" (composition, collaboration, revision, and communication conducted among flash groups of individuals in the network). Castells describes this contradiction in terms of power structures: "cultural and social meaning is defined in place terms, while functionality, wealth, and power are defined in terms of flows" (p. xxxix).

Appadurai (1990) describes this contradiction as disjunction between heterogeneity and homogeneity and emphasizes the networked nature of cultural flows illustrated as "the relationship between five dimensions of global cultural flow which can be termed: (a) ethnoscapes; (b) mediascapes; (c) technoscapes; (d) financescapes; and (e) ideoscapes" (p. 296). These dimensions of cultural flow represent relationships and tensions in continual flux among multiple facets of culture, not binaries in opposition to one another. Castells and Appadurai recognize cultural meanings and economic power flow among and along disjunctions in vast and complex global networks. Students who use GAFE, in turn, enter the space of places at the local level, and join the space of flows as they are connected, through the interface, to larger global systems of network technology and infrastructure, multicultural values and ideologies, and laminated global networks of trade (Appadurai, 1990; Castells, 2010). Students, and their instructors and institutions, negotiate between maintaining a sense of individual identity and needs and fitting those ideas into a more global landscape of what constitutes knowledge, employability, and actualization. The tension and negotiation is not *between* the "world of work" and the "world of school" but more the "world of work" *in* the "world of school." In the space of flows and the space of places, the multiple facets of cultural flow are simultaneously exchanged, enacted and enforced, creating tenuous and negotiated situated identities, individuals within a network, a local within a global.

Cloud-based computing applications such as Google Apps for Education enable and make manifest the networked individualism of glocalization. The student, faculty member, classroom, and writing process and products are always-already part of the global network; GAFE reveals it explicitly. OneDrive's use in educational contexts is a way to support global and networked activity and to develop an awareness of cross-cultural communication and the social nature of composing. When installed as the default file sharing service for an institution, GAFE affords the kind of collaborative composing, reviewing, presenting, and assessing practices encouraged by contemporary composition theory (see Yancey, 2004; J. Rice, 2006; Smith, 2008; Alexander, 2009; and Bridwell-Bowles, Powell, & Choplin, 2009). GAFE represents a space of flows in which composing actor, composing medium, instructor, peers, pedagogy, assessment, and composing practices flow across global networks and local spaces. The local use of GAFE as a composing tool creates a networked learning environment that is a "thoughtful fusion of face-to-face and online learning experiences" (Garrison & Vaughan, 2007, p. 5). As a networked blended learning environment, composition classes that incorporate GAFE rely on socially constructive theories of composition and on the concept of glocalization, through which local activity is seen on a continuum with the global, with local agency reiterated within the larger networked activity of the global through myriad connectivities (Robertson, 1995).

As a composing environment, the networked use of GAFE can create a community of learners. Using sharing permissions among all class members focused on a common assignment or outcome liberates invention, composing, peer review, and revision practices from solitary activities of individual students to social activities within a community of learners. Within this community, concepts sometimes seen as more fixed, such as "student," "teacher," "draft," "process," and "product" are all remediated (Bolter & Grusin, 1996) as students and instructors take advantage of GAFE networked capabilities. Students and teachers alike transition from operating within a high-context classroom environment where meanings are fixed and understood within Hall's (2007) "dominant-hegemonic position" (p. 485) to operating within a low-context classroom environment where meanings and identities are fluid and decoded in a "globally contrary way" (p. 487). In the classroom glocalized using GAFE, classroom concepts and identities are encoded and decoded not via a singular model of changing x to y, but in a dynamic and recursive ecosystem that resonates with Hall's dynamism, Appadurai's scapes, and Castells's intersecting spaces of flows and places.

Collaborative composing is rooted in writing's social aspects (Miller, 1984, 1994; Bazerman, 1994, 2004, 2013; Gaillet, 2009). Collaborating in the same document, on the same assignment, as part of an intentional community of learners, replaces the writer/reader binary and its corollary, "the individual who works in one fixed space within a fixed disciplinary focus with a single identity tied to a singly motivated reading practice tied to a single idea expressed at a single moment" (Rice, 2006), with a far more social actor in a complex, networked space (Latour, 2005). When Bezemer and Kress (2008) consider current and future understandings of "text" and "genre" in composition studies, they invoke the social dimension of composing in multimodal texts: "Every text has a generic form. Each of these frames/genres defines text in terms of activity, of social relations of participants in an event, and in terms of the use of modes and media" (p. 173). Collaborative writing using Google Drive is a frame that defines text in terms of activity (collaboration), social relations (a community of learners), and the use of modes (synchronous or asynchronous commentary, synchronous chat, collaborative revision) and media (the virtual page in a digital network). Collaborative composing is a networked activity (Bazerman, 2004), and by using GAFE in educational settings or similar Google Apps in workplace settings, networked composing activity can easily join similar activity among writers anywhere across the globe, each local group itself functioning within a network or networks.

boyd (2007) notes that digital spaces give young people a sense of autonomy and power. Students who compose with networked technology have access to tools that enable practices and relationships that are unavailable using analog or non-networked composing methods. Using GAFE serves to help level the playing field of access to technology and to powerful digital spaces. However, Vaidhyanathan (2008) points out "the levels of comfort with, understanding of, and dexterity with digital technology varies greatly within every class" (p. B7).

These variances are wider at open access institutions with more diverse student populations. The individual student is the hyper-glocal network node, and although digital technology such as GAFE is implemented on the institutional and classroom level through a connection to the global network of possibilities, the availability of an affordance does not equate to the ability to perceive, access, manipulate, or master it. Social constructionists and postmodernists acknowledge texts are inherently social artifacts, but, as Johnson-Eilola (1998) notes, teachers tend to be rooted to composition practices that privilege individual authorship as final product (p. 17). Using GAFE challenges this bias by enabling access to collaborative process. While meeting the outcomes of the course, students develop skills in workflow process, writing process, and knowledge management. They also practice multimodal literacy ("Council of WPA," 2014) while composing in multiple environments and build digital literacy and collaborative skills that are privileged in a globalized economy and networked society.

IMPLEMENTING GAFE IN THE FIRST-YEAR COMPOSITION CLASSROOM

The authors were engaged in a multi-semester implementation of GAFE in the first-year composition classroom at their respective open-access institutions: a rural/suburban community college and the school of professional and continuing studies at a private liberal arts university. Through a continuous improvement model, the authors have used student feedback from a mixed-methods study, analysis of student artifacts, and participant-observer ethnographic observations and reflections to guide their iterative implementation. Beginning in spring 2014, the GAFE interface was used with students in first- and second-semester composition courses, as well as developmental courses that prepare students for credit-bearing English. Both authors' institutions have adopted GAFE as the primary interface for student email, and all enrolled students have access to the suite of applications and cloud-based storage. Slight variations in the way each author's respective institution implemented GAFE required some customization of the tool to meet the local constraints and student needs.

The extensive use of GAFE made each course section a blended instructional environment. Students used the GAFE interface to interact with course content and each other synchronously as well as asynchronously throughout the semester. Using GAFE leveled access to word processing software, making composing, reviewing, and/or revising available across multiple platforms and allowing students to use their own devices. Teaching with GAFE also taught composing as a network experience. As a result, student familiarity with the composing process and the technology used to create compositions increased throughout the semester with recursive and scaffolded practice.

Two sharing practices were tested with students: one enabled all students and the instructor to view all class members' composing activities; the other allowed the instructor to view all class members' activities and selected members of student groups to view reviewing, revising, and proofreading activities of other students (see Table 15.1). The activity itself was made possible and visible by the web-based tool. The fact that the instructor could observe the traces of a student's activity, even if deleted by the student, led to both a sense of personal accountability and awareness of being watched throughout the composing process, regardless of whether it took place in what may have previously been considered an instructional setting. Glocalization, as enabled by implementing GAFE for collaborative composing in local classes, can replace "one-size-fits-all" implementations of technology with glocalized flexibility. Glocalization as a space of flows represents networked individualism and encourages a localized approach that reflects the specific setting and context in which GAFE is implemented. As a result, the authors were able to respond to local considerations and personal preferences with two different strategies for using GAFE for collaborative composing, as depicted in Table 15.1.

The affordances that make possible collaborative composing in the local classroom also contain the potential for collaborating beyond local boundaries. Composing practices can be traced along a vertical network of power (Castells's "space of flows") running from the student writer through the instructor, the institution, and ultimately to Google; composing in this vertical network required students to monitor and modify

Table 15.1. Differentiating Google Drive Sharing Strategies.

Strategy	Glocal Implementation #1	Glocal Implementation #2
Folder ownership	Single folder shared by instructor with students in a single course section.	Student folders shared with instructor.
Sharing access	All students in class have access to all files by default.	Other students have access to files only with explicit permission.
Institutional configuration	Shared folder created through instructor's institutional account; all students within single Google Apps license and domain.	Student folders (except those of school staff who were students) created through students' institutional account; staff and instructor used personal Google account.
"Pushing" content to students	Students and instructor able to push a single resource to all others via shared drive.	Instructor only able to push resources into individual student shared folders.
Collaboration	Any student could collaborate with any other student at any time. Dynamic, student-selected (but teacher-managed) collaborative groups that changed over time.	Students selected whom to share files with, and when. Primarily worked in teacher-directed groups.
Surveillance	All students and instructor could see all changes made to any document in real time. Entire writing process revealed as it unfolds.	Students decided at what point in composing process to reveal their document with others. Writing process revealed through document history.
Networked activity	Students were connected to all other students in the course as well as the instructor at all times.One main network with composition product as the unit of operations.	Students were connected to selected students in sub-networks within the larger network of the class, visible only to the instructor.Multiple smaller networks linked together; student as the unit of operations.

their behavior in the community, ensuring their activity was circumspect, appropriate, reasonable, and timely. While students composed and collaborated in this vertical network, they also co-created a horizontal network (Castells's "space of places") that led to social learning.

In narrative feedback, students valued participating in networked activities made possible by GAFE. For example, students valued the opportunity to provide and receive feedback beyond the time and space of the class itself, and they appreciated the ability to compose on any Internet-connected device. One student wrote, "I liked that I was able to peer review at home and receive comments on my paper online, so that I could go back and revise my paper" while another appreciated "being able to peer review others work without the pressure of time in the classroom and distractions." Others valued the unique GAFE ability that enables multiple class members, students and instructors alike, to actively compose in a single document synchronously and asynchronously. Students valued specific GAFE functions like "the ability to collaborate with my instructor and classmates on one document" and "being able to partner and communicate with my peers" while recognizing the generalizable value of the composing community to their individual work: "the peer review and comments from our professor were extremely helpful and much appreciated." The GAFE interface places the local within the global, and vice versa, opening opportunities for shared learning whenever two or more collaborators interacted synchronously or asynchronously.

In addition, the lack of anonymity and archiving of network activity allowed for writing and peer review processes to be assessed. Students could see each other's work at all stages of the writing process, from brainstorming and invention to revising and proofreading. Students were asked to comment on a minimum number of peer documents, under deadline constraints, and governed by rubrics concerning peer review activity. These activities were modeled synchronously, during face-to-face (F2F) class-time, often using the projector to view real-time collaboration and the dynamic changes to a document as students offered and accepted feedback. Their activity was visible inside the documents and via revision history to other students in the class.

Opening up to this level of vulnerability required careful attention to building a community of trust, especially during the F2F course sessions, so that it was replicated and recognized within the virtual GAFE network. The glocalized shared community offered a buffer and support network within the Googleverse, and instructors could manage the levels of trust and vulnerability through the sharing privileges of documents within GAFE, so that it would extend to the community created in GAFE. Instructors used F2F classroom sessions to address, assess, and evaluate local student activities while simultaneously explaining, customizing, and implementing the transparent networked GAFE interface. Instructors served as glocalizers for students by connecting the local classroom to the global network through GAFE, by encouraging students to be more aware of their membership in a global community, and by helping students develop a glocal perspective.

APPLICATION

We sought to define questions and considerations about implementing GAFE in the FYC classroom as a collaborative composing medium that would dovetail with composition theory and pedagogical best practices. As such, it could have potentially served as a guideline for others to create their own implementation in other courses and institutions. DePew (2015) notes "individual institutions have to work within their given parameters to create the most effective experiences for all students" (p. 445), reiterating the necessity of glocalization. The heuristic below (Table 15.2) lists questions to ask when considering using GAFE as a pedagogical tool, and breaks them down into three categories related to the institution, faculty, and students. These are divided into the local concerns, where there is agency to affect the implementation, and global concerns, where there is little or no agency, only awareness and mitigation. Together, they offer a way to glocalize GAFE for the specific exigencies and constraints of a given course and institution. The need to introduce explicitly the concept and practice of glocalization in classrooms has emerged as global political and economic systems seek engaged citizens and glocal-aware employees who can understand and manage the flows among and between local and global networks and who can share ideas and information with others through the educational efforts of governments, multinational corporations, and non-governmental organizations (NGOs). (See Spring, 2008; Brooks & Normore, 2010; and Rice & Lauren, 2014, for thorough and ongoing discussions of the value and importance of glocalized educational theory and practice.)

Table 15.2 represents questions that institutions, faculty, and students may address as they consider entering the glocalized "space of flows" of a cloud-based composing platform like GAFE, where students and instructors join an intercultural community of writers who, with appropriate permissions, create a shared audience that flows across time and place. In the space of flows, as Castells (2010) notes, information and identity continually flow between the local and global without being entirely encompassed in either space. As institutions consider implementing GAFE, they create opportunities and limitations that apply to local and global concerns. Local concerns relate to ways the tool gets installed, managed, and used at the institution, while global concerns relate to the way the institution— and the individual—relates to Google as a corporate entity.

As faculty consider implementing GAFE in the classroom, they must address questions of local resources for access and training in using the software suite, as well as for curriculum development, course learning objectives, and assessment. They also face global questions of research and development to stay abreast of software updates, terms of service, and ownership of intellectual property. As students complete classes where GAFE is integrated, they face local issues like access to physical technology and Internet connectivity, universal design, and familiarity with the composing interface and collaborative tools. Students also face

Table 15.2. Heuristic for Implementing Google Drive for Collaborative Composing.

Level	Local Concerns	Global Concerns
Institution	• Does your institution have Google Apps for Education installed? • Are there any restrictions or limits to the way Google Apps for Education will apply to your students? • Who is responsible for the local institutional contract with Google, and what access do you have to this individual or office? • Can you schedule classes in a networked computer classroom or lab? • What are the hours of your Academic Computing Centers and Libraries, for students without computers or reliable Internet access?	• What are the short-term and long-term contractual ownership guidelines for student and instructor data? • What terms of service and privacy policies apply to you and your students, and who is responsible for keeping tabs on changes to those policies? • How will you and your institutional contacts adapt or adopt unexpected and inevitable changes in Google Drive applications and terms of service (TOS)?
Faculty	• How familiar are you with Google Drive? • What resources are available to provide training in the effective use of Google Drive in composition? • How can you adapt and revise your current pedagogical practices to Google Drive? • How can you connect Google Drive as a technology to your learning outcomes and disciplinary practices? • Will you obtain (or are you required to obtain) written student permission to interact in Google Drive?	• How can you implement online writing instruction (OWI) Principles and the Council of Writing Program Administrators (CWPA) Framework for Post-Secondary Education? • What national or international resources can you tap for advice on how to implement Google Drive for collaborative composing? • What Google Apps and third-party plug-ins will you use with your students? • What Google resources can you use to better understand Google's privacy and profiling practices?
Student	• How familiar are your students with Google Drive? What training will you need to provide? • Do your students have access to high-speed Internet outside of F2F classes? • How will you construct and manage deadlines and deliverables? • What will you and your students consider "draft" and "final" products for assessment purposes? • How will you conduct peer review in the collaborative environment? • How will your students submit assignments for grading?	• Are there other students in other institutions composing in Google Drive? Can your students partner with them as resources? • How long will your students have access to their work? What arrangements are made for access after graduation? • When Google changes interfaces or relocates functions, how will you and your students collaborate to remediate? • Is there a plug-in available for Google Drive in the learning management system (LMS)?

global questions of privacy and connectivity, especially to fellow students and collaborators beyond their political, social, and economic borders.

Despite the visual distinction of local and global concerns in the columnar display, the institutional, faculty, and student concerns always exist at both local and global levels at the same time and in the same "real virtualities" (Castells, 2010, p. xxxi), with flow between them. The additional issues raised by the questions in Table 15.2 deserve thorough attention beyond the scope of the chapter. These align in categories of local technical implementation and ongoing support, local intellectual property (IP) rights within globalized cloud storage, accessibility to students and teachers of differing abilities and socioeconomic status, privacy concerns at both local and global levels, and digital asset ownership in cloud-based (rather than locally installed) online learning environments.

Because identities are related to and influenced by technologies (Selfe & Selfe, 1994; Reid, 2008), joining a local network of writers based in the class environment through the global network of Google collaborative composing necessarily influences the identities of class participants and aspects of the class experience. For example, class activities like peer review become student-centered and focused; rather than instructors setting times and dates for peer review, all class participants including the instructor can engage in peer review activities with class members at any stage of the composing process. Deliberately using the collaborative affordances of GAFE for pedagogical goals creates an iterative and participatory composing process that changes the role of instructor, peer reviewer, and writer, as each can simultaneously act as reviewer, writer, and even peer review facilitator. Table 15.3 delineates concepts changed or questioned through using GAFE in the classroom.

Glocalized entities blur their own identities, seen in the close parallels among institution, faculty, and student descriptions throughout Table 15.3. For example, it's never entirely accurate to say that any single entity "owns" a composed artifact. The institution develops account creation procedures locally and implements those procedures in GAFE, and faculty and students use institutionally generated accounts to access GAFE and their content. Google then stores all artifacts in the digital cloud on its physical and virtual servers; faculty and students use institutional and/or personal Google accounts for sharing their work with others of their choosing. Institutional managers, in turn, have access to all accounts and the content created using those accounts, but do not have access to content that is shared by non-institutional account holders with institutional accounts. Finally, Google engineers and administrators have access to everything, but can use the content for narrowly defined purposes set forth in Google's contract and terms of service ("Google apps," n.d.). Thus, glocalization of cloud-based technology co-opts traditional understandings of individuality and privacy and replaces them with networked individualism (see "Google privacy," 2014). Traditional

Table 15.3. Illustration of Glocalized Processes and Entities.

Glocalized Processes (vertical) & Entities (horizontal)	Institution	Faculty	Student
Communication	Installing GAFE integrates communication media and local artifacts into Google networks.	Faculty communication artifacts join student artifacts in Google's network.	Student communication artifacts join other's artifacts in Google's network.
LMS (proprietary software)	Functionality of GAFE may call into question cost-benefit analysis of locally installed LMS.	Maintaining accounts in LMS and GAFE may call into question the need for both in an institutional system or require interaction across systems.	Student frustration with lack of real-time collaborative affordances in LMS or redundancy in dual interfaces may result in questioning value.
Ownership	Institution retains ownership of local work in individual accounts, but stores all work in cloud-based data centers; requires Google's cooperation and intervention to access.	Intellectual property from faculty labor becomes individually owned only through institutional GAFE interface.	Student work represents individual effort, social collaboration among students, and instructor feedback, stored in institutionally defined virtual "place."
Hardware	Optimal implementation of GAFE in F2F classes may require scheduling classes in networked computer classroom with Internet-connected computers.	Faculty computing hardware may require minimal locally installed software. Faculty "office hours" and availability may change as a result of 24/7, multi-device ubiquity.	Student computing hardware requires only an Internet connection and modern web browser or smartphone/tablet app for connecting to the GAFE network.
Training	Individual specialists for training students and faculty in various software titles are not required; instead, institutions can put in place GAFE super-users who carefully follow changes and updates and introduce faculty to Google support sites and GAFE user groups for additional support.	Faculty must become continual learners, regularly updating their skills in GAFE application as they are added and updated at Google's convenience.	Students require training in composing and collaborative affordances. Teachers must teach students the interface they expect them to use, including file naming and folder organization; these skills become useful for other classes and contexts.

continued on next page

Table 15.3—*continued*

Glocalized Processes (vertical) & Entities (horizontal)	Institution	Faculty	Student
Intellectual Property	Institution's locally established GAFE accounts become sole conduit for faculty and student access to their IP.	Faculty may decide to create and use personal Google account(s) for maintaining personal conduits to IP.	Students required to copy all IP to local or personal cloud-based storage to retain rights to IP beyond time as student, or must maintain an institutional account by continually taking classes.
Composing	Integration of GAFE provides a single platform for composing communications independently or collaboratively across offices, departments, populations, and schools.	Teachers engage in students' collaborative composing experiences, providing feedback visible to all class members and modeling reviewing, revising, and commenting functions as a collaborator.	Students compose collaboratively within their own classes and beyond, enabling shared content across political and social boundaries.

institutional policies and procedures related to technology and activities (see Table 15.3) might therefore be unsuitable to authorize access or mediate conflicts when glocalized entities encounter legal agreements and policy statements like FERPA and HIPAA.

Using GAFE as a pedagogical tool combines the local classroom and the global Googleverse to form a glocalized composing community, but this implementation represents a limited networked community. With adequate planning, training, and collaborative pedagogy, we envision and recommend that FYC teachers consider implementing GAFE to create layered glocal networks between the classroom and Googleverse. For example, a writing program administrator (WPA) and instructor might connect multiple course sections with the same teacher at the same institution so students could collaborate across class section boundaries. The WPA and several different teachers at the same institution could connect multiple course sections so students in the same class taught by different instructors could collaborate across instructional and class boundaries. The WPA, department chair or division administrators, and teachers across multiple disciplines in an institution could connect sections of different departments' courses to enable students to cross internal departmental, disciplinary, and divisional borders. Or multiple instructors and/

or WPAs in different institutions could connect classes across boundaries such as institution type or locations, or seek to connect course sections across state, provincial, or national borders, across languages, across levels in schools, and across socioeconomic and political boundaries.

Such boundary-crossing implementations would offer even more layers of glocalized networking to the class experience, benefiting students and teachers alike in their collaborative work through broadened horizons, empathetic responses, and valuable networking connections. Creating layered glocal networks responds to Cargile Cook's (2002) call for "layered literacies" and prepares students for success in current and future writing situations by providing them experiences with "a repertoire of complex and interrelated skills" (p. 7). Our more limited implementation has helped us uncover these broader, multiple-layered networking capabilities that using GAFE enables. As a result, heuristics offered in the chapter also apply to these larger networks available within the Googleverse's supra-network.

CONCLUSION

Global networks operate from locally situated nodes in the network (Castells, 2010, p. xxxv), and the composition class, comprised of students and the faculty member, represents that node. As a node on the global network situated in a local space, composition classes and their content, including argumentation, research, persuasion, expression, and rhetoric, will include and necessarily reflect increasingly glocal thinking. Incorporating GAFE in the classroom places the instructor (as glocalizer) at the intersection of the local and the global: the instructor is the node that connects the horizontal network of the local composing class with the vertical network of the global entity, Google.

Castells (2010) considers this intersection a space of contradiction. The faculty member participates in the composing community through a flattened hierarchy; students often have the same permissions and access to comment and view as the instructor. The faculty member is admitted to—and indeed is responsible for initially creating—the community of trust among the learners. Yet faculty also must enforce the dominant protocols of the course, institution, and society, and they are in the powerful position of assessment. Instructors can be complicit with Castells's vertical network of power, unless they consider the rhetoricity of the technology tool itself, as DePew (2015) suggests. It's also a space of great potential; Castells considers this intersection a key feature of the network society in which networked connectivity works between and among the local and the global. Faculty occupy a unique role that enables them to facilitate awareness of and movement through the two networked worlds, modeling and promoting critical use that empowers participants.

In separate institutional settings, we used Google Drive as the primary composing and collaborating technology for a student-centered learning experience. While the use of Google Drive as a widely available technology is global, its implementation and use, both institutionally and pedagogically, are shaped by local conditions. The heuristics discussed in the chapter demonstrate the faculty's role as this critical network node, as the glocalizer, and guide others in building their own glocalized GAFE networking learning community. They also reveal multiple avenues for further research. Such avenues include the following topics or areas:

- *Issues of transfer*: As a free, available technology, GAFE allows students to develop and hone composing, knowledge management, and workflow processes that can be replicated in other academic, personal, and professional settings. Further research is needed into the extent students' experience composing collaboratively in GAFE influences their future composing decisions and practices, particularly within the disciplines.
- *Ethics, Complicities, and Critical Awareness*: GAFE is offered free to educational institutions, but is a paid product for businesses. Thus, introducing GAFE to students does build a familiarity and affinity with the product. Composition instructors must therefore be aware of the implications of using software provided by a for-profit company whose business model requires data mining and sale of information. They should also seek to foster the critical awareness of technology's hidden ideologies in their students. More research into modifying pedagogical practices to promote this critical awareness is needed.
- *Assessment*: GAFE affords the ability to follow students' composing processes and calls into question the concepts of "draft" and "final." The iterative and archived writing in GAFE creates the opportunity to privilege process over product, which has pedagogical implications for FYC and beyond. It also is an intriguing space for electronic portfolios and capstone projects. Developing strategies and rubrics for assessing process and progress in an online collaborative composing environment is an important avenue for further study.
- *Institutional Collaboration*: Implementing a global technology requires the collaborative, cooperative efforts of multiple campus departments, creating tensions that can be productive (Neff & Whithaus, 2008). These constituencies need agency in local decisions regarding global products. GAFE's flexible and glocalized implementations offer a way to productively encourage cooperation while maintaining individual preferences and needs. Furthermore, GAFE offers the ability

to collaborate *across* and *between* institutions. Opening the composing process to a global, multi-cultural context thus has implications for blending localized norms about writing and world Englishes and opens new areas for related research.

- *Authorship, Agency, and Plagiarism:* Because of the ability to compose simultaneously in GAFE, notions of a single author become complicated. Traditional composition teachers in traditional composition classrooms are invested in the idea of individual students producing single-authored artifacts to assess. If the text isn't composed by a single student writing in a non-networked composition classroom for a single authority figure, we face the prospect of having to rethink the concepts of "author," "owner," "artifact," and "plagiarism." Activity theories complicate agency further by including non-human agents in networked activity (Latour, 2005). The involvement of non-human agents in collaborative composing practice makes assigning credit for aspects of assignments difficult. Furthermore, opening a composing space to collaborative authorship creates the possibility of data manipulation and vulnerability (Chu et al., 2013), even so far as creating "fake collaboratively written documents on collaborative writing platforms" (Lee & Tsai, 2014).

When we compose in digital spaces, our identities and our agency are bound in visible and unseen ways to a network of networks. This entangled position as a node within local networks of students, within a networked institution, within the global network of the Googleverse, can seem alienating and disenfranchising, despite the ability of digital technologies to connect and empower. Yet Wellman et al. (2003) notice that "large institutions have neither destroyed nor withered communal relations."

The collaborative practices enabled by binding composition to the Googleverse also create a glocal community of learners that provides a space of trust, camaraderie, and shared learning that crosses local boundaries in the space of flows. Students not only were networked together through the composition class, they also became a group united via large-scale globalized tool "in response to the pressures, opportunities and constraints of large-scale forces" (Wellman et al., 2003) arising from the confluence of glocal networks in which they were situated. In addition, the community or "support network," bound together by the exigences of the course, creates a buffer against other large-scale forces. Students composing and collaborating in GAFE enact a local community that "provide[s] mutual aid, provide[s] partial identity and a sense of belonging" (Wellman et al., 2003). Binding to the glocal Googleverse also binds students to each other and to replicable, applicable, relevant composing and work processes, benefitting them with ways to navigate networked society as citizens, consumers, and community members.

Note

1. During the process of publishing this chapter, Google rebranded Google Apps for Education (GAFE) as "G Suite for Education." Rather than revising all mentions to match the rebranded identity, we retain the original GAFE throughout to illustrate the point made in Table 15.2 about corporate rebranding as it relates to institutional (and publishing) policies and decisions. We also retain the name of the product as we used it to accurately reflect our use of the tools.

References

Alexander, J. (2009). Gaming, student literacies, and the composition classroom: Some possibilities for transformation. *College Composition and Communication, 61*(1), 35–63.

Appadurai, A. (1990). Disjuncture and difference in the global cultural economy. *Theory, Culture & Society, 7*(2), 295–310. https://doi.org/10.1177/026327690007002017

Bazerman, C. (1994). Systems of genre and the enactment of social intentions. In A. Freedman & P. Medway (Eds.), *Genre and the new rhetoric* (pp. 79–104). London, England: Taylor & Francis.

Bazerman, C. (2004). Speech acts, genres, and activity systems: How texts organize activities and people. In C. Bazerman & P. Prior (Eds.), *What writing does and how it does it: An introduction to analyzing texts and textual practices* (pp. 309–340). New York, NY: Routledge.

Bazerman, C. (2013). *A rhetoric of literate action* (Vol. 1). Anderson, SC: Parlor Press. Retrieved from https://wac.colostate.edu/books/literateaction/v1

Bezemer, J., & Kress, G. (2008). Writing in multimodal texts: A social semiotic account of designs for learning. *Written Communication, 25*(2), 166–195. https://doi.org/10.1177/0741088307313177

Bolter, J. D., & Grusin, R. A. (1996). Remediation. *Configurations, 4*(3), 311–358. https://doi.org/10.1353/con.1996.0018

boyd, d. (2007). Why youth (heart) social network sites: The role of networked publics in teenage social life. In D. Buckingham (Ed.), *Youth, identity, and digital media* (pp. 119–142). Cambridge, MA: The MIT Press.

Bridwell-Bowles, L., Powell, K. E., & Choplin, T. W. (2009). Not just words any more: Multimodal communication across the curriculum. *Across the Disciplines, 6*. Retrieved from https://wac.colostate.edu/atd/technologies/bridwellbowlesetal.cfm

Brooks, J. S., & Normore, A. H. (2010). Educational leadership and globalization: Literacy for a glocal perspective. *Educational Policy, 24*(1), 52–82. https://doi.org/10.1177/0895904809354070

Cargile Cook, K. (2002). Layered literacies: A theoretical frame for technical communication pedagogy. *Technical Communication Quarterly, 11*(1), 5–29. https://doi.org/10.1207/s15427625tcq1101_1

Castells, M. (2010). *The rise of the network society* (2nd ed., vol. 1). Oxford, England: Wiley-Blackwell.

Chu, C.-K., Zhu, W.-T., Han, J., Liu, J. K., Xu, J., & Zhou, J. (2013). Security concerns in popular cloud storage services. *IEEE Pervasive Computing, 12*(4), 50–57. https://doi.org/10.1109/MPRV.2013.72

Council of WPA. (2014, July 17). *WPA outcomes statement for first-year composition.* http://wpacouncil.org/positions/outcomes.html

DePew, K. E. (2015). Preparing for the rhetoricity of OWI. In B. L. Hewett & K. E. DePew (Eds.), *Foundational practices of online writing instruction* (pp. 439–467). Anderson, SC: Parlor Press. https://wac.colostate.edu/books/owi

Feenberg, A. (1991). *Critical theory of technology*. Oxford, England: Oxford University Press

Gaillet, L. L. (2009). A socially constructed view of reading and writing: Historical alternatives to 'bridging the gap'. In L. Ostergaard, J. Ludwig, & J. Nugent (Eds.), *Transforming English studies: New voices in an emerging genre* (pp. 163–178). Anderson, SC: Parlor Press.

Garrison, D. R., & Vaughan, N. D. (2007). *Blended learning in higher education: Framework, principles, and guidelines*. San Francisco, CA: Jossey-Bass. https://doi.org/10.1002/978 1118269558

Google apps terms of service—Google apps. (n.d.). Retrieved from https://www.google .com/apps/intl/en/terms/education_terms.html

Google privacy policy—Google privacy and terms. (2014). Retrieved from http://www .google.com/intl/en/policies/privacy

Hall, S. (2007). Encoding, decoding. In S. During (Ed.), *The cultural studies reader* (3rd ed., pp. 33–44). London, England: Routledge. (Original work published 1973.)

Johnson-Eilola, J. (1998). Negative spaces: From production to connection in composition. In M. Sidler, R. Morris, & E. Smith (Eds.), *Computers in the composition classroom* (pp. 454–468). Boston, MA: Bedford/St. Martin's.

Latour, B. (2005). *Reassembling the social: An introduction to actor-network-theory*. Oxford, England: Oxford University Press.

Lee, Y., & Tsai, W. (2014). A new data hiding method via revision history records on collaborative writing platforms. *ACM Transactions on Multimedia Computing Communications and Applications, 10*(2), 1–21. https://doi.org/10.1145/2534408

Miller, C. R. (1984). Genre as social action. *Quarterly Journal of Speech, 70*(2), 151–167. https://doi.org/10.1080/00335638409383686

Miller, C. R. (1994). Rhetorical community: The cultural basis of genre. In A. Freedman & P. Medway (Eds.), *Genre and the new rhetoric* (pp. 67–78). London, England: Taylor & Francis.

Neff, J. M., & Whithaus, C. (2008). *Writing across distances and disciplines: Research and pedagogy in distributed learning*. New York, NY: Lawrence Erlbaum.

Reid, A. (2008). Portable composition: iTunes university and networked pedagogies. *Computers and Composition, 25*(1), 61–78. https://doi.org/10.1016/j.compcom .2007.09.003

Rice, J. (2006). Networks and new media. *College English, 69*(2), 127–133. https://doi .org/10.2307/25472197

Rice, R., & Lauren, B. (2014). Developing intercultural competence through glocal activity theory using the connect-exchange study abroad app. In G. Verhulsdonck & M. Limbu (Eds.), *Digital rhetoric and global literacies: Communication modes and digital practices in the networked world* (pp. 154–173). Hershey, PA: IGI Global. https://doi.org/10 .4018/978-1-4666-4916-3.ch008

Robertson, R. (1995). Glocalization: Time-space and homogeneity-heterogeneity. In M. Featherstone, S. Lash, & R. Robertson (Eds.), *Global modernities* (pp. 25–44). London, England: Sage. https://doi.org/10.4135/9781446250563.n2

Selber, S. A. (2004). *Multiliteracies for a digital age*. Carbondale, IL: Southern Illinois University Press.

Selfe, C. L., & Selfe, R. J. (1994). The politics of the interface: Power and its exercise in electronic contact zones. *College Composition and Communication, 45*(4), 480–504. https://doi.org/10.2307/358761

Smith, C. C. (2008). Technologies for transcending a focus on error: Blogs and democratic aspirations in first-year composition. *Journal of Basic Writing, 27*(1), 35–60.

Spring, J. (2008). Research on Globalization and Education. *Review of Educational Research, 78*(2), 330–363. https://doi.org/10.3102/0034654308317846

Vaidhyanathan, S. (2008, September 19). Generational myth. *The Chronicle of Higher*

Education, B7. Retrieved from https://www.chronicle.com/article/Generational-Myth/32491

Wellman, B., Quan-Haase, A., Boase, J., Chen, W., Hampton, K., Díaz, I., & Miyata, K. (2003). The social affordances of the Internet for networked individualism. *Journal of Computer-Mediated Communication, 8*(3). https://doi.org/10.1111/j.1083-6101.2003.tb00216.x

Yancey, K. B. (2004). Made Not Only in Words: Composition in a New Key. *College Composition and Communication, 56*(2), 297–328. https://doi.org/10.2307/4140651

AFTERWORD
Navigating Composition Practices in International Online Environments

Kirk St.Amant and Rich Rice

Effective and successful communication involves bridging gaps between writer and reader—between the person who composes an artifact and the audience that interacts with it. As the entries in this collection note, effectively navigating this expanse requires identifying obstacles that could affect the sharing of ideas. Essential to this process is understanding factors or friction points that contribute to gaps that impede communication. The object of this volume is to help readers identify such items. As the contributors note, these factors can sometimes be experiential, such as writer and reader having two very different sets of life experiences from which they approach an issue. In other cases, they can be linguistic: for instance, the writer composing in a language that is not the native tongue of the reader. And in certain instances, factors or friction points could be technological: software (and culture, or "software of the mind") works to simultaneously connect and separate composer from audience. The challenge becomes understanding what these factors are and how they create a separation between writer and reader. The collected ideas in this volume represent important steps toward understanding factors that impede effective communication and measures that help overcome communication gaps.

In many ways, the overall process examined in this text is similar to mapping a terrain. Both require that individuals identify obstacles which can impede movement and then use that information to plot courses for traversing a distance. In the case of writing in online environments, that terrain exists across multiple planes, including language, culture, technology, politics, and economics. Such complexity makes it difficult to know what to focus on when trying to share ideas and foster interaction in these contexts. As editors, our hope is that the contributions in this volume can enhance a writer's understanding of audience in international online spaces. Another of our goals has been that the information presented here helps individuals compose more effectively for international online environments.

RECOGNIZING TERRA INCOGNITA

We have inhabited digital landscapes for several decades. For over twenty years, researchers and teachers in technical communication and writing studies have explored uses of online media in composing processes. Similarly, the study of composing for readers from other cultures is not new; despite being repeatedly examined across technical communication and writing studies for decades, the need for revisiting this topic arises out of continued shifts in methods, modes, and terrains of composing. As such, well-established maps exist for navigating both online and international contexts of writing. They also continue to serve as guides for how to effectively negotiate such contexts and facilitate the effective movement of ideas from writer to reader. Yet understanding composition practices in international online contexts involves more than superimposing the map for writing online over the map of communicating across cultures. As the authors in this collection repeatedly note, the international online environment exists as a new terrain that must be continuously (re)examined and (re)mapped.

Further, these new environments are complex, and understanding them involves knowing ways in which different factors and cultural values contribute to their complexities. A large contributing factor relates to cultures using different technologies to compose for and to engage with audiences online. Individuals in the People's Republic of China, for example, rely far more on WeChat for composing in online social networks, those in India are avid users of WhatsApp, and American counterparts currently rely more on email and text messaging. In other cases, geopolitical factors—such as different national laws regulating what can and cannot be said online—affect composing and reading practices in international cyberspace. And, of course, the language one uses and how and when it is used varies from culture to culture (and within subcultures) according to a range of variables. As such, global online interactions are not simply re-writing the map of composition as we've come to know it. Rather, as our authors point out, such situations are creating an entirely new landscape for us to explore, learn, and understand.

We can begin mapping this landscape by identifying features that jump out at us as we move across this new terrain. We develop understanding by noting those friction points that can slow or stop our composing practices as we attempt to use online media to share ideas in global contexts. Our collection, in turn, represents an initial examination of the friction points one might encounter and suggests a framework for categorizing friction points.

PLOTTING A MAP OF THE NEW INTERNATIONAL ONLINE TERRAIN

As with any exploration, we do not necessarily need to dismiss existing ideas and devise completely novel ones. Rather, as scholars and teachers of writing and communication studies, we need to understand how to adapt current practices to address new contexts. We know, for example, composing practices across media and cultures involves a three-part process: we must be able to (1) *contact* an intended audience, in order to (2) *convey* ideas to them in a way that helps us to (3) *connect* with them and encourage their use of our ideas.

We know why we are traversing the terrain—objectives behind why we are composing in international online spaces. Effective communication solves problems. And problems in our world today are very complex. The entries here begin to address gaps between communication and problem-solving.

As the authors here have repeatedly noted, we need to understand elements that hinder our ability to achieve our objectives for composing. We need to do so in order to develop strategies for achieving the process of contacting, conveying, and connecting in new communication situations. We have two general choices: stumble across and try to address such factors as we go, or build upon others' experiences. It is the latter process that this collection has focused on in examining global communication.

Prior studies can serve as a foundation for the paths we take in our future research (e.g., testing reported trends to see if they hold true, where, when, and for how long) or our future teaching (e.g., using prior work to provide students with suggestions for how to compose in new spaces). Within the context of this collection, each chapter represents an attempt to expand the map of international online composition by using prior research to examine and to understand complex international situations. At the same time, each entry also represents an initial exploration of landscapes and friction points one could encounter when composing in international online contexts. When taken together, these chapters help readers gain a more complete understanding of friction points that can exist (and that need to be considered and accounted for) when seeking to contact, convey, and connect with globally distributed audiences via online media. As such, this text can serve as a guide or map for those of us in technical communication and writing studies.

USING THE COLLECTION TO NAVIGATE
INTERNATIONAL ONLINE SPACES

Each entry in this collection provides unique insights on one aspect of the overall composition dynamic. The chapters in the first section explore the challenges of using online media to make *contact* with audiences from other cultures. The authors in this section identify a particular friction point and note how it affects a writer's ability to contact (i.e., share one's compositions) with an international online audience. When taken together, the five entries in this section provide a framework of factors writers must consider when making such contact. They also present strategies and practices one can employ to avoid or mitigate impediments to access a broader, richer audience of readers.

Once contact is made, the challenge becomes conveying ideas in ways an international online audience views as meaningful and worth considering or acting upon. Thus, the notion of *conveying* becomes a new aspect of the international online landscape writers must negotiate to achieve a particular purpose. The entries in this collection's second section familiarized readers with factors that can impede one's ability to convey ideas once contact with international online audiences has been made. By reviewing such concepts in the aggregate, these entries help readers better understand conditions that affect how one conveys ideas in international online contexts.

Ideally, the international online environment is not one where individuals travel alone. Rather, the true power of such an environment lies in the ability of individuals from different backgrounds and locations to come together and engage in interactions difficult to conceive of in the pre-online age. As such, the mapping of new international online terrain must include understanding factors that could inhibit effective interaction among parties (writer and reader) and prevent the creation of effective international communities that use online composing practices. The entries in this collection's concluding section provided a foundational understanding of this final corner of the map. They note factors that can impede connecting meaningfully in international online contexts. They also provide lessons learned and strategies for how to negotiate this new terrain in order to allow international online communities to grow.

PLOTTING A COURSE AND STEPPING INTO THE NEW LANDSCAPE

As with the exploration of any new terrain, the process is an ongoing one that requires continued, collective work to best understand scope, scale, and complexity. And, as with the exploration of new lands, no one set of experiences from the field can truly be definitive or comprehensive. Rather, such work represents the plotting of one small corner of a greater map—a map all of us as researchers and teachers in technical communication and writing studies need to contribute to in order to fully understand its benefits and limitations. We, the editors, encourage readers not to view this book as a definitive guide to composing in international online contexts. Rather, we wish to present it as an invitation to participate in one's own journey, as an opportunity to expand upon the maps presented here and as a challenge to move into uncharted territories.

Friction points identified by this collection's contributors represent a fraction of what can affect processes of contacting, conveying, and connecting in international online contexts. What is needed now is the opportunity to test these friction points, find solutions to them, and identify and address new ones. Only through doing so can we effectively engage with international audiences when writing online. It is an area large enough that the prospects of exploration and expansion seem almost limitless. Readers must step out into these new spaces to write, test, revise, and write again.

To this end, we ask the reader to use entries in this collection as a map for engaging in their own forays into composing in international online environments. We also encourage readers to share what they discover with others in the field of writing studies and beyond. Readers should thus view their interactions as opportunities to invite individuals from other nations and cultures to explore this new terrain in ways that provide a more complete survey. Further, in our research and through the work of manuscript reviewers and editors, we would like to recommend a few related texts; including *Legal Issues in Global Contexts: Perspectives on Technical Communication in an International Age* (St.Amant & Rife, 2014); *Culture, Communication, and Cyberspace: Rethinking Technical Communication for International Online Environments* (St.Amant & Sapienza, 2011); *Digital Rhetoric and Global Literacies* (Verhulsdonck & Limbu, 2014); and the special issue of *Computers and Composition* called "Online Writing in Global Contexts: Rethinking the Nature of Connections and Communication in the Age of International Online Media" (St.Amant & Rice, 2015).

The task ahead is great, and the scope of it might seem daunting. Yet, by working together and effectively plotting how we contact, convey, and connect in such spaces, we can all collectively advance into and across new environments. By composing to create this new terrain, we help map it and help others negotiate it. And the explorations we can undertake are as vast as our ability to craft texts and read and discuss the writings of others.

References

St.Amant, K., & Rice, R. (Eds.). (2015). *Online writing in global contexts: Rethinking the nature of connections and communication in the age of international online media.* Special issue, *Computers and Composition, 38*(B), v–x. https://doi.org/10.1016/S8755-4615 (15)00104-8.

St.Amant, K., & Rife, C. M. (Eds.). (2014). *Legal issues in global contexts: Perspectives on technical communication in the international age.* Amityville, NY: Baywood.

St.Amant, K., & Sapienza, F. (Eds.). (2011). *Culture, communication, and cyberspace: Rethinking technical communication for international online environments.* Amityville, NY: Baywood.

Verhulsdonck, G., & Limbu, M. (Eds.). (2014). *Digital rhetoric and global literacies: Communication modes and digital practices in the networked world.* Hershey, PA: IGI Global. https://doi.org/10.4018/978-1-4666-4916-3

ABOUT THE AUTHORS

RICH RICE is an associate professor of English at Texas Tech University where he teaches courses in new media, intercultural communication, rhetoric, and composition in the Technical Communication and Rhetoric program. His research interests also include distance education and service-learning, portfolio pedagogy, and professional development. As a U.S. Fulbright-Nehru Scholar, Rich's teaching and research extends to India and China, and he has served as a visiting research professor at three schools in India. He has also served as a visiting research professor in China. Rich's recent publications include an edited special issue of *Computers and Composition* on global technical communication, an edited collection on ePortfolios, and numerous articles and chapters on health and communication, mobile medicine, intercultural communication competence, problem-based universal design for learning, study abroad approaches, remediating photo essays, media labs, faculty professionalization, and hypermediated teaching philosophies. He is a founding member of the Global Society for Online Literacy Educators. (See http://richrice.com.)

KIRK ST.AMANT is the Eunice C. Williamson Endowed chair in Technical Communication at Louisiana Tech University (USA) and an adjunct professor of International Health and Medical Communication with the University of Limerick (Ireland). His primary research interests include international communication and information design for global audiences with a particular focus on the globalization of online education and health and medical communication and e-health for international audiences. (See http://latech.aca demia.edu/KirkStAmant.)

* * *

KATHERINE BRIDGMAN is an assistant professor of English at Texas A&M University at San Antonio. Her research focuses on the use of digital social media by activists with an emphasis on how protestors work across digital interfaces to garner transnational support. She directs the A&M-SA Writing Center and Writing across the Curriculum program. She also teaches classes in composition, writing center practice and theory, and historical and contemporary rhetorical theory. (See http://katherinebridgman.com.)

MAURY ELIZABETH BROWN is an assistant professor of English at Germanna Community College as well as a doctoral candidate in English at Old Dominion University. She researches games in education and culture, multimodal composition, digital and video rhetorics, new media, and business and professional and technical writing. She is co-lead organizer of New World Magischola, a live action role play (LARP) experience exploring affect, agency, and rhetoric in games. She is also the founder and president of Learn Larp, LLC, a company devoted to using intentional rhetorical and instructional strategies to create games that encourage empathy, perspective-taking, and questioning societal norms through embodied roleplay. (See http://odu.academia.edu/MauryBrown.)

KAITLIN CLINNIN is an assistant professor of English and director of composition at the University of Nevada, Las Vegas. She researches identity, bodies, and social interactions in traditional and non-traditional pedagogical environments. Her work has been published in *Composition Studies, Journal of Global Literacies, Technologies, and Emerging Practices,* and *Technoculture.* (See http://kaitlinclinnin.org.)

CYNTHIA DAVIDSON is the Emerging Technologies Coordinator in Writing and Rhetoric and a senior lecturer in the College of Arts and Sciences at Stony Brook University. In 2015, she was the recipient of an S-BOLD grant for WOLFIE (Writer's Online Learning Forum and Information Literacy Environment), a joint project between Writing and Rhetoric and the University Libraries. She has also received two TALENT grants for projects in writing and rhetoric and digital instruction as well as a mini-grant for teaching innovation. She has published in *Computers and Composition Online, Science Fiction Studies,* and many poetry journals She holds a Ph.D. in English from the University of Illinois at Chicago, as well as an advanced certificate in composition studies from Stony Brook University, and has many fond memories of attending the first Digital Media and Composition program at The Ohio State University. (See https://stonybrook.digication.com/cynthia_davidsonpwr.)

SUSAN DELAGRANGE, is an assistant dean and associate professor of English (rhetoric and new media) at The Ohio State University, and she researches, writes, and teaches in the areas of digital rhetoric, visual media, and feminist theory. She has published award-winning articles in *Kairos, PMLA,* and elsewhere. *Technologies of Wonder: Rhetorical Practice in a Digital World,* her book-length digital project, won three national awards, including the 2013 CCCC Outstanding Book Award. Her current project focuses on ethical visual persuasion and the relationship between beauty and justice. (See http://susandelagrange.com.)

SCOTT LLOYD DEWITT is an associate professor of English at The Ohio State University, where he teaches undergraduate and graduate courses in writing and digital media and conducts research on technology and writing pedagogy. He is author of *Writing Inventions: Identities, Technologies, Pedagogies* (SUNY 2002), which won the *Computers and Composition* Distinguished Book Award in 2003. He is also the editor of a scholarly collection of curated exhibits (with H. Louis Ulman and Cynthia L. Selfe), *Stories That Speak To Us: Exhibits from the Digital Archive of Literacy Narratives* (*Computers and Composition* Digital Press, 2013). (See https://english.osu.edu/people/dewitt.18.)

AMBER ENGELSON is an assistant professor of English/communications and director of Writing at Massachusetts College of Liberal Arts. She teaches courses in first-year writing, on the history and global influence of English, and on feminist rhetoric. Articles drawn from her ethnographic research in Indonesia have been published in *College English, Literacy in Composition Studies,* and edited collections. (See http://www.mcla.edu/Academics/undergraduate/englishcommunications/faculty/amberengelson/amber engelson.)

KAY HALASEK is an associate professor of English and director of the University Institute for Teaching and Learning at Ohio State University. She is the author of *A Pedagogy of Possibility: Bakhtinian Perspectives on Composition Studies* (SIU Press, 1999), co-editor of *Landmark Essays on Basic Writing* (Lawrence Erlbaum, 2001), and author or co-author of articles on rhetoric, composition theory, and writing pedagogy appearing in *College English, Composition Studies, Computers and Writing, Journal of General Education, Rhetoric Society Quarterly, WPA Journal,* and *Written Communication.* Her recent work focuses on writing program administration, peer response, and online and distance writing pedagogies. (See https://english.osu.edu/people/halasek.1.)

LAVINIA HIRSU is a lecturer in the School of Education at the University of Glasgow. With a background in rhetoric and composition, she has taught courses in applied linguistics, academic writing, and digital rhetoric. Research interests include language learning and literacies in contexts of voluntary, involuntary, and forced mobilities; digital literacies; and theories of cultural and linguistic diversity. Current projects include a study of student-teachers' ideologies, practices, and networks; literacy work with refugee communities in the UK, Egypt, and Mexico; and a project on the urban engagement role of universities in building sustainable cities in Asia and Africa. She has recently published in *Computers and*

Composition, Peitho, and *The Journal of the Assembly for Expanded Perspectives on Learning.* (See http://laviniahirsu.weebly.com.)

DANIEL HOCUTT is a web manager and adjunct professor of liberal arts at the University of Richmond School of Professional and Continuing Studies. He is also a doctoral candidate studying rhetoric, technology, and technical communication at Old Dominion University. He studies the rhetoric of algorithms and seeks to raise awareness of the persuasive activity of algorithms through emergent networked rhetorical agency. Research interests include Google Docs for collaborative composing, extra-human rhetorics, and describing and tracing agency in complex rhetorical networks. (See http://danielhocutt.com.)

VASSILIKI KOURBANI taught linguistics and composition courses at the American College of Greece from 1991 to 2003. She is co-author of a handbook for teachers of Greek as a Foreign Language, and she has been involved in research in areas such as online foreign language testing and the development of an online platform for the teaching of Greek as a foreign language. At Hellenic American University, she currently serves as director of the Writing Center and the Writing Program. She also teaches linguistics in the undergraduate and graduate programs. She is a member of the European Writing Centers Association (EWCA). (See http://www.hauniv.edu/academics/faculty/item/314-kourbani-vassiliki.)

TIKA LAMSAL is an assistant professor in the Department of Rhetoric and Language at the University of San Francisco. He teaches both undergraduate and graduate courses on multilingual and multimodal writing, academic English for multilingual students, written communication, business communication across languages and cultures, and professional digital communication. His research primarily focuses on multilingual and multimodal literacies, non-Western rhetorics, refugee literacies, cross-cultural and cross-language composition, and South Asian diaspora literature. (See https://tikalamsal.com.)

LIZ LANE is an assistant professor of professional writing at the University of Memphis. Research interests include global and technical communication, new media, and gender theory. Her work has appeared in *Ada: A Journal of Gender, New Media, and Technology;* and *Composition Studies.* (See http://etlane.com.)

BENJAMIN LAUREN is an assistant professor at Michigan State University in the Department of Writing, Rhetoric, and American Cultures. He is also an assistant director of the Graduate Program in Rhetoric and Writing. His work has been published in journals such as *Technical Communication, Computers and Composition,* the *Journal of Technical Writing and Communication,* and *Transactions on Professional Communication.* His book *Communication Project Management* (2018) was published in Routledge's ATTW Series in Technical and Professional Communication. (See http://benlauren.com.)

J. C. LEE is an assistant professor of English and composition coordinator at California State University, Northridge. Research interests include multimodality and public writing, as well as rhetorics of contingency, professional development, and labor in academic environments. Her work has appeared in the *Journal of Popular Culture, Academic Exchange Quarterly,* and *Comparative Literature and Culture.* (See http://www.csun.edu/humanities/english/jennifer-c-lee.)

SUZANNE BLUM MALLEY is senior associate provost and associate professor of English at Columbia College Chicago. She has served as the coordinator of the Professional Writing and the English as an Additional Language (EAL) programs and has taught first-year writing, professional writing, and graduate composition theory and praxis. Areas of research include multilingual and digital/multimodal literacies and globally networked learning environments. She is a founding executive board member (2015–2020) and chair (2017–2018) of the Literacy Studies Forum for the Modern Language Association and has served on the executive committee of the Computers & Writing Graduate Research Network since 2011. (See http://www.sbmalley.com.)

BEN MCCORKLE is an associate professor of English at The Ohio State University. He teaches courses in composition, rhetoric, and digital media studies, primarily at OSU's Marion campus. He is the author of the book *Rhetorical Delivery as Technological Discourse: A Cross-Historical Study*, as well as several articles in publications including *Computers and Composition Online, Rhetoric Society Quarterly,* and *Composition Studies.* Currently, he serves as the Co-Director of the Digital Archive of Literacy Narratives. (See http://u.osu.edu /mccorkle.12.)

JEN MICHAELS is a doctoral candidate in English at The Ohio State University, where she researches ways academics use social media to support scholarly composing. She is the Content Strategist for Learning Experiences at Mindset Digital, a corporate-training firm that helps highly regulated industries embrace social media and other digital innovations. (See http://www.jenmichaels.net.)

MINH-TAM NGUYEN is a user experience researcher and designer. She earned her doctoral degree from Michigan State University in Writing, Rhetoric, and American Cultures, focusing on digital rhetoric and professional writing. Her research focuses on user resistance, power, and ethics in the fields of technical communication and UX. (See http://michi ganstate.academia.edu/MinhTamNguyen.)

BEAU S. PIHLAJA is an assistant professor of Technical Communication and Rhetoric at Texas Tech University. His research explores the mediating effects of communication technologies on intercultural encounters, most recently in a binational company on the U.S.-Mexico border. He has extensive experience teaching and presenting internationally, in south and southeast Asia, as well as Latin America. (See http://beaupihlaja.com.)

Mᵃ PILAR MILAGROS works at Boğaziçi University in Istanbul, Turkey. Her area of specialization is in second language (L2) writing, including ways in which reflection and self-assessment activities have provided L2 students with spaces to engage in negotiations of knowledge and various identities. Research interests include rhetoric, second language (L2) writing, intercultural communication, technology and new forms of digital rhetoric, and reflection and self-assessment and issues of identity positioning and negotiations via language. (See http://westlanglit.boun.edu.tr/people/full-time-faculty.)

CYNTHIA L. SELFE, is blissfully retired. She lives with her partner Dickie Selfe, and two dogs, Lucy and Sparky, on Lake Medora in the Upper Peninsula of Michigan (during the warmer months) and travels in southern climates (during the colder months). She remains eternally grateful for the years she spent with marvelous graduate students and talented and generous colleagues. (See http://dmacinstitute.com.)

HEATHER NOEL TURNER is a doctoral candidate of Rhetoric and Writing and an instructor of Professional Writing in the Writing, Rhetoric, and American Cultures Department at Michigan State University. Her research focuses on design and social justice in technical communication. She is a UX design consultant for the Hub for Innovation in Teaching and Technology; the Writing, Information, and Digital Experience (WIDE) Research Center; and the Hispanic Center of Western Michigan. (See http://heather noelturner.com.)

DON UNGER is an assistant professor of Writing and Rhetoric at St. Edward's University in Austin, Texas, where he teaches courses in rhetorical theory, professional writing, and digital rhetorics. In addition, he serves as a Faculty Fellow of Community Engaged Teaching and Learning for St. Edward's Center for Teaching Excellence, and as the Social Media Editor for *Present Tense: A Journal of Rhetoric in Society.* His work has appeared in *Computers and Composition* and *Kairos: A Journal of Rhetoric, Technology, and Pedagogy.* (See http://donaldunger.com.)

JOSEPHINE WALWEMA is an associate professor at Oakland University. Her teaching and research interests include technical and business communication, intercultural and global rhetorics, communication and information design, and the rhetoric of science. She draws from these research interests in the classes she teaches. Her research is at the intersection of rhetorical theory, the practice of these disciplines, and the emerging roles of professional communication. She has presented at national and international conferences in technical and business communication, and publishes articles in these research areas. (See https://oakland.edu/wrt/top-links/facultystaff-directory/associate-professors/walwema.)

INDEX